Religious Pluralism, Democracy,

and the Catholic Church

in Latin America

RECENT TITLES FROM THE HELEN KELLOGG INSTITUTE FOR
INTERNATIONAL STUDIES

Scott Mainwaring, *general editor*

The University of Notre Dame Press gratefully thanks the Helen Kellogg Institute for
International Studies for its support in the publication of titles in this series.

Katherine Hite and Paola Cesarini, eds.
Authoritarian Legacies and Democracy in Latin America and Southern Europe (2004)

Robert S. Pelton, C.S.C., ed.
Monsignor Romero: A Bishop for the Third Millennium (2004)

Guillermo O'Donnell, Jorge Vargas Cullell, and Osvaldo M. Iazzetta, eds.
The Quality of Democracy: Theory and Applications (2004)

Arie M. Kacowicz
The Impact of Norms in International Society: The Latin American Experience, 1881–2001
(2005)

Roberto DaMatta and Elena Soárez
Eagles, Donkeys, and Butterflies: An Anthropological Study of Brazil's "Animal Game" (2006)

Kenneth P. Serbin
Needs of the Heart: A Social and Cultural History of Brazil's Clergy and Seminaries (2006)

Christopher Welna and Gustavo Gallón, eds.
Peace, Democracy, and Human Rights in Colombia (2007)

Guillermo O'Donnell
Dissonances: Democratic Critiques of Democracy (2007)

Marifel Pérez-Stable, ed.
Looking Forward: Comparative Perspectives on Cuba's Transition (2007)

Jodi S. Finkel
Judicial Reform as Political Insurance: Argentina, Peru, and Mexico in the 1990s (2008)

Robert R. Wilson, Peter M. Ward, Peter K. Spink, and Victoria E. Rodríguez
*Governance in the Americas: Decentralization, Democracy, and Subnational Government in
Brazil, Mexico, and the USA* (2008)

Brian S. McBeth
Dictatorship and Politics: Intrigue, Betrayal, and Survival in Venezuela, 1908–1935 (2008)

Pablo Policzer
The Rise and Fall of Reperssion in Chile (2009)

For a complete list of titles from the Helen Kellogg Institute for International Studies,
see http://www.undpress.nd.edu

Religious Pluralism,

Democracy,

and the Catholic Church

in Latin America

edited by

FRANCES HAGOPIAN

University of Notre Dame Press

Notre Dame, Indiana

Library of Congress Cataloging-in-Publication Data

Religious pluralism, democracy, and the Catholic Church in Latin America /
edited by Frances Hagopian.
    p.   cm. — (From the Helen Kellogg Institute for International Studies)
Based on a conference held Mar. 31–Apr. 1, 2005 at the University of Notre Dame.
Includes bibliographical references and index.
ISBN 978-0-268-03087-2 (pbk. : alk. paper)
1. Catholic Church—Latin America—Congresses. 2. Religious pluralism—Latin
America—Congresses. 3. Democracy—Latin America—Congresses. 4. Religious
pluralism—Catholic Church—Congresses. 5. Democracy—Religious aspects—
Catholic Church—Congresses. 6. Latin America—Church history. I. Hagopian,
Frances.
BX1426.3.R45   2009
282'.8090511—dc22

                                                            2009007122

For Suzanne Berger,

My teacher, who taught me how to teach

Contents

List of Figures

List of Tables

List of Acronyms

ACM	Acción Católica Mexicana (Mexican Catholic Action)
AD	Acción Democrática (Democratic Action, Venezuela)
ANCIFEM	Asociación Nacional Cívica Femenina (National Women's Civic Association, Mexico)
APRA	Alianza Popular Revolucionaria Americana (American Popular Revolutionary Alliance, Peru)
ARENA	Alianza Republicana Nacionalista (Nationalist Republican Alliance, El Salvador)
CCR	Catholic Charismatic Renewal
CDD	Católicas por el Derecho a Decidir (Catholics for the Right to Choose)
CEBs	comunidades eclesiais de base or comunidades eclesiales de base (ecclesial base communities)
CECH	Conferencia Episcopal de Chile (Chilean Episcopal Conference)
CELAM	Consejo Episcopal Latinoamericano (Latin American Catholic Bishops' Council)
CEM	Conferencia del Episcopado Mexicano (Mexican Episcopate Conference)
CEMAN	Comisión Multisectorial de Alto Nivel (Multisectoral High-Level Commission, Peru)

CEP	Conferencia Episcopal Peruana (Peruvian Bishops' Conference)
CEPI	Comisión Especial para los Pueblos Indígenas (Special Commission for Indigenous Peoples, Chile)
CEV	Conferencia Episcopal Venezolana (Venezuelan Episcopal Conference)
CFEMEA	Centro Feminista de Estudos e Assessoria (Feminist Center for Studies and Advisory Services, Brazil)
CGTP	Confederación General de Trabajadores de Perú (General Confederation of Peruvian Workers)
CIMI	Conselho Indigenista Missionário (Indian Missionary Council, Brazil)
CNBB	Conferência Nacional dos Bispos do Brasil (National Conference of Brazilian Bishops)
CNE	Comisión Nacional Electoral (National Electoral Commission, Venezuela)
CNSS	Conselho Nacional de Serviço Social (National Social Service Council, Brazil)
CODEPECA	Consejo de Desarrollo Pesquero Campesino (Council of Fishery and Peasantry Development, Chile)
CONADI	Corporación Nacional de Desarrollo Indígena (National Corporation for Indigenous Development, Chile)
CONFIEP	Confederación Nacional de Instituciones Empresariales Privadas (National Confederation of Private Entrepreneural Associations, Peru)
COPEI	Comité de Organización Política Electoral Independiente (Independent Political Electoral Organization Committee [Christian Democratic Party], Venezuela)
CPT	Comissão Pastoral da Terra (Pastoral Land Commission, Brazil)
CVR	Comisión de la Verdad y Reconciliación (Truth and Reconciliation Commission, Peru)

FMLN	Frente Farabundo Martí para la Liberación Nacional (Farabundo Marti National Liberation Front, El Salvador)
HLI	Human Life International
ILO	International Labor Organization
INCRA	Instituto Nacional de Colonização e Reforma Agrária (National Institute of Colonization and Agrarian Reform, Brazil)
ISET	Instituto Superior de Estudios Teológicos (Higher Institute of Theological Studies)
IU	Izquierda Unida (United Left, Peru)
JOC	Juventude Operária Católica or Juventud Obrera Católica (Catholic Youth Workers)
JUC	Juventude Universitária Católica or Juventud Universitaria Católica (Catholic University Youth)
LOPPE	Ley de Organizaciones Políticas y Procesos Electorales (Law of Political Organizations and Electoral Processes, Mexico)
MCLCP	Mesa de Concertación para la Lucha Contra la Pobreza (Roundtable for the Struggle against Poverty, Peru)
MIMDES	Ministerio de la Mujer y Desarrollo Humano (Ministry of Women and Human Development, Peru)
MRTA	Movimiento Revolucionario Túpac Amaru (Tupac Amaru Revolutionary Movement, Peru)
MST	Movimento dos Trabalhadores Rurais Sem Terra (Landless Workers Movement, Brazil)
MVR	Movimiento Quinta República (Movement of the Fifth Republic, Venezuela)
NAFTA	North American Free Trade Agreement
PAN	Partido Acción Nacional (National Action Party, Mexico)

PASC	Partido Alternativa Socialdemócrata y Campesina (Social-Democratic and Peasant Alternative Party, Mexico)
PCM	Partido Comunista Mexicano (Mexican Communist Party)
PDC	Partido Demócrata Cristiano (Christian Democratic Party, Chile)
PDM	Partido Demócrata Mexicano (Mexican Democratic Party)
PIR	Plan Integral de Reparaciones (Integrated Reparations Plan, Peru)
PJ	Partido Justicialista (Justicialist Party [Peronist Party], Argentina)
PNP	Partido Nacionalista Peruano (Peruvian Nationalist Party)
PNRA	Programa Nacional de Reforma Agrária (National Program for Agrarian Reform, Brazil)
PO	Pastoral Operária (Workers' Pastoral, Brazil)
PPD	Partido por la Democracia (Party for Democracy, Chile)
PRD	Partido de la Revolución Democrática (Party of the Democratic Revolution, Mexico)
PRI	Partido Revolucionario Institucional (Institutional Revolutionary Party, Mexico)
PS	Partido Socialista (Socialist Party, Chile)
PT	Partido dos Trabalhadores (Workers' Party, Brazil)
PUCP	Pontificia Universidad Católica del Perú (Pontifical Catholic University of Peru)
PUSC	Partido de Unidad Social Cristiana (United Social Christian Party, Costa Rica)
RN	Renovación Nacional (National Renovation, Chile)

SINAMOS	Sistema Nacional del Apoyo a la Movilización Social (National System of Support for Social Mobilization, Peru)
SNI	Serviço Nacional de Informações (National Intelligence Service, Brazil)
SNI	Sociedad Nacional de Industrias (National Society of Industry, Peru)
UCCP	Unión de Centro Centro Progresista (Progressive Center Center Union, Chile)
UDI	Unión Demócrata Independiente (Independent Democratic Union, Chile)
UDR	União Democrática Ruralista (Ruralist Democratic Union, Brazil)
UNEC	Unión Nacional de Estudiantes Católicos (National Union of the Catholic Students, Peru)
UNPF	Unión Nacional de Padres de Familia (National Parents Union, Mexico)
UNS	Unión Nacional Sinarquista (National Synarchist Union, Mexico)

Preface and Acknowledgments

The idea for this project was born in a conversation in June 2002 with Rev. John Swope, S.J., who was then executive director of the Secretariat for the Church in Latin America of the United States Conference of Catholic Bishops. (After a period as superior for the Maryland Province of the Society of Jesus, today he is president of Cristo Rey Jesuit High School in Baltimore, Maryland.) Lamenting that at the previous International Congress of the Latin American Studies Association there had been but nine panels on religion, Fr. Swope made me an offer I could not refuse—a cash grant to launch an initiative on religion at the Kellogg Institute (where I was director-designate at the time)—to stimulate more research on the role of the Catholic Church in Latin America.

After many years in which the study of Catholicism had been invigorated by expanding its focus beyond elites and traditional institutional forms to include the "popular" or "progressive" church and the meaning this theology and church infused in the lives and daily struggles of ordinary men and women, scholarship on Catholicism had begun to fracture and flag when the theological, spiritual, social, and political potential of liberation theology that had so excited a new generation of researchers appeared to wane. Some scholars responded to the era of the new evangelization by valiantly pressing ahead with studying grassroots progressive Catholicism. Others, who maintained a deep interest in the individual basis of religious belief, its transformative potential, and its political impact, turned their focus to evangelical and especially Pentecostal Protestant movements, in which they found the religious dynamism Catholic movements appeared to lack in Latin America. But many others abandoned research on religion altogether once democratic regimes had been achieved and turned instead to studying democratic institutions. These students of democracy, mainly political scientists, by and large neglected the role of the Catholic Church in politics because of a perception that Christian Democratic parties in the region were in free fall and political-electoral cleavages today generally do not tend to form along denominational or even religious-versus-secular lines. While the ethnographic case studies of the first two groups of scholars have unquestionably deepened our knowledge of the nature of individual religious belief and religiously motivated action among sectors that the Catholic Church barely reached, illuminating the foundations of a now religiously plural field, the desertion of the latter group has left us without a means of connecting these microlevel processes and the reality on the ground to the broader impacts of religion on politics and politics on religion. We are particularly handicapped in explaining the contemporary responses of the institutional Catholic Church to pluralism—which include efforts to evangelize culture, build civil society, and recover the public sphere for projects of faith—as well as, more profoundly, how democracy has changed the church and how religious change has impacted democratic politics in Latin America.

This state of affairs should bother social scientists. Whatever one's personal beliefs and points of agreement or disagreement with church authorities on matters of public policy in a democracy, abortion laws from El Salvador to Argentina, the fate of the landless, and the electoral future of parties of the traditional right all depend in part on the successes and failures of the Roman Catholic Church to hold rank, mobilize, and fulfill a prophetic as well as a pastoral role. To address these very important questions, we need more than a set of stylized facts that assume Catholics on the ground are progressive, their Protestant counterparts are conservative, and the Catholic hierarchy is suspicious of progressive causes and internal debate. This is the point of departure for this volume.

When I proposed to attempt to raise the profile of the comparative social scientific study of religion in Latin America, the study of Pentecostal beliefs was much in vogue, and, in the post–September 11 world, suddenly the wider community of policy makers and comparative scholars had discovered the importance of Islam, society, and politics and the significance of Christian-Muslim religious dialogue and tolerance. Thus, I needed to convince the skeptical not only that it was still worth studying the Catholic Church in Latin America but also that good scholars were already at work in this field and that others who did not see themselves as students of religion but whose work brought them to the intersection of the religious and the political could be induced to join the project. This volume is the product of four years of planning and mobilizing scholars and practitioners in that effort. Most knew a good deal more about the subject than I did when it all began. The volume's success should be judged, ultimately, not merely on whether or not the questions laid out in the introductory chapter are the right ones to ask, the answers provided by the contributors are the correct ones, or even whether the research agenda offered in the concluding chapter is the most salient and fruitful. Those questions are of course all legitimate, and I invite interested (and appalled) scholars to argue with the book. But my hope is that the volume will spark more interest in the topic, and in the years to come we will see more dissertations produced on the subject of religion and politics and more first-rate social scientists reclaiming the terrain that they abandoned to theologians, historians, and other humanists. As every country in Latin America wrestles with such subjects as religious freedom versus a privileged status for the Catholic majority, public health and the rights of women versus society's norms and morals, and the separation of church and state versus religious education, social science should play a role in explaining what is and informing what will come.

In the course of preparing this volume, I have incurred many debts of gratitude, both to members of the clergy who believed in this project enough to fund it and in me enough to take time to educate a non-Catholic in Catholic ways of thinking and seeing, and to scholars who accepted the trespassing of an amateur. This project's first step was a workshop held at the Kellogg Institute at the University of Notre Dame in October 2003. Daniel Levine and Scott Mainwaring helped me to organize it; several terrific scholars—Carol Ann Drogus, Anthony Gill, Luiz Alberto Gomez de Souza, Mala Htun, Cristián Parker, and Catalina Romero—produced a series of "state-of-the-art" papers; and a stable of distinguished discussants and experts enriched the event, including José Casanova, Margaret Crahan, Ralph Della Cava, Paul Freston, Rev. William Lies, C.S.C., Scott Mainwaring, Rev.

Timothy R. Scully, C.S.C., Timothy Steigenga, and, especially, Rev. Gustavo Gutiérrez, O.P., who mesmerized all those who attended with characteristic brilliance and moral force. I also dragged several authors to a panel at the Latin American Studies Association International Congress in Las Vegas in 2004 in order to fulfill my debt to Fr. Swope. Daniel Levine brought his customary expertise and dry wit to the role of discussant.

The current volume is based on papers presented at a conference entitled Contemporary Catholicism, Religious Pluralism, and Democracy in Latin America, held at Notre Dame from March 31 to April 1, 2005. Funding for the conference was made possible by grants from the Executive Secretariat on Latin America of the United States Conference of Catholic Bishops, Catholic Relief Services, and several units of the University of Notre Dame, including the Joan B. Kroc Institute for International Peace Studies, the Erasmus Institute, the Henkels Lecture Series Fund of the Institute for Scholarship in the Liberal Arts, College of Arts and Letters, and the Helen Kellogg Institute for International Studies, the primary sponsor of the conference. I am grateful for the personal backing of Rev. John Swope, S.J., Daniel Lizarraga, R. Scott Appleby, Rev. Robert Sullivan, S.J., and especially Scott Mainwaring and the Faculty Committee of the Kellogg Institute. This was the latest in a series of great intellectual gatherings made possible by the generous gift of the Coca-Cola Company to Notre Dame's Kellogg Institute.

Several capable colleagues made presentations at the conference and served as discussants, including David Campbell, José Casanova, R. Andrew Chesnut, Robert Fishman, Luiz Alberto Gomes de Souza, Rev. William Lies, C.S.C., Scott Mainwaring, Rev. José Amando Robles, and Sol Serrano. I also wish to acknowledge Rev. Sidney Fones and Rev. Carlos Quintana, secretary and treasurer, respectively, of the Latin American Catholic Bishops' Council (CELAM), who made the journey to Notre Dame—where "the church does its thinking"—and asked nothing in return for their support but the best information a group of scholars could provide. Their honest appreciation of our efforts and their openness to academic inquiry as a prelude to the Fifth General Meeting of the Latin American Episcopate in Aparecida, Brazil, in May 2007 is an example to all who love the Roman Catholic Church not to be afraid of hearing hard truths. I also thank Barbara Hanrahan of the University of Notre Dame Press, who tells a great joke and who had more faith in this project than she probably should have. Two superb editors, Christina Catanzarite of the University of Notre Dame Press and Elizabeth Rankin of the Kellogg Institute, immeasurably improved the readability of the manuscript. I am particularly grateful to Elizabeth for going far above the call of duty in providing the most professional, competent, and timely assistance imaginable in the preparation of this book. The entire text was improved because of the careful readings by Kenneth Serbin and an anonymous reader for the University of Notre Dame Press; they deserve a good deal of credit for rescuing us from assorted mistakes in emphasis and judgment, and none of the blame for the errors that remain.

I also welcome the opportunity to acknowledge publicly the ample support I received in the preparation of the chapters I contributed to the volume. Portions of chapters 1 and 7 appeared earlier as "Latin American Catholicism in an Age of Religious and Political Pluralism: A Framework for Analysis," in *Comparative Politics* (volume 40, issue 2, 2008). Patricia Rodriguez and Cora Fernández-Anderson served as extraordinarily capable and cheerful research assistants. Claudia Maldonado, who reads heavy German texts apparently to relax, supplied the book's epigraph. I am especially indebted to the scholars who educated me on the subject of the Catholic Church in Latin America and commented on earlier versions of my work that appears in this volume. Several generous colleagues—Rev. Ernest Bartell, C.S.C., Susan Fitzpatrick-Behrens, Michael Coppedge, Wendy Hunter, Daniel Levine, Scott Mainwaring, and Kurt Weyland—took the time to comment on a 115-page conference paper and offer encouragement to continue with the project. Ernie and Susan each prepared four pages of single-spaced typed comments on the first draft of my paper, and I am especially grateful to Ernie for patiently instructing me in the evolving attitudes of the hierarchy, clergy, and theologians of the Roman Catholic Church. Thomas Quigley also provided an expert reading of portions of the manuscript. It is not clear for which set of colleagues the task of commenting was the more painful: those who knew next to nothing about the church or those who knew too much. I thank them all.

My greatest and most permanent debt is to Tony and Michael Messina. They are entrusted with the task—which they fulfill exceptionally well—of making sure I do not take myself too seriously. They are also my inspiration to produce work of value and, more importantly, to laugh and to find joy in life. They know I could not live without them. Finally, I want to acknowledge the profound influence on my life exercised by my teacher Suzanne Berger, to whom I owe so much. Perhaps only at this stage of my academic career can I appreciate how extraordinarily fortunate I was to have had a mentor who taught me how to be original, engage questions of significance, question conventional wisdom, and take myself seriously. I do not write as well and, since leaving Cambridge, I do not dress as well (actually, I never did), but I have long attempted to imitate her. To this day I find myself reaching for lines she delivered to me when attempting to prod but not discourage my own graduate students. I have also, step by step, been reproducing her intellectual agenda—from traditional social and political classes to political economy to political representation and, now, to religion and politics. For years, unbeknownst to her, in my own mind I have been thanking her indirectly for her infinite wisdom, patient advice, and boundless generosity by passing along the favor—doing for my students the outrageous things she did for me such as producing a letter of recommendation on a day's notice and editing countless drafts of the same dissertation chapter, for which to this day she has asked nothing in return. I would now like to thank her more directly. With profound gratitude and enduring admiration, I dedicate this book to her.

A powerful religion permeates all the affairs of life and lends color to every movement of the spirit, to every element of culture. In time, of course, those things come to react upon religion, and indeed its living core may be stifled by the ideas and images it once took into its sphere. The sanctification of all the concerns of life has its fateful aspect.

Now, no religion has ever been quite independent of the culture of its people and its time. It is just when religion exercises sovereign sway through the agency of literally written scriptures, when all life seems to revolve round that centre, when it is interwoven with life as a whole that life will most infallibly react upon it. Later, these intimate connections with culture are no longer useful, but simply sources of danger; nevertheless, a religion will always act in this way as long as it is alive.

—Jacob Burckhart, *Weltgeschichtliche Betrachtungen*, 1905

1 | Introduction

The New Landscape

FRANCES HAGOPIAN

As the Roman Catholic Church enters its third millennium, its claims to universalism are both broader and shallower than at any time in recent history. On the one hand, the church has extended its reach from a European center into parts of the developing world where it was once represented by only a handful of dedicated missionaries, with its most dynamic growth in adherents in Africa and Asia. On the other hand, in the heart of the Catholic world the commitment of nominal Catholics to their church has weakened. The process of secularization in western Europe has now advanced to such an extent that it is not hyperbolic to ask if these countries are still "Catholic" in a sense that actually matters.

Today Latin America stands at a crossroads between the decaying core of Roman Catholicism and its vibrant pockets of growth and hope, between a Catholic past and an uncertain future framed by religious and political pluralism. For nearly five hundred years the church enjoyed a near monopoly on religious belief and practice: more than nine out of every ten Latin Americans called themselves Catholic, in many countries presidents and generals had to be Catholic, and children received religious education in private or state schools. Although half of the world's Catholics still live in Latin America, and Latin America has not yet fallen to the tide of secularization that has swept across western and even southern Europe, today's church faces intensifying religious competition and pluralism within these once hegemonic Catholic societies. This pluralism threatens the identity of Latin America as a Catholic region. Across Latin America the days of formal and informal concordats between church and state are over, divorce is legal, and social life is no longer effectively demarcated by religious denomination. Self-identified Protestants now comprise roughly one-fifth of the population of the region, about one in ten Latin Americans identify with no religion at all, and only about 70 percent of the population is nominally Roman Catholic. Practicing Catholics—those who regularly attend Mass, observe Holy Week, and participate in religious movements and church groups—are now a clear minority. Much of civil society—in which the church invested heavily—is now mobilized in organizations that lie beyond the boundaries of ecclesiastical authority. Religious pluralism of a sort that Latin America has never really known, moreover, has grown alongside a democratic pluralism that places limits on state authority—and hence the church's capacity to dictate Catholic norms—over individuals' personal and private lives.

This changing landscape poses unprecedented challenges for the Roman Catholic Church. State-granted privileges are harder to maintain if and as secularization advances and harder to justify when a religious monopoly erodes. A series of direct and indirect state subsidies are endangered, ranging from the salaries of priests to subsidized Catholic education, from tax exemption on church assets to direct public support for Catholic charities and social services, as well as the right to certify marriage and teach Catholic education in the public schools. These benefits were not icing on the cake; they extended the institutional reach of the church and, in turn, helped to keep the faithful in the fold and the church to acquire the degree of influence that allowed it to speak out effectively on those public issues that most deeply concerned it: stopping modern totalitarian projects and moral decay, alleviating poverty, and defending human rights and justice.[1]

If religious pluralism jeopardizes church privileges, secular democracies threaten a moral public sphere (Neuhaus 1984). Center-left and leftist politicians responsive to new demands for social and family policy reform and reproductive rights that run counter to the church's teachings have come to power in municipalities, provinces, and even several national governments in the region. In Chile a Socialist president signed a divorce bill into law after a protracted and bitter debate, and in Argentina a center-left Peronist president confronted the church over sex education, the distribution of condoms, and other moral issues. In Uruguay only the action of the Senate prevented the legalization of abortion; the state legislature of Mexico City, which is dominated by members of the Democratic Revolutionary Party (PRD), legalized abortion during the first trimester of a pregnancy. As the old battle lines of the secular versus the religious, liberal rights versus moral protections, and the rights of women versus the defense of the family re-form, the church brings less to the fight than in decades past. Once the church could count on Catholic public officials to stand firm, and when anticlerical liberals, communists, or dictators—Protestant or Catholic—attacked, the church could credibly threaten to fight back with fury. Now, amid half-empty pews and widespread disobedience among Catholics to church teachings in their daily lives, summoning the faithful for political action to defend the church's policy preferences and institutional interests in the coming battles over stem cell research, emergency contraception, and other bioethical issues; the legalization of abortion and same-sex marriage; the public dissemination of condoms to stop the spread of AIDS; and even state subsidies to religious schools will be problematic.

These societies also are not insulated from broader global influences and constraints, nor can they be. Just as scholars comfortably dismissed as a paper tiger the twentieth-century notion that modern life would inevitably lead to secularization, the global transmission of secular cultures of moral permissiveness and consumerism imported from foreign films, global media networks, and the World Wide Web have renewed this possibility. Globalization has also engendered liberal economic policies and market reforms that have had a salutary effect on resolving public debt, stabilizing prices, and attracting investment, but these same reforms have also led to rising unemployment, poverty, and, especially, inequality (IADB 1998; Korzeniewicz and Smith 2000). International influences per se are hardly a challenge to one of the most truly international institutions in the world, but an international rights discourse that includes reproductive rights and rapid capital mobility that threatens the capacity of states to mount adequate safety nets lie at fundamental odds with Catholic doctrine.

This volume asks how the Catholic Church in various Latin American countries responds to the challenges of secularism and eroding religious hegemony in a context of religious and political pluralism, how democracy has changed the church, and how religious change has impacted democratic politics in Latin America. These are huge questions whose answers are neither obvious nor predetermined. The church could alternately invite more participation from its grassroots members or attempt to impose greater control over them; defend its institutional interests or its social doctrine; or accelerate its pastoral work or seek special protection from secular state authorities to enforce the policy outcomes that it cannot induce through moral persuasion. Democracy could erode hierarchical authority or stimulate greater lay participation in church affairs. And religious change could conceivably prompt electoral realignments, invigorate civil society and engender political participation, loosen state control over private decisions, or exercise very little impact at all. The answers to these questions, moreover, are not necessarily generalizable across Latin America. Though the Catholic Church is a centralized, international institution with a universal worldview, national episcopates and individual bishops navigating different political and social settings may respond to evolving challenges in a wide variety of ways.

We begin our inquiry with a surprisingly thin base of knowledge about the current situation. Although we know something about the institutional health of the church and the trends toward secularism and, in particular, religious pluralism, we know very little about how the changing nature of society impacts religion in the twenty-first century, the way in which the church formulates its responses to these challenges, and the degree of religious influence in politics and public policy. We are also without an analytical road map to guide us in our inquiry. The principal frameworks that for decades have guided our understanding of individual-level religious behavior and the shifting involvements and influence of the Roman Catholic Church in politics and society in Latin America were conceived in times of religious hegemony, corporatism, and dictatorship, when civil society was little more than a hope and democracy a distant goal. The world in which their theoretical expectations were framed has changed, and we need a new set of lenses through which to view church responses to pluralism.

But before we proceed, we should ask if such an inquiry is warranted. If Catholic hegemony has eroded, if the church, apparently weakened by a thinning of its ranks and the flight of the faithful, lacks command over voters or any veto or even influence over public policy, and if religious cleavages are not evidently salient, why should anyone studying Latin American politics particularly care about studying the Roman Catholic Church? In fact, there are many good reasons for doing so. In Colombia, El Salvador, Guatemala, and, most recently, Chiapas, Mexico, the church applied its prestige to bring a halt to political violence and civil conflict—in El Salvador at the great cost of several martyrs. In Chile in 2000 the candidate of the rightist Independent Democratic Union, Joaquín Lavín, a follower of Opus Dei, nearly won the presidency. In Brazil the growth of the leftist Workers' Party (PT) was abetted for many years by a highly effective grassroots campaign by Catholic activists (Ottmann 2002). Though the government of Luiz Inácio "Lula" da Silva moved toward the center after the 2002 presidential election, it nevertheless incorporated many elements of a progressive Catholic agenda, including indigenous land rights and the Fome Zero (Zero Hunger) Program, which was later subsumed under the conditional cash transfer program Bolsa Familia (Family Stipend).[2] Even if the mobilization of Catholic networks and voters did not weigh as heavily on the outcomes of other recent elections as they did in these, if Catholic voters become detached from their traditional partisan alignments their redistribution to another party or across the political spectrum signals possible electoral realignments and new party systems. These alignments might not take on a religious shape initially, but as the range of options available for economic policy narrows due to international economic constraints, political competition for power could spill into the realm of social, cultural, and religious conflict and create a religious cleavage.[3] Apart from electoral politics, as state capacity to deliver social services shrinks with neoliberal state reform, governments are turning to the church to deliver those services through its network of charitable organizations. As the church assumes this role, it will only become more important and influential in the implementation of public health and education programs. Religious social networks, moreover, often provide the socialization and mobilizing force behind tomorrow's political movements. From Mexico to Brazil, Catholic activists with past ties to Catholic Action or liberationist lay groups today lead grassroots movements that are not immediately identifiable as religious but that are inspired by Catholic doctrine and principles.[4] When the Latin American Catholic Church lays claim to a regional Catholic culture, it is essentially correct.

The persistent importance of religious beliefs and divides in society and politics demands that we reframe our questions, revise our frameworks, and update and correct our empirical referents. We need to identify the areas in which more research is needed, stimulate debate, and push outward the boundaries of our scholarship on church, state, and politics in contemporary Latin America. The remainder of this chapter makes a modest start in this direction. It assesses the state of religious pluralism, secularization, and democratic pluralism across Latin America; reviews our paradigmatic explanations for the causes and consequences of religious pluralism and the church's response to it in democratic societies, from the Second Vatican Council to the "new evangelization"; situates the church's responses to religious and political pluralism in its capacity to mobilize society; and partially outlines a new approach to the study of religion, politics, and society while laying out a roadmap for the rest of the volume.

The State of the Church in Society: Religious Pluralism, Secularization, and Eroding Hegemony

From an institutional standpoint, for the first time in decades the future of the church in Latin America looks more promising than the recent past. The number of priests rose in every country in the two decades from 1981 to 2001, and although the increase did not entirely keep pace with population growth, the ratio of priests to Catholics, which had worsened through much of the second half of the twentieth century, leveled off in the 1990s, when more dioceses and parishes were also created (see Table 1.1). The number of religious sisters experienced a modest overall growth of 9 percent in the thirty years between 1972 and 2001, with the sharpest percentage rise taking place in Guatemala, Honduras, and Nicaragua, where numbers doubled (Cleary 2007b). Most encouraging was the rebound in

Table 1.1. The Institutional Reach of the Catholic Church in Latin America, 1950–2001

Country	Catholic Population[a] (2000)[a]	Number of Catholic Priests[b] (1981)[b]	(1997)[b]	(2001)[a]	Ratio of Inhabitants to Catholic Priests[b] (1950)	Ratio of Priests to Catholics[b] (1984)[b]	(1999)[b]	(2001)[a]	Percent Increase in Seminarians (1972–2001)[c]	Replacement Ratio[d] (1977)	(1995)	Number of Parishes[a]	Ratio of Parishes to Parishioners[a]
Argentina	33,549,000	5,450	5,877	5,868	4.3	5.4	5.6	5.7	560	0.07	0.34	2,694	12,453
Bolivia	7,246,000	929	1,058	1,056	6.1	7.0	6.6	6.8	1,357	0.09	0.50	565	12,825
Brazil	143,900,000	13,169	15,577	16,598	6.9	8.7	8.7	8.7	774	0.08	0.44	8,732	16,480
Chile	11,426,000	2,020	2,266	2,298	3.3	4.6	4.9	5.0	596	0.08	0.33	951	12,015
Colombia	37,723,000	5,254	7,316	7,851	3.7	4.9	4.9	4.8	510	0.20	0.63	3,614	10,438
Costa Rica	3,346,000	434	746	770	4.8	4.8	4.0	4.3	421	n.d.	n.d.	258	12,969
Cuba	6,179,000	200	306	296	10.8	19.8	16.7	20.9	106	n.d.	n.d.	264	23,405
Dominican Republic	7,475,000	505	694	817	13.5	11.5	9.4	9.1	866	n.d.	n.d.	485	15,412
Ecuador	11,623,000	1,513	1,795	1,836	3.2	5.5	6.4	6.3	691	0.06	0.43	1,151	10,098
El Salvador	4,986,000	361	592	663	8.7	12.3	8.4	7.5	1,015	n.d.	n.d.	376	13,261
Guatemala	9,471,000	699	916	970	21.2	10.2	9.7	9.8	474	n.d.	n.d.	434	21,823
Haiti	6,778,000	405	593	611	9.3	10.7	10.5	11.1	734	n.d.	n.d.	266	25,481
Honduras	5,362,000	236	327	382	11.9	10.7	14.9	14.0	594	n.d.	n.d.	169	31,728
Mexico	63,347,000	10,087	12,829	14,049	5.8	7.1	6.5	6.4	205[e]	n.d.	n.d.	19,356	15,502
Nicaragua	4,518,000	340	411	418	n.d.	8.1	10.5	10.8	578	n.d.	n.d.	243	18,593
Panama	2,434,000	290	396	392	6.7	6.6	6.2	6.2	654	n.d.	n.d.	176	13,830
Paraguay	4,708,000	543	659	783	6.3	6.0	6.5	6.0	482	0.13	0.47	358	13,151
Peru	23,020,000	2,233	2,505	2,790	6.0	7.7	8.3	8.3	817	0.10	0.54	1,426	16,143
Uruguay	2,507,000	587	536	498	3.7	4.3	5.0	5.0	268	0.05	0.13	229	10,948
Venezuela	21,414,000	1,995	2,419	2,320	6.4	7.5	9.8	9.2	764	0.08	0.45	1,185	18,071

Note: No data available (n.d.) for some categories.

[a]Estimated by Froehle and Gautier (2003, 151–56).

[b]Wilkie (2002, 362–64).

[c]Cleary (2007b).

[d]Seminarians per 10,000/priests per 10,000.

[e]This figure is from 1975 rather than 1972.

seminary enrollments, which rose across the region from 5,334 in 1972 to 28,802 in 2001, an increase of 388 percent. In Bolivia and El Salvador the number of seminarians multiplied tenfold in these three decades from 49 to 714 and 34 to 379, respectively. The number of lay people dedicated to work in church ministries as catechists has also increased over the past twenty years, reaching 1.1 million in 2004 (Cleary 2007a, 169). Meanwhile, the church has maintained its historical channels for extending its reach into society through distributing health, charity, and social services, in some cases funded by national, state, and municipal governments. In Brazil, for example, one study estimated that in the 1970s 10 percent of Brazilians benefited from the church's social action, with 61.6 percent of Catholic assistance works receiving public funds (Serbin 1995, 156–59).[5] Across Latin America, Catholic hospitals and charitable institutions that have served Catholics in times of their greatest need continue to do so today.

Yet the state of the church in society is not as promising. The challenge of religious pluralism is real and self-evident to both religious leaders and scholars alike. Fully cognizant that a church that claims the one true faith cannot justify its privileged status if it cannot maintain its monopoly over worship, the Catholic hierarchy in Latin America has struggled to identify the causes of the swelling ranks of Pentecostal Protestantism and other Christian denominations in Latin America in the past half century, and it has attempted to craft responses to hold on to its rank and file. Though often dismissed by contemporary scholars, the threat of secularism—that the faithful might become quietly detached from *any* religious authority and moral sensibility driven from the public sphere—is at least as great a challenge to the Roman Catholic Church today as religious competition, and it is recognized as such by church officials. It would be difficult otherwise to understand the intensity of church advocacy of religious education and its condemnation of the mass media. There is, moreover, a growing pluralism *within* Catholicism, which challenges not only the position of the institutional church and its reach over public policy but also its hegemony over those who still claim membership in the community of Catholic believers. Secularization and religious pluralism, in turn, carry greater dangers under conditions of political pluralism and democratic politics.

The New Face of Religious Competition

In his 1990 work *Is Latin America Turning Protestant?* David Stoll, extrapolating from the rate of growth of evangelical Protestantism from 1960 to 1985, projected that by the year 2010 four countries—Guatemala, El Salvador, Brazil, and Honduras—would have majority evangelical populations, and in four others—Chile, Bolivia, Haiti, and Costa Rica—evangelicals would make up between one-third and two-fifths of the population. Only Paraguay, Venezuela, Mexico, Uruguay, and Cuba would remain relatively impervious to the Protestant onslaught, although by 1993 Protestant ranks in Venezuela had already exceeded Stoll's projection for 2010; at least a quarter of the Cuban population practices Santería; and more Uruguayans claim no religious denomination at all than claim to be Roman Catholic. While it is improbable that such growth rates would have continued at such a torrid pace, growth itself has not stopped but merely slowed. In El Salvador the Catholic population fell, according to national surveys conducted by the Instituto Universitario de Opinión Pública Universidad Centroamericana (IUDOP-UCA), from 64.1 percent in 1988 to 56.7 percent in 1995, and the percentage of evangelical Protestants rose from 17.8 percent in 1995 to 23.8 percent in 1997 (cited in Stein 1999, 124).[6] In 1985 Protestants had represented less than 13 percent of the Salvadoran population (cited in Stoll 1990; see Table 1.2). In Chile the percentage of the population declaring themselves to be Catholic in the official census declined from 77 percent in 1992 to 70 percent in 2002.

It is a considerable challenge even to describe with any confidence the trends of declining hegemony and growing religious pluralism. Most cross-national databases that offer comparable categories and reporting years depend for their figures on the self-reporting of religious institutions, which notoriously inflate their figures. For example, in El Salvador the Catholic Church reported a Catholic population of 90 percent in 2000, but only 55 percent declared themselves to be Catholic in the 1998 Central American University study (Table 1.2). In any given year, the sum of these self-reported levels of adherence to various denominations would easily exceed 100 percent of the population. Although it may be the case in countries such as

Table 1.2. Religious Pluralism in Latin America, 1980–2002

Country	Index of Religious Fractionalization[a]	Percent Roman Catholic		Percent Evangelical		Percent Pentecostal/ Charismatic	Percent Spiritist/ Other
		(1998–2002)[b]	(2000)[c]	(1985)[d]	(1993)[e]	(1993)	(1993)[f]
Brazil	0.6054	74	85	16.0	17.8	15.6	4.8
Cuba	0.5059	47	n.d.	2.1	2.54	n.d.	25.0
Haiti	0.4704	80	n.d.	14.2	20.7	6.5	75.0
Nicaragua	0.4290	73	85	6.3	14.1	11.0	n.d.
Chile	0.3841	70	n.d.	21.6	26.7	25.4	1.4
Guatemala	0.3753	50–60	83	18.9	23.3	15.8	2.0
El Salvador	0.3559	55	90	12.8	19.8	16.4	n.d.
Uruguay	0.3548	52	69	1.9	2.2	1.6	n.d.
Panama	0.3338	82	73	9.7	1.2	10.6	4.5
Dominican Republic	0.3118	68	89	5.2	n.d.		n.d.
Costa Rica	0.2410	72	92	6.5	9.7	6.8	n.d.
Honduras	0.2357	63	80	8.8	10.4	5.8	3.6
Argentina	0.2236	88	n.d.	4.7	6.9	5.6	1.5
Paraguay	0.2123	n.d.	86	2.5	4.3	2.0	n.d.
Bolivia	0.2085	78	87	6.5	8.4	3.5	15.0
Peru	0.1988	80	94	3.0	5.6	2.5	30.0
Mexico	0.1796	88	n.d.	3.1	4.3	2.6	n.d.
Colombia	0.1478	81	92	2.4	3.1	2.3	n.d.
Ecuador	0.1417	n.d.	93	2.8	3.4	1.4	n.d.
Venezuela	0.1350	70	94	2.0	4.8	3.4	2.4

Note: No data available (n.d.) for some categories.

[a]Alesina et al. (2003, 184–89). The index identifies the percentage of the population of each country that belonged to the three most widely spread religions in the world in 1980—Roman Catholicism, Protestantism, and Islam. For new countries the data are available for 1990–1995. The numbers are in percent (scale from 0 to 100). The residual is called "other religions."

[b]This data come from the following sources: Argentina, 2002 UNCHR report; Bolivia, 2001 survey; Brazil, 2000 census; Chile, 2002 census; Colombia, El Tiempo 2001 poll; Costa Rica, 2003 government figures; Dominican Republic, 1997 IEPD survey; El Salvador, Central American University 1998 survey; Honduras, 2002 survey; Mexico, 2000 census; Nicaragua, 1995 census; Venezuela, 2001 government figures.

[c]World Christian Database, http://www.worldchristiandatabase.org/wcd/.

[d]Wilkie (1995, 346); the original source is Stoll (1990).

[e]Wilkie (2002, 380).

[f]These faiths are defined as follows: Chile—Animist; Guatemala—Animist/Spiritist; Panama—Muslim; Honduras—Baha'i; Argentina—Muslim; Bolivia—Animist; Peru—Christo-Pagan; Venezuela—Animist/Spiritist.

Table 1.3. Religious Denominations as Reported in 2000 World Values Survey

Country	Evangelical	Protestant	Total Protestant	Roman Catholic	Spiritist	None
Colombia	2.0	0.7	2.7	84.0	n.d.	8.3
Peru[a]	6.9	n.d.	6.9	83.6	n.d.	4.7
Argentina	5.0	0.4	5.4	78.4	n.d.	13.0
Mexico	3.3	1.5	4.8	73.9	n.d.	19.4
Brazil	n.d.	3.5	3.5	70.1	14.4	12.0
Venezuela	n.d.	6.7	6.7	65.9	n.d.	27.1
Dominican Republic	6.1	1.7	10.5[b]	59.0	n.d.	24.0
El Salvador[c]	23.0	n.d.	23.0	58.9	n.d.	15.9
Chile	7.6	2.0	9.6	54.1	n.d.	33.9
Uruguay	5.5	1.4	6.9	40.6	n.d.	47.9

Source: Inglehart et al. (2004).
Note: No data available (n.d.) for some categories.
[a]In Peru the other reported religions were 2.7 percent Jehovah's Witness and 1.3 percent Seventh Day Adventist.
[b]Includes 2.7 percent Pentecostal.
[c]Includes 26.5 percent who identify themselves as "Catholic: doesn't follow rules."

Brazil and Cuba that those who identify with Spiritism and Catholicism might genuinely adhere to both religions and see no apparent contradiction between the two, this does not fully account for the discrepancies. National surveys might generate more accurate data, but they often lack comparability. Censuses tend to elicit higher rates of self-identification than other methods because of their official nature. A more accurate measure can arguably be obtained by drawing from responses in World Values Surveys (WVS) to the question, "Do you belong to a religious denomination (If yes, which one?)." Only ten countries (half the total) were included in the 2000 round, but those encompass most of the region's population.

By the criteria of "belonging to a denomination," the most Roman Catholic country of the ten Latin American countries included in the World Values Survey is Colombia, where 84 percent of the population identified itself as such, followed by Peru, Argentina, and Mexico. Brazil and Venezuela were still more than two-thirds Catholic, and the lowest levels of identification with the Catholic Church were registered in El Salvador, Chile, and Uruguay (Table 1.3). These figures corroborate the directional trends and the rank order evident in the national census reports and the reports of churches themselves, if at lower and more realistic levels. In national censuses, Brazil, Cuba, and Haiti, with the largest proportion of Spiritist and Charismatic followers, and Chile, Brazil, Guatemala, El Salvador, and Nicaragua, with the largest representation of Pentecostal and evangelical Protestants, are the countries whose identities as Catholic nations are most threatened (see Table 1.2). In the middle range are Panama, the Dominican Republic, Costa Rica, Honduras, and Paraguay, and at the low end are Colombia, Mexico, and Argentina. Before these countries with proportionally fewer competitors can comfortably be declared as safe for Roman Catholicism, however, we must recognize that self-identification sets a low bar, and religious homogeneity is a rather poor guide to the frequency and intensity of religious practice and to just how strong the bonds of identification with the Catholic Church are among self-identified Catholics.

Whether or not the recent success of religious competitors to the Catholic Church in Latin America should be seen as a novel development depends in part on whether one accepts the view that Latin America was traditionally a deeply Catholic region. During the centuries of Christendom when Roman Catholicism's religious hegemony, originally imposed by conquest, was assured by religious establishment and concordats with states, many scholars now argue, the church only weakly penetrated poor, rural areas and, in particular, indigenous society. From the outset it was severely handicapped by its limited ability to recruit indigenous priests and to import foreign-born ones to take their place. "Quickly disappointed by the indifference and lack of disposition towards a chaste life among the Indians," wrote one historian, Spaniards essentially gave up on the indigenous population after the first fifty years of their empire (Blancarte 2000, 597), concentrating their Christianization efforts instead on mestizos. The church did not develop a true Indian pastoral and essentially excluded the indigenous population from ecclesiastical influence until the second half of the twentieth century. On the Atlantic coast and in the Caribbean, meanwhile, during centuries of slavery and postemancipation oppression, enslaved Africans and their descendants hid their own religious beliefs from

view in synergistic forms of Catholicism, which survive to this day in Santería in Cuba, Umbanda and Candomblé in Brazil, and Diaspora religions
elsewhere in Latin America (Chesnut 2003a). Religious practice was traditionally low among the poor, and local understandings of Catholicism bore
scant resemblance to official Roman doctrine. On such a weak foundation,
the Latin American Catholic Church depended on wealthy landowners and
urban elites and maintained dominance on the "political basis" of its official
status (Vallier 1970, 7). Its religious hegemony may have always been more
an illusion than a reality, based on more of a skin-deep attachment than a
deep and abiding faith (de Groot 1996).

Into this neglected market, argue scholars following the pioneering
work of Finke and Stark (1992), religious competitors entered. The "religious economy thesis" assumes that the demand for an alternative to Catholicism was always there, and once the state-imposed and protected
religious monopoly from which the Catholic Church in Latin America
benefited for centuries was ended and competition was permitted, millions
of low-intensity, nominal adherents seized the opportunity to shop in the
market now open to new offers tailored to them and their needs.[7] Unsurprisingly, the Catholic Church lost part of its market share to competitors
that could match consumer demand for particular forms of worship, promise to heal sick children with faith when quality health care was unavailable,
allow women to use artificial birth control methods, encourage their husbands to end alcohol abuse, and employ a persuasive style of outreach—
with the message carried door to door by family and friends who had done
well by converting (Chesnut 2003a). The demand for these fresh and innovative products also grew as peasants once under the domination of devout
landowners now migrated to cities and became free to worship as they
chose. The dense settlement patterns of urban neighborhoods enabled and
facilitated small Pentecostal operations run out of storefronts or the town
square (Prokopy and Smith 1999, 6–7).[8] They also provided an alternative
religious identity more closely matched to resurgent ethnic identities in
Central America and the Andean nations (Blancarte 2000, 596–97).[9] Baptized Catholic but essentially nonconforming and nonpracticing, indigenous peoples who adopted a new faith and way of practicing it were also
leaving behind a religion that they associated with their peninsular (Iberian) oppressors (Brysk 2004; Corr 2007). Subcultural identity theory—

which contends that social networks and subcultural identities reinforce religious communities by defining both positive reference groups whose opinions they value and negative reference groups that they do not want to be or believe—offers a supporting frame for such a view. External enemies unite believers in their faith, give them strength, and highlight what separates them from outsiders (Prokopy and Smith 1999, 5).

As in any market economy, moreover, suppliers must also reach local markets, and in this regard the Catholic Church is heavily disadvantaged. The church is perennially short of priests (who take years to form), and has too few parishes; the parishes that do exist are too large to reach the faithful in a meaningful way in their daily lives. The problem is particularly acute in poor neighborhoods and rural areas. In Chile there is on average one parish for every 20,658 inhabitants in those areas with less than a 10 percent poverty rate but 73,537 inhabitants per parish in those where the poverty rate exceeds 19 percent (Lehmann 2001).[10] Similarly, in Venezuela there are on average 17,668 persons per parish in the richest quartile of parishes but 42,830 in the poorest (Froehle 1995, 137). Protestant missions also received an early boost from Central American governments that promoted them as a way of making their countries more attractive to the "right" immigrants from the "right" countries. More recently, the U.S. government and various right-wing groups financed Protestant missions in the indigenous highlands of Guatemala and in El Salvador as a way to undermine support for troublesome Catholic opponents of military regimes that were fighting insurgents and to create a support base for a more conservative political order (Stoll 1990; Crahan 1992; Garrard-Burnett 1998).

Thus, the Catholic Church's concern about the inroads made by other religious denominations and missions is not exaggerated or without foundation. But the "false prophets" and "rapacious wolves" of other religious denominations that came to feed on a vulnerable flock, as Pope John Paul referred to them,[11] are not the only threat to the hegemony of Catholicism in society.

Is Latin America Turning Secular?

The giants of early twentieth-century social theory—Max Weber and Emile Durkheim—expected modernity to erode the religious foundations of society. For Weber, human reason, rational calculation, and scientific advancements would explain the mysterious, erode faith in the central claims of religious doctrine, and consign religious authorities to being one, but not necessarily the definitive, source of information in society. Durkheim emphasized that when the modern welfare state and publicly funded and run educational systems in nineteenth- and twentieth-century Europe assumed the functions previously carried out by faith-based voluntary and charitable organizations in the medieval era, the functional need for religious institutions would also erode. Both anticipated that even if citizens still participated in the formal religious rites of birth, marriage, death, and the observance of religious holidays, the public role of religion would inevitably decline. Noted sociologists in the 1960s such as Peter Berger (1967) saw the apparent decline of religious authority and practice as confirmation of the secularization thesis.

In the late twentieth century scholars found, of course, that whether because of church efforts, eternal truths, or the persistent human need to find solace in dreams of another, better world in the face of deprivation and despair, religious belief had not become extinct with the advance of scientific knowledge and capitalist development. Touting the persistence and even revitalization of religion as evidence that the thesis was just plain wrong, many issued calls to bury the secularization thesis once and for all. Indeed, the role of religion in the 2004 U.S. presidential election, the resurgence of Islamic fundamentalism in central Asia and Africa, and the dynamic growth of Protestant churches in Central America do seem to support those who would dismiss the entire notion of secularization. From this perspective, America is not different—western Europe is—and it is the western European pattern of secularization, not American exceptionalism, that needs to be explained (Casanova 1994, 28).

Recent scholarship has called these ready dismissals into question, however. Norris and Inglehart (2004) argue that merely because secularization is not a uniform and universal imperative does not mean that it has not happened in advanced industrial democracies. Unlike vulnerable populations in poorer nations, among whom religious observance is still strong, religiosity *is* in decline among populations that have known material security in their personal lives and their communities. The United States, with its high rates of religiosity and apparently majoritarian views in favor of blurring the separation of church and state, is the clear exception. Most Europeans still express formal belief in God or identify themselves as Protestants or Catholics on official forms, but church attendance has fallen, the clergy have largely lost influence over the public on a series of moral issues, and religious vitality and influence over how people live their daily lives have gradually eroded (Norris and Inglehart 2004, 25). Even in once strongly Catholic Ireland, there are only 3.6 seminarians per 100 priests (compared with 10 in the United States and 22.5 in Poland) and weekly church attendance has experienced its steepest decline in Europe (from 91 percent in 1973 to 34 percent in 2005) (Shorto 2007, 42, 63). For Norris and Inglehart, the secularization thesis needs to be updated and secularization redefined not as something born of confidence in science or the acquisition of material wealth but rather a result of existential security—the "feeling that survival is secure enough that it can be taken for granted" (2004, 4).

It might be tempting to think that with two decades of economic crisis and civil violence, Latin Americans would be short on existential security and clutching onto their religious beliefs. In some senses they are: according to the World Values Survey conducted in ten Latin American countries in 2000, 97 percent of respondents reported that they believe in God and 84 percent that they draw comfort and strength from religion; 79 percent consider themselves religious persons, and 75 percent say God is very important in their lives (Inglehart et al. 2004).[12] Very high totals believe that people have a soul (86 percent), in heaven (81 percent), and in life after death (71 percent); fewer, but still a majority, believe in hell (55 percent). By contrast, only 53 percent of respondents in Spain, 47 percent in Portugal, 45 percent in France, 44 percent in Belgium, and 39 percent in Germany—once the core of Catholic Europe—believe in life after death, to take just one indicator.

The degree to which religiosity has declined in Latin America is hard to gauge, in part because our knowledge of Latin America's past is, frankly, sketchy at best. The World Values Survey, our source for current levels of self-reported practice and political involvement, began modestly in Latin America twenty-five years ago in only two countries, Argentina and Mexico. In Chile, one of the few Latin American countries with a long tradition of survey research (the premier polling firm of Eduardo Hamuy operated as early as the late 1950s), we know that 33.2 percent of the Catholic population in greater Santiago in 1958 practiced; in 1998 that figure had dropped to 18.5 percent in Santiago and to 14 percent nationwide (down from 21 percent in 1995) (Lehmann 2001). In more recent years the picture is mixed. On the one hand, an average of just over 40 percent of respondents in the ten countries included in the 2000 round of the WVS attend religious services of any kind once a week or more (Table 1.4). Only in El Salvador, Mexico, and the Dominican Republic do a majority attend services. In Uruguay, where a mere 14 percent attend religious services with any regularity, a majority (54.5 percent) report that they *never* do so. Moreover, just over half of all Latin Americans and barely more Roman Catholics reported that

Table 1.4. Devotion of Latin American Catholics, as Reported in 2000 World Values Survey

Question: *How often do you attend religious services?* (Percent answering once a week or more often)

Country	Catholics	Total Population
Mexico	62.3	56.4
El Salvador	61.1	58.1
Dominican Republic	50.0	44.8
Colombia	47.5	45.9
Peru	45.9	47.4
Chile[a]	38.3	31.1
Brazil	36.2	36.1
Venezuela	35.2	30.6
Argentina	23.9	24.5
Uruguay	17.6	13.6
Latin American Average	*45.0*	*41.3*

Source: Inglehart et al. (2004).
[a]Figures for Chile vary considerably from earlier World Values Surveys (Lehmann 2002, 31–32), when only 14 percent of Roman Catholics and 19 percent of all Chileans reported attending religious services at least once a week.

religion is very important to their lives, and less than half cite religious faith as a quality that is important to encourage children to learn at home (Table 1.5). On the other hand, although those who self-identify as religious people, find comfort and strength in religion, and pray to God outside religious services declined in Chile from 1990 to 2000, private devotion appears to have held steady in Argentina, Brazil, and Mexico.[13]

If most scholars are ready to bury concerns about secularization, the Catholic Church, long preoccupied with the crisis of modernity, is not. To the church the danger in secularization is not merely that people will abandon their faith in God and no longer call themselves Catholic, or even that members will make up their own brand of Catholicism as they go along; rather, the church is concerned that society will become morally corrupted if Catholics neglect to observe their faith, privatize it, and loosen religious constraints on their personal ethical behavior. The church, in other words, understands secularization, like Weber, as the decline of religious vitality and the importance of religion to public and private life, or, in Casanova's (1994) words, the "privatization of religion." In the past two decades the church's concern that secularization threatens Catholic culture and public morality more broadly has only grown.

An Erosion of Hegemony or the Decline of Authority?
The Pluralism Within

The crisis of declining religious hegemony confronting the Roman Catholic Church in Latin America is manifested in the success of religious competitors and a decline in the religious self-identification of the population, a lessening of the intensity of belief in God among Catholics, and the declining rates of religious observance duly reported here; however, its origins run deeper. A plurality of religious belief has invaded Catholicism itself. Some currents such as Catholic Charismatic Renewal (CCR), a dynamic movement of small communities that shares with Pentecostalism a spirituality emphasizing *glossolalia* (speaking in tongues) and faith healing as gifts of the Holy Spirit, have readily deferred to and accepted hierarchical authority, in effect "recentralizing" the church by "affirming and reproducing the power of the church hierarchy" (Peterson and Vásquez 2001, 199). But other contemporary Catholic movements pose a challenge to the

Table 1.5. Importance of Religion in People's Lives in Ten Latin American Countries, 2000 (in percent)

	Evangelical	Pentecostal	Protestant	Spiritist	Catholic "Doesn't Follow Rules"	Roman Catholic	No Denomination	All Respondents
Importance of religion in life								
Very important	76.5	54.5	68.8	74.5	83.3	56.8	30.8	54.3
Rather important	17.6	36.4	19.5	19.4	10.9	31.9	27.6	29.8
Not very important	4.2	9.1	9.5	5.5	3.9	9.7	25.6	11.8
Not at all important	1.8	0.0	2.2	0.6	1.8	1.6	64.1	4.1
Cite religious faith as a quality that is important to encourage children to learn at home[a]	61.2	81.8	58.4	64.2	63.0	48.6	27.0	46.5
Spend time with people at church								
Weekly	51.0	n.d.	n.d.	48.9	n.d.	23.7	6.9	22.8
Once or twice a month	24.2	n.d.	n.d.	20.3	n.d.	23.9	12.8	21.6
Only few times a year	13.9	n.d.	n.d.	17.3	n.d.	21.4	20.7	20.6
Not at all	10.9	n.d.	n.d.	13.5	n.d.	31.0	59.6	35.0
Say God is very important in their lives[b]	90.9	100.0	92.3	93.9	83.4	77.1	56.9	74.9
Draw comfort and strength from religion	96.6	90.0	86.2	92.1	85.4	91.2	47.4	84.4

Source: 2000 World Values Surveys (Inglehart et al. 2004).

Note: No data available (n.d.) for some categories.

[a] Respondents were asked to indicate the five most important qualities to encourage children to learn at home. The other options were good manners, independence, hard work, feeling of responsibility, imagination, tolerance and respect for other people, thrift, perseverance, unselfishness, and obedience.

[b] Respondents were asked to rate the importance of God in their lives on a scale of one to ten, with one representing not at all important and ten representing very important. Only responses of ten are included here.

church's traditional hegemony. In these postmodern times, when globalization and its attendant migration of people and secular ideas via the mass media are claimed to have transformed education, generated a global culture of consumerism, fragmented identities, and stoked indigenous demands, Parker (2003, 2004; see also chap. 4 in this volume) argues that globalization has not destroyed religion but rather created new spiritualities and, in particular, a syncretic Catholicism that has blended old and new, Catholic and non-Catholic beliefs. Catholics who have passed through non-Catholic educational institutions, both public and private, and who belong to new women's and indigenous social movements are especially likely to pick and choose from a smorgasbord of religious beliefs rather than practice a traditional variant of Catholicism. This "heterodox" Catholicism poses a major challenge to the cultural hegemony of a church that jealously protects its "brand"—Catholicism does not permit just anyone to call herself and whatever she believes Catholic—as well as its control over the institutions in which collective beliefs are formed.

The origins of Catholic heterodoxy may lay with the decline of the subcultural institutions of the church that traditionally socialized Catholics for public life. Although the church is still reasonably capable of reaching school-aged children in Nicaragua, Bolivia, and Venezuela—where in 1999 participation rates in parochial secondary educational institutions ranged from a quarter to a little over a third—fewer than one in ten children were educated in Catholic secondary schools in Brazil, Mexico, Panama, Costa Rica, Uruguay, Honduras, and Peru (Table 1.6). Where the population was already reasonably literate and well educated, the proportion of students enrolled in Catholic educational institutions has remained relatively steady or even modestly increased. But where there were substantial gains in the public educational system—especially among the social strata that cannot afford the tuition fees of private religious schools—as there were in Brazil in the 1990s, the decline has been dramatic; the percentage of Brazilian secondary school–aged students in Catholic schools dropped off from 21.9 percent in 1985 to 4.8 percent in 1999. Such low percentages of students now brought into the Catholic orbit does not augur well for the church's capacity to shape culture in the continent's large, pluralistic countries. Loosened from their moorings in Catholic educational institutions and social organizations that for centuries transmitted religious instruction and

Table 1.6. The Reach of the Church: Educational Institutions, 1985–1999

| | Percent of Students in Catholic Schools | | | |
| | Primary Schools | | Secondary Schools | |
	1985	1999	1985	1999
Argentina	13.7	13.9[b]	17.5	n.d.
Bolivia	7.6	8.9[b]	29.0	27.4
Brazil	4.3	2.8	21.9	4.8
Chile	12.4	15.6	13.8	16.8
Colombia	16.3	9.5	26.1	20.8
Costa Rica	2.3	2.7	8.0	8.3
Dominican Republic	6.2[a]	5.6[b]	9.5[a]	13.8[b]
Ecuador	11.3	12.3	15.9	16.1
El Salvador	4.8	3.5	14.0	18.8
Guatemala	9.2	5.5[b]	29.4	n.d.
Haiti	35.6	42.8[c]	11.2	20.4[c]
Honduras	0.9	1.0	6.0	9.0[d]
Mexico	3.7	4.9	3.9	5.6
Nicaragua	15.2	10.0	25.1	26.0
Panama	3.8	6.5	10.9	6.5
Paraguay	10.0	5.4	17.2	19.0
Peru	5.9	4.9	12.2	10.6
Uruguay	14.8	11.8	9.9	9.2
Venezuela	7.4	5.7	36.9	35.0

Sources: For Roman Catholic educational institution enrollments, see Wilkie (1990, 311–13; and Wilkie 2002, 368–72). For total enrollments in primary- and secondary-level education, see UN-ECLAC (2003, 517–19).

Note: Secondary school enrollment figures for Argentina and Guatemala not available (n.d.) for 1999.

[a]Figure reflects 1986 enrollment.
[b]Figure reflects 1997 enrollment.
[c]Figure reflects 1990 enrollment.
[d]Figure reflects 2000 enrollment.

values, Catholics are now not only more open to new religious missions but also more likely to develop their own pastiche of beliefs.

What is harder to measure is the qualitative change in the nature of a distinctively Catholic "spiritual capital"[14] and the degree to which the church may be losing its grip over social movements, parishioners, and parties. The apex of church influence over the social and political life of Latin America's Catholics may have come in the middle of the twentieth century, when the church's renewed mission to evangelize Latin American society, replicating the integralist project launched in Europe in the 1920s, began to bear fruit. Beginning in the 1930s, the church invited lay participation and fostered the invigoration of Catholic civil society through a dense network of organizations that blanketed Latin America under the rubric of Catholic Action. It organized workers into Catholic labor unions known as Círculos Católicos de Obreros, or Operários in Brazil (Catholic Worker Circles); youth into Catholic University Youth (JUC) and Catholic Youth Workers (JOC); and peasants into Rural Catholic Action movements and Catholic Peasants Leagues, which laid roots from the northwestern Mayan departments of Guatemala (Calder 2004, 95–96, 104) to the Chilean countryside. Trade unions were particularly important to forestall the possibility of socialist unionization, and youth organizations served to insulate university students from radical ideologies and socialize them to become future Catholic lay leaders (Gill 1998, 35). Alongside these movements, numerous missionary expeditions branched out to remote rural areas to educate and develop skills among the rural population and ensure that local Catholic practice conformed to Roman orthodoxy.

Eventually these movements dissipated, their demise hastened by military repression and the withdrawal of hierarchical support. The generation of Catholic activists who had answered the church's initial call to action fanned out to join and even organize the continent's most prominent Catholic lay organizations and political parties. Eduardo Frei and Rafael Caldera, inspired by the ideological influence of their priests (Hawkins 2003), went on to lead two of Latin America's most important Christian Democratic parties in Chile and Venezuela. Church leaders backed the new parties not as an unintended, defensive response to a liberal onslaught, as they had in Europe in the late nineteenth century (Kalyvas 1996), but as a bulwark against communism—though communism was not in an immediate position to threaten the church, except as understood by Archbishop Mariano Rossell (1964 [1954]) in Guatemala in 1954 and eventually in Cuba. Others went left and staffed the liberationist church. Brazil's Catholic Youth Worker movement, for instance, has been called one of the "most important precursors to the popular Church of the 1970s" (Mainwaring 1986, 116). But lay activists did not always stay in the fold, and as they migrated to secular organizations, even with their Catholic guiding principles and beliefs in tow, the church was not always satisfied with the results. A parallel process in France sent former integralists in what Suzanne Berger (1985) has referred to as a pattern of "centrifugal dispersion" into leftist parties and movements. As she put it, from the church's standpoint the subcultural organizations that had been mandated to do the church's work in the outside world were pulled into it, "assimilated by the natives they had come to convert" (37–38). Although the presence of committed Catholics dramatically transformed these parties and organizations in a fundamentally more humanist direction, the integralist project was judged a failure, doomed by secularization, affluence, and the erosion of the anticlerical and Jacobin features of French society that had posed obstacles to the integration of Catholics into republican France (S. Berger 1985).

Beginning in the 1960s, the Latin American church tried again, this time creating new grassroots church communities that became famously known as "ecclesial base communities" (comunidades eclesiais de base, or CEBs). Appearing first in Brazil, the CEBs were intended to foster new forms of participation that would intensify the religious experience in places where priests were scarce. Many, guided by the precepts of the theology of liberation, also were expected to re-energize the faith by connecting it to daily practice, hand the people the tools to discover the word of God on their own by replacing catechism with the Bible, and empower the poor and oppressed by inviting participation (Levine 1981b). In Colombia bishops retained control of these organizations (Levine 1981b, 1993), but in Brazil and even in Venezuela the CEBs carved out a reasonable degree of autonomy from ecclesiastical authorities. The fact that the church by and large did not control the CEBs as it once had the Catholic Action network allowed a measure of creativity in the groups, empowered their members, and energized lay participation in the church (Levine 1981a). But it also diluted the capacity of religious associations to hold the line against pluralism from without and within. This was especially so once democratic openings created space in which social movements could safely operate without church protection. Unlike during the years of dictatorship, when Catholic churches in some countries enjoyed privileged positions at the head of broad alliances encompassing human rights groups, democratic politicians, and lay activists, religious leadership of civil society organizations now would have to be earned, not assumed. Indigenous movements from Guatemala to Chile, which the church had protected from military-nationalist projects, slipped outside the church's reach, both organizationally and theologically (cf. Parker 2004). Moreover, democratic openings revealed cracks in alliances that had been papered over during authoritarian regimes. To take one notable example, women's movements that once allied with the church over the economic survival of their families and communities when dictators were determined to drive down wages came to challenge the church's moral/family agenda in demanding access to artificial and even emergency contraception, the option of voluntary sterilization, the right to dissolve a marriage (and gain state backing for child support), and even the legal right to terminate a pregnancy.

The outwardly visible sign that the church is losing its influence over the faithful is the emerging gap between the views of the laity and those of the hierarchy on a series of moral issues. A major survey of Catholic opinion in six major metropolitan areas of Brazil, which elicited opinion about a broad range of issues and connected opinion about church influences on an issue-by-issue basis, uncovered a growing gulf between church teachings and the views of Catholics on divorce, birth control, and even a celibate priesthood (Table 1.7). In a broader sample of ten countries, Catholic opinion overwhelmingly rejects the notion that an abortion can ever be justified, but significant minorities of the population believe that transgressing the church proscriptions on homosexuality and euthanasia can sometimes be justified, and only roughly one-third of Latin Americans oppose divorce in all circumstances (Table 1.8). If Catholics side with the church on the issue of the sanctity of life in the womb in surveys, however, they do not in practice. Across Latin America, rates of clandestine abortions are among the highest in the world.[15] On those issues on which the two sides are farthest apart, Catholics think the church should either attempt to influence the public debate but not exercise any undue influence over public policy or that it should not even attempt to influence public opinion on these subjects. The WVS data show that a strong majority of Venezuelans, three-fifths of Mexicans, and two-thirds of Chileans believe that the church should not influence government or how people vote in elections. Roughly the same percentage of Argentines agreed that the church should not attempt to influence government, but as many as three-fourths felt the church should not influence how people vote in elections (Table 1.9).

Table 1.7. Catholic Opinion in Brazil: Moral Issues and Church Involvement, 2000

	Individual Conduct		Institutional Role[a]		
	In Favor	Opposed	Should Not Be Involved	Should Debate, without Imposing	Should Impose Its Vision
Family Planning	77.5	4.2	29.4	57.4	8.1
Contraception	73.2	11.7	28.8	50.8	10.9
Abortion	12.8	71.8	16.3	36.9	37.0
Premarital Sex	43.6	27.4	35.6	42.9	12.9
Homosexuality	10.0	60.6	27.0	28.0	33.1
Celibate Priesthood	33.1	34.5	22.7	36.0	22.9
Second Marriage	62.7	16.2	38.7	33.0	9.0
Divorce	59.4	20.1	31.9	39.0	10.9
Extramarital Affairs[b]	12.4	70.4	n.d.	n.d.	n.d.
Adultery	6.0	80.0	19.3	31.2	38.5
Euthanasia	15.5	61.3	17.7	32.6	35.1
Death Penalty	27.8	53.3	17.7	34.5	34.9
Human Genetic Manipulation	7.3	67.6	16.9	27.8	38.7

Source: Cabral Medeiros (2002, 201–47).
Note: Survey instrument was administered to 5,218 respondents in six metropolitan areas: Belo Horizonte, Porto Alegre, Recife, Rio de Janeiro, Salvador, and São Paulo. Here, only responses of Catholics (n = 3,513, 67.3 percent of the total sample) are included.
[a]Options: (1) religion should not be involved with this question, which is a personal, intimate one; (2) the position one adopts should depend on one's own conscience; religion should be allowed to debate, orient, and suggest a line of conduct to its faithful without "imposing" its vision; (3) religion should "impose" its vision of conduct on the faithful; and (4) I cannot judge how religion should act.
[b]Question not asked about role of religion in extramarital affairs.

Table 1.8. Catholic Views on Moral Issues, as Reported in 2000 World Values Survey

Question: Please tell me for each of the following statements whether you think it can always be justified, never be justified, or something in between. (in percent)

	Homosexuality			Abortion			Divorce			Euthanasia			"Morality Index"[a]
	Never Justifiable (1)	(5-6)	Always Justifiable (10)	Never Justifiable (1)	(5-6)	Always Justifiable (10)	Never Justifiable (1)	(5-6)	Always Justifiable (10)	Never Justifiable (1)	(5-6)	Always Justifiable (10)	
Argentina	39	28	14	67	18	3	24	34	18	49	20	13	45
Brazil	55	17	7	76	8	3	30	24	18	61	12	8	56
Chile	38	25	7	71	9	2	31	20	20	49	16	7	47
Colombia	61	14	4	75	8	1	33	23	14	45	15	14	54
Dominican Republic	48	20	5	60	11	8	23	29	18	53	13	9	46
El Salvador	78	7	4	92	2	2	55	12	15	83	4	6	77
Mexico	53	17	10	70	9	6	41	20	15	40	24	10	51
Peru[b]	54	19	3	73	7	1	40	24	10	n.d.	n.d.	n.d.	56
Uruguay	48	16	13	53	18	10	26	21	27	42	23	21	42
Venezuela	63	9	1	71	8	2	29	31	9	55	10	8	55

Source: Inglehart et al. (2004).

Note: Figures do not add up to 100 because only the extreme (1,10) and center positions (5-6) on a scale of 1 to 10 were included. There were few responses from 2-4 and 7-9 on these issues.

[a]Average of "never justifiable" responses to all four questions. Peruvian case averaged across three available issue areas.

[b]Question concerning euthanasia not asked in Peruvian survey.

The church is also losing political agents that protected its interests and carried forth its principles into the public sphere. Conservative parties close to the church in Colombia and Uruguay are not guaranteed a share of national power as they once were. Christian Democratic parties that once flourished by promising a "third way" (Sigmund 2003) have similarly lost ground. Once competitive parties in El Salvador, Guatemala, and Venezuela have been reduced to rump parties, and those that have survived thus far are also losing seats in Congress, religious voters, and their distinctive identities (Mainwaring and Scully 2003). The Chilean Christian Democratic Party (PDC), once a party identified with an ideology of freedom, community, development, and social justice based on the tenets of Christian humanism that inspired millions of Chileans and other Latin Americans, today transmits only the sort of technocratic, depoliticized message that devastated its Venezuelan counterpart, the Social Christian Party (COPEI) (Crisp, Levine, and Molina 2003). The exceptions—the Mexican National Action Party (Partido Acción Nacional, or PAN), the Costa Rican United Social Christian Party (Partido de Unidad Social Cristiana, or

Table 1.9. Should the Church be Involved in Politics? Catholic Views as Reported in 2000 World Values Survey

Question: *How much do you agree or disagree with each of the following statements? Religious leaders should not influence . . .*

	How People Vote in Elections			Government		
	Agree[a]	Neither[b]	Disagree[c]	Agree[a]	Neither[b]	Disagree[c]
Argentina	76	10	14	63	15	22
Chile	67	7	26	67	6	28
Mexico	61	10	29	63	9	28
Venezuela	56	15	28	58	15	27

Source: Inglehart et al. (2004).
[a]Percent who agree strongly and agree.
[b]Percent who neither agree nor disagree.
[c]Percent who disagree and disagree strongly.

PUSC), and Christian Democratic fragments in new Peruvian movements and parties (Schmidt 2003)—are few and far between. There is also no hope of renewal. The church no longer supports partisan political ventures and will not encourage Christian Democratic parties to recreate themselves under new party labels (Mainwaring 2003, 377–78). Although there are good reasons why the church should not allow itself to become identified with any one party or government, the decline of parties once identified with the church does carry a cost. If church leaders were once fearful of Catholic parties over which they had no control, now they must rely to an even greater extent on parties that accept church help but owe the church little in return. The disappearance of these parties, which were embedded in the larger Catholic world built by the laity and priests on the ground, has left no explicitly Catholic space in political society. Even Catholic politicians respond to voters, not bishops.

It is difficult to overstate the gravity of the implications of this shifting terrain for the Catholic Church and Latin American states and societies. Against the reality of a growing minority of the population that belong to other faiths, the shrinking majority of Catholics, and the growing independence of the faithful, political pluralism has sparked national debates about where the line separating church and state will be drawn and the degree to which state policy should reflect a Catholic society or maintain religious neutrality. At issue, at least for the moment, is less whether the church will be able to maintain state subsidies for the salaries of priests, Catholic educational institutions, and charities (Table 1.10) than whether religious competitors should be placed on an equal footing. Constitutional and ordinary legislation governing religious freedom and nondiscrimination, the process of registering religious institutions, and even the enforcement of local ordinances that can have differential impacts on different religious traditions have come under intense scrutiny and discussion in a number of countries, including Venezuela (Smilde 1999), Colombia (Brusco 1999), and Argentina (Bonino 1999). These and other countries are also experiencing heated debates about the appropriate boundaries of religious influence in the design of public policies that in other pluralist democracies privilege rights to privacy.

If democratic politics has raised many new dilemmas for the Roman Catholic Church in Latin America, it has also renewed many familiar ones.

After a checkered history with respect to democracy and political pluralism, in *Gaudium et Spes* (the Pastoral Constitution on the Church in the
Modern World), produced in 1965 by the Second Vatican Council, the
Catholic Church embraced democracy without qualification as the form of
governance that best allowed human beings to fulfill their nature by freely
participating in the political community and that best guaranteed the
church autonomy, integrity, and freedom. But the fit between a hegemonic
church and a democratic political order has always been a bit uncomfort-
able. Today is no different.

How democracy and pluralism have already changed the church, how
religious change is shaping democratic politics, and how the Catholic
Church in various Latin American countries will respond to the challenges
of pluralism—whether bishops will become more or less apt to ally with
conservative political authorities; focus their energies on achieving social
justice or upholding moral values; impose hierarchy or lend autonomy to
grassroots and lay initiatives; fall in step with the Vatican or chart regional
and even national courses—are open questions. Before we address these issues, however, we need to review the church's trajectory in the past quarter
century.

The Latin American Catholic Church: From Hegemony to Pluralism

If this were a novel rather than a work of social science, we would
begin, "When we last left the church, its Brazilian, Chilean, Peruvian, and
Salvadoran branches, spurred on by their liberationist grassroots, were
breaking with the centuries-long tradition of reinforcing the traditional oligarchical order (epitomized by the highly conservative Colombian church),
as well as with counterparts in Argentina and elsewhere who backed brutal
military dictatorships, to bravely oppose authoritarian regimes." We would
then be obliged to note that this much-heralded trend did not continue.
By and large, a church that declared a "preferential option for the poor" in
1979 self-consciously pulled back from the social justice commitments it
had made in the preceding decade, and bishops withdrew support for the
legions of liberationist activists—clergy and laity, men and women—the

Table 1.10. Contemporary Church-State Relations in Latin America

	Catholicism Official Religion	State Support/ Public Subsidies for Catholic Church	Catholic Education/Media/Charities
Argentina	No; constitution stipulates that federal government "sustains the apostolic Roman Catholic faith"	Subsidies for church by Secretariat of Worship (in Ministry of Foreign Affairs) amount to $4 million per annum	Secular public education but religious instruction may be requested in school or religious institution
Bolivia	Yes, constitution recognizes Catholicism as official religion If president attends Mass as part of official functions, by tradition all cabinet members accompany him	Priests receive stipends from state (in part a compensation for land expropriation in past)	Only Catholic religious instruction provided in public institutions; though optional by law, students face strong peer pressure to participate
Brazil	No favored or state religion, although government maintains a concordat with the Vatican	None mentioned	Government subsidies to education, health, and philanthropy programs of Catholic Church; in 1998, 92 percent of Catholic Children's Pastoral funding provided by federal government Public schools are required to offer religious instruction, which is optional for students
Chile	No, church and state are officially separate. 1999 law on religion prohibits religious discrimination; however, the Catholic Church enjoys a privileged status and occasionally receives preferential treatment	None mentioned	In 2002 church opposed bill that removes property tax exemption of private schools charging over $75/month Schools are required to offer religious education twice a week through middle

	Catholicism Official Religion	State Support/Public Subsidies for Catholic Church	Catholic Education/Media/Charities
Chile	Membership in the Catholic Church is considered beneficial to a military career; in the navy, it is said to be almost a requirement for advancement to the highest posts		school (participation is optional with parental waiver) and teach the creed requested by parents; 92 percent of public schools and 81 percent of private schools offered instruction based only on the Catholic faith
Colombia	No (since 1991), but Catholic Church retains de facto privileged status	None mentioned	Catholic Church has agreement with government to provide (tax-exempt) schools in rural areas without state-run schools Catholic Church and other religious groups may provide optional religious instruction in public schools
Costa Rica	Yes, constitution requires state to contribute to maintenance of Catholic Church	Tax exemption on property directly used for worship (full exemption ended in 1992) Land can be conveyed to Catholic Church through development grants (state retains title) or outright title grant Government subsidies to church decided through annual and semi-annual legislation	Catholic instruction provided in public schools, but not mandatory; religious education teachers in public schools must be certified by Catholic Bishops' Conference; only graduates of Catholic University are eligible; teachers from other religious groups are not certified
Dominican Republic	No state religion, but 1954 concordat with Vatican made Catholicism official religion and extended special privileges to church	Public funds to underwrite church expenses, rebuilding of facilities not available to other groups; automatic waiver of customs duties for imported goods (other churches must request exoneration)	Law requires Bible to be read in public schools but is not enforced

Table 1.10. Contemporary Church-State Relations in Latin America (*cont.*)

	Catholicism Official Religion	State Support/Public Subsidies for Catholic Church	Catholic Education/Media/Charities
Ecuador	No	None mentioned	No religious instruction permitted in public schools; private schools may provide religious instruction; some receive public funds from Ministry of Education
El Salvador	Constitution explicitly recognizes Catholic Church and grants it legal status; civil codes give equal status to churches as nonprofit foundations	Exempt from government regulation of church finances (1997 law); church enjoys tax-exempt status	Public education is secular
Guatemala	No state religion, but constitution recognizes "distinct legal personality of Roman Catholic Church"	Government does not subsidize religious groups, and no groups have reported receiving national funding	Some financial assistance to private religious schools Religious instruction permitted but not required in public schools
Honduras	No state religion Government consults with Catholic Church and appoints Catholic leaders to quasi-official commissions Armed forces have official Catholic patron saint	All religious institutions eligible for tax exemption	Subsidies for Catholic schools; In 2000 Congress passed (but did not put into effect) law requiring ten minutes of Bible reading in schools Religious instruction part of curriculum in public schools
Mexico	No, constitution provides for separation of church and state, bars clergy from holding public office and advocating partisan views or supporting political candidates	1992 constitution lifts restrictions on Catholic Church; religious buildings constructed after 1992 are property of religious association that built them (pre-1992 buildings are state-owned and tax exempt)	Religious instruction not allowed in public schools Religious groups may not own or administer broadcast radio or television stations

	Catholicism Official Religion	State Support/Public Subsidies for Catholic Church	Catholic Education/Media/Charities
Nicaragua	No official state religion, but Catholic Church "enjoys a close relationship" with government; political influence of Catholic Church is "significant"; leaders "routinely" meet with senior government officials	All religious institutions eligible for tax exemption	Government pays teacher salaries for Catholic primary and secondary schools Religion not taught in public schools
Panama	No official state religion, but constitution recognizes Catholicism as "religion of the majority"	None mentioned	Constitution requires that Catholicism be taught in public schools, but exemptions allowed upon parental request
Paraguay	No (since 1992); constitution recognizes "historical role of Catholic Church in public life"; Catholic priests perform Mass at government functions, but government is secular Armed forces have an extensive Catholic chaplain program	None mentioned	Government imposes no curriculum requirements regarding religion
Peru	No, but close relationship with state; constitutionally recognized role of Catholic Church in history, culture, and morals of Peru	Earnings of Catholic priests/bishops exempt from income tax; all 52 bishops and priests in towns and villages in border zones additionally receive state remuneration All dioceses receive small monthly institutional subsidy	1998 General Education law mandates all schools to impart religious education; Catholicism only religion taught in public schools (non-Catholic religious and secular private schools have been granted

Table 1.10. Contemporary Church-State Relations in Latin America (*cont.*)

	Catholicism Official Religion	State Support/Public Subsidies for Catholic Church	Catholic Education/Media/Charities
Peru	Military may employ only Catholic clergy as chaplains; Catholicism only recognized religion of military personnel Church officials play "high profile role in public sector"	Real estate, buildings, and houses owned by Catholic Church are exempt from property taxes (other religious groups must pay property taxes for schools and clergy residences)	exemptions); Education Ministry mandates that presiding Catholic bishops recommend and approve religious education teachers in public schools Catholic charities do not have to pay customs duties Non-Catholic missionaries claim immigration discrimination
Uruguay	No, strict separation of church and state	Property-tax exemption for all religious groups if registered as nonprofit entity	Religious instruction prohibited in public schools
Venezuela	No, 1964 concordat governs relations between government and Vatican; Military chaplain corps opened to evangelicals in 2005	All registered religious groups are eligible for government subsidies to support religious services, but most money goes to Catholic organizations because assigned shares are fixed	In 2001 $1.5 million in subsidies to Catholic social programs/schools; other religious groups received only assistance for building repair; in 2004, state urged to pay subsidies to Catholic schools (for poor) on time

Sources: Information culled from U.S. Department of State (2006) and Serbin (1995).

church had unleashed during the 1970s (Ottmann 2002; Drogus and Stewart-Gambino 2005). Although, as one prominent expert on progressive Catholicism in Latin America put it, "the Catholic movement lives on, not only in the visible organizational forms of Christian base communities . . . but in the sensibilities of the millions of people who lived through the last 30 years in some form of engagement with the progressive church" (Burdick 2000, 206), even this observer acknowledges that, shorn of institutional support, the base communities have clearly declined in numbers and militancy.

Alongside this familiar story another has developed. In the quarter century since the Third General Meeting of the Latin American Bishops' Conference at Puebla, Mexico, arguably the more significant shift of the church was not to the right on the ideological spectrum as we know it, as has often been popularly alleged, or even back up the vertical axis from greater lay participation to submission to hierarchical authority. Rather, in 1992 the church launched an encompassing strategy to reclaim the public sphere for religious morality through civil society.

From State to Civil Society, from Politics to Culture

For centuries the Latin American Catholic Church benefited from a cozy relationship with the state. During the period of empire, through the institution of the *patronato* (*padroado* in Portuguese), the Spanish and Portuguese Crowns established the Catholic Church and protected its religious monopoly. To be sure, patronage was a double-edged sword; during this era of Christendom, the church was dependent in the New World on the Crown, which exercised a strong influence on the appointment of bishops, controlled monasteries, authorized religious orders, and placed strict limits on creating new dioceses and recruiting foreign-born priests. Although many priests sympathized with or openly supported independence movements, the church hierarchy took the side of the Crown during the wars of independence and suffered the adverse effects of its strategic miscalculation in country after country at the hands of the liberals.[16] Conservative restorations reinstated church perquisites for a while, at least until the late-nineteenth-century liberal heyday when outward-looking leaders who wished to cultivate trade with Protestant nations disestablished the Catholic Church in country after country.[17]

The effects of disestablishment were at worst ambiguous. In Colombia a new concordat in 1857 protected the Catholic Church's monopoly. Elsewhere, the church rebuilt its institutions and infrastructure with and without state help. In Brazil, under the masterful strategy of Cardinal Sebastião Leme of Rio de Janeiro, the church flourished after the Positivist founders of the republic lifted the *padroado* in 1890 (Mainwaring 1986; Serbin 1995). It created dozens of new bishoprics, imported thousands of European priests and nuns, and organized its own pressure group, the Liga Eleitoral Católica. This strategy was so successful that by the time of Getúlio Vargas's ascendancy to the presidency in 1930, the church "stood poised to reenter national politics as a formidable institution" (Serbin 1995, 155–56). The church won the promulgation of the constitution in the name of God, the indissolubility of marriage, the restoration of military chaplaincies (which had been banned under the republic), renewed state subsidies, and the placement of religious crucifixes in public buildings. The most radical separation of church and state took place in Mexico, where the 1917 constitution proscribed state recognition of religious marriages, disenfranchised priests, prevented church authorities from speaking about politics, and disallowed church ownership of property. But even there, church and state reached a modus vivendi after the 1940s, an arrangement that a Vatican delegate likened to "an unmarried couple living together" (Camp 1997, 32).

This traditional landscape appeared to change irrevocably, at least in some countries, with the combined impact of Vatican II, dictatorship, and the emergence of progressive Catholic churches. Legions of grassroots activists supported by liberation theologians and sympathetic bishops (who also sheltered striking workers and human rights activists) turned the notion of a hierarchical and ritualistic church on its head. But retaliatory attacks on church workers and property, as well as the favorable treatment of religious competitors, by civil authorities from Guatemala and Nicaragua to the Southern Cone soon reminded church leaders of their immense vulnerability to their allies' opponents when the church took sides. The church hierarchy concluded it was right and proper to withdraw from politics. This withdrawal from the political, however, was not merely a defensive maneuver, and it was not understood to mean a withdrawal from the public.

Facing the rapid advance of secularism, the church set out to combat the crisis of modernity. Its project became one of evangelizing society and reclaiming the public sphere for projects of faith and, secondarily, realizing the church's social doctrine and principles of economic justice.

The New Evangelization and Recovering the Public Sphere in a Time of Democratic and Religious Pluralism

In *Evangeli Nuntiandi* (1977) Pope Paul VI had admitted the possibility of accepting a secular cultural domain and resigned the church to the "impossibility of achieving a Christian social order" (Ghio 1992, 197). In the late twentieth century, under the papacy of John Paul II, the church confronted its old nemesis, modernity—which had subordinated the religious to the scientific, extirpated the sacred from daily life, and relegated moral authority only to a private domain now walled off from the public sphere—with new institutional weapons and a new strategy. Having concluded that the defensive project of the first half of the century, which sought to segregate Catholic society from the pernicious influences of modern life, had failed, as had the radical successor projects in Europe and the liberationist projects in Latin America, the church justified mounting an ambitious offensive to chart a new course to deepen church influence over society—the new "evangelization of culture." "Culture" is an overarching concept that encompasses political institutions, economic activities, science, and, at its core, religion; the "evangelization of culture" refers to a project to organize the public sphere upon the principles of faith (Ghio 1992, 195), or, in Casanova's (1994) terms, that religion become "deprivatized" and take its place center stage in the modern world.

The project to evangelize culture was built on an updated social doctrine elaborated in the papal encyclical *Laborem Exercens,* issued in 1981 on the ninetieth anniversary of Pope Leo XIII's encyclical *Rerum Novarum.* In a context of technological, economic, and political change, *Laborem Exercens* called attention to the dignity and rights of those who work, asserting that "human work is a *key,* probably *the essential key,* to the whole social question" (John Paul II 1981, §3). The encyclical established the *"principle of the priority of labor over capital"* (§12); laid out a Catholic understanding of property ownership that "diverges radically from the *collectivism* as proclaimed by Marxism and . . . *capitalism* practiced by liberalism" in asserting that in the Christian tradition "*the right to private property* is" not absolute or untouchable but "*subordinated to the right to common use*" (§14); and affirmed the right of association in labor or trade unions "for the purpose of defending the vital interests of those employed in the various professions" (§20). The pontiff was clear that unions are not a "mouthpiece for *class* struggle, but for the struggle for *social justice . . . not a struggle against others,*" but a "constructive factor of *social order* and *solidarity*" (§20). The document forcefully defends the dignity of agricultural work and agricultural workers, who are made to "feel that they are social outcasts," subject to "*objectively unjust situations,*" and often left "defenseless against the 'land hunger' of more powerful individuals or groups" (§21; all emphases in the original).

The pontiff's elaboration of the church's social doctrine made three necessary, forward-looking connections that laid the foundation for restoring the sacred to modern life. First, it reconciled the church to the slice of modernity—technology and scientific progress—that it had previously viewed with suspicion. Second, it inverted what it perceived to be the tendency of liberation theology to subordinate faith to politics by taking the opposite tack: in seeking to integrate the social world into the realm of faith, the new project sought to reduce the political to the religious (Ghio 1992, 190–91). Third, in renewing Christian precepts of justice that would appeal to the poor, it established a way for the project to be communicated to society as a whole, which it had to do if it were to be successful.

In their Fourth General Meeting in 1992 in Santo Domingo, the Latin American Bishops' Conference embraced the new evangelization project. Latin America was considered a "privileged context for the implementation of the program" to combat secularization via the evangelization of culture, and the time—the dawn of the church's third millennium and its second five hundred years in Latin America—was appropriate to force the bishops "to think of vast and radical perspectives for a civilizing re-foundation," as a former president of the Latin American Catholic Bishops' Council (CELAM) put it (qtd. in Ghio 1992, 194, 196). Europe was already too secular, and the rest of world was not Catholic enough. By contrast, it was assumed that Latin America had entered into modernity without eliminating popular Catholic traditions inherited from Spanish colonialism. Popular Catholicism, however, had not penetrated the network of social institutions due to "internal and foreign domination" (Ghio 1992, 195).

Reclaiming the public sphere as sacred implied most fundamentally that the church not merely maintain influence over the state but that it also extend its influence deep into civil society. Following the principle of subsidiarity in Catholic social teaching as established in *Rerum Novarum,* the church reserved a special role for—and sought to promote—intermediate organizations in civil society. But unlike the integralist project in which Catholics walled themselves off from the secular world and encapsulated themselves in a Catholic subculture within civil society, the new evangelization required that Christianity penetrate the totality of the public sphere, including all forms of public institutions on the cultural, economic, and social levels (Ghio 1992, 195–96). Reinstating the sacred did not imply abandoning the political realm. The "ultimate goal," as Ghio put it, was to place the church "at the core of society and to transform the institution's social doctrine into an ordering and legitimizing principle for society" (1992, 198). This "daring strategy" to construct an "ethical utopia" (198), as Ghio called it, returned the church to a preconciliar tradition but was not, as he rightly claims, simply conservative or a mere step back into the past. Unlike the old integralist projects, the episcopate defended social reform and representative democracy, particularly its participatory dimension.

There is little evidence that this ambitious project has been successful in stemming the tides of both secularization and increasing religious pluralism, as the continuing decline of Catholic religious hegemony in Latin America has shown. But the new evangelization has not been abandoned, and it is already clear that bishops in different countries have followed different paths in attempting to fulfill its promise. Some, such as the Brazilian, have stressed the church's social justice commitments, while others, such as the Chilean, have retreated from them. Moreover, the church has had greater success in enshrining moral principles in national legislation in some countries, such as El Salvador and Nicaragua, than it has in others, such as Argentina and Chile. We turn our attention in the following section to identifying an appropriate theoretical frame for discerning church strategies and their likely impact on both religion and politics in Latin America in the twenty-first century.

Paradigms before Pluralism

The most important theoretical frameworks for understanding the Catholic Church in Latin America were developed in earlier times to address questions such as whether the church could be an agent of modernization and under what conditions it might abet democratization rather than buttress authoritarian regimes. Whether or not these frames are suited to addressing the questions that anchor this volume—how will the church respond to religious and political pluralism, how have democracy and pluralism changed the church, and how has religious change shaped democratic politics—we shall now examine.

Institutional Interests and the Role of the Hierarchy

A long intellectual tradition has viewed the Roman Catholic Church as an institution that, like most other institutions, will act to defend its institutional interests and advance its agenda in the world of politics and affairs of state. Unlike some other organizations, however, because the Roman Catholic Church is a hierarchical institution, its agenda and interests are defined by its leadership—the Roman pontiff, the curia, and several hundred bishops. The pope inspires and enforces doctrine through papal encyclicals, declarations, and other authoritative definitions of Catholic faith, and the Congregation for the Doctrine of the Faith can, in rare but necessary occasions, squelch dissenting theologians. Critically, the pope appoints bishops, who orient pastoral work, supervise seminaries, administer schools, and speak out on issues of national significance.

The institutionalist paradigm situates the responses of the church hierarchy in organizational interests, not visions of faith. One of the pioneers of this approach, Ivan Vallier, flatly attributed the tendencies of the church hierarchy "to ally with conservative states to preserve privilege as well as to pull incipient lay movements under ecclesiastical control"—what he called "Catholicism's resistive tendencies"—not to "the content of the beliefs nor the way in which they define the relation of this world to the other-worldly sphere . . . but rather [to] the institutional paths that Church elites have followed in their attempts to preserve a religious monopoly and to insulate the 'faithful' from contaminating influences" (1970, 9). Although the church in this view is generally seen to be a lumbering, inherently conservative, and antimodern institution that changes not at all or only at a glacial pace when Rome permits, in extraordinary times, and when provoked, the church may change course. Brian Smith (1982) interpreted the opposition of the Chilean Catholic Church to the Pinochet dictatorship as a change of this nature; in this case, the church's actions were a form of institutional self-defense. As Smith argued, when the repressive apparatus of the military was turned on the clergy—when bishops were insulted, Christian Democratic leaders exiled, and religious workers tortured—the church closed ranks, turned its back on the dictatorship (which at least some in the hierarchy had welcomed), provided protection to victims in the Vicaría de la Solidaridad, and became a forceful advocate for the defense of human rights.

After the ferment of Medellín, the stance of many national episcopates against dictatorship in the 1970s, and the apparent flourishing of the popular church—Smith's important work aside—the field distanced itself from this view primarily because it seemed impossible ever again to equate the church with an inherently conservative hierarchy. Yet the church's redirection after the 1979 Puebla meeting of Latin American bishops appeared to vindicate the older view. The turn toward restoring hierarchical authority, removing the church from partisan politics, clericalizing grassroots pastoral initiatives, and controlling local religious practices (Vásquez 1998, 216) was interpreted as a regression to the historical mean steered by a more conservative Polish pope who in the first fifteen years of his papacy alone appointed conservative bishops to head close to 50 percent of Latin America's dioceses (Daudelin and Hewitt 1995, 179). Whether he transformed the once progressive, popular church into a bastion of reaction (Della Cava 1992; Ghio 1992, 185–87) or merely reaffirmed the presumption of religious hegemony and hierarchy in a church in which progressive currents at no point represented more than a "small, chartered experiment," as Daudelin and Hewitt (1995) assert, does not matter.

The extraordinary power of Rome and national bishops to censor dissidents, remove priests, and close programs of course must be factored into any explanation for the course taken by the church. But papal beliefs and even the views of bishops provide only very rough guides, not specific blue-prints, for national episcopates to resolve the many complex problems aris-ing from the challenges posed by pluralism. The pontificate of John Paul II stressed a *range* of issues, and along with its strong position on issues of personal morality and the family it also championed the causes of eco-nomic justice, the dignity of work, and opposition to all forms of violence. Church social doctrine, as framed by the papal encyclicals *Rerum Novarum* and *Laborem Exercens,* claims the supremacy of labor over capital, favors a relative, not absolute right, to private property, and brands both capitalism and socialism as "institutional injustice" (Ghio 1992, 191–92). The fact that these issue positions are spread around the ideological spectrum could, in principle, create possibilities for different forms of political action. More-over, if the Vatican was instrumental in facilitating a conservative restora-tion, it had allies within the clergy and national episcopates making calls for precisely these shifts. Indeed, Latin American bishops had taken the lead in reversing Medellín before the Polish pope traveled to Puebla. Addi-tionally, the hierarchy does not always speak with one voice. Within some churches, such as the Brazilian, as Mainwaring (1986) showed, competing visions of faith and religious models divide the church not horizontally be-tween the hierarchy and the base but vertically. Factions within countries may hold different viewpoints and construct alliances to gain position against rivals.

On an empirical level, any view that privileges the role of the Vatican in setting church strategy implies that a uniform response by the church across countries should be evident, which is also not the case. The Brazilian na-tional episcopate has managed to retain a progressive posture on many socioeconomic and political issues, not to mention an internal church or-ganization that reserves important spaces for popular participation, while several other episcopates in the region have not. To say that the church will defend itself against perceived attacks, moreover, does not imply what is its best strategy for doing so. This approach, in short, does not generate clear predictions about why national episcopates would clamp down or encour-age theological ferment and plural voices from within and lurch to the left or right or out of politics altogether, or why responses of the institutional church, parish priests, lay politicians, social movement leaders, and voters should differ across Latin America.

Rational Choice and Religion: The Church as a Rational Actor

The religious economy paradigm applies rational choice analysis developed to explain individual-level behavior in the religious marketplace specifically to predict the responses of national episcopates to political and institutional challenges. Much as in any microeconomic model of utility maximization, but in clear violation of the key rationalist premise of methodological individualism, in this approach episcopal responses are driven by the logic of the market and, specifically, the degree of competition for consumers of religious offerings. In a seminal work, Anthony Gill (1998, 7–8) explained the willingness of bishops in some countries to take progressive theological and political stances in defiance of authoritarian regimes as a function of the degree of religious competition they encountered, especially from evangelical Protestants. Where competition was weak or nonexistent, bishops could slip into easy, historic alliances with the military and with wealthy, conservative elites who could support the church and its organization financially and protect the church's institutional interests, without much fear of losing parishioners to other denominations. On the other hand, where competition was more intense, the church was motivated to seek a more active following among nominal Catholics, especially the rural and urban poor who historically had received only weak pastoral care, which brought it into conflict with military regimes that set out to suppress "subversive" activities among the lower classes. Given the long history of neglect, the church also had to make strong public statements on behalf of the poor to make its commitment to serve them credible. This, of course, increased the risk of a repressive response from the government, but not doing so would have led to a greater loss of poor parishioners to competing evangelical groups. In this way Gill explained church opposition to the Pinochet dictatorship in Chile and its acquiescence to an even more brutal one in Argentina.[18]

In the decade since its appearance, Gill's powerful and parsimonious framework has attracted many adherents as well as its share of critics. From our perspective, it is not theoretically self-evident that the church's best strategic option when faced with religious competition should be to respond to the *political* needs of its poor parishioners and, in addition, that these would be on the political left. Among its other options, it could create more parishes, build more churches, and deploy more priests, nuns, catechists, and other religious workers to the most contested areas, a strategy it apparently pursued in Guatemala (Steigenga 1999, 165) and elsewhere (Gill 2002, 196, 205).[19] It could attempt to gain legal advantages over its opponents, making it more difficult for Protestants to convert Catholics (such as by preventing preaching in public squares during lunchtime), another possibility later admitted by Gill (2002, 196). It could also invest in new product lines and back other movements such as the Catholic Charismatic Renewal, which has shown some promise in stemming the tide of Catholic defections in Guatemala, Mexico, and Brazil, where it has attracted more than twice the number of adherents than the CEBs (Chesnut 2003b). Though some bishops and episcopates were slow to endorse the CCR (Cleary 2007b), they have in fact since recognized its potential; the charismatic movement has been successfully incorporated into the institutional church in El Salvador and elsewhere and has become central to efforts to revitalize the church (Peterson and Vásquez 2001, 190, 192). The inculturation project, which aims to redefine the indigenous past to conform to a Christian one, can be seen as a long-standing attempt to reach indigenous peoples. By contrast, there is little evidence that a turn to the left maintained the faithful in its ranks and arrested the growth of Protestantism, and it may have even cost the church other supporters. In Guatemala, when lay religious workers threatened with kidnapping and death fled the highlands, they left religious institutions in the hands of the local population, which left an increased space for the Mayan lay brotherhoods (*cofradías*) and traditional religious beliefs and practices (*costumbre*) that the church had sought to rein in decades earlier, as well as a void in which Protestantism and Pentecostal churches expanded markedly (Calder 2004, 109).

In fact, the religious economy paradigm does not specify an ordering of the preferences of the poor, though it assumes that respect for human rights appears at the top of the list. In times of highly repressive dictatorships, this is a reasonable assumption. But under conditions of democracy, the poor may prioritize something else. It is not clear that church leaders have up-to-date information about what the poor want and need or that leaders would be willing to change their message if this information were available to them. It is improbable, for instance, that bishops would flout church teachings and loosen the ban on artificial birth control methods, a ban that the poor generally oppose. The religious economy thesis does not provide a guidepost to explain church responses when preferences are multiple, when issues of grave concern to the church do not map easily onto existing political space, and when for some of these issues there can be no compromise.

This framework also did not stand the test of time. Religious competition is more intense today than in the 1970s, yet there is scant evidence that in those countries in which competition is fiercest the national episcopates tend more to the left—in other words, to champion the issues of economic and social justice or the needs of the poor more today than in the past, with the sole exception of Brazil. Although parish priests in Chile preach in the direction of their poor parishioners (and often against the hierarchy) in those neighborhoods where Pentecostal conversions run high (Lies 2003), bishops have moved to the right, deemphasizing the issue that had won the church such moral authority during the dictatorship—the defense of human rights (Cruz 2004)—and instead have chosen to advocate the censorship of films and oppose the legalization of divorce. In Guatemala and El Salvador national episcopates have also pulled back from sympathy with popular causes, and in Nicaragua, despite a revved up competition, younger, native-born diocesan priests, in particular, have grown increasingly less politically tolerant (Stein 1998). On the other hand, in Ecuador, where religious competition is comparatively minimal, the church has long maintained an important relationship with the indigenous population, a relationship its counterparts in Bolivia and Peru do not have—though their Protestant populations are larger (Yashar 2005; Brysk 2004).

In a subsequent work Gill (2002, 209) contended that in a democratic polity, church incentives are inverted. Still unable to meet competition and now lacking resources once proffered by international donors to fight authoritarian regimes, state protection and support become all the more valuable, the costs of criticizing government rise, and church leaders will seek accommodation with elites (Gill 2002, 177–78, 184). Since the church must now act more like a specialized interest group in order to promote the missionary and doctrinal goals of Catholicism, and church leaders seek to unify the voice of the Catholic Church behind a more moderate political message, Gill reached the "paradoxical conclusion" that "as society becomes more pluralistic, the Catholic Church must become less so to be politically effective" (2002, 196–97, 209). If this argument is correct, the logic of religious competition and resource scarcity should have produced a uniform pattern of retrenchment from popular causes as well as from confrontations with political authorities. Yet some national conferences, such as the Brazilian, have retained progressive postures, while others have not, and some, such as the Argentine, have openly confronted governments over moral and cultural policies that others have dissented from less publicly. Moreover, theoretically, there is no intrinsic reason why the resource constraint under democracy should be hard and inelastic, and why in democratic regimes other, nonfinancial resources, such as foot soldiers, could not serve as effective substitutes for international aid, especially if the church's goals are broader than maintaining buildings and membership rolls, as anyone who believes in the sincerity of the church's mission would attest.

Competing Visions of Mission

Dissatisfied with the inability of the institutionalist paradigm to explain the emergence of the popular, liberationist church, as well as a focus on the Catholic Church that denied the enormous transformative potential that religious beliefs can carry when ordinary people find meaning in religious commitment, a contending approach attributed divergent church priorities and episcopal responses to authoritarian regimes to the particular understandings of faith and the church's evangelizing mission, which motivated not merely church leaders but also parish priests, nuns, and the laity. In this framework ideas are, to use the language of social science, independent variables in their own right that act upon individual priests and bishops, as well as on national episcopates as collectives.

As with any theory that assigns great weight to the independent role of ideas, it is incumbent upon this framework to explain from where beliefs emanate, how they evolve, why old ones lose credibility and new ones arise to conform to new realities, how they are reproduced or recycled in new guises, and why certain ideas can prevail and guide church responses to religious and political pluralism in some contexts but not others. The most intriguing answer to this series of questions was offered by Mainwaring

(1986, 12, 15) and Mainwaring and Wilde (1989), who argue that during dictatorial regimes, conceptions of faith and mission were transformed by political struggles of the grassroots that generated new conceptions about society and the church's role within it. Whether the church dared to oppose dictators or chose to ally with them against leftist insurgents was in effect attributable to the prevalence of voices within the church espousing one course of action or the other. The progressive church was more vulnerable and its liberationist wing more easily reined in where its conceptions of faith and mission were not shared by bishops (the case in Peru, El Salvador, and Nicaragua) than where they were, as in Brazil (Mainwaring and Wilde 1989, 19–21). Even in Colombia, where the Catholic Church is widely viewed as the most conservative in Latin America, Alexander Wilde (1987) has argued that grassroots groups were no less present in the church than in other Latin American countries, but key bishops deliberately recreated "neo-Christendom" in the context of an oligarchical political order that the church had a stake in maintaining.

This view of competing visions of mission explained national differences in the short term, but in a brief time, as we know, the popular church appeared to collapse. Scholars working within the ideational paradigm divided between those who placed emphasis on the quality of the ideas associated with liberationism and the way they were transmitted to the faithful and those who attributed the triumph of conservative ideas to the institutional power behind them. For Vásquez (1998), the utopian vision that propelled the liberationist project shared the weakness of all modern emancipatory ideologies in believing that a rational mastery of the world was possible; this vision did not and could not resonate with the radically altered life circumstances of the urban poor that followed from the profound changes in global capitalism in the 1980s. A competing, widely held view joins with the institutionalists to explain the marginalization of the ideas that animated the popular church as resulting from the use of papal authority and the determination of more conservative bishops to quell debates about the church's mission. The problem with this view is that the appointment of scores of like-minded bishops in the past quarter century by two more conservative pontiffs should have by now produced convergent episcopal responses to the challenges of secularism and pluralism—but this is not the case. Although we might be tempted to explain the divergence of national episcopates as assuming a path-dependent course—that is, that once liberationist groups had been expelled and conservative clerics promoted to the ranks of the hierarchy, the church's next steps might not be severely constrained—in fact the paths of national bishops' conferences do not necessarily follow their trajectories of a quarter century ago. An alternative explanation might postulate an interplay between ideas and the institution. Gomez de Souza (2003) suggests that because the progressive wing and moderate sectors of the Brazilian episcopate made the correct strategic decision to eschew separatism and ally in National Conference of Brazilian Bishops (Conferência Nacional dos Bispos do Brasil, or CNBB) elections, radicals did not become isolated from the mainstream, an interpretation confirmed by Serbin (2000, 150).[20] In Central America (and especially Nicaragua), by contrast, leftist clergy became disjoined from their confreres, in effect pushing the entire episcopate toward the right in a dynamic not unlike the centrifugal tendencies of party competition that Valenzuela (1978) used to characterize the polarization of the Chilean party system.

However plausible this particular explanation is for the Brazilian anomaly, we need a new framework to explain new patterns of church-state relations and the broader, changing role of the church in society. As the church faces the challenges of secularization and globalization, intensifying religious competition, and a new matrix of political competition, which way it will turn and how much of an impact it will have on public policy and in the lives of the faithful are complex questions not easily answered by paradigms written in earlier, less plural times.

A Paradigm for Pluralism: The Embedded Church

We may summarize the unresolved debates of existing paradigms in two fundamental questions. First, does the church act as its hierarchy believes it should, or in a way its hierarchy perceives will serve the church's institutional interests? Second, does it matter what the laity believes, or which course it would prefer, with or without competition? Whereas the institutionalist and rational choice frameworks explain church positions as a function of the calculations of its hierarchy, regardless of beliefs, and the "competing visions of mission" explains its positions in terms of the ideas of both the hierarchy and base (with those of the former weighing more heavily), in our view, it is neither impossible nor assured that the grassroots may permeate the hierarchy and its decision-making processes. Rather, the influence of the base varies over time and across political and social settings. The central premise of this volume is that in these times of religious pluralism and democracy, the responses of the church in different countries to the challenges posed by pluralism and their likely impact cannot be understood without reference to the beliefs, motivations, and commitments of ordinary people.[21] What we have in mind is more than a barometer of public opinion on controversial issues that church leaders may review; it is, rather, the church's ability to connect with, mobilize, and even learn from its faithful in civil society. At times those connections may pose constraints on the hierarchy, but the room for maneuver afforded by their absence may bring with it a different sort of constraint on the effectiveness of church intervention in the public sphere and, ultimately, its own future.

Let us assume a simple model of decision making in the church. On one axis, church leaders may act according to their perception of what is in the church's institutional interests, or in line with their beliefs and understandings of their mission. On the other, the calculations of the hierarchy (pope and national bishops) matter more at one extreme, and the views of the grassroots at the other. Our argument here is simple: when the Catholic Church holds a religious monopoly and operates in an authoritarian regime, the views of the hierarchy will be dominant, and their perceptions about where the church's interests lie will prevail over their personal beliefs. As religious hegemony erodes and political pluralism expands, beliefs matter more, as do the views of the grassroots—in the lexicon of Vatican II, the "people of God"—in the overall life of the church. At this point, the church hierarchy will take the ideas and aspirations of civil society into account. We may visualize this argument as in Figure 1.1.

What we mean by taking these views into account is this: The hierarchy holds certain core beliefs, about God, life, and salvation, that are immutable or at minimum change only very slowly and usually not as a result of lay intervention. But other ideas, such as those about property and labor rights, just wages, and even democracy, are more fungible. The interplay between beliefs and institutional interests is a strategic calculation, and

Figure 1.1. A Simple Model of Ideas, Institutions, and Influence

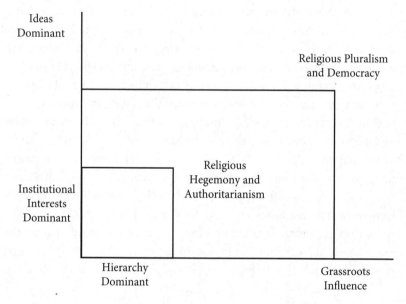

often the ideas that win out will be those that are perceived as giving the church its best shot to confront the most pressing challenges it faces—today that would be pluralism, secularism, and an erosion of hegemony. But it is also the case that ecclesiastical authorities may be influenced about theological principles or the merits of seizing a piece of land by the parish priests, catechists, politicians, benefactors, teachers, lay workers, and believers within their orbit, for two distinct but related reasons. In anticipating the reactions of their bases, national church leaders may constrain their own ambitions in light of what is possible, or, alternatively, they may use that information as an asset in pressing their preferred strategies with each other, their regional counterparts, and even Rome.

A key argument of this volume is that the church's calculations, likely effectiveness in the public sphere, and even its long-term viability as a religious institution depend on the degree to which the hierarchy can mobilize the faithful for its projects, or, conversely, the faithful can move the hierarchy to its preferred theology and policy prescriptions. This relationship would be important in any case, but it is especially so under conditions of religious and political pluralism. In Albert Hirschman's (1970) classic scheme, the faithful have the option of exit, voice, and loyalty. In our view, by making the threat of exit more credible, religious pluralism enhances the voice, and the bargaining position, of the grassroots. Competition may matter at least as much or more for opening the church to meaningful lay participation and influence, for according the laity autonomy from the hierarchy, and even for allowing national churches to gain a measure of flexibility from Roman doctrine, than for whether the church positions itself on the left or right as the religious economy paradigm presumed.

Political pluralism and the loss of state protection characteristic of the days of modern-day concordats and neo-Christendom, moreover, mean that the church can no longer automatically expect to dictate its preferences as law and public policy. Under conditions of democratic competition, the church must win political allies, which in turn depends on its ability to rally the faithful to its side. The evangelizing project the church has defined, which brings it into the public, political arena, requires bridges to the voluntary associations of civil society. The church must win its contemporary goals, in other words, in the multidimensional space of electoral and party politics. But the complexity of Catholic doctrine does not readily map onto the single left-right dimension in existing political space and could conceivably be used to justify either a concern with unemployment, inequality, and especially poverty and its attendant threats to human dignity associated with a revved up market model or such traditional moral issues as divorce, contraception, and, especially, the same-sex marriage and abortion debates. Institutional interests and the moral agenda often overlap in political space, while moral issues and economic justice issues often do not. In order to assess the likely effectiveness of church responses to pluralism, we will need to build into our framework not merely whether or not the church can mobilize its rank and file but also whether it can summon allies, sway voters, capture politicians, and influence bureaucracies responsible for policy implementation. We expand on this framework in chapter 7.

Plan of the Volume

Taken together the essays in this volume move beyond existing paradigms to illuminate the challenges facing the Latin American Catholic

Church and its ideological, institutional, and policy responses. All of the contributors are cognizant that the church is a part of and responds to civil society. Suspicious of the trend that reduces religiously motivated collective action to degrees and sources of competition, the authors tackle the nature of religious beliefs and democratic values at the individual level in Latin America today, drawing in many cases from original surveys, as well as on the core nature of the hierarchy-base relationship. Several authors bring their considerable expertise to bear in country case studies that both illustrate many of the broader themes and also answer specific questions about why the responses of national episcopates to common regional challenges sometimes diverge.

The essays in part 1 lay out the nature of the pluralist challenges facing the Roman Catholic Church in Latin America today. Ronald Inglehart, in chapter 2, draws from his pioneering frameworks about culture and politics and from World Values Survey data to characterize the sort of cultural change that is underpinning democracy in Latin America today. This chapter is followed by case studies of modernization in Mexico and Chile and its attendant consequences for religious observance and especially for religious deference in the private and public sphere. In chapter 3 Soledad Loaeza elegantly charts the monumental transformation of the roles of Mexican women, whether affluent or poor, from a culture of femininity and subservience to male family members and parish priest—in which marriage or a religious life were the only realistic options—to one replete with greater access to higher education, paid work, and artificial birth control. Given the role that women traditionally played as pillars of the church, such profound changes raise obvious dilemmas for the church. Similarly, in chapter 4 Cristián Parker draws from recent surveys conducted among Chilean youth of various social strata and argues convincingly that socialization in public and private lay institutions of higher learning has not so much diminished religious belief—though it has somewhat done that as well—as it has undermined the trust of youth in religious authority. Parker's innovative survey questions enable him to bring to light in a systematic way what many have long suspected. From the derisive term "cafeteria Catholics" (those who pick and choose the aspects of church teachings that have resonance as the precepts to follow), Parker discovers the explosion of a new category of self-identified Catholics: "Catholic in my own way."[22]

Part 2 examines church responses to the changing landscape and their impacts from the perspective of church visions and frames, institutions for hierarchy-base communication, and alliances with political actors. In chapter 5 Patricia Rodriguez takes up a fascinating comparative study of church responses to land-based movements and conflicts in Brazil and Chile. There are few examples imaginable that test the commitment of the church's preferential option for the poor more than the posture of national episcopates and parish priests toward land-based movements. Were bishops' responses to the powerless strictly a function of competition from other sects, we would expect the responses of the church in Brazil and Chile to converge. Yet Rodriguez finds that the church in Brazil has honored its commitment to the landless to a far greater extent than in Chile. Rodriguez shows that organizational structures of the church, and the way these channel participation and information flows from laity to the clergy, the clergy to the hierarchy, and back again, matter for shaping church responses to the pressing social justice needs of the faithful.

In chapter 6 Roberto Blancarte examines the approach taken by the hierarchy of the Mexican Catholic Church to the constitutional reform of church-state relations and the end of the regime of the officially anticlerical but practically accommodating the Institutional Revolutionary Party (Partido Revolucionario Institucional, or PRI). His analysis of the most important statements of the hierarchy shows that the way in which nations, states, and religious freedom are defined in any society is hotly contested. From these understandings flow legal precedent and interpretation, the limits of state support for religious institutions, and whether or not freedom is defined in liberal terms. His chapter also soberly conveys the difficult truth that on these hard issues compromise is not always possible. The vision of church leaders for the role of the Roman Catholic Church simply cannot be reconciled with that of a liberal vision of religious freedom and a separation of the religious and the public spheres. Survey research strongly suggests that public opinion in Mexico does not favor a stronger role for religion in public policy.

In the larger context of explaining variation in church responses to policy challenges in democratic polities, chapter 7 examines the church in civil society, including its degree of religious hegemony, capacity to mobilize civil society, and the political orientation of the Catholic grassroots, particularly on issues of economic justice and morality. The church finds it-self occupying politically lonely ground when it defends social justice, re-strictions on liberal rights, and its institutional interests—namely, main-taining its status as the dominant religion, favorable tax policies, subsidies for salaries and buildings, and religious instruction in private and public schools. National episcopates may share these goals, but the church has very different capacities in different countries to rally society to realize these aims simultaneously. Whether bishops prioritize and remain true to the church's moral agenda, social doctrine, or the church's institutional interests—particularly when those clash—depends in large measure on the capacity of the church to mobilize the faithful, as well as the directions in which the faithful pull it. Where its subcultural organizations are weak, church leaders will be more likely to seek strategic allies on the political right that can protect the institutional church and promote a public policy agenda consistent with the most central tenets of church teachings. Where, on the other hand, religious pluralism is high and the church must be atten-tive to the possibility of defection—*and,* in addition, Catholic religious and lay activists lead a dense network of civic and political associations that are reasonably autonomous from the control of religious authorities—its base has more potential leverage and can pull church leaders in a more progres-sive direction.

Part 3 considers the impact of the contemporary Catholic Church and Catholicism on public policy and democracy itself. There is no area in which the clash of modernizing influences, transformation of traditional gender roles, and expansion of educational opportunities with the public policy agenda favored by church authorities is greater than in the area of policies governing reproduction and sexuality. Ranging the gamut from the availability of artificial contraception, the public distribution of condoms to stop the spread of HIV/AIDS, and the morning-after pill to embryonic stem cell research to the conditions for legal abortion, the church in every country in Latin America has spoken out forcefully in recent years to en-shrine church teaching in public law and the implementation of public policy. This has engendered highly visible clashes between bishops and ministers of public health in many countries of the region. In chapter 8 Mala Htun does not shy away from the most controversial of all these pub-lic policy measures: the availability of legal abortion and the legal recognition of same-sex unions. She contends that whereas bishops have not been able to circumscribe public debates about sensitive moral issues, they have effectively exercised indirect vetoes to slow and stop legislative change.

Catalina Romero's case study, in chapter 9, of the deeply divided Catholic Church in Peru returns to what scholars enamored of liberation theology in an earlier era left dangling as a hypothetical possibility: the contribution of religious persons to the construction of democracy in society. Drawing from original surveys to show that an important segment of Catholic opinion, held by those who learned their Catholicism from catechists formed after Vatican II, has eluded the antiliberationist turn of the Peruvian hierarchy, she shows the ways in which Catholicism's internal pluralism has exercised an impact on the democratization of civil society. While the institutions of the formal Peruvian political system have been essentially failing, these holdouts, in alliance with members of other religious organizations, have built and reinforced civil democratic institutions from the ground up during a decade of national crisis by backing three major initiatives: the Truth and Reconciliation Commission, the National Accord, and the *Mesa de Concertación y la Lucha contra la Pobreza* (Roundtable for the Struggle against Poverty).

The fourth and final part of the work looks back as well as ahead. In chapter 10 Daniel Levine draws upon decades of study and reflection about the changing nature of religious belief, participation, and the institutional landscape to remind us all that pluralism in the religious sphere brings not only nettlesome challenges but also opportunities that should be embraced. Religious pluralism affords the opportunities for many voices to be heard, for civic capacities and social capital to be created, and for groups to establish ties and relationships that facilitate the flow of information and undergird the possibilities for common action. Religious pluralism, in effect, carries the seeds of what in other contexts we might call a democratic political culture. If the church can be good for democracy, can democracy similarly be good for the church? If the church is understood as the ability of its most visible institutional representatives to lead its faithful as well as those outside its sphere, then perhaps not. But if church leaders believe they can learn from the people of God, then meeting the challenge of political pluralism might free the Catholic Church from its status of "lazy monopolist." The concluding chapter summarizes the most important themes and findings of the volume, speculates about the possible future scenarios confronting the church and the democracies in which they are located today, and lays out an agenda for future research. If this volume spawns such research, our ambition will have been fulfilled.

Notes

1. The need for state support has been all the more urgent in Latin America because the church there never developed the tradition of broad-based private financial support that it did in the United States.

2. For a fascinating insider's account of the diminished role played by religious and secular social movements during the Lula government's first two years in office, see the diary of Frei Betto (2007), who served as special presidential advisor, coordinator of social mobilization for the Zero Hunger Program, and informal liaison to social movements before his resignation in December 2004.

3. In Chile the rightist Independent Democratic Union party has cultivated the vote of Catholics and successfully courted the support of many bishops in its fight against divorce, abortion, and other personal morality issues, threatening a key voting base of the centrist Christian Democratic Party and even political realignment.

4. This is apparently true of many Maya movements of war widows, the displaced, and rural workers and for human rights (Calder 2004), as well as progressive and militant opponents of the Chilean dictatorship (Dixon 2000). In Brazil for the past twenty years, grassroots church groups are credited with stoking the campaigns and boosting the electoral fortunes of the leftist Workers' Party in their fights for land, against hunger, and even against government corruption, as well as feminist movements. "Nudged out of the Church," these Catholic activists were "increasingly forced to anchor their projects in the secular realm" (Ottmann 2002, 163).

5. The church-state partnership that Serbin (1995) called the "moral concordat," established during the Vargas dictatorship (1930–1945), enabled the state to funnel resources through the Conselho Nacional de Serviço Social (CNSS, or National Social Service Council) to Catholic charities and other social service organizations.

6. Figures for Catholics are higher in studies conducted in 1991 in the capital and nationally in 1995 by the University of Pittsburgh (72.3 percent in the earlier year and 69.5 percent in the later one) but even lower in a special study conducted in 1994 by FLACSO (57 percent). IUDOP's 1997 figures for Catholics are not cited (Stein 1999, 124).

7. Gill (2002, 201, 204) contends that once onerous government restrictions on registration requirements, zoning laws, and limits on media access that make it difficult for new religious organizations to expand were lifted in Colombia, Argentina, Bolivia, Ecuador, Paraguay, and elsewhere, evangelical Protestant growth "took off."

8. In El Salvador Catholics are reported to have converted to Protestantism because they had migrated from rural to urban areas, they were unfamiliar with Catholic doctrine, and they had a dislike for restrictions on the priesthood, the church's prohibition on birth control and divorce, and its "cold style of worship" (Stein 1999, 125).

9. Blancarte (2000) asserts that the countries most susceptible to Protestant incursions have been those with the highest proportion of indigenous peoples, such as Guatemala and Bolivia. He estimates (in his view, conservatively) that in the Mexican state of Chiapas, 40 percent of the population has converted, a rate well above the national average.

10. The correlation between the poverty of an area and the ratio of inhabitants per parish is 0.62. Eighty-two percent of the upper class but 78 percent of the middle class and only 69 percent of the lower class self-identify as Catholics (and within these groups the rate of practice drops from one-third to one-fifth to one-tenth).

11. When asked to whom he was referring when he spoke of "false prophets," John Paul replied the Seventh Day Adventists, the Mormons, and the Jehovah's Witnesses (Stoll 1990, 49). The metaphor of "rapacious wolves," of course, was later used by the pope in Santo Domingo in 1992 to refer to evangelical Protestant sects more broadly.

12. The latter question asked respondents to rank the importance of God in their lives on a scale of 1 to 10, with 10 being very important. When those responding with scores of 7, 8, and 9 are added, the total rises to 91 percent.

13. These four countries were the only ones in Latin America in which these questions were asked in 1990 and 2000.

14. The term is a play on "social capital," as made popular by political scientist Robert Putnam. The Metanexus Institute on Religions and Science, which sponsors a "Spiritual Capital Research Program" inspired in part by Putnam's finding that "religion is by far the largest generator of social capital in the United States, contributing to more than half of the social capital in the country," defines "spiritual capital" as "the effects of spiritual and religious practices, beliefs, networks and institutions that have a measurable impact on individuals, communities and societies" (http://www.metanexus.net).

15. The Alan Guttmacher Institute reported that approximately 35 percent of pregnancies in Chile, 31 percent in Brazil, 30 percent in Peru, 28 percent in the

Dominican Republic, 26 percent in Colombia, and 17 percent in Mexico were terminated by abortion from 1989 to 1991. Estimates are that 4,000,000 abortions were performed across Latin America during this period. Unlike in developed countries, most women undergoing abortions are married, over the age of twenty, and already have at least one child. (Data available at http://www.guttmacher.org/, retrieved on February 16, 2005.) Opponents of abortion dispute these figures, which are gathered from women hospitalized as a result of complications from clandestine procedures.

16. Many priests, such as Father Hidalgo, who were killed for supporting independence movements also advocated land reform, republicanism, an end to slavery, and many other liberal reforms. But many priests who chose insurgency (by one careful estimate, approximately one in twelve in Mexico) were also motivated by the restrictions placed on the priesthood and religion in public life by the Bourbon reforms, which blurred responsibilities and sharpened disputes between parish priests and district governors (Taylor 1996, 449–57).

17. Churches were disestablished in Colombia in 1848 and 1853, in Argentina in 1853 and 1884, in Mexico in 1857 and 1910, in Costa Rica in 1860 and 1871, in Paraguay in 1870, in Guatemala and El Salvador in 1871, in Honduras in 1880, in Chile in 1884 and 1925, in Brazil in 1889, in Nicaragua in 1894, in Cuba in 1902, in Panama in 1904, in Ecuador in 1906 and 1937, in Bolivia in 1906, and in Uruguay in 1917 (Gill 1998, 32).

18. Though the contrast between the episcopates in Argentina and Chile is aptly drawn, Gill may have mischaracterized the stances of several other bishops' conferences in his study as pro- or anti-authoritarian (Lies 2003, 57).

19. Gill (2002, 205) notes that bishops have made a concerted effort to meet the spiritual needs of more Catholics by increasing the number of dioceses, parishes, and seminaries.

20. The Brazilian episcopal conference elected Dom Lucas president to "placate the Vatican," and Dom Jayme Chemello, from the popular church, was elected vice president. As Serbin put it, "Tensions arose between Dom Lucas and this group, but the balance of power preserved the CNBB's basic structure" (2000, 150).

21. I am grateful to Ernie Bartell for informing me that there is a long tradition in Catholic theology of regard for the *"sensus fidelium"* ("sense of the faithful") with respect to the understanding of doctrine, even in deliberations among the hierarchy.

22. The 2000 round of the World Values Survey offered respondents in El Salvador a similar option: "Catholic, doesn't follow the rules." More than one-quarter of Salvadorans identified themselves in this way, compared with about one-third who described themselves as "Roman Catholic" without qualification. Villa and Mallimaci refer to such Argentines as *"católicos cuentapropistas"* (2007,

126). The term *"cuenta propria"* is usually employed as a census category to refer to the self-employed; here, we might translate their expression as "Catholics by their own account."

References

Alesina, Alberto, Arnaud Devleeschauwer, William Easterly, Sergio Kurlat, and Romain Wacziarg. 2003. "Fractionalization." *Journal of Economic Growth* 8: 155–94.

Berger, Peter L. 1967. *The Sacred Canopy.* Garden City, NY: Doubleday.

Berger, Suzanne. 1985. "Religious Transformation and the Future of Politics." *European Sociological Review* 1, no. 1: 23–45.

Betto, Frei. 2007. *Calendário do Poder.* Rio de Janeiro: Editora Rocco.

Blancarte, Roberto J. 2000. "Popular Religion, Catholicism and Socioreligious Dissent in Latin America: Facing the Modernity Paradigm." *International Sociology* 15, no. 4: 591–603.

Bonino, José Miguez. 1999. "Argentina: Church, State, and Religious Freedom in Argentina." In Paul E. Sigmund, ed., *Religious Freedom and Evangelization in Latin America: The Challenge of Religious Pluralism,* 187–203. Maryknoll, NY: Orbis Books.

Brusco, Elizabeth E. 1999. "Columbia: Past Persecution, Present Tension." In Paul E. Sigmund, ed., *Religious Freedom and Evangelization in Latin America: The Challenge of Religious Pluralism,* 235–52. Maryknoll, NY: Orbis Books.

Brysk, Alison. 2004. "From Civil Society to Collective Action: The Politics of Religion in Ecuador." In Edward L. Cleary and Timothy J. Steigenga, eds., *Resurgent Voices in Latin America: Indigenous Peoples, Political Mobilization, and Religious Change,* 25–42. New Brunswick, NJ: Rutgers University Press.

Burdick, John. 2000. "Afterword." In John Burdick and W. E. Hewitt, eds., *The Church at the Grassroots in Latin America: Perspectives on Thirty Years of Activism.* Westport, CT: Praeger.

Cabral Medeiros, Katia Maria. 2002. "Orientações Etico-Religiosas." In Luiz Alberto Gomez de Souza and Silvia Regina Alves Fernandes, eds., *Desafios do catolicismo na cidade: Pesquisa em regiões metropolitanas brasileiras,* 199–251. Rio de Janeiro/São Paulo: CERIS/Paulus.

Calder, Bruce J. 2004. "Interwoven Histories: The Catholic Church and the Maya, 1940 to the Present." In Edward L. Cleary and Timothy J. Steigenga, eds., *Resurgent Voices in Latin America: Indigenous Peoples, Peasant Mobilization, and Religious Change,* 93–124. New Brunswick, NJ: Rutgers University Press.

Camp, Roderic Ai. 1997. *Crossing Swords: Politics and Religion in Mexico.* New York: Oxford University Press.

Casanova, José. 1994. *Public Religions in the Modern World*. Chicago: University of Chicago Press.

Chesnut, R. Andrew. 2003a. *Competitive Spirits: Latin America's New Religious Economy*. New York: Oxford University Press.

———. 2003b. "A Preferential Option for the Spirit: The Catholic Charismatic Renewal in Latin America's New Religious Economy." *Latin American Politics and Society* 45, no. 1: 55–85.

Cleary, Edward L. 2007a. "The Catholic Charismatic Renewal: Revitalization Movements and Conversion." In Timothy J. Steigenga and Edward L. Cleary, eds., *Conversion of a Continent: Contemporary Religious Change in Latin America*, 153–73. New Brunswick, NJ: Rutgers University Press.

———. 2007b. "Catholic Church in Latin America." Religion in Latin America—Statistics. Accessed May 20, 2007, from http://www.providence.edu/las/Statistics.htm.

Corr, Rachel. 2007. "Conversion to Native Spirituality in the Andes." In Timothy J. Steigenga and Edward L. Cleary, eds., *Conversion of a Continent: Contemporary Religious Change in Latin America*, 174–95. New Brunswick, NJ: Rutgers University Press.

Crahan, Margaret E. 1992. "Religion, Revolution, and Counterrevolution: The Role of the Religious Right in Central America." In Douglas A. Chalmers, Maria do Carmo Campello de Souza, and Atilio A. Boron, eds., *The Right and Democracy in Latin America*, 163–82. New York: Praeger.

Crisp, Brian F., Daniel H. Levine, and José E. Molina. 2003. "The Rise and Decline of COPEI in Venezuela." In Scott Mainwaring and Timothy R. Scully, eds., *Christian Democracy in Latin America: Electoral Competition and Regime Conflicts*, 275–300. Stanford, CA: Stanford University Press.

Cruz, Maria Angélica. 2004. *Iglesia, represión y memoria: El caso Chileno*. Madrid: Siglo Veintiuno.

Daudelin, Jean, and W. E. Hewitt. 1995. "Churches and Politics in Latin America: Catholicism at the Crossroads." *Third World Quarterly* 16, no. 2: 221–36.

de Groot, C. F. G. 1996. *Brazilian Catholicism and the Ultramontane Reform, 1850–1930*. Amsterdam: Center for Latin American Research and Documentation.

Della Cava, Ralph. 1992. "The Ten-Year Crusade Toward the Third Christian Millennium: An Account of Evangelization 2000 and Lumen 2000." In Douglas A. Chalmers, Maria do Carmo Campello de Souza, and Atilio A. Boron, eds., *The Right and Democracy in Latin America*, 202–22. New York: Praeger.

Dixon, Dave. 2000. "From Option for the Poor to Evangelization of Culture: Silent Conflicts and Comings-of-Age." In John Burdick and W. E. Hewitt, eds., *The Church at the Grassroots in Latin America: Perspectives on Thirty Years of Activism*. Westport, CT: Praeger.

Drogus, Carol Ann, and Hannah Stewart-Gambino. 2005. *Activist Faith: Grassroots Women in Democratic Brazil and Chile.* University Park: Pennsylvania State University Press.

Finke, Roger, and Rodney Stark. 1992. *The Churching of America, 1776–1990: Winners and Losers in Our Religious Economy.* New Brunswick, NJ: Rutgers University Press.

Froehle, Bryan T. 1995. "Religious Competition in Contemporary Venezuela." In Satya R. Pattnayak, ed., *Organized Religion in the Political Transformation of Latin America,* 125–52. Lanham, MD: University Press of America.

Froehle, Bryan T., and Mary L. Gautier. 2003. *Global Catholicism: Portrait of a World Church.* Maryknoll, NY: Orbis Books.

Garrard-Burnett, Virginia. 1998. *Protestantism in Guatemala: Living in the New Jerusalem.* Austin: University of Texas Press.

Gaudium et Spes. 1965. Pastoral Constitution on the Church in the Modern World, promulgated by His Holiness, Pope Paul VI. (December 7). Available at http://www.vatican.va/archive/hist_councils/ii_vatican_council/documents/vat-ii_cons_19651207_gaudium-et-spes_en.html.

Ghio, José-Maria. 1992. "The Latin American Church and the Papacy of Wojtyla." In Douglas A. Chalmers, Maria do Carmo Campello de Souza, and Atilio A. Boron, eds., *The Right and Democracy in Latin America,* 183–201. New York: Praeger.

Gill, Anthony. 1998. *Rendering Unto Caesar: The Catholic Church and the State in Latin America.* Chicago: University of Chicago Press.

———. 2002. "Religion and Democracy in South America: Challenges and Opportunities." In Ted Gerard Jelen and Clyde Wilcox, eds., *Religion and Politics in Comparative Perspective,* 195–221. Cambridge: Cambridge University Press.

Gomez de Souza, Luiz Alberto. 2003. "Institutional Church Politics in Latin America." Paper presented at the workshop Contemporary Challenges to Catholicism in Latin America, Kellogg Institute, University of Notre Dame, October 2–3.

Hawkins, Kirk A. 2003. "Sowing Ideas: Explaining the Origins of Christian Democratic Parties in Latin America." In Scott Mainwaring and Timothy R. Scully, eds., *Christian Democracy in Latin America: Electoral Competition and Regime Conflicts,* 78–117. Stanford, CA: Stanford University Press.

Hirschman, Albert O. 1970. *Exit, Voice, and Loyalty: Responses to Decline in Firms, Organizations, and States.* Cambridge, MA: Harvard University Press.

Inglehart, Ronald, Miguel Basáñez, Jaime Díez-Medrano, Loek Halman, and Ruud Luijkx. 2004. *Human Beliefs and Values: A Cross-Cultural Sourcebook Based on the 1999–2002 Values Surveys.* Mexico: Siglo XXI.

Inter-American Development Bank (IADB). 1998. *Facing Up to Inequality in Latin America: Economic and Social Progress in Latin America, 1998–1999 Report*. Washington, DC: Johns Hopkins University Press and the Inter-American Development Bank.

John Paul II. 1981. *Laborem Exercens*. Rome: Libreria Editrice Vaticana. Available at http://www.vatican.va/holy_father/john_paul_ii/encyclicals/documents/ hf_jp-ii_enc_14091981_laborem-exercens_en.html.

Kalyvas, Stathis N. 1996. *The Rise of Christian Democracy in Europe*. Ithaca, NY: Cornell University Press.

Korzeniewicz, Roberto Patricio, and William C. Smith. 2000. "Poverty, Inequality, and Growth in Latin America: Searching for the High Road to Globalization." *Latin American Research Review* 35, no. 3: 7–54.

Lehmann, Carla. 2001. "Chile: ¿Un País Católico? *Puntos de Referencia 249*. Santiago: Centro de Estudios Públicos.

———. 2002. ¿Cuán Religiosos Somos Los Chilenos? Mapa de Religiosidad en 31 Países." *Estudios Públicos* 85: 21–40.

Levine, Daniel H. 1981a. *Religion and Politics in Latin America: The Catholic Church in Venezuela and Colombia*. Princeton, NJ: Princeton University Press.

———. 1981b. "Religion, Society, and Politics: State of the Art." *Latin American Research Review* 16, no. 3: 185–209.

———. 1993. "Popular Groups, Popular Culture, and Popular Religion." In Daniel H. Levine, ed., *Constructing Culture and Power in Latin America*, 171–225. Ann Arbor: University of Michigan Press.

Lies, William M. 2003. "Counting Sheep: Religious Socialization, Competition, and Chilean Politics." Ph.D. diss., University of Pittsburgh.

Mainwaring, Scott. 1986. *The Catholic Church and Politics in Brazil, 1916–1985*. Stanford, CA: Stanford University Press.

———. 2003. "The Transformation and Decline of Christian Democracy in Latin America." In Scott Mainwaring and Timothy R. Scully, eds., *Christian Democracy in Latin America: Electoral Competition and Regime Conflicts*, 364–83. Stanford, CA: Stanford University Press.

Mainwaring, Scott, and Timothy R. Scully, eds. 2003. *Christian Democracy in Latin America: Electoral Competition and Regime Conflicts*. Stanford, CA: Stanford University Press.

Mainwaring, Scott, and Alexander Wilde. 1989. "The Progressive Church in Latin America: An Interpretation." In Scott Mainwaring and Alexander Wilde, eds., *The Progressive Church in Latin America*, 1–37. Notre Dame, IN: University of Notre Dame Press.

Neuhaus, Richard John. 1984. *The Naked Public Square: Religion and Democracy in America*. Grand Rapids, MI: W. B. Eerdmans.

Norris, Pippa, and Ronald Inglehart. 2004. *Sacred and Secular: Religion and Politics Worldwide*. Cambridge: Cambridge University Press.

Ottmann, Goetz Frank. 2002. *Lost for Words? Brazilian Liberationism in the 1990s*. Pittsburgh, PA: University of Pittsburgh Press.

Parker, Cristián. 2003. "Cultural and Religious Pluralism and Challenges of Cultural Institutions in Societies within a Process of Globalization." Paper presented at the workshop Contemporary Challenges to Catholicism in Latin America, Kellogg Institute, University of Notre Dame, October 2–3.

———. 2004. "¿América Latina ya no es católica? (Cambios culturales, transformación del campo religioso y debilitamiento de la Iglesia)." Paper presented at the International Congress of the Latin American Studies Association, Las Vegas, NV, October 7–9.

Peterson, Anna, and Manuel Vásquez, 2001. "'Upwards, Never Down': The Catholic Charismatic Renewal in Transnational Perspective." In Anna Peterson, Manuel Vásquez, and Philip Williams, eds., *Christianity, Social Change, and Globalization in the Americas*, 188–209. New Brunswick, NJ: Rutgers University Press.

Prokopy, Joshua, and Christian Smith. "Introduction." 1999. In Christian Smith and Joshua Prokopy, eds., *Latin American Religion in Motion*, 1–16. New York: Routledge.

Rossell y Arellano, Mons. Mariano. 1964 [1954]. "A Pastoral Letter on Catholic Social Justice and the Struggle Against Communism." In Frederick B. Pike, ed., *The Conflict Between Church and State in Latin America*, 175–82. New York: Knopf.

Schmidt, Gregory D. 2003. "The Great Minority: Christian Democracy in Peru." In Scott Mainwaring and Timothy R. Scully, eds., *Christian Democracy in Latin America: Electoral Competition and Regime Conflicts*, 330–63. Stanford, CA: Stanford University Press.

Serbin, Kenneth P. 1995. "Brazil: State Subsidization and the Church Since 1930." In Satya R. Pattnayak, ed., *Organized Religion in the Political Transformation of Latin America*, 153–76. Lanham, MD: University Press of America.

———. 2000. "The Catholic Church, Religious Pluralism, and Democracy in Brazil." In Peter R. Kingstone and Timothy J. Power, eds., *Democratic Brazil: Actors, Institutions, and Processes*, 144–61. Pittsburgh, PA: University of Pittsburgh Press.

Shorto, Russell. 2007. "Keeping the Faith." *New York Times Magazine*, April 8.

Sigmund, Paul E. 2003. "The Transformation of Christian Democratic Ideology: Transcending Left and Right, or Whatever Happened to the Third Way?" In Scott Mainwaring and Timothy R. Scully, eds., *Christian Democracy in Latin America: Electoral Competition and Regime Conflicts*, 64–77. Stanford, CA: Stanford University Press.

Smilde, David A. 1999. "Nationhood, Patronage, and the Conflict over New Religious Movements." In Paul E. Sigmund, ed., *Religious Freedom and Evangelization in Latin America,* 269–83. Maryknoll, NY: Orbis Books.

Smith, Brian H. 1982. *The Church and Politics in Chile: Challenges to Modern Catholicism.* Princeton, NJ: Princeton University Press.

Steigenga, Timothy. 1999. "Guatemala," In Paul E. Sigmund, ed., *Religious Freedom and Evangelization in Latin America,* 150–74. Maryknoll, NY: Orbis Books.

Stein, Andrew J. 1998. "The Consequences of the Nicaraguan Revolution for Political Tolerance: Explaining Differences among the Mass Public, Catholic Priests, and Secular Elites." *Comparative Politics* 30, no. 3 (April): 335–53.

———. 1999. "El Salvador." In Paul E. Sigmund, ed., *Religious Freedom and Evangelization in Latin America,* 113–28. Maryknoll, NY: Orbis Books.

Stoll, David. 1990. *Is Latin America Turning Protestant? The Politics of Evangelical Growth.* Berkeley: University of California Press.

Taylor, William B. 1996. *Magistrates of the Sacred: Priests and Parishioners in Eighteenth-Century Mexico.* Stanford, CA: Stanford University Press.

United Nations Economic Commission for Latin America and the Caribbean (UN-ECLAC). 2003. *Statistical Yearbook.* New York: UN-ECLAC.

U.S. Department of State. 2006. *International Religious Freedom Report 2006.* Available at http://www.state.gov/g/drl/irf/rpt/.

Valenzuela, Arturo. 1978. *The Breakdown of Democratic Regimes: Chile.* Baltimore, MD: Johns Hopkins University Press.

Vallier, Ivan. 1970. *Catholicism, Social Control, and Modernization in Latin America.* Englewood Cliffs, NJ: Prentice-Hall.

Vásquez, Manuel A. 1998. *The Brazilian Popular Church and the Crisis of Modernity.* Cambridge: Cambridge University Press.

Villa, Martha, and Fortunato Mallimaci. 2007. "Las Comunidades Eclesiales de Base y el Mundo de los Pobres en la Argentina: Conflictos y Tensiones por el Control del Poder en el Catolicismo." Available at http://www.ceil-piette.gov.ar/docpub/libros/cebs.pdf.

Wilde, Alexander. 1987. "Creating Neo-Christendom in Colombia." Kellogg Institute Working Paper #92 (March), Kellogg Institute, University of Notre Dame.

Wilkie, James W., ed. 1990. *Statistical Abstract of Latin America. Vol. 28.* Los Angeles: University of California, Los Angeles, Latin American Center Publications.

———, ed. 1995. *Statistical Abstract of Latin America, Vol. 31, Part I.* Los Angeles: University of California, Los Angeles, Latin American Center Publications.

———, ed. 2002. *Statistical Abstract of Latin America, Vol. 38.* Los Angeles: University of California, Los Angeles, Latin American Center Publications.

Yashar, Deborah. 2005. *Contesting Citizenship in Latin America: The Rise of Indigenous Movements and the Postliberal Challenge.* Cambridge: Cambridge University Press.

PART I

Pluralist Challenges to the Contemporary Catholic Church in Latin America: Institutions and Beliefs in a Context of Religious and Social Change

2 | Cultural Change, Religion, Subjective Well-Being, and Democracy in Latin America

RONALD INGLEHART

Introduction

This chapter argues that Latin America constitutes a distinctive global cultural region, characterized by strong emphasis on traditional values such as religion as well as free choice and self-expression, which is normally found in high-income societies. These attributes are conducive to high levels of subjective well-being and to the functioning of democracy. Our analysis is based on a body of survey evidence that represents almost 90 percent of the world's population. Data from successive waves of the World Values Survey (WVS) and European Values Study (EVS) indicate that major cultural changes are occurring—*and* that a society's religious tradition, colonial history, and other historical factors give rise to distinctive cultural traditions that continue to influence a society's value system despite the forces of modernization. Thus, though Latin America spans a vast geographical distance, from Tijuana to Patagonia, with considerable cultural variations within and among nations, the publics of Latin American countries have relatively similar basic values in comparison with other societies. On the one hand, they emphasize traditional religious and social values more strongly than most other societies. On the other hand, they

also rank relatively high on another important dimension of modernization, emphasizing a syndrome of "self-expression values" more strongly
than their economic level would predict. This dimension is strongly linked
with both subjective well-being and the emergence and flourishing of
democratic institutions.

Strong emphasis on religion is perfectly compatible with democracy *if*
the top religious authorities accept the principle that elections, and not the
word of God, should decide who holds secular power. Thus, stable democracies exist in highly secular societies, such as Sweden and Japan, and in
relatively religious societies, such as Ireland, the United States, and Latin
America. A crucial factor shaping democracy today is the extent to which
people emphasize the syndrome of tolerance, trust, and political activism
that is tapped by self-expression values. Although basic values change over
time, the impact of a society's historical heritage remains clearly visible in
the contemporary value systems of its public. In this regard, Latin America
continues to constitute a distinct cultural region.

Modernization and Cultural Change

In the nineteenth and early twentieth centuries, modernization
theorists from Marx to Weber tried to predict the future of industrial society, emphasizing the rise of rationality and the decline of religion. In the
twenty-first century it is clear that modernization is more complex than
these early views anticipated. Today, hardly anyone views the abolition of
private property as the solution to society's ills, and it is increasingly evident that religion has not vanished, as predicted. Moreover, it is apparent
that modernization cannot be equated with Westernization. Non-Western
societies in East Asia have surpassed their Western role models in key aspects of modernization, such as rates of economic growth and high life
expectancy. And few observers today would attribute moral superiority to
the West.

Although the original Marxist version of modernization theory is un-
tenable today, one of its core concepts remains valid: the insight that, once
industrialization begins, it produces pervasive social and cultural consequences, from rising educational levels to changing gender roles. Industri-

alization is the central element of a modernization process that impacts on most other elements of society. Marx's failures as a prophet are evident, but he correctly foresaw that industrialization would transform the world. When he was writing *Das Kapital* only a handful of societies were industrialized; today, almost every society on earth is at some stage of the industrialization process.

This chapter focuses on cultural changes in Latin America through examination of the distinctive position of this region in the light of evidence from the World Values Surveys, which have measured the beliefs and values of scores of societies containing most of the world's population. These surveys provide time series data from the earliest wave in 1981 to the most recent wave completed in 2007, offering an unprecedented rich source of insight into the relationships between economic development and social and political change. The surveys show that substantial changes have occurred in the values and beliefs of the publics of these societies during the years since 1981. These changes are closely linked with the economic changes experienced by a given society, but we find evidence of both massive cultural change *and* the persistence of traditional values. As we will demonstrate, economic development is associated with predictable changes away from absolute norms and values and toward a syndrome of increasingly rational, tolerant, trusting, and postindustrial values.

The evidence indicates that when socioeconomic development reaches the postindustrial phase, it produces rising emphasis on "self-expression values" (described more fully below). These values give high priority to the civil and political liberties that are central to democracy, so the cultural shift from emphasis on survival values to self-expression values is inherently conducive to democracy. As we will see, the prevalence of self-expression values among a society's public is strongly correlated with societal-level democracy. This correlation reflects a causal process through which economic development gives rise to increasing emphasis on self-expression values, which in turn leads to the emergence and flourishing of democratic institutions. Liberal democracy guarantees civil and political rights that enable people to make autonomous choices in their private and public activities: it institutionalizes freedom of action. Although the desire for freedom is a universal human aspiration, it does not take top priority when people grow up with the feeling that survival is uncertain. When survival seems secure, however, increasing emphasis on self-expression values makes the emergence of democracy increasingly likely where it does not yet exist and makes democracy increasingly *effective* where it already exists.

Conversely, adopting democratic institutions does not automatically make self-expression values people's top priority. These values emerge when socioeconomic development diminishes material, cognitive, and social constraints on human choice, thereby nourishing a sense of existential security. This can occur under *either* democratic or authoritarian institutions, depending on whether they attain high levels of socioeconomic development. Rising emphasis on self-expression does not reflect the prior existence of democracy; quite the opposite—it can emerge under either democratic or authoritarian institutions, and when it does, it generates mass demands for democracy. Demonstrating that the rise of self-expression values is conducive to democracy, rather than the other way around, requires a complex empirical analysis (see Inglehart and Welzel 2005, chaps. 7 and 8). Latin America is a distinctive cultural region because its people place relatively strong emphasis on traditional religious values, but they also emphasize self-expression values more heavily than other societies at comparable levels of economic development, making the outlook for democracy relatively favorable. Let us examine each of these factors more closely.

Modernization and Cross-Cultural Variation

The World Values Survey data demonstrate that the worldviews of the people of rich societies differ systematically from those of low-income societies across a wide range of political, social, and religious norms and beliefs.[1] In order to focus our comparisons on a small number of important dimensions of cross-cultural variance, we carried out a factor analysis of each society's mean level on scores of variables, replicating the analysis in Inglehart and Baker (2000).[2] The two most significant dimensions that emerge reflect, first, a polarization between *traditional* and *secular-rational* orientations toward authority and, second, a polarization between *survival* and *self-expression* values. By *traditional* we refer to orientations that place strong emphasis on religion, male dominance in economic and political life, and respect for authority; have relatively low levels of tolerance for abortion and divorce; and have high levels of national pride. More modern societies, or *secular-rational* societies, have the opposite characteristics.

The second major dimension of cross-cultural variation is linked with the transition from an industrial to a postindustrial society. This transition produces a polarization between *survival* and *self-expression* values, which are emerging among generations who have grown up taking survival for granted. Self-expression values give high priority to environmental protection, tolerance of diversity, and rising demands for participation in decision making in economic and political life. They emphasize gender equality as part of a broader syndrome of tolerance of out-groups, including foreigners, gays, and lesbians. The shift from survival values to self-expression values also includes a shift in child-rearing values, in particular, a shift from emphasis on hard work toward imagination and tolerance as important values to teach a child. In addition, this shift leads to a rising sense of subjective well-being that is conducive to an atmosphere of tolerance, trust, and political moderation, in which people place a relatively high value on individual freedom and self-expression and have activist political orientations. These are precisely the attributes that the political culture literature defines as crucial to democracy.

The unprecedented wealth that has accumulated in advanced societies during the past generation means that an increasing share of the population has grown up taking survival for granted. Thus, priorities have shifted from an overwhelming emphasis on economic and physical security toward an increasing emphasis on subjective well-being, self-expression, and quality of life. Inglehart and Welzel (2005) demonstrate that orientations have shifted from *traditional* toward *secular-rational values,* and from *survival* toward *self-expression values* in almost all advanced industrial societies that have experienced economic growth. But modernization is not linear—when a society has completed industrialization and starts becoming a postindustrial society (or "knowledge society"), it moves in a new direction.

Figure 2.1 shows a two-dimensional cultural map on which the value systems of eighty societies are depicted. The vertical axis represents the traditional/secular-rational dimension, and the horizontal axis reflects the

Figure 2.1. Global Cultural Map, 2000

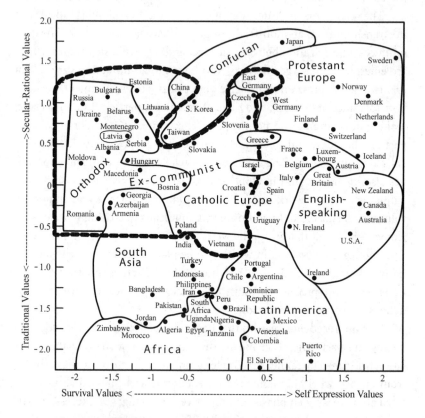

Source: Data from the 1995 and 2000 waves of the World Values Survey and European Values Study.

survival/self-expression values dimension. Both dimensions are strongly linked with economic development: the value systems of rich countries differ systematically from those of poor countries. Germany, France, Britain, Italy, Japan, Sweden, the United States, and all other societies with an annual per capita gross national product (GNP) over $15,000[3] in 1995 rank relatively high on both dimensions: without exception, they fall in a broad zone near the upper-right-hand corner. Conversely, every one of the societies with per capita GNPs below $2,000 fall into a cluster at the lower left of the map; cutting across the African, South Asian, ex-communist, and Orthodox cultural zones, India, Bangladesh, Pakistan, Nigeria, Ghana, and Peru are all part of this category. The remaining societies fall into intermediate cultural-economic zones. Based on this analysis, then, economic development seems to move societies in a common direction, regardless of their cultural heritage.

Economic Development Interacts with a Society's Cultural Heritage

Nevertheless, distinctive cultural zones persist two centuries after the onset of the industrial revolution. Different societies follow different trajectories even when they are subjected to the same forces of economic development, in part because situation-specific factors, such as a society's cultural heritage, also shape how a particular society develops. Huntington (1996) emphasized the role of religion in shaping the world's eight major civilizations, or "cultural zones": Western Christian, Orthodox Christian, Islamic, Confucian, Japanese, Hindu, African, and Latin American. These zones were shaped by religious traditions that are still powerful today, despite the forces of modernization.

Because a society's cultural heritage as well as its economic development influence cultural change, the eleven Latin American societies fall into a coherent cluster showing relatively similar values. As stated above, they rank high on traditional religious values but place stronger emphasis on self-expression values than their economic levels would predict. Economic factors are important, but they are only part of the story; other factors—for example, the common Iberian colonial heritage across these societies—seem to have left an impact that persists centuries later (and Uruguay actually falls between Spain and Portugal in Figure 2.1). Similarly, despite their wide geographic dispersion, the English-speaking countries constitute a relatively compact cultural zone, as do the historically Roman Catholic societies of Western Europe (Italy, Portugal, Spain, France, Belgium, and Austria), which display relatively traditional values when compared with Confucian or ex-communist societies with the same proportion of industrial workers. Virtually all of the historically Protestant societies (West Germany, Denmark, Norway, Sweden, Finland, and Iceland) rank higher on both the traditional/secular-rational dimension and the survival/self-expression dimension than do the historically Roman Catholic societies. And all four of the Confucian-influenced societies (China, Taiwan, South Korea, and Japan) have relatively secular values, constituting a Confucian cultural zone despite substantial differences in wealth. The Orthodox societies constitute another distinct cultural zone, as Huntington argued.

Each society's religious and colonial heritages seem to have had an enduring impact on their contemporary value systems. But a society's culture reflects its entire historical heritage. A central historical event of the twentieth century was the rise and fall of a communist empire that once ruled one-third of the world's population. Communism left a clear imprint on the value systems of those who lived under it, and these societies are encircled by a heavy broken line on Figure 2.1. East Germany remains culturally close to West Germany despite four decades of communist rule, but its value system has been drawn toward the communist zone. And although China is a member of the Confucian zone, it also falls within a broad communist-influenced zone. Similarly, Azerbaijan, though part of the Islamic cluster, also falls within the communist "superzone" that dominated it for decades. Thus, again we can see that changes in GNP and occupational structure have important influences on prevailing worldviews, but traditional cultural influences persist.

The ex-communist societies of Central and Eastern Europe all fall into the upper-left-hand quadrant of our cultural map, ranking high on the traditional/secular-rational dimension (toward the secular pole) but low on the survival/self-expression dimension (falling near the survival-oriented pole). Although they are by no means the poorest countries in the world, the societies of Central and Eastern Europe have recently experienced the collapse of communism, which shattered their economic, political, and social systems and engendered a pervasive sense of insecurity. Thus, Russia, Ukraine, Bulgaria, Romania, and Moldova rank lowest of any countries on the survival/self-expression dimension; they exhibit lower levels of subjective well-being than much poorer countries such as India,

Bangladesh, Zimbabwe, Uganda, and Pakistan. People who have experienced stable poverty throughout their lives tend to emphasize survival values, but those who have experienced the collapse of their social system (and may, as in Russia, have living standards and life expectancies far below where they were fifteen years ago) experience a sense of unpredictability and insecurity that leads them to emphasize survival values even more heavily than those who are long-accustomed to an even lower standard of living.

Not surprisingly, communist rule was conducive to the emergence of a relatively secular-rational culture. As Figure 2.1 demonstrates, the ex-communist countries in general, and those that were part of the Soviet Union in particular (and thus experienced communist rule for seven decades rather then four) rank higher on secular-rational values than noncommunist countries. And to an equally striking extent, ex-communist countries in general, and former Soviet countries in particular, emphasize survival values more heavily than societies that have not experienced communist rule. But there is wide diversity within the former communist zone as well. The basic values prevailing in the Czech Republic, Slovenia, Croatia, and East Germany are very close to those of Western European societies on both major dimensions. Significantly, these societies have experienced relatively successful transitions from communism to market economies, and they were historically shaped by the Protestant or Roman Catholic religious traditions rather than by the Orthodox tradition. This is part of a broader pattern. The historically Protestant or Roman Catholic ex-communist societies show a marked tendency to rank higher on self-expression values than the historically Orthodox societies. A society's position on this dimension has important political implications: we find a strong correlation between self-expression values and how democratic a given society is, as measured by its political rights and civil liberties ratings.

When the broad "noncommunist" category is broken down into these finer categories, it is clear that both Protestant Europe and the Confucian cultural region are even more secular than the Orthodox cultural region: the repression of religion that occurred under communist rule probably contributed to the relatively secular worldviews held by the publics of Orthodox societies, but the forces of modernization seem to have secularized

Protestant Europe even more effectively than the conscious efforts that communist regimes made to stamp out religion. The Confucian cultural heritage, of course, has emphasized a relatively secular, this-world orientation for many centuries. The English-speaking publics remain significantly more traditional in their orientations than those of other rich countries— though they are markedly less so than the publics of developing societies in South Asia, the Islamic region, Latin America, and Africa, the most traditional cultural region of all.

Though they lag behind other rich societies in their degree of secularization, the English-speaking societies place greater emphasis on self-expression values than the people of any other cultural region. Protestant Europe comes next; on the two-dimensional map, this region exhibits the most modern outlook of any cultural region. Latin America ranks third, though it is not nearly as rich as the English-speaking or west European zones.

The Orthodox societies rank at the opposite extreme, placing less emphasis on self-expression values (and more on survival values) than the people of any other cultural zone. Catholic Europe as a whole places relatively strong emphasis on self-expression values, despite the fact that roughly half the members of this group have experienced communist rule (along with two societies of Protestant Europe). Decades of communist rule had a significant impact on the values and beliefs of those who experienced it, but a given cultural heritage can partially offset or reinforce its impact. Thus, as Inglehart and Baker (2000) demonstrate, even when we control for level of economic development and other factors, a history of communist rule continues to account for a significant share of the cross-cultural variance in basic values. In addition, an Orthodox tradition seems to reduce emphasis on self-expression values in comparison with societies historically shaped by a Roman Catholic or Protestant cultural tradition.

Religion and Happiness in Latin America

We have compared the belief systems of the people of Latin American societies with those of other regions on two major dimensions of cross-cultural variation. This provides a useful overview, but it remains at a high level of generalization. Now let us examine how these societies differ on some specific variables linked with each of the two main dimensions.

Table 2.1 shows the percentage of people worldwide who say that "God is very important in my life"—a variable that is closely linked with the traditional/secular-rational dimension. In the world as a whole, about 36 percent of the public says that God is very important in their lives. The Latin American peoples rank far above this level: among the twelve Latin American societies for which we have data, this figure ranges from a low of 37 percent in Uruguay to a high of 91 percent in Puerto Rico. Latin American publics hold relatively traditional values—in fact, they rank almost as high as the Islamic publics in their emphasis on religion.

As one would expect, living under communist rule was conducive to secular values, and the publics of the Soviet successor states are less than half as likely to say that "God is very important in my life" than are the publics of noncommunist societies. But high levels of economic development have had a secularizing impact fully as strong as that of seven decades of communist rule (see Norris and Inglehart 2004). Thus, the publics of Denmark, Norway, Sweden, France, the Netherlands, and Japan are even *less* likely to say that God plays an important role in their lives than are the publics of most ex-communist countries.

Table 2.2 gives a detailed picture of one of the variables closely linked with the survival/self-expression dimension: people's sense of subjective well-being. This index is based on each public's combined scores on self-reported happiness and life satisfaction, with these two indicators given equal weight.[4] The survival/self-expression values dimension taps emphasis on postmaterialist values, interpersonal trust, tolerance of out-groups (such as foreigners, homosexuals, and women), political activism, and subjective well-being. We focus on subjective well-being scores here because they reveal an important feature of Latin American publics: they show higher scores on subjective well-being than their economic level would predict.

Economic development, as we have seen, is conducive to high levels of subjective well-being (though it reaches a point of diminishing returns). Across the more than eighty societies for which we have data, the correlation between subjective well-being and gross domestic product (GDP) per capita is a robust $r = 0.62$. Accordingly, all of the high-income societies

Table 2.1. Percentage of People Who Say That "God Is Very Important in My Life"

Jordan	98	Mexico	64	Montenegro	22
Pakistan	97	Chile	61	Hungary	21
Morocco	95	Azerbaijan	61	Tambov	20
Algeria	95	Argentina	59	Switzerland	20
Saudi Arabia	94	Cyprus	58	Belarus	20
Iraq	92	United States	57	Serbia	20
Puerto Rico	91	Romania	57	Andorra	20
Tanzania	90	Israel	55	Britain	19
Indonesia	90	Poland	54	Spain	18
Trinidad	90	Kyrgyzstan	48	Russia	18
El Salvador	89	Bosnia	42	Thailand	18
Bangladesh	89	Macedonia	40	Finland	16
Zimbabwe	88	Malaysia	40	Slovenia	16
Brazil	87	India	38	Latvia	16
Ghana	87	Georgia	38	Belgium	15
Philippines	87	Canada	37	Iceland	15
Guatemala	87	Uruguay	37	Luxembourg	15
Nigeria	85	Ireland	36	South Korea	14
Colombia	83	Portugal	36	Vietnam	14
Egypt	82	Moldova	35	West Germany	12
Iran	82	Italy	33	Bulgaria	12
Turkey	80	Greece	31	Netherlands	11
Venezuela	80	Armenia	31	Norway	11
Dominican Republic	80	Slovakia	30	France	10
Rwanda	79	Northern Ireland	29	Taiwan	10
Uganda	76	Singapore	29	Czech Republic	9
Zambia	71	Croatia	29	Estonia	9
Burkina Faso	70	Lithuania	26	Sweden	8
South Africa	69	Austria	25	Denmark	7
Peru	69	Albania	25	Japan	6
Mali	68	Australia	24	East Germany	6
Malta	67	Ukraine	24	Hong Kong	6
Ethiopia	67	New Zealand	24	China	5

Source: Combined data from World Values Survey and European Values Study, 1995–2007 surveys.

Note: Percentages are based on those respondents who chose ten on a ten-point scale. Latin American countries are shown in **bold**.

Table 2.2. Subjective Well-Being Rankings of Latin American Countries and the Rest of the World

Denmark	4.24	Malaysia	2.61	Croatia	0.87
Puerto Rico	**4.21**	West Germany	2.60	Morocco	0.87
Colombia	**4.18**	Vietnam	2.52	India	0.85
Iceland	4.15	France	2.50	Uganda	0.69
Northern Ireland	4.13	Philippines	2.47	Zambia	0.68
Ireland	4.12	**Uruguay**	**2.43**	Algeria	0.60
Switzerland	3.96	Indonesia	2.37	Burkina Faso	0.60
Netherlands	3.77	**Chile**	**2.34**	Egypt	0.52
Canada	3.76	**Dominican Republic**	**2.29**	Slovakia	0.41
Austria	3.68	Japan	2.24	Hungary	0.36
El Salvador	**3.67**	Spain	2.16	Montenegro	0.19
Malta	3.61	Israel	2.08	Serbia	0.18
Luxembourg	3.61	Italy	2.06	Tanzania	0.13
Sweden	3.58	Portugal	2.01	Azerbaijan	0.13
New Zealand	3.57	Taiwan	1.83	Macedonia	-0.06
United States	3.55	East Germany	1.78	Rwanda	-0.15
Guatemala	**3.53**	Slovenia	1.77	Pakistan	-0.30
Mexico	**3.52**	Ghana	1.73	Ethiopia	-0.30
Norway	3.50	Poland	1.66	Estonia	-0.36
Belgium	3.40	Czech Republic	1.66	Lithuania	-0.70
Britain	3.39	China	1.64	Latvia	-0.75
Australia	3.26	Mali	1.62	Romania	-0.88
Venezuela	**3.25**	Kyrgyzstan	1.59	Russia	-1.01
Trinidad	3.25	Jordan	1.46	Georgia	-1.01
Finland	3.24	Greece	1.45	Bulgaria	-1.09
Saudi Arabia	3.17	South Africa	1.39	Iraq	-1.36
Thailand	3.02	Turkey	1.27	Albania	-1.44
Cyprus	2.96	**Peru**	**1.24**	Ukraine	-1.69
Nigeria	2.82	South Korea	1.23	Belarus	-1.74
Brazil	**2.81**	Hong Kong	1.16	Moldova	-1.74
Singapore	2.72	Iran	1.12	Armenia	-1.80
Argentina	**2.69**	Bangladesh	1.00	Zimbabwe	-1.92
Andorra	2.64	Bosnia	0.94		

Source: Combined data from World Values Survey and European Values Study, 1995–2007 surveys.
Note: Figures are mean scores on subjective well-being index, based on each respondent's reported happiness and satisfaction with life as a whole being equally weighted. Negative scores indicate that a majority of respondents are unhappy and dissatisfied. Latin American countries are shown in **bold**.

shown in Table 2.2 rank above the median on subjective well-being. But because cultural and historical factors also play an important role, although
they are not "high-income countries" as classified by the World Bank, two
of the three countries with the highest levels of subjective well-being are
Latin American, and all twelve of the Latin American societies included in
the survey rank above the median level for the world as a whole. Looking at
it from another perspective, *all* twenty-five societies with the highest levels
of subjective well-being are either (1) high-income countries or (2) Latin
American countries. Being Latin American seems to provide a bonus in
subjective well-being, which moves these countries up to the level of high-
income countries.

As Figure 2.2 demonstrates, subjective well-being increases with rising
levels of GNP per capita, but the relationship is curvilinear, as the regression line on Figure 2.2 indicates. All twelve of the Latin American societies
for which we have data fall above the regression line: they all show higher
levels of subjective well-being than their economic level would predict.
Puerto Rico and Colombia, in particular, show some of the highest levels of
subjective well-being in the world, though their economic levels are much
lower than those of the United States, Canada, western Europe, and Japan.
Conversely, the ex-communist societies in general, and the Soviet successor states in particular, show much lower scores than their economic level
would predict. Thus, in countries that never experienced communist rule,
33 percent of the public describes themselves as "very happy," as compared
with only 7 percent in the ex-Soviet societies and 16 percent in the other
former communist societies.

For the former communist societies, this finding is not surprising. In
1989–1991 communism collapsed throughout Central and Eastern Europe.
In the Soviet successor states this brought drastic decreases in standards of
living, stagnant or falling life expectancies, and the traumatic experience of
the collapse of the social, political, and belief systems under which people
had lived for many decades. The prevailing sense of existential security and
individual control over one's life fell sharply, and the collapse of faith in the
communist ideology seems to have left a spiritual vacuum. Although these
societies are far from the poorest countries in the world, their publics' recent experience has been of a sharp downward shift from the levels of

Figure 2.2. Economic Development and Subjective Well-Being in Latin America and Other Countries

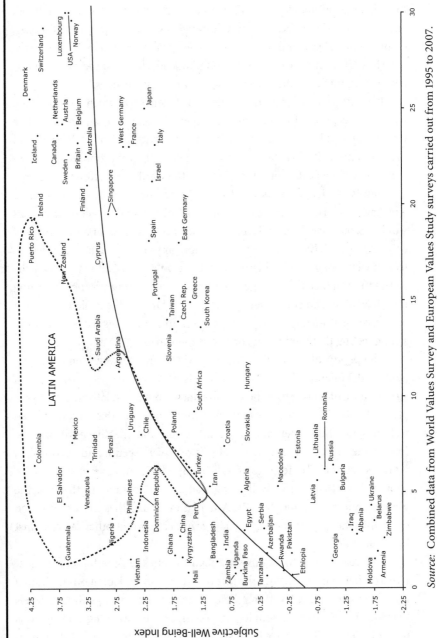

Source: Combined data from World Values Survey and European Values Study surveys carried out from 1995 to 2007.

income, security, and sense of meaning to which they had been accustomed. Thus, although Vietnam, China, East Germany, Slovenia, Poland, and the Czech Republic have middle-range levels of subjective well-being, all of the other ex-communist societies, especially the ten ex-Soviet states, have low levels of subjective well-being. Indeed, twelve of the fourteen unhappiest countries in the world are ex-communist societies.

In contrast, all of the Latin American societies for which we have data, with the exception of Peru, rank well above the global mean on subjective well-being—and even Peru ranks higher than its economic level would predict. The revised version of modernization theory proposed by Inglehart and Welzel (2005) provides a straightforward explanation for the ex-communist societies' low scores on subjective well-being, and it hints at why Latin American societies tend to be happier than their economic levels would predict: as societies develop economically, a sense of autonomy—of controlling one's life—plays an increasingly important role in shaping subjective well-being. And it happens that the publics of Latin American societies rank higher than the people of most other cultural zones in feeling that they are in control of their lives. This only moves the explanation back one step, for it is not entirely clear *why* Latin Americans have a relatively strong feeling that they are in control of their lives.

The people of the Nordic countries (Sweden, Norway, Denmark, Iceland, and Finland) also show high levels of subjective well-being and a strong sense of having free choice and control, but it is relatively easy to explain why this is so: they live in high-income countries that have advanced welfare states, little internal conflict, and stable and effective governments. Life in the Nordic countries actually *is* relatively secure and predictable, which is conducive to feelings of well-being. The Latin American countries show levels of subjective well-being that are comparable to those of the Nordic countries although Latin America in general has *not* experienced economic stability or good governance, indicating that other factors must be influential here.

One reason why the Latin American societies rank so high on subjective well-being is linked with the fact that they also rank high on traditional religious values: high levels of religiosity tend to be linked with high levels of subjective well-being. Religion serves important psychological functions for its believers. It can provide a sense of security and predictability in an uncertain world. Religions tend to establish a sense of community and social solidarity, and they provide explanations for the meaning and purpose of life. Thus, empirical studies have found that those who adhere to some religion tend to have higher levels of subjective well-being than those who do not (Ferriss 2002).

This is not true in all societies, however. Figure 2.3 shows the strength of the correlation between happiness and emphasis on religion (as measured by the percentage saying that God is important in their lives) in both rich and poor countries. The vertical axis in the middle of this graph shows the zero point where there is no correlation between religiosity and happiness. The people living in the countries located to the right of this line have a positive correlation between religion and happiness (which gets stronger as one moves to the right). In the countries located to the left of this line, there is a negative correlation between religion and happiness (which gets stronger as one moves to the left). In the overwhelming majority of countries, we find a positive correlation: in sixty-nine of the eighty-three societies for which we have data (including all Latin American countries), religious people are happier than those who are not. This provides strong support for the claim that religion is conducive to happiness.

In fourteen societies, however, the relationship is negative or neutral, and twelve of these fourteen cases are ex-communist countries: Russia, China, Bulgaria, Romania, Macedonia, Moldova, Vietnam, Albania, Lithuania, Hungary, Slovenia, and Montenegro. Why are religious people happier almost everywhere except in ex-communist countries? We believe this reflects an interesting dynamic. In the long run, religion does tend to be conducive to happiness, but the ex-communist countries are a special case. Until about 1990 they were dominated by a Marxist ideology that once filled the function of a religion, providing psychological security, predictability, and a sense of meaning and purpose in life for many people. It is impossible to understand the rise to power of communist movements in many of these countries without recognizing the motivating power that the communist worldview once had. But during the 1970s and 1980s this ideology began losing credibility; fewer and fewer people believed that communist regimes were building an ideal society that represented the wave of the future. By 1990 communism was generally discredited, and communist regimes collapsed throughout the Soviet Union and Eastern Europe or, as in China and

Figure 2.3. Religion and Happiness in Eighty-Three Countries

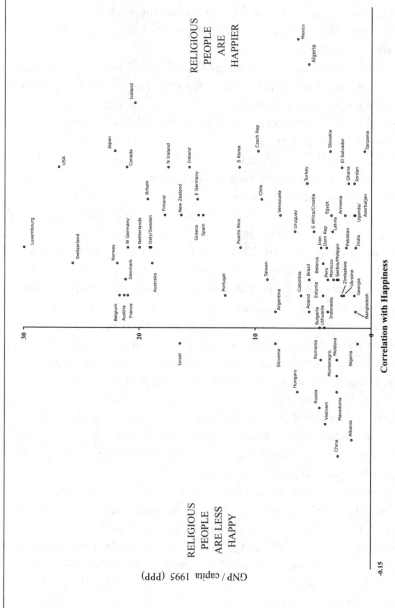

Correlation with Happiness

Source: Combined data from World Values Survey and European Values Study surveys carried out from 1995 to 2007.
Note: Placement of countries indicates correlations between responses to "How important is God in your life?" and reported happiness.

Vietnam, were replaced by nominally communist regimes that have become increasingly pragmatic and market-oriented in practice. The collapse of communist regimes was accompanied by severe economic and social decline in the former Soviet Union and Eastern Europe and left an ideological vacuum everywhere.

The communist regimes had systematically repressed religion, which they viewed as a misleading competing ideology (though the degree of repression varied from relatively little in Poland to a great deal in the Soviet Union and China). But since the collapse of communism, religion has been making a comeback in most ex-communist countries. It has not recruited equally from all strata: it has tended to attract the *least* happy people—those who feel the greatest need for a sense of meaning, reassurance, predictability, and social support. We hypothesize that, in the ex-communist countries, a disproportionate share of those who emphasize religion are new recruits who have been drawn to religion because they are unhappy and disoriented. For the time being, this creates a negative correlation between religion and happiness in these countries.

This explanation depends on the assumption that religion has been growing recently in former communist countries, which is up for debate. Figure 2.4 shows the extent to which the publics of given countries have come to emphasize religion more strongly (or less strongly) since 1981. The graph shows the difference between each country's mean score on the "Importance of God" scale in the earliest and latest available survey for each country in which at least two surveys were carried out in waves scheduled at least ten years apart (the average number of surveys is 3.7 and the mean time span is seventeen years). For example, the mean score of the Bulgarian public (at the top of the graph) increased from 3.56 in the 1990 survey to 5.15 in the 2006 survey—a gain of more than two points on the ten-point scale.

We do not find a global resurgence of religion, as some observers have claimed. Fully 72 percent of the western European countries show *declining* emphasis on religion, as do the publics of Australia, Canada, and the United States. But many countries show increases, and all of the six countries showing the greatest gains are ex-communist: Bulgaria, Russia, China, Belarus, Serbia, and Romania. Overall, the publics of 78 percent of the ex-communist countries placed increasing emphasis on religion. This is consistent with the hypothesis that religiosity is linked with unhappiness in these countries because those who are religious consist disproportionately of new, relatively unhappy recruits. This hypothesis gains further support from the fact that emphasis on religion increased most in countries with relatively low levels of happiness ($r = 0.5$).

Their relatively high levels of religiosity are not the only reason why Latin American countries tend to show higher levels of subjective well-being than their economic level would predict. An even more important

Figure 2.4. Changes in Emphasis on Religion in Fifty-Two Countries, 1981–2007

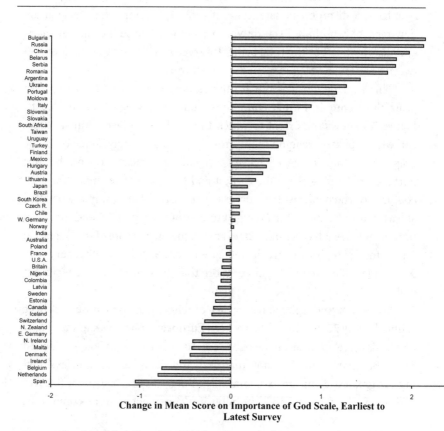

Change in Mean Score on Importance of God Scale, Earliest to Latest Survey

Source: Combined data from World Values Survey and European Values Study surveys carried out from 1981 to 2007.

factor is the fact that the publics of these countries tend to feel that they are in control of their lives. The WVS asked respondents to what extent they feel that they have free choice and control over their lives. Table 2.3 shows the percentage of respondents indicating that they have relatively high levels of free choice (placing themselves at points eight to ten on a ten-point scale). As one might expect, the publics of high-income societies are relatively likely to feel that they have control over their lives: the objective reality is that having abundant economic resources expands one's range of choices. Nevertheless, all four of the publics showing the highest levels of free choice and control are from Latin American countries, and all twelve Latin American publics rank above the global median in their sense of having free choice. All twenty of the highest-ranking publics are from either (1) high-income countries or (2) Latin America. As Inglehart et al. (2008) demonstrate, the extent to which people feel that they have free choice and control over their lives is the most important single factor shaping a country's level of subjective well-being, even more than the country's level of economic development. At this point in history the Latin American publics have the best of both worlds in certain respects. They continue to have relatively strong religious orientations—a traditional source of subjective well-being. But they also tend to have a relatively strong sense that they are in control of their lives, which tends to be most widespread in high-income societies where religion and other traditional sources of solidarity play a diminished role.

A strong sense of freedom and control seems to be an enduring characteristic of Latin American societies, but it also reflects, to some extent, the recent wave of democratization in the region. The public of Mexico, for example, has not always shown the high levels of subjective well-being that it now manifests. The transition to democracy in 2000 was accompanied by a sharp rise in feelings of both free choice and subjective well-being, and this persisted through the 2006 survey. Democratization in the former Soviet Union, by contrast, was accompanied by economic and social collapse and, therefore, did not bring rising feelings of subjective well-being.

The finding that Latin American publics tend to register relatively high levels of subjective well-being is a robust phenomenon and a major reason

Table 2.3. The Sense That One Has Free Choice and Control over One's Life in Latin America and the Rest of the World

Puerto Rico	74	**Peru**	48
Venezuela	71	West Germany	47
Mexico	69	South Africa	47
Colombia	69	**Chile**	47
New Zealand	66	Malaysia	47
Trinidad	64	Luxembourg	46
United States	63	South Korea	45
Iceland	61	Thailand	45
Guatemala	61	Greece	44
Canada	60	Philippines	43
Finland	60	Uganda	43
Dominican Republic	60	Singapore	43
Australia	59	Egypt	43
Andorra	59	Iran	43
Brazil	58	Algeria	42
Denmark	57	Croatia	40
Northern Ireland	56	Belgium	39
Norway	56	Czech Republic	39
El Salvador	56	East Germany	39
Malta	56	Tanzania	39
Jordan	56	Saudi Arabia	39
Cyprus	56	Poland	37
Sweden	55	Zimbabwe	37
Argentina	55	Portugal	36
Switzerland	54	Moldova	36
Taiwan	54	France	35
Austria	54	Netherlands	35
Uruguay	54	Turkey	35
Ghana	53	Georgia	35
Britain	51	Hungary	34
Nigeria	51	Lithuania	34
Slovenia	51	Slovakia	34
Romania	51	Italy	33
China	51	Spain	33
Indonesia	51	Russia	33
Ireland	50	Azerbaijan	33
Kyrgyzstan	50	Macedonia	33
Zambia	50	Morocco	33
Vietnam	49	Serbia	32

Table 2.3. (Cont.)

Mali	32	Burkina Faso	27
Rwanda	32	Latvia	26
India	30	Ethiopia	25
Bangladesh	30	Ukraine	24
Montenegro	30	Japan	22
Bosnia	30	Belarus	21
Estonia	29	Albania	18
Armenia	28	Pakistan	5
Iraq	28		
Hong Kong	28		
Bulgaria	27		

Source: Combined data from World Values Survey and European Values Study, 1995–2007 surveys.
Note: Percentages indicated those placing themselves at points eight through ten on a ten-point scale indicating to what extent one has free choice and control, with ten indicating a great deal of free choice. Latin American countries are shown in **bold**.

why they rank disproportionately high on the broader syndrome of self-expression values. The fact that they do has significant implications, for there is a remarkably strong linkage between self-expression values and stable democracy.

Self-Expression Values and Democracy

A society's position on the survival/self-expression index is strongly correlated with its level of democracy, as indicated by its ranking on the Freedom House political rights and civil liberties scores. This relationship is remarkably powerful, and it is clearly not a methodological artifact since the two variables are measured at different levels and come from entirely different sources. Virtually all of the societies that rank high on survival/self-expression values are stable democracies, while virtually all of the societies that rank low on this dimension have authoritarian governments.

The Freedom House measures are limited by the fact that they only measure the extent to which civil and political liberties are institutionalized, which does not necessarily reflect the extent to which these liberties are actually respected by political elites. Noteworthy recent literature has emphasized the importance of the distinction between formal democracy and genuine liberal democracy (Ottaway 2003; O'Donnell, Vargas Cullel, and Iazzetta 2004). In order to measure liberal democracy, we need a measure of "effective democracy," which reflects not only the extent to which formal civil and political liberties are institutionalized but also the extent to which these liberties are actually *practiced*—indicating how much free choice people really have in their lives. To construct such an index of effective democracy, Inglehart and Welzel (2005) multiply the Freedom House measures of civil and political rights by the World Bank's anticorruption scores (Kaufmann, Kraay, and Mastruzzi 2003), which they see as an indicator of "elite integrity," or the extent to which state power actually follows legal norms.[5] When we examine the linkage between this measure of genuine democracy and mass self-expression values, we find a remarkably strong correlation of $r = 0.90$ across seventy-three nations. This reflects a powerful cross-level linkage, connecting mass values that emphasize free choice and the extent to which societal institutions actually provide free choice.

Figure 2.5 depicts the relationship between this index of effective democracy and mass self-expression values. The extent to which self-expression values are present in a society explains fully 80 percent of the cross-national variance in the degree to which liberal democracy is actually practiced. These findings suggest that the importance of the linkage between individual-level values and democratic institutions has been underestimated. Mass preferences play a crucial role in the emergence of genuine democracy.

The linkage between mass self-expression values and democratic institutions is remarkably strong and consistent, with only a few outliers such as China, Iran, and Vietnam showing lower levels of democracy than their publics' values would predict. These countries have authoritarian regimes that are under growing societal pressure to liberalize. Authoritarian rulers of some Asian societies have argued that the distinctive "Asian values" of these societies make them unsuitable for democracy (Lee and Zakaria 1994; Thompson 2000). But in fact the position of most Asian countries on Fig-

Figure 2.5. Impact of Self-Expression Values on Effective Democracy

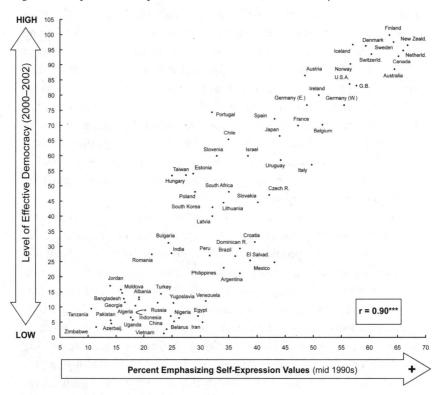

Source: Inglehart and Welzel (2005, 155).

ure 2.5 is about where their level of socioeconomic development would predict. Japan ranks with the established Western democracies, both on the self-expression values dimension and on its level of democracy. And Taiwan's and South Korea's positions on both dimensions are similar to those of other relatively new democracies such as Hungary or Poland. The publics of Confucian societies are more supportive of democracy than is generally believed.

We now turn to the question of what comes first—a democratic political culture or democratic institutions? The extent to which people emphasize self-expression values is closely linked with the flourishing of democratic institutions. But what causes what? We have argued that economic development interacts with a society's cultural heritage, so that high levels of development (linked with the rise of the knowledge society) bring growing emphasis on self-expression values, which, in turn, produces strong mass demands for liberalization and democratic institutions. The reverse interpretation would be that democratic institutions give rise to the self-expression values that are so closely linked with them. In other words, democracy makes people healthy, happy, nonsexist, tolerant, and trusting and instills postmaterialist values. This interpretation is appealing, and if it were true it would provide a powerful argument for democracy, implying that we have a quick fix for most of the world's problems: adopt democratic institutions and live happily ever after.

Unfortunately, the experience of the Soviet Union's successor states does not support this interpretation. Since their dramatic move toward democracy in 1991, the peoples of these nations have not become healthier, happier, more trusting, more tolerant, or more postmaterialist; in fact, many have moved in exactly the opposite direction. In these cases, economic and physical insecurity seems to have more impact on the development of self-expression values than the fact that leaders are chosen in reasonably free elections. Moreover, the WVS demonstrates that growing emphasis on self-expression values emerged in these states through a process of intergenerational change within the authoritarian communist regimes: democratic regimes do not necessarily produce self-expression values, and self-expression values can emerge even within authoritarian regimes if they produce rising levels of existential security.

Democratic institutions do not automatically produce a culture that emphasizes self-expression values. Instead, it seems that economic development gradually leads to social and cultural changes that make democratic institutions more likely to survive and flourish. That would help explain why mass democracy did not emerge until a relatively recent point in history, and why, even now, it is most likely to be found in economically more developed countries—in particular, those that emphasize self-expression values over survival values.

During the past few decades, most industrialized societies have moved toward increasing emphasis on self-expression values in an intergenerational cultural shift linked with economic development. This trend is at work in Latin America. Throughout this region, the younger generations place greater emphasis on self-expression values than do the older generations. This relationship is found in all of the Latin American countries for which we have data, being strongest in Uruguay, Argentina, and Colombia and relatively weak in Peru and Venezuela. In this region as a whole, only 41 percent of those aged sixty-five and over rank above the worldwide mean in emphasis on self-expression values, while among those under thirty-five years of age, 54 percent rank above the global mean. In the long run, the process of intergenerational population replacement tends to make these values more widespread. The flourishing of democratic institutions is also contingent on economic development and political stability, but other things being equal, the intergenerational shift toward increasing emphasis on self-expression values produces growing mass pressures in favor of democracy.

Conclusion

Modernization is not linear. It goes through various phases, each of which brings distinctive changes in people's worldviews. The Industrial Revolution was linked with a shift from traditional to secular-rational values, bringing the secularization of authority. In the postindustrial phase of modernization, another cultural change becomes dominant—a shift from survival values to self-expression values, which brings increasing emancipation *from* authority. Rising self-expression values makes democracy increasingly likely to emerge—indeed, beyond a certain point it becomes increasingly difficult to *avoid* democratization.

Cross-cultural variation is surprisingly coherent, and a wide range of attitudes (in such different life domains as the family, work, religion, environment, politics, and sexual behavior) reflect just two major underlying dimensions: one that taps the polarization between *traditional values* and *secular-rational values,* and a second dimension that taps the polarization between *survival values* and *self-expression values.* The world's societies cluster into relatively homogenous cultural zones reflecting their historical heritage, and these cultural zones persist robustly over time.

Latin American societies have a distinctive character in global perspective. They emphasize traditional religious values more strongly than most other cultural zones, while also emphasizing the self-expression values linked with postindustrial societies far more strongly than other societies at comparable levels of economic development. The fact that they continue to emphasize traditional religious values *and* modern values such as free choice and self-expression leads them to have much higher levels of subjective well-being than other societies at comparable levels of economic development. Their emphasis on self-expression values also has important political implications, for these values are—to a remarkably strong degree—linked with the emergence and flourishing of democracy.

Notes

1. The World Values Surveys and European Values Study have been carried out in more than ninety societies containing almost 90 percent of the world's population. In order to analyze changes, they have conducted multiple waves, with a first wave in 1981–1982, a second in 1990–1991, a third in 1995–1997, a fourth in 1999–2001, and a fifth in 2005–2007. For detailed information about these surveys, see the WVS Web site at http://www.worldvaluessurvey.org and the EVS Web site at http://www.europeanvalues.nl/.

2. For details of these analyses at both the individual level and the national level, see Inglehart and Baker (2000) and Inglehart and Welzel (2005).

3. We use the 1995 level of GNP to reflect the time lag between economic development and cultural change.

4. Respondents were asked (1) "Taking all things together, would you say you are: very happy, rather happy, not very happy, or not at all happy?" and (2) "All things considered, how satisfied are you with your life as a whole these days? Using this card on which 1 means you are 'completely dissatisfied' and 10 means you are 'completely satisfied,' where would you put your satisfaction with your life as a whole?" Happiness was rated on a four-point scale, on which high scores indicated low levels of happiness; life satisfaction was rated on a ten-point scale on which high scores indicated high levels of satisfaction. Thus, to give both variables equal weight, the mean scores on the happiness scale were multiplied by 2.5 and subtracted from the life satisfaction scores.

5. See Inglehart and Welzel (2005, chap. 7) for a more detailed discussion of this index.

References

Ferriss, Abbott L. 2002. "Religion and the Quality of Life." *Journal of Happiness Studies* 3, no. 3: 199–215.

Huntington, Samuel P. 1996. *The Clash of Civilizations and the Remaking of World Order.* New York: Simon and Schuster.

Inglehart, Ronald, and Wayne Baker. 2000. "Modernization, Cultural Change and the Persistence of Traditional Values." *American Sociological Review* 65, no. 1 (February): 19–51.

Inglehart, Ronald, Roberto Foa, Christopher Peterson, and Christian Welzel. 2008. "Development, Freedom, and Rising Happiness: A Global Perspective, 1981–2007." *Perspectives on Psychological Science* 3, no. 4 (July): 264–85.

Inglehart, Ronald, and Christian Welzel. 2005. *Modernization, Cultural Change and Democracy.* New York: Cambridge University Press.

Kaufmann, Daniel, Aart Kraay, and Massimo Mastruzzi. 2003. "Governance Matters III: Governance Indicators for 1996–2002." World Bank Policy Research Department Working Paper No. 2195. Washington, DC: World Bank.

Lee, Kuan Yew, and Fareed Zakaria. 1994. "Culture Is Destiny: A Conversation with Lee Kuan Yew." *Foreign Affairs* 73, no. 2: 109–26.

Norris, Pippa, and Ronald Inglehart. 2004. *Sacred and Secular: Religion and Politics Worldwide.* New York: Cambridge University Press.

O'Donnell, Guillermo, Jorge Vargas Cullel, and Osvaldo Miguel Iazzetta, eds. 2004. *The Quality of Democracy: Theory and Applications.* Notre Dame, IN: University of Notre Dame Press.

Ottaway, Marina. 2003. *Democracy Challenged: The Rise of Semi-Authoritarianism.* Washington, DC: Carnegie Endowment for International Peace.

Thompson, John B. 2000. "The Survival of Asian Values as 'Zivilisationskritik.'" *Theory and Society* 29: 651–86.

3 | Cultural Change in Mexico at the Turn of the Century

The Secularization of Women's Identity and the Erosion of the Authority of the Catholic Church

SOLEDAD LOAEZA

In the last thirty years of the twentieth century Mexican society underwent a process of change that transformed the knowledge, attitudes, and values concerning social norms and hierarchies, the economy, political institutions, religious beliefs, the family, and women's rights. In sharp contrast to the stereotypical images of a traditional society stagnating in conservative values tightly controlled by the Catholic Church, in Mexico today individual autonomy, diversity, and self-expression—all features of Ronald Inglehart's "postmodern value syndrome"—are generally pursued as positive social goals (Inglehart 1997). Thus, the Mexican experience illustrates Inglehart's claim that although the shift from modern to postmodern culture—or postmaterial culture—has taken place mainly in industrial countries that have solved the basic problems of survival (7–10), industrializing countries have not remained outside what appears to be a global process (49). The latter are moving in the same direction as the former in spite of varying cultural traditions and initial levels of change; industrializing countries are also experiencing "the rise of *new* values and lifestyles, with greater tolerance for ethnic, cultural, and sexual diversity and individual choice concerning the life one wants to lead" (23). This evolution shows that poverty and inequality do not necessarily hamper value change; these two general conditions add complexity to the understanding of societies in which significant percentages of the population have not yet solved basic problems of well-being. For instance, the postmodern value syndrome has created new sources of internal differentiation within Mexican society and deepened its heterogeneity.

In Mexico all institutions have been shaken by this process of change, from the family to the Catholic Church. However, the latter seems to be most affected by the ongoing secularization that accentuates a long-standing trend of separation between religious and civil institutions and values, further undermining the church's authority and influence and its historical position of privilege in the definition of social norms. In this type of environment the Catholic Church has become just one among a number of other cultural institutions, such as other religious denominations, the media, or an increasingly diverse school system, competing for the socialization of Mexicans. The church finds this state of affairs difficult to accept in light of its historical cultural hegemony and because of the fact that according to the 2000 census, 89 percent of the population self-identifies as Catholic.

Cultural change has always been a threat to the Catholic Church. However, in the past the church was able to moderate the consequences of this change for its authority by joining the state's social and political stabilization efforts after periods of civil war, political turmoil, or intense social mobility. This happened during the Porfirio Díaz dictatorship (1886–1910) and during the apogee of the one-party hegemonic political system (1945–1970). In both instances church and state found a formula for accommodating the grievances resulting from past confrontations, and the two worked together in the preservation of a traditional set of values in order to prevent uncontrolled change (see Loaeza 1988).

However, the circumstances in which the Catholic Church faces the challenge of secularization today are different from previous episodes. First, in contemporary Mexico secularization is not a state policy per se—as it was in the past when the state sought to enforce a rigorous anticlerical legislation—but rather a spontaneous process sustained by economic transformation, migration, the development of the media, and the opening of Mexico to globalization. Second, political democratization tends to reinforce social tolerance toward diversity, including religious diversity; it also promotes pluralism and participatory attitudes and demands and erodes rigid hierarchies in general and strict gender role differentiation in particular. This context does not favor the church's—or any institution's—monopoly on social values and creates tensions within the institution, such as those generated by discussions about artificial contraception or the legalization of abortion.

This chapter hypothesizes that the Catholic Church in Mexico does not have the resources to fight or even slow down a secularization process that poses a major challenge to its claims of value hegemony and political influence. As mentioned before, in previous episodes the Catholic Church and the authoritarian state formed an implicit alliance in support of a hierarchical and paternalistic social order and of principles such as the subordinate status of women. Nevertheless, in a democratized political system built on the basis of pluralism and a participatory society, formerly mutual interests have dissolved. Furthermore, the Mexican state does not have the means nor the interest to sustain the church's aspirations of cultural restoration, and there is growing evidence of long-term tendencies in Mexican society that point toward the consolidation of postmodern values within the dominant culture, in particular those related to sexual behavior, gender equality, and the position of women in the family. This is the culture that is transmitted by the media, the government, political actors, and an increasing number of interest groups; their influence on social values has been a central result of the democratization process.

To illustrate the steady decline of the Catholic Church's influence in Mexican society, this chapter describes and discusses the change in the last two decades in values and attitudes regarding the status of women in society. It also identifies emerging notions of femininity and examines women's patterns of economic and reproductive behavior that indicate a significant and profound cultural transformation and a pronounced intergenerational shift associated with higher levels of education.[1] Traditionally in Mexico, as in every Catholic society, the bond between the church and women was very strong. Women were responsible for the transmission of religious beliefs and for the observance of religious rites and norms in the family, and religious practice was an important aspect of domestic life. In addition, religious symbols were at the center of the definition of the normative feminine identity, and religiosity was a factor in gender differentiation. Mexican women participated actively with the church in its battles against anticlerical and secularization policies. During the Cristero rebellion—which erupted in 1926 in central Mexico when the government tried to enforce anticlerical legislation—women were the church's most valued allies and agents. Likewise, in the 1950s and 1960s women played a key role in the organization of broad anticommunist campaigns that were primarily religious crusades.[2] The loss of women's support has weakened the church's influence and capacity to mobilize public opinion.

Issues related to women and gender are reliable indicators of the social influence of the Catholic Church because until the 1970s the normative definition of the feminine identity had a strong religious component, closely associated with the role of the Virgin Mary as a model for young girls and women. This association was reinforced by the preeminence of maternity in the determination of a woman's social status and by the bonds that tied women to the family. The traditional normative "ideal woman" did not see women as individuals; they were either part of the mother/child duo or of the family set. Until the 1970s a woman's identity was the product of a relationship: she was mother, wife, daughter, or sister. Therefore, the secularization of the feminine identity and of the social status of women has been a process by which women have succeeded in being perceived as individuals with legitimate claims to personal welfare and happiness, even if these claims are different from those of their families.

Mexico's recent experience of cultural change is relevant to our attempts to gain a better understanding of this process. First, it is an industrializing country that in the last two decades has had a mediocre economic performance; however, this did not prevent the emergence of new attitudes and values, in seeming contradiction with the notion that cultural change only occurs in a context of economic expansion. Second, after centuries of hegemonic control of values and social norms, the Catholic Church is being overcome by the forces of modernity and postmodernity. Also, this analysis calls attention to the need to revise myths, stereotypes, and clichés about Mexican culture at the turn of the century.

The first part of this chapter describes economic performance and the main features of cultural change in Mexico in the last two decades; the second part looks at the religious component in the normative definition of the feminine identity prevailing in Mexico until the 1970s; the third part examines the diminishing gender differentiation derived from the emergence of women as individuals resulting from changes in education, women's participation in the labor force, and the demographic transition; and lastly, the chapter analyzes the impact of these changes on the influence of the Catholic Church in relation to women's political participation.

Cultural Change in Mexico after the 1970s

At the beginning of the twenty-first century in Mexico, far-reaching cultural changes can be recognized in the everyday life of expanding cities and industrial activities, in improved life expectancy and levels of formal education, in diminishing gender differentiation, and in the dissemination of foreign music, food, television programs, and films that familiarize Mexicans with the outside world. The majority of the population still self-identifies as Catholic, but if Mexicans continue to be deeply religious people they are also increasingly pluralist—with greater numbers joining evangelical or Protestant denominations—and increasingly secularized. Mexicans defend freedom of conscience and "emphasize more and more the importance of the separation of the Church and state, of the public and the private" (Blancarte 2006, 428).

Significant changes can be traced to the open economy, which has introduced a greater choice of consumer goods in local markets. Changes have also occurred in a democratized political system in which mass loyalties to political parties have eroded, respect for authority has weakened, and mass participation is encouraged in order to challenge elites. At the same time diversity and political mobility have encouraged party pluralism and the emergence of a diverse set of nongovernmental organizations that emphasize issue-specific forms of participation. All of these are features of a postmodern culture, according to Inglehart's definition (Inglehart 1997, 47).

The Mexican experience of cultural change confirms the relationship of this process to events in the economy. First, the long period of economic expansion that began in 1945 was accompanied by accelerated urbanization, bureaucratization, extension of formal education, improvement in life expectancy, and growing secularization; then, in 1982 a violent financial crisis put an end to sustained rates of economic growth and inaugurated almost two decades of economic instability and low rates of growth. Economic discontinuity did not halt cultural change, however. The experience of Mexico in the 1980s and 1990s shows that both economic crisis and economic reform can induce a transformation of attitudes and values as meaningful as that occurring in the context of an expanding economy. The content of the changes may vary, but these differences do not make them less significant.

During the last two decades of the twentieth century the Mexican economy went through a deep transformation that affected both "the economic policy framework and the structure of economic activity" (Werner, Barros, and Ursúa 2006, 88). In 1982 the development model of extended state intervention and high protectionism showed dramatic signs of exhaustion that for five years plunged the country into unprecedented high rates of inflation and negative rates of growth. In order to stabilize the economy, solve severe problems of fiscal deficit and an unmanageable public debt, and assure economic recovery, three successive administrations between 1982 and 2000 maintained anti-inflationary policies and introduced a number of reforms: trade liberalization, privatization, and deregulation. These led to a change in the country's economic model that has affected many Mexicans' everyday lives—for instance, by transforming the job market—so that at the beginning of the twenty-first century there is a greater demand for skills and expertise in computing services, telecommunications, and export-import activities than in agriculture.

The most consequential of these reforms was the opening of the Mexican economy to international trade. In less than twenty years Mexico went from decades of protectionism to radical trade liberalization: "The volume of trade (exports plus imports) as a share of GDP went from 20 percent in 1980 to 40 percent in 1994 and 70 percent in 2003" (Werner, Barros, and Ursúa 2006, 78). By 2006 Mexico had signed free-trade agreements with seventeen countries, a policy in itself significant for a country that used to be taken as an example of extreme economic nationalism. However, from a cultural perspective the North American Free Trade Agreement (NAFTA) stands out because it represents a substantial discontinuity in Mexican attitudes toward the United States, especially among the Mexican elite for whom in the 1980s closer ties with the United States began to be perceived more as an opportunity than as a national security threat (see Loaeza 1994).

Migration rates to the United States indicate that it was perceived by many poor Mexicans more as a land of opportunity than as an enemy well before the elite decided to adopt a policy of integration. Since the mid-1960s migration to the United States—legal and illegal—has increased steadily, going from 350,000 in the five-year period from 1965 to 1969 to over 400,000 annually in recent years. According to the U.S. Census Bureau, between 2000 and 2005 two million Mexicans migrated to the United States, increasing their number from 9.17 to 10.96 million, which represents 30 percent of all foreign-born individuals living in the United States (U.S. Census Bureau 2006).[3]

Almost two million households in Mexico (out of a total of 22 million) are directly connected to migration, and remittances from the United States reach an impressive $14 billion *per year* (Santibañez Rosellón 2004, 9). Given the dimensions of the phenomenon it can be presumed that migration has brought a substantial number of Mexican households into contact with the United States; this closeness has also been a vehicle for the dissemination of U.S. popular culture even among the lower social strata, as shown by preferences in music, dress, and fast food over the more vernacular alternatives that are perceived as old-fashioned or "traditional." In this respect Mexican society has become better disposed to accept change and more respectful of diversity; however, the ascent of individualism as a powerful and legitimate social value seems to be the more far-reaching influence of U.S. culture in Mexican society, given the latter's long-standing community and corporatist traditions.

From 1984 to 2004 the Mexican economy performed poorly. Between 1984 and 1994 the average annual growth of the gross domestic product (GDP) was just 2.7 percent, with 3.3 percent the following decade; in those same years GDP per capita grew at an annual rate of 0.8 and 1.8 percent, re-spectively. These low rates of growth were also the consequence of two deep financial crises—1982–1987 and 1994–1995—that thrust millions of Mexicans into poverty. In 1994, 64 percent of the population lived in poverty, and yet, in spite of the low-performing economy, ten years later this proportion had been reduced to 50 percent (World Bank 2006).

It is remarkable that in these inauspicious conditions literacy rates and levels of education continued to improve. In 2000 the average number of years of schooling of those aged fifteen and above was 6.6. In 2005, 90 percent of the population had completed primary school. The expansion of the educational system has benefited women in particular. In the past they were consistently less schooled than men; however, by the year 2000 it was already difficult "to identify educational differences between boys and girls" (Parker and Pederzini Villarreal 2000, 98). The average number of years of school attendance was 7 for women and 7.6 for men. Women's education has a direct effect on the improvement of their living conditions and those of their children; for instance, it has an immediate impact on reproduction and infant mortality. As will be shown below, survey information confirms the findings of historians, sociologists, and demographers: increased levels of women's education are determinant of the transformation of women's self-perceptions, of their status in society, and of their behavioral patterns concerning reproduction and the family.[4]

To deal with economic adversity Mexicans developed survival strategies that had significant implications in terms of attitudes and values. For instance, to face the crises of the 1980s many married women entered the workforce, breaking with a tradition according to which men were the sole breadwinners in the family. The growing incorporation of women into the labor market was also possible because of the broad acceptance of the use of artificial contraceptives. In the two decades from 1980 to 2000, "the increase in women's employment is one of the most important transformations in labor markets in Mexico," according to Cerrutti and Zenteno (2000, 90). In the thirty years from 1970 to 2000, the percentage of women who were economically active went from 19 to 31.5 percent (Rendón Gan 2004, 16). In the past, although many women, mostly from the lower classes, worked (see Gonzalbo 1987; Giraud 1987; Carner 1987; Ramos Escandón 1987), most of them were single and childless. This changed at the turn of the twentieth century, when many married women with children entered the labor market. In the decade between 1987 and 1997, the growth of married women engaged in extra-domestic work grew 32 percent, whereas the percentage of unmarried daughters of the household in the workforce increased 28 percent in those same years.

Although the majority of married women in the workforce still depend on their husbands because their earnings are lower than those of the head of the family, their contribution to the family income modifies domestic hierarchies and weakens gender differentiation. However, in the year 2000 the nuclear family—head of family with spouse and children, or head of family and children—was still predominant. Accordingly, in 1997 divorce rates were among the lowest in Latin America—only 70 out of 1,000 marriages were dissolved *per year* (Quilodrán 2001, 50). This percentage is also interesting because divorce laws in Mexico, first introduced in 1915, are markedly relaxed and protective of women. But family stability is more than the result of religious obedience; it is also a response to adverse economic conditions in which the family provides the individual with protection in case of layoffs, unemployment, and low wages. In addition, families working as an economic unit tend to improve their living standards through the accumulation of the salaries or wages of several of their members.

Mothers, Wives, Daughters: Repressing Women's Identity

The history of Mexican church-state relations from the mid-nineteenth to the mid-twentieth century is plagued with conflict. The confrontation derived from the opposition of the church to the secularization policies pursued first by the liberals and then by postrevolutionary governments, some of whose anticlerical measures were incorporated into the 1917 constitution. After 1940 the reconciliation between the church and state was an important facet of the stabilization process undertaken by the elite in power. However, the anticlerical legislation was neither modified nor enforced. As a result of this arrangement, cooperation and mutual support between church and state developed within a framework of informal rules: the authoritarian political regime found a reliable support in the patriarchal social order promoted by the church, and the conservatism and passivity necessary for the acceptance of the set of values associated with Catholicism contributed to the support of an authoritarian political order. After 1946 church activities, most of which were concentrated on education, were tolerated. Thanks to this policy of tolerance, the church achieved institutional restoration and reestablished its quasi-monopoly over social values and patterns of behavior. It was also able to resist the undermining effects of social change. Thus, the golden years of Mexican authoritarianism (1945–1970) also marked the peak of the social influence of the Catholic Church in the twentieth century.

Thanks to this close collaboration between church and state, until the beginning of the 1970s the main normative notions and images concerning women and femininity were those disseminated by the Catholic Church. However, the real influence of these norms and ideals on women's behavior varied according to social class: since colonial times the upper and middle classes seemed to have been more responsive to this authority than women from the lower classes. For instance, common-law unions, premarital conceptions, and single mothers were frequent among the urban poor and in rural communities. Their number is a reflection of the limited resources of the Catholic Church in Mexico; only widespread education and a state policy oriented toward family planning or the regularization of unions could reduce the occurrence of these phenomena (Ramos Escandón 1987, 147).

Since the nineteenth century the church's norms of feminine behavior and women's rights—or rather, duties—found juridical support in the civil code or in general legislation based on an assumption of women's subordinate status (Ramos Escandón 1987, 147). The revolution brought about some legal changes, mostly in divorce laws; however, women continued to be treated as lifelong minors who depended on men for their protection. During the 1947 debates on women's suffrage, Manuel Gómez Morín, at the time president of the conservative opposition party Partido Acción Nacional (National Action Party, or PAN), asked party members whether it would be right to expose "our daughters, our wives, our mothers and sisters to the filth of politics" (Gómez Morín 1950). This view did not represent a major difference between political parties; rather, it was dominant across the political spectrum. In 1939 President Lázaro Cárdenas, who is mostly remembered for his radical reforms, halted the constitutional amendment that would have introduced women's suffrage, fearing that women would be an instrument of the church. Others opposed women's voting rights because they believed that "spiritual values represented by feminine virtues would be lost" (cited in Ramos Escandón 1998, 99). During the 1945 presidential campaign, Miguel Alemán, who at the time led the more ambitious modernizing wing of the official party, Partido Revolucionario Institucional (Institutional Revolutionary Party, or PRI), supported legislation that granted women full participation in municipal elections. Nevertheless, he also stated his pride in Mexican women "by tradition immemorial incomparable mothers, abnegated and industrious wives, loyal sisters, and chaste daughters" (cited in Ramos Escandón 1998, 100).

The works of Mexican writers such as Rosario Castellanos (1979), Inés Arredondo (1988), and Agustín Yáñez (1993) vividly portray the subordinate status of women and the strict moral standards that were applied to judge their behavior. Sociologists, anthropologists, and literary critics have observed that in the 1950s and 1960s the normative model of the ideal woman prevailing in Mexican society was characterized by passivity, self-denial, modesty, and chastity (see Pescatello 1973; Fowler-Salamini and Vaughan 1994; Tuñon Pablos 1999, 88). These traits correspond to the motherly figure symbolized by the Virgin Mary or her more vernacular representation, the Virgin of Guadalupe, who provided the essential reference for femininity and as such was forcefully disseminated by the church.

The implications of the presence of a strong religious component in the ideal feminine identity were manifold and far-reaching in terms of the rules governing women's behavior. They were expected to be a reference of moral superiority and a source of spiritual strength (Stevens 1973). These characteristics entailed boundless generosity and patience, as well as unlimited understanding for the failings of men who were morally weak. The fact that the reference of the ideal woman was a religious symbol of sanctity also explains the severity of girls' education compared with boys' and the rigid demands on girls' self-control. Upper- and middle-class women bore strong pressures from the family and their social environment to conform to church prescriptions, the trespassing of any of which was in many cases tantamount to social degradation because only women from the lower classes rejected these rules or were too weak to observe them.

The primacy of a woman's chastity over any other personal quality justified that girls be kept in complete ignorance of sexual matters. To prevent "strange ideas" from getting into young women's heads, only rarely were they given sexual information by the family, at school, or even in women's magazines. In this respect postrevolutionary governments were markedly puritanical. In 1941 the government suppressed coeducation in public schools because, according to President Manuel Ávila Camacho, it was an institution "repulsive to the Nation's feelings" (Ávila Camacho 1942, 15).

Marriage followed by motherhood was a woman's natural goal and destiny. Matrimony was a promised land for women both rich and poor, but they were expected to remain virgins until they married. Virginity was a highly valued treasure. In many cases it was the only "treasure" a young woman could bring to the marriage, and it was a matter of honor for men to guard their girlfriend's or sister's virtue. Virginity meant obedience to the church's teaching, but it was also an important piece of the "macho" culture that still prevails in Mexico. This would explain why for women in the year 2000, "first sexual encounter" and the "first marriage/cohabitation" were events closely related in time (see Solís, Gayet, and Juárez 2005).

Whether rich or poor, until the 1970s a woman who married was fulfilling her duty as intended by God. However, while matrimony was the only life option—other than religious life—for single women in a middle-class family, for women of lesser means matrimony was an attractive alternative to low-paid domestic service or factory work. For those who had to make a living, finding a husband was tantamount to having more freedom since they were promised a steady income. Ideally, marriage meant no longer having to clean other peoples' homes, waiting on strangers, or spending entire days in front of a machine. According to the prevalent stereotype, marriage provided protection and respectability. A man in the house was a principle of order because the male figure was by definition a figure of authority and the family backbone. Maternity was the next "natural" stage for young Mexican women. Very few couples used artificial contraceptives, and abortion was a word not spoken out loud, and much less in front of young women.

The notion that a woman's place was at home was an argument against the education of women. In the 1950s women represented a little more than half of the total population, yet only in primary schools did the proportion of girls to boys reproduce the demographic ratio; the presence of girls in the educational system decreased significantly in high school. In 1970 only 17 percent of women between twenty-five and forty years of age had a high school or college education; twenty-five years later this number had climbed to 66 percent (Parker and Pederzini Villarreal 2000, 105). A poor family that could not afford a college education for all their children would automatically give precedence to the sons over the daughters. In the 1950s and 1960s middle-class working women had a short preprofessional education: they were engaged in clerical work or were nurses, accountants, or preschool or elementary school teachers. Women were educated to carry out support activities, not to make executive decisions (Castellanos 1973). Lower-class women worked as domestic servants or market vendors or held low-paid jobs, such as seamstresses, and many were denied marriage or maternity because they could not reconcile their activities with family life.

Most women's low educational level kept them in a state of perpetual childhood, but their lack of education was not a stigma in a value system where even ineffectuality was considered an "endearing" feminine quality (Flora 1973). Most middle-class women grew up still holding puerile notions of love relationships; this was only a facet of the childish world to which they had been condemned by the church and by a political system whose presidents referred to society as the "great Mexican family." This metaphor is a reflection of the patriarchal structure of Mexican society, a hierarchical organization presided over by the authority of a mother and a father and within which male children gradually reached adulthood whereas female children remained minors throughout their lives. As observed by Cornelia Butler Flora in an analysis of women's magazines in Latin America in the 1960s, although a woman's status varies by culture and by class, "there remains the large residual status factor of sex, which is more important than either culture or class in determining female status characteristics" (Flora 1973, 61).[5]

The role the church played in the dissemination of values, symbols, and norms relative to women and the family accounts for the weakness of the social class variable in the differentiation of female social status because the church message was sent across class divisions and was reinforced by women's magazines and the popular press. The church focused on women and relied on them for the development and consolidation of its social influence (see Loaeza 2005). In 1953, 286,273 women represented 80 percent of the membership in Acción Católica Mexicana (Mexican Catholic Action, or ACM), the lay organization that was the church's main instrument of influence. The number of nuns shows their significance in the clergy: in 1945 there were 8,123 nuns in Mexico; in 1960, 19,400. In other words, within a period of fifteen years their number rose almost 139 percent, and there were three times as many nuns as priests.[6]

The astonishing increase in the number of nuns was also an indirect reflection of one of the teachings of the church: that God had a *life plan* for every one of His daughters. In this program not to marry was not a choice for women. In any case, in the Mexico of the 1950s women did not make decisions by themselves. Either there was something very wrong with a woman who did not marry or God had other plans for her: a religious life. By entering a religious order a woman was responding to God's calling. However, for more down-to-earth single women, the convent was also an honorable way out that sanctified their "bad luck"; the convent could help them disguise their incompetence at finding husbands. The religious profession was also an alternative for young women from poor families who wanted to continue their studies, or for whom a convent provided stable employment, a bed, and board. A "decent" woman did not live by herself. Rather, respectable single women remained at home with their family, taking care of their aging parents or ailing relatives or looking after nephews and nieces.

The desirability of a dependent status for women can also be traced in popular literature and romance novels. Flora's findings in Mexico and Colombia show that "the plot of the majority of the stories in each class and culture group centered upon the female achieving the proper dependent status either by marrying or manipulating existing dependency relationships to reaffirm the heroine's subordinate position. The male support— monetary, social and psychological—was generally seen as well worth any independence or selfhood given up in the process" (Flora 1973, 71).

Before 1970 Mexican women were expected to be the anchors of social stability. The "mother saint" was responsible for the preservation of the family as a strong, united institution; she was also in charge of keeping traditions alive, guarding memories dear to the heart, and encouraging everything that strengthened family unity. In this axiomatic context it took enormous courage from a woman to sue for divorce. All the images, values, and preconceptions that governed women's behavior constituted more complex realities than those pictured in romance novels or in the magazines and leaflets distributed in parochial churches every Sunday after Mass. Women were expected to be mothers and teachers. But there were many that could not fulfill this exemplary role, and when they did not they had to learn to live with the shame and guilt of having failed. The punishment for not following the rules was greater subordination and marginality.

Vatican II, the consequential assembly launched in 1961 by Pope John XXIII that set down the guidelines for Catholics in the second half of the twentieth century, should have changed the perceptions within Mexican society of the church's message to women. However, in those years the church in Mexico had other priorities. The first echo of Vatican II in Mexico was the episcopate's 1968 pastoral letter *Carta Pastoral sobre el desarrollo e integración de la patria* (Pastoral Letter on the Development and Integration of the Fatherland; Conferencia del Episcopado Mexicano 1968), which offered a critical view of social conditions in the country and of the "civic poverty" of society and proposed a "democratic plan or program" in search of an intermediate way "between individualistic liberalism and totalitarianism." This document suggested that, for the first time in decades, the church was assuming social leadership. However, when in the summer of 1968 a severe crisis derived from university students' challenge to authoritarianism, which threatened the basic stability of the political system, the hierarchy renewed its support of the government as well as its distrust of political "radicalism" and retreated to a more subdued attitude.

Vatican II had an important impact on the Mexican Catholic Church, but its reach and significance were shaped by the local circumstances, namely, the authoritarian political system and the particular features of state-church relations, which since the 1940s had stabilized due to a policy of cooperation that overcame the confrontation of the 1920s and 1930s. (Loaeza 1984). As in other countries, the council had a divisive effect on the Mexican clergy and laity: a radical interpretation of the church's documents encouraged the emergence of a progressive wing that became associated with popular movements and organizations and tended toward the option for the poor and liberation theology, while the majority followed the more cautious line of most of the hierarchy. In effect, Vatican II precipitated an ideological cleavage within the church in Mexico. In the 1970s the church's potential influence was contained by the increase in internal tensions derived from this division. In those years there was a dramatic increase in differences of opinion and conflicts within the hierarchy—between bishops and priests, between the hierarchy and lay organizations, and between Catholics themselves. This situation further weakened the church's position. The relatively unstable position of the church and the fact that it did not have full legal status according to the Mexican constitution bolstered the position of the more conservative members of the episcopate.

Women: The Transition from Dependents to Individuals

In the last thirty years one of the most salient transformations of Mexican society has been a general—if unequal—improvement in women's lives and social status. This process is associated with an important rise in the level of education among women. Between 1970 and 1997 the percentage of illiterate women fell from almost 30 percent in 1970 to 13 percent in 1997 (Figure 3.1). The years of schooling for women increased by 122 percent, going from an average of 3.2 years to 7.1 (CONAPO 2005; see Figure 3.2.). Also, the participation of women in the labor force grew from 21 percent in 1970 to 34 percent in 2000 (CONAPO 2005).

The education of women and their participation in the economically active population are widely accepted in Mexican society. In a survey on the social status of women conducted in 1999, the statement "It is not worthwhile to spend on a daughter's education because she will marry" was agreed with by 5 percent of women with a high-school education or more and 8 percent of men with the same level of education. The same survey also reported that a majority disagreed with the following statement: "The responsibility for the economic maintenance of the home lies exclusively on the man of the family" (Grupo Interdisciplinario de Mujer, Trabajo y Pobreza 1999). In this case it is worth noting that women's disagreement was significantly higher than men's; thus, among 18–24 year olds, 73 percent of women disagreed while only 52 percent of men disagreed; the same gap appears in the 25–34 and 35–44 age groups. The percentage of dis-agreement was below 70 percent only among women 45 years old and older (62 percent).

An analysis of the World Values Surveys (WVS) shows that 82 percent of women agree with the statement "both the husband and the wife should contribute to household income." This answer is consistent with views re-garding the shared responsibility for the household held by 85 percent of women and 79 percent of men surveyed. These attitudes toward responsi-bility for the household suggest that women are not perceived as dependent members of the family (Inglehart, Basáñez, and Moreno 1998, Table V223). It could not be otherwise in a society where in the last twenty-five years the percentage of households headed by women has risen from 14 to 21 per-cent. The pace of increase in households headed by women accelerated after 1990; while in that year three million households fell into that cate-gory, today there are five million households headed by women.

In addition to the changes in women's education and participation in economic activities, over the last thirty years women's life trajectories have also been affected by changes in mortality, marriage, and fertility patterns

Figure 3.1. Illiterate Mexican Population Fifteen Years Old and Older, 1970–1997 (in percent)

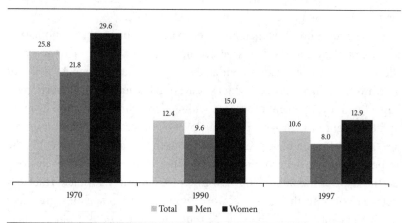

Source: Dirección General de Estadística (1970); INEGI (1995, 1999).

due to significant variations in life expectancy and age patterns of marriage, divorce, and widowhood (CONAPO 2002). Between 1970 and 2000 the life expectancy of fifteen year olds rose from fifty-seven to sixty-three; even if the average woman in Mexico today marries at twenty, the same age as her mother, she has fewer children. In 1970, 45 percent of married women in their fifties had five or more children and only 21 percent had just one or two children. Today only 11 percent of married women in their fifties have five children or more, while 40 percent have one or two children. In 1970 the fertility rate, which stood at forty-five births per thousand, had not changed since 1945; in effect, by the end of their reproductive life (forty-nine years of age) Mexican women on average had given birth to seven children (Alba 1993, 136).

The self-confidence women derive from being better educated and from participating in the labor force and earning an income has been substantially enhanced by the widespread use of contraception. The Catholic Church has little influence on family size. The church opposes reproductive choice; however, the reproductive patterns of Mexican women show that they prefer to decide freely whether to have children or not and when.

Figure 3.2. Average Number of Years in School of Mexican Population Fifteen Years Old and Older, 1970–1997

(in percent)

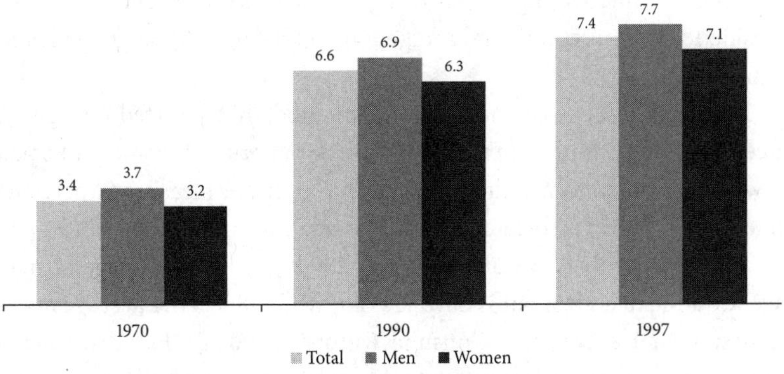

Source: Dirección General de Estadística (1970); INEGI (1995, 1999).

Every indicator of the use of birth control is also an indicator of the reach of the social influence of the church. Women who decide how many children they want to have go against the teachings of the Catholic Church and, furthermore, are not passive subjects who accept a preordained destiny. These women have substantive control over their bodies and over a fundamental aspect of family life, and they refuse to put decisions concerning such crucial matters into the hands of others. A survey conducted in 2003 shows that a majority of Catholics in Mexico (84 percent) believe that a "person can use contraceptives and still be a good Catholic" (Belden Russonello and Stewart Research 2003, 33). Thus, Mexican Catholics do not seem to find a contradiction between their religious beliefs and their birth control practices.

Since family planning became a governmental policy in the early 1970s, it has steadily gained social acceptance and support. According to a survey conducted by Consulta Mitofsky in 2004, 79 percent of Mexicans approve of the pill and 87 percent approve the use of condoms (Consulta Mitofsky 2004a). This explains why the percentage of women of childbearing age living in stable relationships who use contraceptive methods has risen from 30 percent in 1976 to 71 percent in 2000 (Figure 3.3). It is noteworthy that this aspect of the demographic transition undergone by Mexican society in the last thirty years may have been reinforced by economic adversity and that public policy on contraception was not modified by Vicente Fox, the first member of the conservative PAN to be elected president and a devout Catholic. It should also be noted that knowledge of contraceptive methods by women of childbearing age is strongly associated with schooling, place of residence (urban/rural), and indigenous (non-Spanish) language ability (Figure 3.4).

The extended use of contraceptive methods has induced changes in perceptions of sex and in sexual behavior. A majority of women associate sex with love (47 percent), the couple (22 percent), or pleasure (9 percent), while only 3 percent associate sex with procreation and marriage and 2 percent with the family (Consulta Mitofsky 2004a). The average age of marriage for a Mexican woman is 20 years old, while 18.5 is the average age of her first sexual encounter (Consulta Mitofsky 2004a). The discrepancy between these two averages suggests that virginity has lost the importance it had in the past for women who wanted to marry, as indicated by the

Figure 3.3. Mexican Women of Childbearing Age Living in Stable Relationships Who Use Contraception, 1976–2000

(in percent)

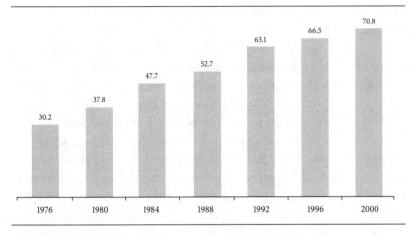

Source: CONAPO (2005).

Figure 3.4. Mexican Women of Childbearing Age Who Do Not Use Contraception, 1997

(in percent)

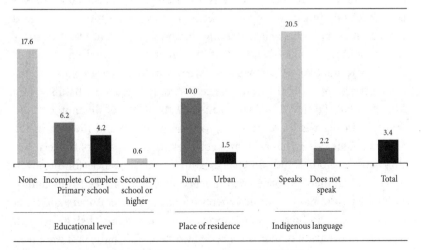

Source: Consejo Nacional de Población. Estimates based on INEGI (1999).

increase in premarital conceptions. According to a demographic study conducted in 1990, "consensual premarital sex is an extended practice on the increase, the opposite of what happens in Asian societies" (Quilodrán 2001, 51). Also, the diminished value of virginity indicates that chastity is not a sine qua non attribute of Mexican brides as it used to be in the past. However, this does not mean that there has been a radical transformation of sexual mores. The World Values Survey shows that only 31 percent of Mexicans agree with the statement that individuals should have the chance to enjoy complete sexual freedom without being restricted. Nonetheless, this percentage places Mexico in eleventh place in the international ranking, right after France and six places above the United States (Inglehart, Basáñez, and Moreno 1998, Table V197). Other surveys indicate that the vast majority of Mexican women (80 percent) are monogamous, having been married to or lived with only one partner throughout their lives (Quilodrán 2001, 60).

Nevertheless, the ability women have acquired to assume responsibility for their own lives has induced and reinforced changes in attitudes and values regarding women in general. In addition, the attributes of Mexican femininity have been modified by the emergence of women as individuals distinct from their family relationships; that is, the notion that women have an identity independent from their role in the family has also reduced gender differentiation.

A comprehensive overview of WVS findings provides valuable information for building a preliminary sketch of emerging attitudes with regard to women as individuals. It is striking that only 52 percent of Mexicans—women and men alike—believe that "a woman needs children to be fulfilled," a result that places Mexico in a position closer to most of the industrial countries and below France and Italy (Inglehart, Basáñez, and Moreno 1998, Table V215). This means that the image of the mother/child duo that in the past gave meaning to a woman's life and identity in the Mexican value system has been broken. The new perception of the relationship between woman and child has meaningful consequences for the development of an identity for women independent of their role in the family. This change also has important repercussions for a better understanding of maternity as a choice; as well, it improves the social status of single women with no children and of infertile married women, who in the past were seen as cursed.

Women's new independence from the mother/child identity is only one aspect of a more general cultural transformation taking place in Mexico, by which the importance of individualistic values is increasing. This change should not be underestimated in a society that comes from a resilient corporatist culture—dominated by family, union, party, and religious organizations—in which individual initiative and preferences were subordinate to collective decisions and rules typically restricted individual development. The WVS shows that 70 percent of Mexicans believe that they have "a great deal" of choice over the way their life turns out (Inglehart, Basáñez, and Moreno 1998, Table V95). This percentage places Mexico in seventh place in the international ranking. Interestingly enough, the percentage of women who believe they have free choice over their lives is slightly higher than the men's percentage (70 versus 69 percent). Evidence of the strengthening of the individual in Mexican culture is found in the view of 88 percent of Mexicans that "greater emphasis on the development of the individual" would be a good thing (Inglehart, Basáñez, and Moreno 1998, table V267).

Religion continues to be a factor in gender differentiation. However, the gap between men and women is not as wide as that between younger and older generations. While 47 percent of women and 36 percent of men attend church more than once a week, 32 percent of those between the ages of eighteen and twenty-nine do so, whereas 57 percent of those fifty years old and over attend church more than once a week (Consulta Mitofsky 2004b). Women pray more often than men, find more comfort in religion than men, and believe in God more than men; more women than men declare that God and religion are very important in their lives (see Inglehart, Basáñez, and Moreno 1998, Tables V9, V166, V177, V178, V179). However, this religiosity does not imply submission to the church's authority but rather a personalized and direct relationship with God.

Attitudes concerning abortion show that for a vast majority of Mexicans the woman as an individual takes precedence over the woman as mother. Although 43 percent stated that abortion was never justified, when presented with qualifying conditions, these attitudes changed. Among five possible situations in which abortion could be an option, 82 percent approved it when the mother's health was at risk; 58 percent would approve it if the child would be born physically handicapped; 19 percent approved abortion when the married couple do not want any more children; and a very low 17 percent approved it when the mother was unmarried. However, Mexico's abortion rate ranks among the lowest in Latin America: only seventeen abortions per ten thousand pregnancies (see Guillaume, Lerner, and Salas 2005). The rate could be explained by the extensive use of contraceptives or higher levels of education; it could also be the result of difficulties in gathering accurate information concerning abortion rates.

Views on the relationship between women and the family have also undergone meaningful changes. For most women—as for the vast majority of Mexicans—family is "very important" in their lives; however, this does not prevent them from seeing divorce as a legitimate alternative. The World Values Survey shows that only 29 percent of Mexicans believed that divorce is never justified—below Argentina, Brazil, and Chile; however, while 34 percent of women agreed, only 26 percent of men did. This result does not alter the basic observation that the perceptions of women's role within the family are very different today to what they were in the past. There is a growing belief in the equal responsibility of wives and husbands for the welfare of the family; there is also an increasing acceptance of new roles for women in the labor force, roles that are not perceived as compromising a woman's femininity. The information provided by the WVS regarding attitudes toward contribution to the household income, the satisfactions of domesticity, and the advantages of working women and working mothers reveals an emerging notion of femininity that departs from the religious ideal of the past and responds to a more realistic notion of women and their rights (see Inglehart, Basáñez, and Moreno 1998, Tables V215, V218, V219, V128, V237, V220, V221, V222).

This information also indicates a pronounced intergenerational shift between the responses of the sixteen to twenty-nine age cohort and that of respondents over fifty years old: the old notions seem to prevail among the older generation, while the younger generation has embraced a more egalitarian and secular view of women's role and status. This intergenerational shift is also present in education. In 2000, 30 percent of Mexicans over sixty years old (born in or before 1940)—and 36 percent of women—were illiterate; by contrast, only 4 percent of Mexicans between fifteen and twenty-nine years old (born after 1970) were illiterate—and the percentage was nearly the same for men and women in this age group (Table 3.1).

The Catholic Church and Women's Political Participation

The increased participation of women in the public arena has been an important aspect of the secularization of normative femininity and the diminishing gender differentiation brought about by the cultural change of the last thirty years. The democratized political system continues to privilege men, but the number of women in positions of governmental responsibility at the municipal, state, and federal levels has grown significantly. Women have become more vocal and active in all political parties; however, many politically oriented women have found in nongovernmental organizations a propitious environment to develop their abilities and organizational skills (see Camp 1998; Massolo 1998; Tarrés 1998).

The incorporation of women into the democratization process marks an important discontinuity with the majority of women's apparent passivity or dependence in the past: the initial strategy for achieving incorporation, followed by feminist groups in the 1980s, was to assimilate their demands to those of indigenous and sexual minorities as well as to more general democratic claims (Tarrés 1998). Nevertheless, there is continuity in terms of the issues that induce women to participate, most of which are associated with "everyday family life and with domestic tasks" (Massolo 1998, 193). In this respect gender differentiation persists because of "the social and cultural baggage embedded in the roles of mother, wife, and housewife" (Massolo 1998, 193), and women's responsibility for the control and improvement of the spaces immediately surrounding them—the neighborhood, the vicinal

Table 3.1. Illiteracy Rates in Mexico, 2000
(in percent)

Age Group	Females	Males	Females per 100 Males
15–29	3.9	3.3	118
30–44	8.6	5.3	162
45–59	19.5	11.3	173
60 and over	35.5	23.9	149

Source: INEGI (2000).

community, and the locality—has led them to develop a political identity of their own. This differentiation is confirmed by their struggles around issues, such as sexual and reproductive behavior, that concern their individual development. The position of the church on these matters has further loosened its traditional bond with Mexican women. The Catholic Church has consistently opposed women's rights since the policy of family planning was introduced in the 1970s. "The Episcopate went so far as to declare that demographic policies, contraceptive campaigns, and sterilization and abortion campaigns were all part of a conspiracy 'of dominant countries'" (Blancarte 2006, 430). These positions have alienated many women from the church, so much so that the church can no longer count on their support.

Mexican women were granted the right to vote and to run for office in two stages: they gained the right to vote in municipal elections in 1948, and in 1953 the right was extended to the federal level. Until then, the assumption that women were political instruments of the Catholic Church had provided strong arguments against women's suffrage. This assumption was not entirely unfounded. Women had participated very actively in conservative movements. During the Cristero rebellion (see Meyer 1971), they played a decisive role in the organization of clandestine networks. They helped hide the priests and nuns who were being persecuted and provided underground contacts and meetings between bishops and priests and their faithful. Women were couriers, spies, and uniform and flag seamstresses; they sewed the banners of Christ the King soldiers, dressed their wounds, found places to perform religious services, transmitted the insurgents' secret messages, and fueled hatred against the "anti-Christ," as they called President Calles. In 1928 a nun, Mother Conchita, plotted the murder of President-elect Alvaro Obregón. The militancy of Mexican Catholic women in defense of the church's rights was zealous and at times frenzied. The U.S. ambassador in Mexico, Dwight S. Morrow (1927–1929), who actively promoted an agreement between church and state, complained bitterly of Catholic women who opposed the conflict's resolution and boisterously expressed their antagonism in front of the U.S. embassy in Mexico City.

Historical experience also accounted for the widespread presumption that the Catholic Church was a powerful political actor. The memories of the *Cristiada*, the bitter and bloody war that, according to Jean Meyer

(1971), cost fifty thousand lives in central Mexico between 1926 and 1929, as well as the images of the effective peasant mobilizations organized in the 1940s by the Unión Nacional Sinarquista (National Synarchist Union, or UNS)—the heirs of the Cristeros—fed the presumption that the church maintained considerable potential to influence the political behavior and preferences of Mexicans. However, by the 1950s this alleged political power was more hypothetical than real.

The dominant position of the Catholic Church in the values and belief system of Mexican society in the years prior to 1970 gave it important leverage in its relations with government authorities. The real political power of the Catholic Church rested in its position within the political system and in the privileged access ecclesiastical authorities had to Mexican elites. However, this privileged access did not translate into the capacity to intervene in policy making. For example, in 1974 church authorities were powerless in the face of family planning legislation introduced by the Echeverría administration (1970–1976) that, in an effort to cut explosive rates of population growth that could jeopardize any plans for economic development, massively promoted the use of contraceptives through a broad media campaign and the public health services. The magnitude of the "birth control offensive" undertaken by the government simply overwhelmed any action attempted by the church to counter the new policy.

Until the political openings of the 1970s, the PRI's tight control of electoral participation and the opposition could support claims of the existence of a *Catholic electorate* by bishops, priests, and lay leaders of Catholic organizations. Observers and commentators alike shared in the belief that such an electorate existed and that the PRI hegemony and the electoral system were powerful impediments to the expression of Catholic voting preferences. The only evidence they provided to support their allegation was the national census, according to which the vast majority of Mexicans self-identified as Catholics. The implications of these claims were unsustainable. Had they been true, Mexico would have had a political system not very different from the one it had—a one-party hegemony—only that party would have been Catholic. As long as elections were rigged, this hypothesis could not be tested.

As suggested above, in the 1970s the church seemed to lose its previous self-confidence. Internal turmoil and political turbulence surrounding the

1968 crisis of the political system triggered by a students' movement in Mexico City shook the ground on which the church based its ability to influence social values and behavior. Nevertheless, the cautiousness exercised by the hierarchy in that political crisis helped it maintain its capacity to influence governmental policies. In 1972 the episcopate presented its position on family planning, *Mensaje del Episcopado al pueblo de México sobre paternidad responsable* (Message from the Episcopate to the Mexican People on Responsible Parenthood; Conferencia del Episcopado Mexicano 1973), in terms that were considered equivocal by the Vatican, in that it was ambiguous with respect to the use of artificial contraceptives. As the document had not been previously approved by the Vatican it was withdrawn (Loaeza 1984, 154–55). Nevertheless, the 1973 "Ley General de Población" (General Law on Population; Gobierno Mexicano 1974) promoted "responsible paternity," a formula that had first appeared in the 1968 encyclical *Humanae Vitae,* and, more importantly, the cooperative attitude the church showed toward the government's family planning policies prevented the legalization of abortion, which had been advanced by several members of the PRI, at the time the hegemonic party.

In the following three decades political reforms and noticeable transformations in attitudes regarding political participation gradually weakened emblematic authoritarian institutions, such as the PRI. In this context the Catholic Church maintained harmonious relations with the state while at the same time working more consistently toward the modification of anticlerical legislation. It is worth noting that during the protracted process of democratization that led to the establishment of a multiparty system (1979–2000), the Catholic Church added its demands to those of opposition parties and organized minorities clamoring to open up the political system to represent a diverse society. That is, it abandoned the strategy that it had followed in the past of defending its particular cause in the name of its particular rights.

In contrast with past experiences, there was no lay mobilization to support the Catholic Church's specific demands related to its status, rights, and privileges. The constitutional reform of 1991 that replaced legislation from the time of the revolution and gave juridical status to all churches in Mexico was negotiated by President Carlos Salinas (1988–1994) with ecclesiastical authorities within the framework of the government's modernization program; it did not result from popular demand.

Whatever political influence the Catholic Church may have had in the past, it has been eroded by the continuing pace of secularization. Surveys measuring attitudes toward the church show that generally Mexicans believe that the church should concentrate on helping the poor, promoting the defense of human rights, and providing moral guidance to Catholics. A majority of Mexicans believe that the church provides adequate answers to people's spiritual needs (80 percent) and that it should speak out on racial discrimination (76 percent), abortion (73 percent), the Third World (66 percent), disarmament (65 percent), and environmental issues (69 percent). But these high percentages tend to diminish when respondents are asked about the church speaking out on social problems (47 percent), and the percentage falls sharply when the question is "Do you think it proper for churches to speak out on government policy?" (34 percent) (Inglehart, Basáñez, and Moreno 1998, Tables V156, V158, V161, V165, V154, V155, V157). In all these responses there is a clear gender differentiation: women show a better disposition toward and more confidence in church guidance and intervention than men. Nonetheless, the gender difference is very narrow concerning the intervention of the church in government policy: 36 percent of women and 32 percent of men agreed with church intervention. These responses are consistent with the results of other surveys that indicate that Catholics in Mexico, as in other Latin American countries, do not believe that the church should play a political role or that they need its political advice: "they do not approve of their using the pulpit to promote or oppose political candidates. Mexicans are the most emphatically opposed to clerical involvement in the political sphere" (Belden Russonello and Stewart Research 2003, 20).

The results of the 1979 federal elections, organized in the framework set out in the political reform law of 1977 known as LOPPE (Ley de Organizaciones Politicas y Procesos Electorales, or Law of Political Organizations and Electoral Processes), showed that the Mexican electorate was diverse and did not follow the political advice of bishops who had spoken against the candidates of the Mexican Communist Party (Partido Comunista Mexicano, or PCM). PAN won more seats than the left; nevertheless, the party could hardly boast of representing the Mexican Catholic majority, and the PCM won enough votes to be represented in Congress. The electoral diversity and relative indifference of a great part of the electorate to the political guidelines of the church that emerged in the 1979 elections set a long-term pattern in the behavior of Mexican voters. Some studies show that women tend to support PAN more than other parties. However, the difference between female PAN voters and female PRI voters is not significant, while it tends to be greater when PAN voters are compared to the Partido de la Revolución Democrática (Party of the Democratic Revolution, or PRD). In the 2006 presidential elections exit polls indicated that women voted less than men (44 percent vs. 56 percent) and had a small preference for the PAN candidate, Felipe Calderón (32 percent); 29 percent voted for the PRD candidate, Andrés Manuel López Obrador; and 3.4 percent voted for Patricia Mercado, the only woman who ran for the presidency, supported by the Partido Alternativa Socialdemócrata y Campesina (Social-Democratic and Peasant Alternative Party, or PASC) (Consulta Mitofsky 2006).

The relative appeal of PAN to women is to some extent consistent with the responses cited above regarding women's positive attitudes toward the church's political advice, given the identification of this party with Catholic values and the close association between PAN and lay organizations such as the Asociación Nacional Cívica Femenina (National Women's Civic Association, or ANCIFEM) or the Unión Nacional de Padres de Familia (National Parents' Union, or UNPF). However, the political preferences and attitudes of Mexican women tend to be a reflection of the country's political diversity as is suggested by the ties between many women's and feminist organizations and the PRD or the PRI. This pluralism is in itself an expression of the emergence of women as individuals.

Conclusion

At the beginning of the twenty-first century Mexican society showed numerous signs of an emerging postmodern culture conducive to a change in a number of traditional values and attitudes that for centuries were identified as distinctively Mexican. Most of these derived from the

Catholic Church's hegemony in the definition of social norms and ideal models. Women's rights, gender differentiation, and the normative images of femininity provide a powerful example of value transformation and of the corresponding erosion of Catholic authority over women's behavior and attitudes, as shown by their reproductive and sexual behavior and by changes in their position within the family. The emergence of women as individuals independent of the family unit is a facet of a more general process of secularization that has engulfed Mexican society as a whole.

The transformation of women's position in society and of the notions of femininity brought about significant discontinuities with notions and norms that for centuries had been upheld by the Catholic Church with the support of the state. The origins of these changes can be traced to public policies that were designed to meet the needs of Mexican society in the 1970s, namely, the improvement of women's education and family planning. These policies were not seeking to undercut church authority; nevertheless, that was their inevitable side effect. Thus, the Mexican experience shows that secularization is a spontaneous process resulting from broad social change. The church has tried to respond to this challenge and to many of the issues raised in this chapter, for instance, in general terms by incorporating itself and participating—even if hesitantly—in the anti-authoritarian mobilizations of the 1980s; however, in the deeply partisan context of Mexico today, this involvement has led to an inevitable politicization of the church that has further weakened its authority. Moreover, the church does not have the material resources to oppose general trends toward social change (Loaeza 1996).

Empirical evidence shows that cultural transformation in Mexico was propelled by public policies that were sustained in times of economic expansion (such as the 1970s) and in times of economic crisis and poor economic performance. However, these policies only supplemented women's and families' responses to adverse economic conditions. From this perspective the Mexican democratization process that led to party pluralism and the demise of the PRI was only one aspect of the broad cultural change that took place in the last quarter of the twentieth century. It was a necessary adjustment of political institutions to a society more urbanized and more educated, with greater economic complexity and openness to globalization. In a democratic political context the trends toward cultural change are strengthened and in some cases accelerated. Liberal political institutions foster the development of a liberal society. The Mexican experience also shows that such an environment does not destroy women's identity. Contrary to traditional belief, it provides instead a strong framework for the protection of women's autonomy and rights.

Notes

1. This analysis has been based on empirical evidence from Inglehart, Basáñez, and Moreno (1998); Mexico's National Census of 2000 (INEGI 2000); Belden Russonello and Stewart Research (2003); and CONAPO (2005) reports on women's work, health, and sexual and reproductive patterns. Surveys by Consulta Mitofsky (2004a, 2004b) on sexual behavior and attitudes toward the church have also been consulted to examine these changes.

2. For an analysis of the political implications of this bond in the cold war context, see Loaeza (2005).

3. A majority of Mexicans express this knowledge of the United States when they consider migration to that country as an option. See Basáñez (2006, 24).

4. See, for instance, Cerrutti and Zenteno (2000); Parker and Pederzini Villarreal (2000); Quilodrán (2001); and Solís, Gayet, and Juárez (2005).

5. At least three generations of Mexican women—and Latin American women—of the postwar period were educated by Spanish romantic novels exported by a publishing company called Bruguera or published by a women's magazine called *Vanidades;* they were first published in Cuba in 1951 and distributed throughout the entire Latin American market. In 1962 UNESCO declared Corín Tellado—who became the star of the romance novel in Spanish and who in the 1950s published a weekly novel—the most widely read Spanish author, after the Bible and Cervantes. Corín Tellado began her career as a novelist in 1945, at the age of eighteen. By 2005 she had published over 2,300 novels.

6. In 1910 there were 8,000 citizens per religious female in Mexico; by 1946 this ratio had decreased to 3,000, and by 1960 to 2,000. See Ramos, Alonso, and Garre (1963, 88).

References

Alba, Francisco. 1993. "Evolución de la población: realizaciones y retos." In José Woldenberg and José Joaquín Blanco, eds., *México a fines de siglo,* vol. 1: 130–51. Mexico City: Fondo de Cultura Económica/CONACULTA.

Arredondo, Inés. 1988. *Los Espejos*. México: Joaquín Mortiz.

Ávila Camacho, Manuel. 1942. "Exposición de Motivos." In *Ley Orgánica de Educación Pública, Secretaría de Educación Pública*. Mexico City: Ediciones de la SEP.

Basáñez, Miguel. 2006. "Ideologies and Values." In Laura Randall, ed., *Changing Structure of Mexico: Political, Social, and Economic Prospects*, 19–31. New York: M. E. Sharpe.

Belden Russonello and Stewart Research and Communications. 2003. *Attitudes of Catholics on Reproductive Rights, Church-State and Related Issues: Three National Surveys in Bolivia, Colombia and Mexico Conducted for Catholics for Free Choice and Católicas por el Derecho a Decidir en Bolivia, Colombia and México*. Accessed April 15, 2007, from http://www.catholicsforchoice.org/topics/abortion/documents/2004latinamericapoll_000.pdf.

Blancarte, Roberto. 2006. "Religion, Church, and the State in Contemporary Mexico." In Laura Randall, ed., *Changing Structure of Mexico: Political, Social, and Economic Prospects*, 424–34. New York: M. E. Sharpe.

Camp, Roderic Ai. 1998. "Women and Men, Men and Women: Gender Patterns in Mexican Politics." In Victoria Rodríguez, ed., *Women's Participation in Mexican Political Life*, 167–78. Boulder, CO: Westview Press.

Carner, Francoise. 1987. "Estereotipos del siglo XIX." In Carmen Ramos Escandón, ed., *Presencia y Transparencia: Mujer en la Historia de México*, 95–110. Mexico City: El Colegio de México.

Castellanos, Rosario. 1973. *Mujer que sabe latín . . .* Mexico City: SepSetentas.

———. 1979. *Oficio de Tinieblas*. Mexico City: Promexa.

Cerrutti, Marcela, and René Zenteno. 2000. "Cambios en el papel económico de las mujeres entre las parejas mexicanas." *Estudios Demográficos y Urbanos* 15, no. 1: 65–96.

Conferencia del Episcopado Mexicano. 1968. *Carta Pastoral sobre el desarrollo e integración de la patria*. México.

———. 1973. *Mensaje del Episcopado al pueblo de México sobre paternidad responsable*. Cuernavaca: Centro Intercultural de Documentación.

Consejo Nacional de Población (CONAPO). 2002. *Las madres en México. Información con Motivo del Día de las Madres*. Accessed March 29, 2005, from http://www.conapo.gob.mx/prensa/2002/2002may02.htm.

———. 2005. *Situación Actual de la Mujer en México. Diagnóstico Sociodemográfico*. Accessed March 29, 2005, from http://www.conapo.gob.mx/publicaciones/cuaderno3.htm.

Consulta Mitofsky. 2004a. *Primera Encuesta Nacional Sobre Sexo. Primera Entrega año 2004*. Accessed March 29, 2005, from http://www.consulta.com.mx/interiores/99_pdfs/12_mexicanos_pdf/mxc_NA20040808_FDS_1era.pdf.

———. 2004b. *Quienes asisten a misa?* Accessed March 29, 2005, from http://www.consulta.com.mx/interiores/12_mex_por_consulta/mxc_misa0804.html.

———. 2006. *2 de julio 2006. Análisis de la Elección. Encuesta de Salida.* Accessed April 15, 2007, from http://www.consulta.com.mx/interiores/99_pdfs/11_elecciones_pdf/20060702_ExitPoll_PerFilVotante.pdf.

Dirección General de Estadística. 1970. *IX (noveno) Censo General de Población, 1970.* México.

Flora, Cornelia Butler. 1973. "The Passive Female and Social Change: A Cross-Cultural Comparison of Women's Magazine Fiction." In Ann Pescatello, ed., *Female and Male in Latin America: Essays,* 59–85. Pittsburgh, PA: University of Pittsburgh Press.

Fowler-Salamini, Heather, and Mary Kay Vaughan, eds. 1994. *Women of the Mexican Countryside, 1850–1990.* Tucson: University of Arizona Press.

Giraud, Francois. 1987. "Mujeres y familia en Nueva España." In Carmen Ramos Escandón, ed., *Presencia y Transparencia: Mujer en la Historia de México,* 61–78. Mexico City: El Colegio de México.

Gobierno Mexicano. 1974. "Ley General de Población (1973)." *Demografía y Economia* 8, no. 1: 93–109.

Gómez Morín, Manuel. 1950. "Informe a la V Convención Nacional de Acción Nacional, rendido el 5 de febrero de 1947." In Manuel Gómez Morín, ed., *Diez Años de México,* 199–222. Mexico City: Editorial Jus.

Gonzalbo, Pilar. 1987. "Tradición y ruptura en la educación femenina del Siglo XVI." In Carmen Ramos Escandón, ed., *Presencia y Transparencia: Mujer en la Historia de México,* 33–60. Mexico City: El Colegio de México.

Grupo Interdisciplinario de Mujer, Trabajo y Pobreza (Fundación McArthur-Comisión Nacional de la Mujer). 1999. *Observatorio sobre la Condición de la Mujer en México.* Accessed March 29, 2005, from http://dgcnesyp.inegi.gob.mx/sisesim/bibliografia/BHogFamViv.html.

Guillaume, Agnes, Susana Lerner, and Guadalupe Salas. 2005. *El Aborto en América Latina y el Caribe.* CD-ROM. Paris: Les Numériques du CEPED.

Inglehart, Ronald. 1997. *Modernization and Post Modernization: Cultural, Economic and Political Change in 43 Societies.* Princeton, NJ: Princeton University Press.

Inglehart, Ronald, Miguel Basáñez, and Alejandro Moreno. 1998. *Human Beliefs and Values: A Cross-Cultural Sourcebook.* Ann Arbor: University of Michigan Press.

Instituto Nacional de Estadística, Geografía e Informática (INEGI). 1995. *Censo General de Población y Vivienda, 1990.* Aguascalientes, Mexico.

———. 1999. *Encuesta Nacional de la Dinámica Demográfica, 1997.* Aguascalientes, Mexico.

————. 2000. *Censo general de población y vivienda 2000.* Accessed March 29, 2005, from http://www.inegi.gob.mx/est/librerias/tabulados.asp?tabulado= tab_ed02b&s=est&c=11466.

Loaeza, Soledad. 1984. "La Iglesia católica Mexicana y el reformismo autoritario." *Foro Internacional* 25, no. 2: 138–65.

————. 1988. *Clases Medias y Política en México. La Querella Escolar, 1959–1963.* Mexico City: El Colegio de México.

————. 1994. "The Changing Face of Mexican Nationalism." In Delal Baer and Sidney J. Weintraub, eds., *The NAFTA Debate: Grappling with Unconventional Trade Issues,* 145–47. Boulder, CO: Lynne Rienner.

————. 1996. "Las relaciones Estado-Iglesia católica en México, 1988–1994. Los costos de la institucionalización." *Foro Internacional* 36, nos. 1–2: 107–32.

————. 2005. "Mexico in the Fifties: Women and Church in Holy Alliance." *Women's Studies Quarterly* 33, nos. 3–4 (Winter): 138–60.

Massolo, Alejandra. 1998. "Women in the Local Arena and Municipal Power." In Victoria Rodríguez, ed., *Women's Participation in Mexican Political Life,* 193–203. Boulder, CO: Westview Press.

Meyer, Jean. 1971. *La Cristiana.* 3 vols. Mexico City: Siglo XXI Editores.

Parker, Susan W., and Carla Pederzini Villarreal. 2000. "Género y educación en México." *Estudios Demográficos y Urbanos* 15, no. 1: 97–122.

Pescatello, Ann, ed. 1973. *Female and Male in Latin America: Essays.* Pittsburgh, PA: University of Pittsburgh Press.

Quilodrán, Julieta. 2001. *Cien Años de Matrimonio en México.* Mexico City: El Colegio de México.

Ramos, Rutilio, Isidoro Alonso, and Domingo Garre. 1963. *La Iglesia en México: Estructuras Eclesiásticas.* Bogotá: Febres.

Ramos Escandón, Carmen. 1987. "Señoritas porfirianas: Mujer e ideología en el México progresista, 1880–1910." In Carmen Ramos Escandón, ed., *Presencia y Transparencia: Mujer en la Historia de México,* 143–62. Mexico City: El Colegio de México.

————. 1998. "Women and Power in Mexico: The Forgotten Heritage, 1880–1954." In Victoria Rodríguez, ed., *Women's Participation in Mexican Political Life,* 87–102. Boulder, CO: Westview Press.

Rendón Gan, Teresa. 2004. "Doble jornada femenina y bajos salarios." *Demos. Carta Demográfica sobre México* (Instituto de Investigaciones Sociales, Universidad Nacional Autónoma de México) 16 (2003–04): 16.

Santibañez Rosellón, Jorge. 2004. "De no tener política a aceptar su importancia." *Demos. Carta Demográfica sobre México* (Instituto de Investigaciones Sociales, Universidad Nacional Autónoma de México) 16 (2003–04): 9.

Solís, Patricio, Cecilia Gayet, and Fátima Juárez. 2005. "Las transiciones a la vida sexual, a la unión y a la maternidad." Unpublished paper, El Colegio de México.

Stevens, Evelyn P. 1973. "Marianismo: The Other Face of Machismo in Latin America." In Ann Pescatello, ed., *Female and Male in Latin America: Essays,* 89–102. Pittsburgh, PA: University of Pittsburgh Press.

Tarrés, María Luisa. 1998. "De la identidad al espacio público: las organizaciones no gubernamentales de mujeres en México." In José Luis Méndez, ed., *Organizaciones Civiles y Políticas Públicas en México y Centroamérica,* 101–36. Mexico City: Editorial Porrúa.

Tuñon Pablos, Julia. 1999. *Women in Mexico: A Past Unveiled.* Austin: University of Texas Press.

U.S. Census Bureau. 2006. *American Community Survey 2005.* Accessed August 17, 2006, from http://www.census.gov/acs/www/Products/users_guide/2005/index.htm.

Werner, Alejandro M., Rodrigo Barros, and José F. Ursúa. 2006. "The Mexican Economy: Transformation and Challenges." In Laura Randall, ed., *Changing Structure of Mexico: Political, Social, and Economic Prospects,* 67–90. New York: M. E. Sharpe.

World Bank. 2006. *Key Development Data and Statistics.* Accessed August 17, 2006, from http://web.worldbank.org/WBSITE/EXTERNAL/DATASTATIS TICS/0,,menuPK:232599~pagePK:64133170~piPK:64133498~theSiteP K:239419,00.html.

Yáñez, Agustín. 1993. *Al Filo del Agua.* Mexico City: Consejo Nacional para la Cultura y las Artes.

4 | # Education and Increasing Religious Pluralism in Latin America

The Case of Chile

CRISTIÁN PARKER GUMUCIO

At the end of the 1980s, according to some scholars, Latin America was becoming Protestant (Martin 1990; Stoll 1990). However, in the first decade of the twenty-first century the growth of evangelical churches has stopped, or at least their rate of growth has slowed. At the same time, it is evident that in the last century the rate of growth of Catholics has systematically declined. The Latin American context has changed: it has passed from being a "Catholic continent" to being an increasingly religiously pluralist region.

Indeed, Latin America has ceased to be "Catholic" in the traditional sense of the term. The decline of Catholics has been paralleled by the increase in other religious expressions. Latin American countries vary considerably in their history and in the social and political weight of the institutional Roman Catholic Church and of Christian traditions in the collective mentality and civil society. Nevertheless, some general and common dynamics must be examined. With the exception of Cuba and Uruguay, in the last three or four decades the alternatives to Catholicism have come not mainly from the growth of nonbelievers and atheists but from the expansion of evangelicals, in particular, Pentecostals. Nevertheless, Latin America is more "evangelical" only in relative and partial terms. The continent still remains a privileged space within world Catholicism: in 2004 the Catholic population of nineteen Latin American countries was approximately 447 million, or 48 percent of the nearly 932 million Catholics in the world. Yet, if Latin America has not become "Protestant," neither does it continue to be "Catholic" in the same sense that it was at the beginning of the twentieth century.[1]

These data suggest that the continent is *becoming increasingly religiously plural*. In other words, Latin America is still a majority-Catholic region—its religious and cultural mainstream is neither Protestant nor secular—but it is becoming more religiously diverse. The Catholic Church has recognized the challenges it faces. Using new methods, it has renewed its classical skirmish against secularism ("evangelization of culture"), and, beginning with the Medellín bishops' conference (1968) and continuing with the Puebla (1979), Santo Domingo (1992), and Aparecida (2007) conferences, the church has acknowledged the threat of competition and religious pluralism (for example, the challenges of sects, new religious movements, and Pentecostals). But beneath the surface and less widely recognized in the media and in academic and public debate is the rise of such nonorthodox religious expressions as "diffuse religiosity," "popular religiosity," and other hermetic and New Age expressions. These have developed not as independent institutions, churches, or cults but often as syncretic mixtures in the minds of the faithful, who identify themselves as nominally "Catholic" and even "Protestant."

Throughout Latin American history popular Catholicism has coexisted with various forms of syncretisms.[2] This is in fact one of the distinguishing features of Latin America's history and sociology. In another work (Parker 1996b) I analyzed the emergence of new syncretisms, which aggregate traditional and historical forms. These new syncretic forms are, of course, much more tied to the process of modernization and educational reform than traditional and popular syncretisms whose origins lay in a distinct sociohistorical dynamic.

How do we explain these changes? What are the main social and cultural factors that are influencing these new tendencies toward religious pluralism among Latin Americans? Among the cultural factors that influence religious change are the consumer culture promoted by the market and the new economy; the mass media and the revolution in communications and electronics; rapid changes in education; and the renewal of social and ethnic movements that affect the religious field (see Parker 2005). All these social and cultural factors are affecting the way the people represent themselves in their religious beliefs and practices—the social construction of their symbolic reality (see Berger and Luckmann, 1966)—with the consequence that many of the Catholic faithful no longer reproduce conventional forms of religious affiliation or adhere to the faith received from their parents.

As we shall see, there has been a boom in new "underground currents" of "superstitions" or "neopagan" contemporary religious tendencies.[3] Nearly a third of Catholics, and even those who practice regularly, now adhere to these tendencies (see Parker 1999). There is not merely growing pluralism within institutional Catholicism and an increase of new religious movements or cults; in addition, ways of believing that are far removed from the institutional churches have emerged: for example, self-professed "Catholics in my own way," or "believers without belonging" (to a church), as they are also termed (see Davie 2004).

The current decline of Catholicism can be traced in part to the church's trajectory of the past four decades. But our hypothesis is that its decline did not originate in politics, historical processes, or conjectural crises—as happened in the 1960s when national churches were confronted with political change and revolutionary movements, and in the 1970s and mid-1980s when they confronted authoritarian governments over human rights abuses.[4] There have been many factors that have contributed to contemporary Latin American religious change—to opening up new ways of thinking and feeling about and acting on one's relationship with the supernatural. Beyond the aforementioned changes in the culture of the market, the media, and the new technologies of communication and information—as well as ethnic issues and new social and ecological problems—the role of education, and the mental change it introduces, stands out as critical in enhancing religious pluralism.

In this chapter I contend that cultural factors involved in educational change set in motion a complex process in and through which religious expressions in the "religious field"[5] have become more diverse. Cultural factors also explain the related and simultaneous tendency toward rationalization (the appearance of nonbelievers and atheists) and spiritual revivals (of old currents such as popular mysticism and shamanism and popular new ones such as syncretism and New Age practices) that tend to delegitimate the central place official churches historically occupied in the religious socialization process. More specifically, modern education permits the individual to explore a wider cultural horizon with diverse lifestyles and opens him or her to a critical appraisal of things that tend to annihilate traditional morals, norms, and dogmas. Moreover, higher levels of schooling and the diversification of educational alternatives help to redefine cultural patterns and give rise to pluricultural societies.

Indeed, modern educational reforms that have been implemented in recent decades throughout Latin America under the auspices of the World Bank have introduced a different rationalization of schools and educational management and have diversified the educational supply. They have also introduced a more liberal culture that, in turn, has facilitated a greater acceptance of messages, beliefs, and heterodox rituals and a certain distrust of ecclesiastical institutions. These cultural changes have precipitated an increase in those who believe in religion "in my own way." Additionally, educational reforms, especially the pluralization and privatization of schools and universities, have facilitated the penetration of diverse religious confessions, congregations, and lay alternatives in the field of education. Structural changes such as the rise in enrollments at different educational levels and educational reforms may prove to decisively affect culture. Specifically, they might modify the mentality of young people and make them more open to change and diversity. This openness, in turn, legitimates different options in the spiritual and religious field.

This chapter proceeds as follows. In the first part I review how classic social theory looks at modernization and religious belief. Next, drawing on original survey data, I highlight the growing tendency of well-educated Chilean youth to identify themselves with self-styled religious beliefs. The third part examines in greater detail the role of education in framing religious options. The fourth part extends the analysis to consider other cases and speculates about the future of religious belief in Latin America given the increase in educational enrollments and the growing diversity of higher education.

Religion and the Rationalization of Social Life

Contrary to the classical secularization thesis (Martin 1978), Latin America has undergone several processes of modernization and rationalization in the last two decades that have not diminished the presence of religion in private and public life (Parker 1996b). What has changed, however, is the composition of the Latin American religious field itself (Parker 1998) and the significance of different institutional or noninstitutional religious orientations. The Latin American cases do not show the simple persistence of traditions that we find in diverse sociocultural contexts where traditional values have persisted alongside modernization and cultural changes (Inglehart and Baker 2000). What we are observing are specific religious changes.

The continuing importance of religion in the context of the different processes of modernization that are presently underway in Latin America, and the diversification of religious expressions, are not exclusively due to new evangelical preachers and the growing influence of Pentecostals.[6] Other deep cultural factors are involved that are influencing the new, pluralistic religious panorama. In addition to the remaining importance of the churches—that is, the "official" religions—we must consider the increasing revitalization of numerous mass phenomena: namely, traditional popular religions or new syncretic forms associated with new religious movements or spiritual tendencies such as New Age or contemporary esotericism (Guerreiro 2003; Trombetta 2003; Carozzi 1999, 2000; Tavares Gomes 2000; Frigerio 1999; Van Hove 1999).

In this chapter I argue that these expressions are manifestations of the cultural changes that are being experienced by the younger generation in societies in which the religious field has historically been dominated by Catholicism, as was true in Chile and many other Hispanic countries. Indeed, young people are not immune from the complex influences of globalization (Pace 1997; Castells 1999), which, paradoxically, simultaneously facilitates the introduction of more pragmatic and secularized rationalities, on the one hand, and new spiritual currents and the revival of diverse faith expressions, on the other. Indeed, one of the principal debates concerning the relationship between religion and modernity is centered precisely on the problem of the "rationality" of religion and its relationship with the rationalization of social life derived from modernization.

When discussing the relationship between religion and politics and religion and fanaticism, conservatives have attributed the source of many conflicts to a kind of irrational hatred (what Nietzsche would have called "resentment") that is directed toward Western secularism, material wealth, and technology. The irrationality of this attitude is said to come from the rejection of the rationalization of social life, which, as we know, was studied by Weber (1958, 1963). Rationalization, a tendency based on the efficient calculation of means and the willingness to substitute alternative ends as equally valuable pursuits, manifests itself most saliently in capitalist economic activity and the global marketplace. As Pecora put it, "We then have a whole structure of explanation that juxtaposes anachronistic allegiance to what Weber called the *Wertrationalität* (or value-oriented rationality) of religious absolutes with the *Zweckrationalität* (or purposive rationality) of modern, capitalist, instrumental reason" (2003, 2).

According to Weber, the rationalization of social life in Western historical, capitalist contexts will bring about the *disenchantment of the world*. Asceticism—carried out of monastic cells into everyday life—began to dominate the "worldly morality" of the modern economic order. But as the modern economic order was bound to the technical and economic conditions of machine production, and determined the lives of individuals in ways that were broader than those aspects of one's life directly influenced by the economic market, the spirit of religious asceticism became progressively divorced from any economic motivations. Thus, religious asceticism lost its symbolic power to legitimize the economic spirit. Capitalism, which rests on mechanical foundations, emerged victorious, and the capitalist mode of production did not need religious legitimation of any sort. Material goods gained an increasing and ultimately an inexorable power over the lives of humans in a way without precedent in human history. For Weber, the mechanical foundations of industrial capitalism had its own forms of legitimation:

> The rosy blush of its laughing heir, the Enlightenment, seems also to be irretrievably fading, and the idea of duty in one's calling prowls about in our lives like the ghost of dead religious beliefs. Where the fulfill-

ment of the calling cannot directly be related to the highest spiritual and cultural values, or when, on the other hand, it need not be felt simply as economic compulsion, the individual generally abandons the attempt to justify it at all. (Weber 1958, 182)

If this was true of the modern capitalist societies that Weber studied, what then would we expect to happen in a developing society undergoing a rapid process of modernization *and* globalization?

Increasing Religious Alternatives among Chilean Youth

Contrary to Weberian secularization theory, in a country such as Chile, which is representative of the way in which the developing countries of Latin America are becoming integrated into global markets, cultural change takes forms that illustrate different trends. Among Chilean youth we find that the purposive rationality of market-oriented culture and its logic of competition is growing as a source of meaning for social action. And yet, in their religious orientations, Chilean youth neither reject value-oriented rationality nor do they fall into an irrational fanaticism. Rather, the more formally educated manifest an increased rationalization and a general tendency to open the scope of religious alternatives to include new types of diffused and syncretic religious expressions that have components of New Age beliefs and rituals and to reject beliefs related to institutionalized religions (that is, the churches).

The growing pluralization of religious alternatives among youth is confirmed by the Chilean National Censuses of 1992 and 2002 (INE 2003). Table 4.1 contrasts both age poles (the younger and the older generations) according to religious affiliation. In both 1992 and 2002 the highest proportion of evangelicals was found in the 15–29 age stratum. But the most salient tendency is the rapid increase among the "indifferent" (also termed "non-religionists"), "atheists," and those claiming affiliation to "other religions." The proportion of Catholics fell in this decade (Lehmann 2001, 2002; Parker 1996a) from 74 to 66 percent in the younger age cohort (those from 15 to 29 years old), a rate that contrasts sharply with that of the older generation (among whom it dropped only from 81 to 77 percent). Among

Table 4.1. Religious Affiliation by Age in Chile, 1992–2002
(in percent)

	1992		2002	
	15–29	*60+*	*15–29*	*60+*
Catholic	74.1	80.8	66.2	76.9
Evangelical	14.1	12.1	15.4	13.7
Non-Religionist/ Atheist	7.4	3.3	11.1	4.5
Other Religion	4.5	3.7	7.3	4.9

Source: Chilean National Census 1992, 2002 (INE 2003).

the younger generation the proportion of Catholics is decreasing more rapidly than evangelicals are growing. The alternative religions are rising slightly, and the number identifying as "indifferent" and "atheists" is growing steadily.

At first glance the data seem to suggest that the classic secularization thesis may have some merit after all. But this is not the case. In both 1992 and 2002 the census did not offer an alternative for people that, on the one hand, did not want to be identified with a church but, on the other, did not want to be considered antireligious. The only option on the census questionnaire for these people was "indifferent or atheist." Data from other surveys, as we will see, suggest that the so-called non-religious or indifferent should be distinguished from antireligious atheists. Qualitative data has shown that most of the self-declared "indifferent" are indeed believers categorized as "without religion." This means that they believe in God and in the majority of the basic Christian beliefs (having been born and socialized in a Christian culture), and they may even have a "spirituality of their own"; yet, at the same time, they distance themselves from churches and church doctrines, ethics, and clergy, which they consider to be alienating, repressive, or anachronistic. By contrast, atheists are a very small percentage of younger people. The general tendency of secularization to produce cultural change, which in the 1960s and 1970s predicted a large percentage of atheist and antireligious affiliations in surveys and polls (see B. Smith 1982), has not been borne out.

Today, as many studies have suggested, the participation of youth in a variety of different religious expressions is very important. The Chilean National Youth Survey of 2000 (INJUV 2001) (N = 3,701) reveals that the majority of young people aged 15 to 30 identify themselves with some religion: Catholics account for 53 percent and a majority among women (58 percent) and the middle socioeconomic strata (56 percent) (Table 4.2). Evangelicals account for 11.7 percent, with the percentages even higher among women (13 percent) and the lower socioeconomic stratum (17 percent). The other religious groupings include the Mormons, Jehovah's Witnesses, and other types of religious affiliation ("Believes in God and has another religion"). Nonbelievers constitute just fewer than 5 percent.

These data show the importance of the category of people who are believers but do not identify with any church. To underscore this point, the

Table 4.2. Belief in God and Religious Affiliation in Chile, 2000 (in percent)

| Type of Believer | Total | Sex | | Socioeconomic Level | | |
		Men	Women	High	Middle	Low
Catholic	53.0	48.6	57.5	54.3	55.5	46.8
Believes in God, without church	26.3	29.4	23.2	33.7	25.5	27.4
Evangelical	11.7	10.5	12.9	3.6	9.8	17.1
Doesn't believe in God	4.8	6.7	2.8	6.8	4.7	4.7
Believes in God, other denomination	1.6	2.3	0.9	0.1	1.5	2.1
Jehovah's Witness	1.3	1.3	1.4	0.0	1.5	1.2
Mormon	1.2	1.3	1.0	1.5	1.5	0.7
No Response	0.1	0.0	0.1	0.0	0.1	0.0

Source: Third National Youth Survey, 2000 (INJUV 2001).

2000 survey included a new category, "Believes in God, without church." Remarkably, more than a quarter of young respondents (those between 15 and 30 years old) chose this alternative. Men from the higher socioeconomic stratum predominate in this category. Generally speaking, these individuals have had more formal education and enjoy a higher standard of living—in other words, these are the individuals who are the most integrated into the modernization process.

In the past eight years I have conducted five surveys about religious affiliation (Table 4.3 reports results from the most recent four) in which I have introduced new measurements that reveal a great deal about the nature of religious change—in particular, that youth still believe but distance themselves from and distrust religious authorities.[7] The data from the National Youth Survey utilizes the modified measures we first used in our Popular Religion Survey in 1997–1998 in a municipality of Santiago, Chile (Parker 1999) and in 1998–1999 for our Secondary Students Survey, a study requested by the National Planning Ministry and that focused on new cultural traits of students in Chile (Parker 2000). The "believer without religion" category borrowed from previous qualitative research as a form of self-identification for people who did not want to be identified as affiliated with a church but also did not consider themselves to be antireligious, and the "Catholic in my own way" category was used to capture the views of Catholics who wish to stress their autonomy from the official positions of their church. These categories offer an innovative methodology for measuring religious affiliation that contrasts with the classical form of religious affiliation measurement that asks only about affiliation with established churches. The introduction of this new measure for the survey responses also introduces a new sociological perspective on the complexity of religious identity and the limits of the role that institutional churches play in the social construction of religious meaning by ordinary people.

The Secondary Students Survey (Parker 2000) conducted in 1998–1999 was administered to 643 secondary school students from different socioeconomic backgrounds and two different parts of the country: the Metropolitan Region (Santiago) and the VIII Region (Concepción Province). The University Sample Survey, conducted in 2001, consisted of a sample of 515 university students from the Universidad de Santiago de Chile, one of the main public universities in the country (Parker, Peña, and Barría 2002).

The Metropolitan Region Survey, from which we draw our religious data, was a study of public opinion about the penal system conducted for the Department of Justice in October 2004 (Parker and Peña 2005; religious data available from author). It was based on a general representative sample (N =1,202) of the entire population of the metropolitan region (the greater Santiago area of six million people and its surroundings). Finally, the National University Student Survey (Parker 2007) was conducted in 2005 using a representative sample of university students from the twenty-five main universities in Chile.

In these studies we asked secondary and university students, as well as the general population, about their religious self-identification. Unsurprisingly in a Latino and mestizo culture, we found that religious affiliation continues to be a characteristic trait of the cultural identity of the majority of the younger generation. We were able to distinguish between believers (mainly among Catholics) and those who are not affiliated with any ecclesiastic institution by establishing the categories "Catholic in my own way" and "believer without religion," options that come from the common-sense language analyzed in previous qualitative research. These alternative religious options—present in everyday discourse—augment the traditional categories of "Catholic," "evangelical," "nonbeliever," "atheist," and so forth. By opening the umbrella of religious options, we can explore the diverse religious identifications and meanings of today's young people.

Between 25 and 30 percent of the student sample from the secondary schools and universities declare themselves to be simply "Catholic" (Table 4.3). Between 26 and 31 percent of the secondary and university students identify themselves as "Catholics in my own way," suggesting that they distance themselves from official and ecclesiastical Catholicism. Between 15 and 25 percent of the students identify themselves as "believers without religion," while only 5 percent of secondary students and 11 to 17 percent of university students identify themselves as either "nonbelievers" or "atheists."[8]

Although our secondary (1999) and university student (2002) samples are not representative of the entire country, our 2004 survey of the metropolitan region is, which enables us to draw some conclusions with confidence. In our comparison of the national university sample of 2005 with the 2004 survey, we were able to identify some general tendencies. First,

Table 4.3. Religious Self-Identification in Chile, 1999–2005
(in percent)

Type of Believer	Age Group	Secondary Students[a] Sample (Two Regions) (1999) 16–20	University Students[b] (One University) (2002) 17–29	Metropolitan Region[c] (Total Population) (2004) 18–29[e]	(2004) 18–99	University Students[d] (National) (2005) 17–29
Catholic		29.1	25.8	26.7	37.4	30.1
Catholic "in my own way"		31.0	31.5	29.9	29.0	25.8
Believer "without religion"		15.1	24.5	21.6	13.9	17.1
Evangelical		14.6	4.4	5.5	8.7	5.7
Protestant		2.3	0.8	0.6	0.5	1.0
Another Religion		2.1	1.9	3.2	2.6	2.4
Jewish		0.8	0.4	0.0	0.0	0.7
Atheist		2.1	5.7	8.0	4.3	6.4
Nonbeliever		3.1	5.0	4.6	3.7	10.8

[a]Sample of schools in Metropolitan Region and Concepción Province, from Secondary Students Survey, 1999 (Parker 2000).
[b]Representative sample of a main state university in Santiago, from University Sample Survey, 2002 (Parker, Peña, and Barría 2002).
[c]Representative sample of whole population in the region, from Metropolitan Region Survey, 2004 (Parker and Peña 2005; religious data available from author).
[d]Representative sample of all students attending the twenty-five main universities in Chile, from National University Student Survey, 2005 (Parker 2007).
[e]This group is a subsample of the general sample.

there are significant differences between secondary and university students, the most substantial being in the categories "atheist" and "nonbeliever," which are both higher for university students. The sum of these two categories is also greater than the sum of the values for the sample of the population of the metropolitan region as a whole.

In the Fourth National Youth Survey conducted by the government in 2003 (INJUV 2004) ($N = 7,189$), which had another classification for religious affiliation, 23 percent of respondents affirmed that "I do not feel close to any religion," but only 4.5 percent declared themselves to be a "non-believer in God or any type of divinity." In our 2005 National University Student Survey (Parker 2007), of the 17.2 percent of "nonbelievers" and "atheists," at least 28 percent (4.8 percent of the total) acknowledged believing in God; the proportion of genuine nonbelievers represented only 12.2 percent of the entire sample. The "Catholic" category is higher (37 percent) for the total sample of the metropolitan population than any value in the other sample of youth or student groups. "Believers without religious affiliation" (which is 14 percent for the entire metropolitan population) tends to be higher in the different youth samples: 15 percent for secondary students, and 17 percent for the sample of national university students.

Evidence from the metropolitan region sample (see Table 4.4) suggests that while the "believers without religion" are found mostly among young people, self-identified Catholics are found mostly among their elders. Self-declared "Catholics in my own way" are slightly more prevalent among

Table 4.4. Religious Affiliation by Age in the Santiago Metropolitan Region, 2004

Type of Believer	Age									
	18–29		30–49		50–59		60+		Total	
	#	%	#	%	#	%	#	%	#	%
Agnostic, Atheist	44	12.7	16	6.5	17	6.0	16	5.6	93	8.0
Believer "without religion"	75	21.7	36	14.7	29	10.3	21	7.4	161	13.9
Catholic	93	26.9	74	30.2	117	41.6	148	52.1	432	37.4
Catholic "in my own way"	104	30.1	88	35.9	78	27.8	67	23.6	337	29.2
Evangelical	21	6.1	29	11.8	33	11.7	25	8.8	108	9.3
Other Religion	9	2.6	2	0.8	7	2.5	7	2.5	25	2.2
Total	346		245		281		284		1,156	

Source: Metropolitan Region Survey, Santiago, Chile, 2004 (Parker and Peña 2005).

young and middle-aged adults in the 30- to 49-year-old range (36 percent) and in younger individuals (30 percent) rather than in the older age strata (24 percent). These data are statistically significant (Chi^2[10] = 97.63, p = 0.000).

The general tendency to widen the scope of religious options (and the decline in the number of Catholics) is greater among students and youth. With the exception of the 1999 Secondary Student Survey (due to the type of schools chosen for the sample) this trend cannot be attributed to a higher proportion of evangelicals but rather to the growing number of students with higher education who tend to identify themselves as "believers without a church" or simply as "nonbelievers." It seems that individuals with a higher level of formal education will tend to opt for more rationalized and noninstitutional forms of beliefs ("in my own way" or "without religion" believers) or for abandoning all references to religion in their life (agnosticism or atheism). The percentage of "believers without religion" should make us pause: if we observe religious affiliation from an institutional point of view according to the distance from the official religion—Catholicism is the predominant religion in Chile—we have a very high percentage of young people whose religious identification points toward an extra-institutional affiliation (or at least to one distant from the mainstream institutions).

In fact, the Metropolitan Region Survey (see Table 4.5) shows that declaring oneself to be "Catholic" means that an individual has a greater degree of confidence in the church and its religious hierarchy—that is, Catholic priests. Asked about their trust in priests, 46 percent of "Catholics" respond they have "much confidence," while only 26 percent of "Catholics in my own way" respond the same. The distrust is logically greater among agnostics and atheists (67 percent), but interestingly 53 percent of believers that declared themselves to be "without religion" distrust Catholic priests (all data are statistically significant: Chi^2(10) = 193.371, p = 0.000; Pears = 0.06697, p = 0.029; Spear = 0.0496, p = 0.030) (Parker and Peña 2005). Clearly, "without religion" must be interpreted as a position held by individuals who want to stress dissidence toward the official Catholic Church in a country where this church has a monopoly on the goods of salvation. Indeed, we have observed in other surveys that this type of believer generally acknowledges faith in a Christian God.

Responses from the 2005 National University Student Survey (Parker 2007) are consistent with these general trends (see Table 4.6). In the context of falling rates of trust in the church, 37 percent of "Catholics in my own way" express distrust in the church (versus only 19 percent of those who declared themselves simply "Catholics"). These rates were even higher than the distrust expressed by evangelicals (classic adversaries of Catholics in past decades).[9] As might be expected, agnostics and atheists exhibited the highest degree of distrust in the Catholic Church—69 and 77 percent, respectively. Consistent with the evidence from the 2005 survey, a high proportion of believers "without religion" (61 percent) exhibit a high level of distrust toward the church.

Returning to the data in Table 4.3, 46 percent of high school students and 43 to 56 percent of university students are either "Catholics in my own way" or "believers without religion." As we have mentioned, from the point of view of the sociological theory of the religious field (Bourdieu 1971), these data could be interpreted as forms of "religious dissidence" in a nation in which Catholicism is dominant in cultural terms. The data from the 2004 Metropolitan Region Survey move in the same direction: 51 percent of people between 18 and 29 years of age can be classified as "dissidents" from official Catholicism, as can 43 percent of the population as a whole above the age of 18 (Parker and Peña 2005).

Table 4.5. Confidence in Catholic Priests in the Santiago Metropolitan Region, 2004 (in percent)

Type of Believer	Distrust	Some Confidence	Much Confidence	N
Agnostic, Atheist	67.0	26.6	6.4	94
Believer "without religion"	52.8	29.2	18.0	161
Catholic	18.0	36.0	46.0	433
Catholic "in my own way"	26.8	47.2	26.0	339
Evangelical	45.4	44.4	10.2	108
Other Religion	51.9	37.0	11.1	27
Total	32.7	38.4	28.9	1162

Source: Metropolitan Region Survey, Santiago, Chile, 2004 (Parker and Peña 2005).

Table 4.6. Degree of Distrust in Churches among Chilean University Students, 2005

Level of Distrust		Percent of Group Expressing Distrust[a]	Percent of Whole Sample
High	Atheist	76.6	6.3
	Agnostic, Nonbeliever	69.4	10.9
	Believer "without religion"	61.3	17.0
Moderate	Other Religion	48.3	3.2
	Catholic "in my own way"	37.3	25.7
Low	Evangelical	26.8	6.7
	Catholic	19.3	30.2
	Mean	41.4	

Source: University Student Survey (Parker 2007).
[a]Responses generated from question on confidence in institutions: *How much confidence do you have in: churches (government, parliament, universities, the police, etc.)?* Possible responses were *a lot, some, none.* The percentage responding "none" is represented here.

As in North America, attendance at traditional mainline churches is falling. But this fact does not suggest a lack of religious interest but rather a shift of interest in new directions. In Europe, especially in France, such a shift is manifested in what Lambert (2003) has called the "cultural Christians" or the "Deist Christians." This phenomenon is important in Chile in that it reveals distrust in public institutions, a growing feature of political disengagement and disenchantment among Chilean youth in a society that is rapidly modernizing and integrating into the global economy and society.

Like their European and U.S. counterparts, younger Chileans lack interest in classic civic engagement. They tend to avoid traditional civic institutions and conventional types of civic activism in growing numbers, and they distance themselves from classical forms of participation that were common among previous generations (Balardini 2000; Lamanna 2003; Parker 2003). Young people in Chile tend to voice their public concern, show their political involvement, and create social capital in new ways and channels, especially in and through new social movements, sports, and religion. In this way they differ from young North Americans and Europeans, who tend to channel their public concerns into leisure and consumption.

Education as a Factor that Influences Religious Options

Modern education is a factor of secularization that reduces religiosity and promotes rational choices and the critique of tradition. In the Chilean data we observe that the educational factor is relevant for changes in religious mentality: to some extent education increases antireligious rationalism, but it also promotes new religious alternatives and spiritual choices. One of the main indicators of the process of modernization in Chile is the country's high rate of literacy. According to the official census, Chile's literacy rate rose from 94.6 to 95.8 percent between 1992 and 2002. Additionally, a very significant increase has taken place in the level of formal education. The 2002 census indicates that the number of children attending preschool almost doubled, and the number of people receiving high school and university education increased from 1,072,198 in 1992 to 2,284,036 in 2002 (INE 2003). In the same period the higher education enrollment rate increased from 9 to 16.4 percent.

In the context of the census data we can analyze religious identification among 15 to 29 year olds nationwide (see Table 4.7). We find that a higher level of formal education produces more people who declare themselves as not having any religion or as atheists or agnostics. Among those with only a primary education, atheists and agnostics represent only 9.5 percent of the total. The percentage increases to 9.9 percent among respondents who reached secondary school and to 15.3 percent among those who had some higher education. If we look now at the census data for the metropolitan region,[10] we find further evidence of this trend among "nonbelievers" and "atheists" (see Table 4.8). Evangelicals, who are more prevalent among the least educated, are significantly influenced by formal education, but Catholics are not. In addition, as the younger generation increasingly experiences the modern educational system, this tendency is evident in the corresponding data for people between 15 and 29 years old (see Table 4.7). Catholics with less formal education are underrepresented relative to the total Catholic population, and evangelicals are overrepresented relative to their overall numbers. Also, proportionally fewer evangelicals have had access to a university education.

This tendency coincides with the one observed in the Third National Youth Survey (INJUV 2001) and the 1999 Secondary Students Survey (Parker 2000). When the educational factor is cross-tabulated with other variables (such as gender, family income strata, type of school, and so forth), we find that men with higher income levels who attended elite schools are disproportionately Catholic. Women from the lower income strata and from lower-class schools are disproportionately evangelical. Protestants and Jews are slightly better represented among women, among higher-revenue strata, and among those who attended schools for the upper class. "Believers without religion" are also more numerous among women and those educated in schools for the middle and lower classes; and the nonbelievers prevail in middle-class and elite income levels and schools. Atheists are for the most part men from middle- and high-income strata and schools. Alternative religions are preferred by women from lower strata and schools. Finally, those identifying as "Catholic in my own way" prevail among the male youths of middle and high strata and schools.

Table 4.7. Education and Religion among 15 to 29 Year Olds in Chile, 2002 (in percent)

Educational Level	Catholic	Evangelical	Other Religion	None or Atheist
8th Grade or Less	61.8	22.2	6.5	9.5
Secondary School	67.2	15.9	7.0	9.9
Tertiary Education	67.3	8.7	8.6	15.3
Total *(mean)*	66.2	15.4	7.3	11.1

Source: Chilean National Census 2002 (INE 2003).

Table 4.8. Religion by Educational Level in the Santiago Metropolitan Region, 2002

Educational Level	Catholics		Evangelicals		Other Religion		Atheist, No Religion		Total
	#	%	#	%	#	%	#	%	#
Primary (8th grade or less)	814,308	66.8	234,442	19.2	86,905	7.1	83,853	6.9	1,219,508
Secondary (9th–12th grades)	1,468,781	69.6	277,466	13.1	161,951	7.7	202,798	9.6	2,110,996
Technical and University	846,160	69.3	83,265	6.8	106,672	8.7	185,366	15.2	1,221,463
Total	3,129,249	68.7	595,173	13.1	355,528	7.8	472,017	10.4	4,551,967

Source: Chilean National Census, 2002 (INE 2003).

The Metropolitan Region Survey (Parker and Peña 2005), conducted in October 2004 with a representative sample of the region's entire population, allows us to build on these empirical observations and determine their significance with statistical correlations. If we correlate religion with age it is clear (as we observed before) that age is influencing religious options in terms of diminishing Catholicism and increasing "other alternatives," but this is the case mostly among nonbelievers and "believers in my own way." Cramer's correlation test gives significant results. On the other hand, if we correlate religion with educational level, we find a very significant result (see Table 4.9.) In order to avoid the bias of age in the causal relationship between education and religion, we have applied a nominal by nominal Cramer's Correlation test to each age strata with the following results: 18 to 29 years old, CrV = 0.162, p = 0.052; 30 to 49 years, CrV = 0.197, p = 0.000; 50 to 59 years, CrV = 0.173, p = 0.410; more than 60 years old, CrV = 0.181, p = 0.687.

This means that both the age and education variables are influencing religion. With a nominal by nominal correlation test we verify that education is significantly correlated with religion among 18 to 29 year olds, and even more strongly among 30 to 49 year olds, but not in the other age cohorts (those between 50 and 59 and above 60). In other words, this survey shows us that modern and formal education significantly influences religious choices among the young and middle-aged but not older people. This is very important because of the great changes in educational systems during the last half of the twentieth century. Members of the older generation (those 50 and above) who were able to get an education attended school forty to sixty years ago when cultural and religious options and pedagogical conditions were more traditional and the educational culture had not absorbed the impact of today's mass media and new technologies. The cultural influence of globalization on education and socialization beginning in the 1980s (affecting individuals who are from 20 to 40 years old) is more evident in the younger generation.

The survey evidence permits us to develop the hypothesis for future research that higher levels of education are generating religious changes in Latin America by increasing the alternatives to "orthodox," traditional Catholicism. These rising alternatives are self-descriptive: "Catholic in my

Table 4.9. Religion by Educational Level in the Santiago Metropolitan Region, 2004

Educational Level	Agnostic/ Atheist		Believer "without religion"		Catholic		Catholic "in my own way"		Evangelical		Other Religion		Total
	#	%	#	%	#	%	#	%	#	%	#	%	#
8th Grade or Less	5	2.1	28	11.8	106	44.7	60	25.3	34	14.4	4	1.7	237
Secondary School	29	5.3	73	13.4	204	37.6	165	30.4	57	10.5	15	2.8	543
Tertiary Education	59	15.2	61	15.7	128	33.0	115	29.6	17	4.4	8	2.1	388
Total	93	8.0	162	13.9	438	37.5	340	29.1	108	9.3	27	2.3	1,168

Source: Metropolitan Region Survey (Parker and Peña 2005).

own way"; a "believer without religion," "agnostic," or "atheist"; and the nebulous category of "other religions."

A parallel tendency—and presumably exercising a great impact on religion in Latin America—is that there is an inverse relationship between educational level and the proportion of evangelicals. But does this mean that as educational reforms continue in Latin America and formal education increases among new waves of young people, the religious scene will become even more diversified, and evangelicals will decrease just as did the proportion of faithful Catholics? If we focus on students (17 to 25 year olds), a clear example of an elite in a developing country, we must ask, Is it the sole effect of a higher level of education that produces religious pluralism, or is it the type of education supplied (more diverse, religious or not) that is broadening the scope for religious alternatives?

Let us examine the empirical data we have, first for secondary students and then for university students, and cross-tabulate the type of believer with the type of institution—public (lyceums), private secular, or Catholic (see Table 4.10.) In both wholly private Catholic schools and those in which the state subsidizes tuition for low- and lower-middle-income families, the percentage of Catholics is higher (55 percent) but the difference is not pronounced. Only in one lay, private, upper-class school do we find a higher proportion of Catholics (72 percent). This is probably due to the fact that Catholicism is a cultural trait of the upper classes in Chile and the school we are analyzing is a very typical elite school. In most of the secular or public schools of different social strata we find a higher proportion of "Catholics in my own way"—approximately 63 to 65 percent. This is the case with the lay subsidized private secondary schools and many of the public high schools known as *liceos* (lyceums).[11] Lower-class public secondary school students in the Concepción region, 66 percent of whom are Catholic, constitute an exception, probably due to local cultural dynamics. The association of non-Catholic schools (private lay and public) and the greater presence of "Catholic in my own way" students is relevant. In six of the ten non-Catholic schools, this kind of believer constitutes more than 60 percent of self-declared Catholics. The association between Catholic schools and the presence of "Catholics"—that is to say Catholics close to official Catholicism—is important but not as clear as one would expect: only 55 to 56 percent of students in these schools self-identify as Catholics.

Table 4.10. Type of Catholics by Types of Secondary Schools in Chile, 1999 (in percent)

Socioeconomic				Type of Believer	
Level	Region	No. of Schools	Type of School	Catholic	Catholic "in my own way"
Lower	Santiago	2	Public—Lyceum*	35.4	64.6
Concepción		2	Public—Lyceum*	65.7	34.3
Middle	Santiago	1	Catholic—Private *	55.6	44.4
	Concepción and Santiago	2	Lay—Private*	35.4	64.6
	Concepción	1	Public—Lyceum*	52.6	47.4
High	Santiago	1	Lay—Private Paid**	71.7	28.3
	Concepción and Santiago	2	Lay—Private Paid**	36.9	63.1
	Concepción	1	Catholic—Private Paid**	55.9	44.1

Source: Survey of Secondary Students (Parker 2000).
*These schools are subsidized partially or wholly by the state.
**These schools are wholly private and independent.

This evidence suggests that the general tendency may be for the number of "Catholics in my own way" to increase proportionate to the expansion in private lay or public secondary institutions. Nowadays, the correlation is not absolute and direct: there are important exceptions (private lay schools with a higher percentage of Catholics; public lyceums with more Catholics), but these exceptions are due to local culture and/or to class-specific cultural variables that are conditioning this phenomenon. Even in Catholic schools cultural values are a very important influence that generate "in my own way" believers (at least 44 percent), which implies that whether or not a school is Catholic, although relevant, is not the exclusive factor conditioning the religious consciousness of secondary school students.

Does the type of educational institution have a similar impact on the religious affiliation of university students? Are university students educated in lay institutions more likely to be Catholics "in their own way" or believers without religious affiliation than students educated in traditional Catholic institutions? Our 2005 National University Student Survey (Parker 2007) reveals that Catholic institutions do tend to "produce" (that is, generate the favorable conditions for the social production of) "plain" Catholics—that is, persons of faith who indeed identify with their church—but not a proportionately high number of them (see Table 4.11). The Catholic university, as a "confessional institution,"[12] has as its main purpose promoting faith and religious adhesion to "straight" catechismal teachings and morals. The fact that 50 percent of the students are "in my own way believers" rather than "Catholics" (38 percent) means that this type of university is in fact generating a more pluralistic education.

On the other hand, secular universities generate a social space where we find the social conditions more likely to produce alternatives to Catholicism, such as believers "in my own way," adherents of other religions, and atheists. In particular, a variety of lay institutions are increasing the ranks of adherents to other faiths (Protestants, including Pentecostals, Mormons, Jews, etc.) and believers "in my own way." Traditional secular institutions (some of them state universities, some private universities promoted by lay movements such as the Masons), which originated as alternatives to confessional institutions and often with an anticlerical stance, are not generating the social conditions for atheism. Rather, they are stimulating religious alternatives to Catholicism.

Table 4.11. Religious Affiliation by Type of University in Chile, 2005 (in percent)

Type of University	Atheist	"In my own way" believer[a]	Catholic	Other Religion
Lay	7.04	55.0	26.8	11.2
Catholic	4.7	50.1	38.4	6.8

Source: National University Student Survey (Parker 2007).
[a]This category is the sum of the "Catholics in my own way" and "believer without religion" categories.

In recent years new institutions have appeared. Indeed, the privatization of the educational system and the introduction of educational reforms have created more diverse types of private schools and universities. Some of these are Protestant colleges and universities, which were practically non-existent in Latin America during the nineteenth and most of the twentieth centuries. In some countries even Catholic universities did not exist in the nineteenth century: given the *patronato* regime (the special accord between the state and the Vatican), public national universities included departments of (Catholic) theology, helping give rise to the notion of the "Catholic continent."

But let us take a closer look at what is happening with those self-identified Catholics who want to distance themselves from their church—the "Catholics in my own way." As the National University Student Survey shows, whereas in lay universities the difference between "Catholics" and "Catholics in my own way" is insignificant (26.8 percent vs. 25.5 percent, respectively), in Catholic universities substantially more students self-identify as "Catholic" (38.4 percent) than as "Catholic in my own way" (26 percent) (Parker 2007).

If the type of institution at the tertiary level (confessional or not) does not explain how "in my own way" Catholics are produced, then the emergence of this religious identification—which, as we have seen, indicates distrust in the institutional church—must be attributable to other social factors. Our hypothesis is that the general exposure to a more liberal and critical culture within circles of highly educated elites (such as the university students studied) affords the opportunity to question traditional religious identification. The "Enlightenment" culture in this case does not produce secularization (understood as a dissipating of faith) but rather self-styled forms of believing and classical critiques of the concept of authority.

Educational Change in Latin America: More Religious Changes in the Future?

Beginning in the 1980s (and picking up steam in the 1990s), educational reforms have been transforming educational systems in Latin

America.[13] Educational reforms backed by the World Bank and other international organizations have followed the neoliberal prescriptions that began with Margaret Thatcher's educational reforms in Britain. These policies reduced government financial support to educational institutions, introduced accountability for the use of public funds, and required educational institutions to turn to the market as the main factor shaping their future.

Structural adjustment measures were undertaken by Latin American countries in the 1980s and 1990s in order to stabilize the economy, liberalize trade, and become integrated into the global market. Great efforts were also made to advance educational reforms in all sectors. Programs to increase primary and secondary education coverage and quality have been implemented all over the region in the past fifteen years. In the ten years from 1994 to 2004, when World Bank lending for tertiary education averaged US$343 million per year, Latin America and the Caribbean received the largest share (33 percent) of bank lending for tertiary education, followed by East Asia and the Pacific (29 percent) and South Asia (15 percent).

In its support for the actual implementation of higher educational reforms, the World Bank gives priority to programs and projects that focus on increasing institutional diversification; establishing sustainable financing systems to encourage responsiveness and flexibility; strengthening management capacities; improving the quality and relevance of tertiary education; and supporting research and development capacity. It also promotes programs aimed at achieving greater equity by assisting disadvantaged students. In recent decades there has been an impressive growth of enrollments, "together with the multiplication of universities, creating greater institutional differentiation and increasing regionalization and privatization" (Torres and Schugurensky 2004, 37).

The main result of these reforms has been educational pluralization. For decades the developmentalist or populist states in Latin America were in charge of education. Many countries were proud of their public schools and universities. But the crisis of the 1970s and 1980s affected educational systems, and their recovery began with the implementation of neoliberal reforms and structural readjustment measures that reduced public funding for social policy, including education, and promoted different ways of financing private investment in this area (CTERA et al. 2005). The presence of the private sector in the field has been growing to different degrees in different countries. In general, private education today is represented by a larger percentage of institutions of higher learning than of primary and secondary schools (González 2002).

The state continues to support the educational system but the door is clearly open to the private sector and for different types of private-public combinations. More private corporations and enterprises are committed (totally or partially) to financing, administering, and promoting private schools. This privatization of education stems from the interest of the private sector in skilled labor and its perception that education is a lucrative business. Private investment in education has also been supported by increased public subsidies and tax breaks.

Whereas Catholic institutions were traditionally the main components of the private educational sector, today there is a growing presence of Protestant and secular institutions. Even within Catholicism there is increasing diversification because liberal educational norms allow for the implementation of different educational programs coming out of different dioceses, Catholic congregations, and lay movements. The direct consequence of these developments in terms of religion is primarily that private education is ceasing to be a monopoly of traditional Catholicism.

The data we have marshaled in the preceding section, however, suggests that the type of educational institution that students attend is not the most important source of religious change. Religious pluralism increases not only because the number of Catholic schools and universities are declining, their influence is reduced, or there are fewer "religious classes" in the schools. Rather, religious pluralism is growing because of the population's increased symbolic production of diverse forms of religious beliefs and types of spiritual searching that are often distrustful of religious institutions. And, in turn, the increase in the educational levels is affecting positively the social conditions that produce these diverse religious alternatives. We refer here to the general impact of education on religious consciousness, not to explicit religious teaching or catechism received in "religion classes" in public or confessional establishments.

Since colonial times—following the Christendom model—religious instruction in public educational institutions was the norm. In fact, during the nineteenth century most governments continued to depend on the church to provide education, and secular public schools only appeared with the reforms pushed through by liberal governments in the second half of the nineteenth century. In many countries, however, in spite of the separation of church and state, religious teaching continued to be a Catholic monopoly, even in public schools. In Mexico (Loaeza 2003) the Catholic order essentially underpinned the authoritarian regime, even though the regime was allegedly anticlerical. This picture shifted in the second half of the twentieth century, and "religion classes" are now optional or elective (depending on the student's professed confession) in many public educational systems in Latin America. This transformation of religious instruction in schools toward the end of the twentieth century coincided with the above-mentioned educational reforms that tend to diversify educational offerings, thus considerably reducing the reach and influence of confessional education.

These changes took place in the context of the diminishment of traditional family religious socialization (see Loaeza, chap. 3 in this volume). Especially against the backdrop of the diminishing importance of the extended family vis-à-vis the nuclear family in today's Latin American societies, the role of grandparents has been transformed. Whereas traditionally Latin American children received their religious socialization at home from their grandmothers, today, with the breakdown of the extended family, children and youth are much more exposed to the messages coming from school, television, and the Internet.

If explicit religious teaching in school is a secondary factor that brings about religious pluralism, and traditional family religious socialization is diminishing, then our attention must focus on the general educational changes in the region and to what has happened, in general terms, with formal education and its influence on the Latin American masses. The general level of education of the Latin American population has increased systematically in the past two decades. The illiteracy rate is now much lower—in 2000 only 12 percent of the population aged 15 and above was illiterate, compared to 18.5 percent in 1980 (ECLAC 1999). In 2004 only 4 percent of youth aged 15 to 24 were illiterate (the world average was 12 percent) and the gender parity index was 1.01 (UNESCO 2005, 132). Moreover, enrollments in primary, secondary, and tertiary schools have all increased as well. On average for all Latin American countries, enrollment in primary schools has increased from 85 percent in 1980 to 94 percent in 2000 and enrollment in secondary schools has increased from 38 percent in 1980 to 60 percent in 2003. The current rate of primary education enrollment (above 95 percent) is similar to that registered in developed countries.

In comparative terms educational changes in Latin America have been clear and vigorous. As we can observe in Table 4.12, information provided by the World Education Indicators (WEI) program (a joint UNESCO Institute for Statistics [UIS] and Organization for Economic Cooperation and Development [OECD] project) for 2002–2003 permits us to compare the progress of Latin American countries participating in this program (Brazil, Chile, Paraguay, Peru, and Uruguay) with the mean of all countries that participate in the project, including some African, Asian (WEI mean), and OECD countries (OECD mean). The table clearly illustrates that the annual growth rate in enrollment (2.94 percent) is higher for Latin American countries as a whole than for the WEI countries (2.08 percent) and the OECD countries (0.65 percent). It continues to be high for primary (0.68 percent) and for secondary education (4.74 vs. 3.04 for all WEI and 0.26 for all OECD countries). Only in tertiary education is the rate of enrollment growth in Latin American countries surpassed by other developing and developed countries (the sample included China, India, and Russia).

Table 4.12. Average Annual Growth Rate of Enrollment at Different Levels of Education, 1995–2003

	Latin America WEI	*WEI Mean*	*OECD Mean*
Total	2.94	2.08	0.65
Preprimary	3.80	3.90	0.75
Primary	0.68	−0.01	0.23
Lower Secondary	3.90	2.28	−0.28
Upper Secondary	6.04	4.32	0.24
All Secondary	4.74	3.04	0.26
Tertiary[a]	5.54	n.d.	−0.85
Tertiary and Advanced Research Programs	3.46	9.80	4.15
All Tertiary	4.70	7.64	4.16

Source: World Education Indicators (UIS-OECD 2005).
[a]WEI mean for tertiary level not available.

Table 4.13 shows the 2004 net school enrollment by age of children between the ages of 7 and 17 years old for MERCOSUR (*Mercado Común del Sur, or the Southern Common Market*) members (Argentina, Brazil, Uruguay, and Paraguay) and an associated member country (Chile).[14] The schooling rates for secondary and especially for higher education continue to be lower in Latin America than in the more economically developed countries. Nonetheless, according to Muñoz and Márquez Jiménez (2000), at the end of the twentieth century these differences between Latin America and the developed countries were narrowing (57.2 versus 100 percent in secondary education, and 18.4 versus 50.5 percent in higher education, for the 1998–1999 period).

According to recent data on the gross and net enrollment ratios for secondary education in Latin America furnished by UNESCO, there are evident differences among countries (see Table 4.14). By 2002–2003, whereas the net enrollment ratio of Cuba, Argentina, Chile, and Brazil had exceeded 75 percent, that of Guatemala, the Dominican Republic, and Nicaragua was less than 40 percent. But the gap between South America and the United States is becoming smaller. In 1998–1999 the net enrollment ratio for South America was 62 percent, while in the United States it was 88 percent. By 2002–2003 (the last years for which data are available) this rate had reached 71 percent in South America while remaining stationary in the United States at 88 percent. This increase of 9 percent between 1998 and 2003 is

Table 4.13. Net Enrollment by Age, 2004
(in percent)

Country	Age	
	7–14	*15–17*
Argentina	104.3	79.8
Brazil	97.0	80.6
Chile	95.6	89.2
Paraguay	96.1	64.7
Uruguay	100.9	76.3

Source: MERCOSUR (2004).

larger than the mean for all of the Latin American countries, which moved from 53.5 percent in 1998–1999 to 60.1 percent in 2002–2003, an increase of 6.64 percentage points.

The expansion of education to a greater segment of the population is not without problems. Educational coverage has expanded in the last thirty years, but educational quality has not kept pace: the teaching of language, mathematics, and the sciences is weak even in many of the most advanced

Table 4.14. Secondary Education in Latin America, 1998–1999 and 2002–2003

	1998–1999		2002–2003	
	Gross Enrollment Ratio	*Net Enrollment Ratio*	*Gross Enrollment Ratio*	*Net Enrollment Ratio*
Argentina	89	74	100	81
Bolivia	72	n.d.	86	71
Brazil	n.d.	n.d.	110	75
Chile	80	70	89	79
Colombia	71	54	71	55
Costa Rica	57	49	66	53
Cuba	79	75	93	86
Dominican Republic	56	40	59	36
Ecuador	56	46	59	50
El Salvador	50	40	59	49
Guatemala	31	21	43	30
Mexico	69	55	79	63
Nicaragua	48	n.d.	61	39
Panama	68	60	71	63
Paraguay	51	42	65	51
Peru	82	62	90	69
Uruguay	88	66	106	73
Venezuela	57	48	70	59
United States	95	88	94	88
North America[a]	81	71	84	74
South America	85	62	97	71

Source: UIS (2005); author's calculations.
Note: No data (n.d.) available for some countries.
[a]Includes Canada, the United States, and Mexico.

countries of the region. Access to education is still unequal. Opportunities to access secondary education and especially higher education continue to be strongly concentrated in the upper-income groups (Muñoz and Márquez Jiménez 2000).

Notwithstanding the lack of equity and quality, the rising levels of education in Latin America in the last thirty years have had an impact on the growth of Protestants (especially Pentecostals) among the lower classes. As we have seen in the Chilean case, all the evidence points to the fact that higher levels of formal education produce fewer evangelicals. It is well known that lower levels of formal education and especially illiteracy are generally associated with poverty. Similarly, among lower social strata with low levels of formal education, as levels of education rise, the rate at which people join evangelical and especially Pentecostal churches—those often found in this social milieu—falls.

As for tertiary education, in 1950 only one country had 10 percent of the population between 19 and 22 years of age attending institutions of higher learning; in a second, 8 percent were; in most countries, less than 4 percent of the population had had any higher education. In 1997 the rate of enrollment in higher education had reached 22 percent in Latin America. By 2002–2003 the gross rate of enrollment of university and other post-secondary students in fifteen selected countries had reached 30 percent, still far from the U.S. rate of 83 percent but certainly much higher than even the 1998 rate of 24 percent. Overall, the number of undergraduate students rose sharply from 270,000 in the 1950s to almost 10 million by the year 2000. Higher education has become a mass phenomenon in Latin America (C. Rama 2002).

Educational reforms have had a great impact on tertiary education: the alternatives have multiplied with the expanded capacity of the education supply brought about by the increasing number of private universities supplementing the traditional public system. In light of the growing demand for higher education, national and regional governments, and a considerable number of private initiatives, have responded with diverse institutional offerings (Burbano López 1999).

The number of higher educational institutions in the entire region rose from 75 (mostly universities) in 1950 to around 6,000 diverse tertiary institutions in the mid-1990s. By 1994 there were more than 800 universities, approximately 60 percent of which were in the private sector. The number of other tertiary institutions rose from "a few units" to more than 4,000, of which the preponderance were private, "lucrative types of institutions" (Tünnermann 1997, 99). This trend continued into the next decade. By the beginning of the twenty-first century, the massive institutional expansion and diversification of education had produced more than 8,000 institutions of higher learning in the region, compared with the few that had existed just decades earlier. Today the region's universities, institutes, polytechnic schools, public and private professional colleges, and for-profit and non-profit institutions present an extremely diverse educational landscape. According to UNESCO data for 2002–2003, over half (53.5 percent) of students in a sample of Latin American countries enrolled in tertiary educational institutions attended public institutions, as compared to 76.3 percent in the OECD countries and 74.7 percent in a sample of Asian and African countries. The mean proportion of students enrolled in government-dependent private institutions in Latin America (42 percent) was much higher than the mean for the OECD countries (12 percent) and the developing countries of Asia and Africa (32 percent) (UIS 2005).[15]

The diversity in the tertiary educational system in Latin America extends beyond the nature of the institutions of higher learning. The ownership and cultural and ideological orientation of private schools and universities is nowadays much more pluralistic than it was in the middle of the twentieth century. Some churches, especially the Catholic Church, have increased their presence, but other, mainly Protestant and evangelical, churches have also recently begun to develop activities in this domain.

Catholic institutions themselves are becoming more diverse. In addition to universities supported by the Vatican, the National Bishops' Conferences, and even some dioceses, a number of universities have also been founded by different religious orders and lay movements covering the entire spectrum, from the very conservative Legionaries of Christ and Opus Dei to the very progressive Jesuits and Dominicans, as well as other religious orders such as the Salesians and Franciscans and doctrinal and ideological religious groups. Options in higher education are multiplying beyond confessional institutions. Indeed, since the 1980s many universities have been founded by private companies and ideological groups such as the Masons.[16]

I believe there are a number of outstanding factors influencing religious options that can be generalized to all Latin American countries, as explained in the following hypotheses[17]:

(a) *The deficiencies in education that are evident in many respects in the region have not been and will not prove to be obstacles to modern schools influencing the culture of new generations with the codes and values of modernity.* Culture has had a decisive impact on religious beliefs and practices since, as we have suggested, education has significantly opened up religious options, all the more among young people.

b) *The pluralization of public and private options in the local educational system not only creates alternatives to the classical confessional school but also questions the classic model of confessional schools.* The reproduction of religious beliefs and morals no longer depends exclusively on classic family socialization patterns or exposure to traditional catechism and religious instruction in school.

c) *Contemporary educational content and pedagogy that tends to elevate the autonomy of the subject being educated[18] breed a critical attitude and skepticism toward received narratives, in addition to the critical spirit already stimulated by today's scientific spirit and method.* In the formal socialization process there is space for creativity, which in religious and spiritual matters undoubtedly prompts the young to distance themselves from conventional preaching, catechetical practices, and the old-fashioned presentation of church dogmas and doctrine.

d) *If there is indeed an inverse correlation between the number of evangelicals and levels of education, if this tendency is generalizable to different cultural and educational contexts across Latin America, and if with modernization and globalization educational levels continue to show improvement throughout the region, then we may have reached a ceiling in the continued growth of evangelicalism (mostly of Pentecostal inspiration).*

e) *Lastly, if the observed tendency for more highly educated Catholics to identify as believing "in my own way," and this type of religious option has significant interaction with other "nonorthodox" and nonconventional beliefs and practices ("believers without religion," New Age spirituality, and new popular syncretic practices), and if we can expect educa-*

tional levels to improve throughout Latin America, then we should witness an increase in religious pluralization in and through the expansion of nonconventional beliefs and practices.

Unquestionably, the changes within churches, which follow from the specific historical dynamics of Catholicism and evangelical denominations, are key to understanding transformations in the field of religion. Another notable source of change is the religious competition among churches. Finally, notwithstanding the weakening of Catholic hegemony from without by evangelical and missionary churches, which many see as "besieging the church," Catholic hegemony is also being "tunneled out" by new cultural patterns reproduced in socialization and pedagogical processes in modern schools and universities. Most importantly, educational reforms are undermining Catholic hegemony. For the great majority of Latin America's youth, who are raised in Catholic families, the access to school and to higher levels of formal education—in the context of the new educational conditions—encourages them to search for new religious beliefs, distrust traditional religious authorities, and accept alternative, sometimes syncretic and "self-styled," ways of believing.

Responses to the 2005 National University Student Survey (Parker 2007) illustrate in particularly dramatic fashion the birth of different types of syncretic beliefs drawn from East Asian and local folk traditions. When asked about heterodox beliefs, more than half of the students in the sample responded that they believed in one or more of the following: black magic, witches, spirits, reincarnation, astrology, aliens, and traditional shamans (Table 4.15). Cluster analysis allowed us to construct a typology: those who believe in supernatural or mysterious realities (Cluster 1) and those who do not believe (Cluster 2). The cross-tabulation with the type of believer reveals that believers "in my own way" and "without religion" tend to hold heterodox beliefs.[19]

Empirical data provided by the 2003 Chilean National Youth Survey (INJUV 2004) for young people (sixteen to twenty-nine years old) who have thirteen or more years of formal education (including at least one year of tertiary education) confirm that people with this level of education tend to hold syncretic beliefs: 54 percent acknowledge believing in an assortment of concepts, including astrology, reincarnation, aliens, "self knowledge,"

Table 4.15. Heterodox Beliefs among University Students in Chile, 2005

Type of Believer	Believes (Cluster 1)	Does Not Believe (Cluster 2)
Atheist	27.2	72.8
Agnostic, nonbeliever	38.4	61.6
Believer "without religion"	62.4	37.6
Catholic "in my own way"	63.4	36.6
Catholic	56.8	44.0
Evangelical	47.9	52.1
Other Religion	41.6	58.4
Mean	54.5	45.5

Source: National University Student Survey (Parker 2007).
Note: Based on responses (affirmative and negative) to question, *"Do you believe in black magic, witches, spirits, reincarnation, astrology, aliens, and shamans?"* Clusters represent groups of believers and nonbelievers in these supernatural entities.

and magic. All those surveyed had a Christian background. The general observed tendency holds even for Catholics—50 percent hold heterodox beliefs. Furthermore, 59 percent of those declaring "I don't feel close to any religion" (33 of the total in this survey) adhere to this type of heterogeneous belief.

Indeed, Catholics are setting out on an internal path toward dissidence when they declare themselves to be Catholic "in my own way"; but the path to dissidence stretches even further when they switch to other churches or when they join the group of "believers without religion" (mostly nominal Catholics still considering themselves to be believers in God and Jesus Christ but not part of the Catholic Church). This type of belief constitutes a form of dissidence from Catholic orthodoxy because in their syncretic views the faithful blend some theological truths and official dogma (believing in God, Jesus Christ, and even the Virgin Mary) with a variety of popular or folk beliefs (traditional shamanism, healing, black magic, and so forth) and "postmodern" beliefs (astrology, witchcraft, aliens, and other types of occultist or New Age components). These self-styled believers combine a variety of different religious or traditional beliefs into a unique fusion that suits their particular experience and context. In other words, while atheism is growing slowly, the faithful whose beliefs are "diffuse" and who only nominally recognize their affiliation to Catholicism are growing more palpably. Meanwhile, popular Catholicism, with all its syncretism and heterodoxy, continues to make inroads even among the better educated and urban elite.

In all these new religious expressions the changing pattern of global culture is made manifest. The development of beliefs and rituals is being influenced and made possible by the new technologies of information and communication that are ever more available to the more educated younger generation. In this context horizontal and decentralized networks that represent a growing resistance to hierarchical authority are proliferating. New real and virtual rituals and supernatural realities are born and entire worldviews are transformed. It is within this religious diversity that individuals search for alternative answers to institutionalized and rationalized religions and promote syncretism and pluralism. Multiple affiliations, interactions among religions, the neo-magic (hermetic and magico-ritual mysticism), all the Pentecostals (Catholic or evangelical), ethnic shamanism, and varied popular religions and new spiritualities coexist and develop within this complex (often called "postmodern") panorama. Formal educational changes are altering the cultural patterns where religious shifts are taking place. Sometimes higher levels of education promote religious pluralism directly; at other times, educational changes generate new conditions conducive to the blossoming of religious diversity.

I have based my analysis and interpretation mostly on evidence from the Chilean case; therefore, generalizations should be made with caution. I have underscored the impact of educational changes that create favorable conditions for the acceptance of the global cultural marketplace that is driving religious and cultural change. If other Latin American countries follow the Chilean model of reform, they, too, will undoubtedly experience these global cultural factors. Indeed, experts consider Chilean educational reform a model that is being followed by many countries in the region. Torres and Schugurensky, who analyze university restructuring in comparative perspective, conclude that in Latin America this process "is following a model of privatization probably most advanced in Chile, where the 1981 reform . . . can be interpreted as the reverse of the Argentinean 1918 university reform" (2004, 38).[20] Nevertheless, as can well be imagined, each country has its own local cultural and religious history and traditions that can develop the general tendency toward religious pluralization in many different but specific directions.

What we have learned from the Chilean case in particular is that there is a positive and complex (while not necessarily direct and causal) relation between the increase in educational opportunities and the diversification of educational systems, on the one hand, and the increase in religious pluralism in the mentality of young people, on the other hand. This general tendency permits us to predict, as a working hypothesis, that if general sociological and historical conditions evolve along similar lines in the different countries, the changing religious panorama of Latin American countries will continue to become more pluralistic. Catholicism will remain the main religious option for most Latin Americans for many years to come; however, Catholicism itself will be increasingly challenged by diverse religious alternatives (often heterodox beliefs) even among its own adherents.

Conclusion: Religious Pluralism as Political Pluralism?

In highly developed societies, especially in Europe (and to a notably lesser extent in the United States), Weber's observation in the early twentieth century rings true: "the pursuit of wealth, stripped of its religious and ethical meaning, tends to become associated with purely mundane passions, which often actually give it the character of sport" (Weber 1958, 182).

Our study of Chile suggests that along with economic growth and socioeconomic prosperity in recent decades, a consumer society has changed the lives of the people. But contrary to Weberian expectations, religious expressions have not vanished. Rather, they have become diversified and are still a source of meaning for the people. Because the country's religious roots are Catholic rather than Protestant, religious beliefs have spread neither asceticism nor the idea of "the calling" (or the Protestant work ethic and the spirit of capital accumulation) in this cultural context. But because the process of secularization was not tightly connected to and did not follow directly from economic compulsion, as it did for Weber, the secularized idea of fulfillment of the calling has been replaced by the hedonistic

spirit of consumerism, without need of any justification. Thus, religious beliefs have been developed in a parallel world to everyday economic life. The
transformation of the system toward a postmodern culture has guaranteed
the renewal of ancient values in new conditions, akin to what Debray called
"postmodern archaism" (1996).

According to Weber, rationality was supposed to engender antireligious attitudes or at least diminish religion's great influence. In contrast,
what we have observed in this chapter is that, at least in the Latin American
context, rationality brings new religious expression and spirituality. Thus,
rationality and spiritualism can coexist. What has happened here to create
this situation, and why are these findings important? Weber believed that
the mechanical nature of industrial capitalism would inevitably impact society's worldview and expel all religious meaning. But he was also aware of
the possibility of change created by historical processes. He once wrote,
"No one knows who will live in this cage in the future, or whether at the
end of this tremendous development, entirely new prophets will arise, or
there will be a great rebirth of old ideas and ideals, or, if neither, mechanized petrification, embellished with a sort of convulsive self-importance"
(Weber 1958, 182).

What Weber did not or could not have imagined was the new technological information and communication revolution of the last half of the
twentieth century. The new globalized capitalism is not based on mechanical forms of production but rather on technotronic forms that stress symbolic and virtual realities. New religious expressions have been nurtured by
educational transformation in a society that has been exposed to a radical
cultural change: the culture of images and symbols and a new consumer society in which all sorts of electronic devices pervade everyday life. There is
no longer a risk of Weber's "mechanized petrification" of social meaning.
Instead, the risk is the chaotic multiplication of "new prophets" and an excessive diversification of all sorts of "ideas and ideals."

In the context of Latin culture, educational transformation—the increase of educational levels and access to institutions of higher education,
changes in pedagogy and the reform of traditional patterns, and the opening to new technologies and science—leads to the autonomy of a "postmodern" Latin subject who searches "in her own way" for new modes of
believing. Educational change also explains why education and rationality

generate distrust of religious institutions (and dogma) but not religion and religious belief itself. If we expect educational levels to improve throughout Latin America, then we should also anticipate not merely the spread of the classic, secular Enlightenment mentality but also that of nonconventional ("postmodern") beliefs and practices.

The new religious panorama in Latin America, taking into account the particularities of each country and region, is evidence of a decline of Catholicism and a consequent diminishing of the cultural and political influence of the Catholic Church. As mentioned at the beginning of this chapter, this change does not mean that we are facing a "Protestant continent" or secularization. Rather, we are confronted with a complex process in which the marked tendency is toward a constant increase in religious pluralism—the result of ongoing educational change—but the presence of a Catholic Church that continues to maintain certain symbolic (and sometimes even political) privileges as the once "official religion" of Latin American societies is maintained.

Much of the existing religious diversity is expressed in such examples as the devotion to the Virgin of Guadalupe; Umbanda, Candomblé, Santería, and Spiritism; "Pare de Sufrir"; televangelism; "Prosperity Theology"; Pentecostalism; and Father Rossi, Mother Angelica, and the popular "saints"[21]—Sarita Colonia (Peru), Romualdito (Chile), María Lionza (Venezuela), and the Difunta Correa (Argentina), to mention some of the most famous. Some of these religious manifestations come under the umbrella of a Catholicism that is nominally "Roman Catholic" but is often referred to as "Popular Catholicism," while others are clear expressions of new religious movements or cults. Many of them are—in the minds of the faithful—just different ways of constructing or reconstructing their own self-styled religious meaning. Higher levels of formal education do not threaten these types of cults, but education is transforming the ways in which meaning is produced: the faithful reconstruct (and reform) in their own minds and in their own way the official and conventional meaning these realities have had for institutional churches or cults or for the traditional popular worldview. Younger believers are distancing themselves from long-established official or popular beliefs and rituals and creating new types of syncretic beliefs in a style that combines many symbolic elements from different traditions. Indeed, the symbolic goods offered by consumer society are more diverse and alluring than ever before. However, diversity has always been part of the spiritual landscape, and people have always built their personal religious convictions and beliefs in the intimacy of their hearts, with creativity and the symbolic raw materials (codes, traditions, patterns, signs, and languages) they find close at hand: "What is different today is that the traditional Christian churches have lost the power to impose their 'orthodoxy' and to suppress those 'heterodoxies' of people" (D. Smith 2001).

The impact produced by the plurality of religious choices as well as changes in religious mentality does not necessarily point to certain political views or involvements. We must remember that the field of religion has a much more complex and indirect (certainly not direct or casual) relationship with the field of politics. Therefore, it follows that we cannot deduce a direct increase in political pluralism from the increase in religious pluralism. Rather, we need to examine each national case in order to determine the relationship between religion and politics. Although general cultural tendencies may impact religious change across national borders, when we speak of politics we must take into consideration the changing conditions of specific conjunctural and institutional dynamics in each country (see Hagopian, chap. 1 in this volume).

The capacity of the Catholic Church to influence politics depends on many factors, including the church's relationship with the state, its own institutional strength, and its relationship with civil society. In democratic contexts pluralist religious options have different forms of expression, which diminish the impact of moral and social messages of the hierarchy, who are constrained by that plural base. The church can participate in public debates but will not always have a decisive influence in political decisions and outputs—even vis-à-vis Catholic politicians. The capacity for mobilizing civil society will depend on grassroots organization generated in parishes, base communities, lay movements, and other initiatives inspired by Christianity, but it will be more likely motivated by secular social and political interests inspired by moral doctrine rather than by direct religious expression of beliefs, rituals, and faith.

The reality is that these societies are now dealing with a weaker Catholic Church in cultural and political terms. This fact will certainly shape twenty-first-century societies. The Catholic Church, which provided stability and social cohesion in the context of the political cycles of instability in the twentieth century, may not be able to perform this role in the future as it did in the past. This transformation of the Latin American religious scene— that is, the declining influence of Catholicism and the increase of religious pluralism—is a challenge for sociologists and political scientists inasmuch as they have to analyze and evaluate these changes in terms of the costs and benefits for the development of democracy (McCarthy 1993). Growing religious pluralism could be a sign of democracy's advance, but only to the extent that different religious currents promote an ecumenical attitude of tolerance—including tolerance for heterodoxies—and so long as they do not fall captive to fundamentalist perspectives.

Notes

This chapter is a revised and updated version of a paper presented at the conference Contemporary Catholicism, Religious Pluralism, and Democracy in Latin America: Challenges, Responses, and Impact held at the Kellogg Institute for International Studies, University of Notre Dame, March 31–April 1, 2005. The author uses empirical data from previous research he has conducted in Chile, especially the FONDECYT No. 104261 Research Project, "Scientific and Political Collective Representations of University Students in Chile," conducted from 2004 to 2006, in which the author was the principal investigator.

1. For the historical context see Dussel (1972, 1985) and Prien (1985).

2. Latin America as a region cannot be historically considered fully "Catholic" because a mixture of religious beliefs and practices coexisted, among them Catholic, indigenous, Afroamerican, and even an Old World popular religion that the Tridentine reformers wished to abolish. Nonetheless, the Catholic Church from the Conquest on was dominant and exercised a Catholic hegemony over culture and civic and political life. The church's authority and orthodoxy was often challenged, and popular religion was always dynamic and syncretizing with native and African religions. Nonetheless, the church at no time was confronted by the scope and nature of challenges that have arisen from the new religiously pluralist panorama.

3. "Superstition" and "neopagan" are charged concepts used by churches to denigrate or disqualify these religious expressions.

4. Many authors have analyzed the historical confrontation of the Catholic Church and authoritarian regimes in Latin America; Christianity and revolutionary movements; and liberation theology, the church, and politics from the 1960s to the 1990s. Among them see Klaiber (1999); Mignone (1999); Sigmund (1999);

Pierucci and Prandi (1996); Sonería (1996); Oxhorn (1995); Romero (1989); Maduro (1987); Mainwaring (1986); De Roux (1983); Muratorio (1982); Richard and Meléndez (1982); IEPALA (1982); Levine (1981a, 1981b); Lalive (1975); and Landsberger (1970).

5. In this chapter I use "religious field" as developed in the theory of sociologist Pierre Bourdieu (1971). The religious field is a complex phenomenon: it refers to the set of religious actors (priests, religious, lay people, magicians, etc., as well as institutions) that interact in a dynamic and competitive division of religious labor for the social production of religious meaning.

6. About the growth of Pentecostals and other religions in Latin America, see Sanpedro (1986); Lagos (1987); Martínez (1989); Martin (1990); Stoll (1990); Canales, Palma, and Villela (1991); Cleary and Stewart-Gambino (1992); Marostica (1994); Mariz (1995); B. Gutiérrez (1995); T. Gutiérrez (1996); Freston (1994, 1998); Oro (1999); Carozzi (1999); Frigerio (1999); Masferrer (2000); Barrera (2001); Mafra (2001); and Guerreiro (2003).

7. The five surveys are Popular Religion Survey, 1998 (Parker 1999); Secondary Students Survey, 1999 (Parker 2000); University Sample Survey, 2002 (Parker, Peña, and Barría 2002); Metropolitan Region Survey, 2004 (Parker and Peña 2005; religious data available from author); and National University Students Survey, 2005 (Parker 2007).

8. For our quota sample of secondary students, we looked for a comparative database with a high expression of religious diversity within schools and *municipalidades* (counties) from the Metropolitan Region and Concepción. In this sample 60 percent of the students identify themselves as Catholic. According to the National Youth Survey of 1997 (INJUV 1999), among those that completed secondary education, 70.9 percent were Catholic, 19.2 percent evangelical, 6 percent "no religion," and 3. 4 percent "other religion."

9. This cross-tabulation is statistically significant: Pears = 0.0084, p = 0.013.

10. The Metropolitan Region refers to the city of Santiago and all its municipalities, a total of 6,038,947 inhabitants (INE 2003). The religious affiliation data comes from people 15 years old or older.

11. Lyceum are Chilean public secondary schools in the European tradition developed in the nineteenth century. Currently the lyceum—public high schools— are totally subsidized by the state and run by the local town governments (municipalities). Many of them are attended by the lower classes, but a few are excellent elite public high schools attended by upper-middle-class or upper-class students.

12. In Spanish, *instituciones confesionales* refer to schools (or universities) that are run by a religious institution and that follow a religious orientation and philosophy (Catholic, Protestant, or evangelical vs. lay or public).

13. See G. Rama (1994); Braslavsky (1995); Puiggrós (1999); Rodríguez Gómez (2001); Álvarez Gallego (2001); Arellano Marín (2002); Ricci (2003); CTERA et al. (2005).

14. The secondary school gross enrollment ratio (GER) is the total secondary school enrollment (both sexes), regardless of age, expressed as a percentage of the secondary school–age population. GER values can be over 100 percent due to the inclusion of overage and underage students in enrollment statistics. Ratios of 100 percent or more indicate that a country is, in principle, able to accommodate all of its school-age population (that is, it has a high educational capacity). When net (age-based) enrollment data are not available, GER data can be used as a substitute indicator to express general levels of participation in education. The difference between GER and net enrollment values estimates the extent of overage and underage enrollment.

GER is calculated by dividing the number of students enrolled in secondary education, regardless of age, by the total population of secondary school–age students. This ratio is multiplied by 100 to produce the final percentage. Population data used in calculations are obtained from different national or international databases, many from the United Nations Population Division or UNESCO.

15. *Government-dependent* private institutions—as opposed to independent private institutions—are subsidized by the state and must follow special government regulations.

16. In Latin America Masonry has been an important secret society that has influenced elites throughout the history of the republics. Adhering to an anti-Catholic ideology, it has been open to liberal (even radical) and anticlerical political options.

17. The Chilean case is not necessarily representative of the rest of Latin America today; Chile is more modernized and its educational reforms, including the expansion of private education, have gone farther. Yet it is plausible to imagine that other Latin American countries will converge on this structural model once educational reform and modernization advance, especially since the weight of the evidence suggests that these reforms and processes will follow broadly similar patterns.

18. These concepts are associated with the important principles coming out of the World Conference on Education for All, Meeting Basic Learning Needs, held in Jontiem, Thailand, in 1990. Its main resolutions were a statement on the inherent right of all children to a full cycle of primary education; commitment to a child-centered concept of education in which individual differences are accepted as a source of diversity and a challenge rather than a problem; improvement in the quality of primary education, including improvements in professional training and the provision of more flexible schooling with respect to organization, process, and content; greater parental and community participation in education;

recognition of the wide diversity of needs and patterns of primary school children's development, necessitating a wider and more flexible range of responses; and commitment to a developmental, intersectoral, and holistic approach to education and care of primary school children.

19. There is a positive difference of 9 and 8 points, respectively, and the correlation (Pearson's $r = 0.078$) is statistically significant at the 0.05 level ($p = 0.013$).

20. In 1918 a group of students at the Universidad de Córdoba, in northern Argentina, launched a movement that would have vast consequences for universities across the entire continent. In addition to societal democratization, the student movement advocated for the secularization and democratization of universities, which up to that point had been very elitist and traditional.

21. These were ordinary people with extraordinary life stories and often with tragic fates, in whom other people see signs of a miraculous intervention by God. After death they have been "canonized" by popular faith (although regarded with mistrust by the Catholic Church) and have been turned into massive objects of popular devotion in their respective countries.

References

Álvarez Gallego, Alejandro. 2001. "Del Estado docente a la sociedad educadora: ¿un cambio de época?" *Revista Iberoamericana de Educación* 26 (May–August). Available at http://www.rieoei.org/rie26f.htm.

Arellano Marín, José Pablo. 2002. "Competitividad internacional y educación en los países de América Latina y el Caribe." *Revista Iberoamericana de Educación* 30 (September–December). Available at http://www.campus-oei.org/revista/rie30f.htm.

Balardini, Sergio. 2000. *La Participación Social y Política de los Jóvenes en el Horizonte del Nuevo Siglo*. Buenos Aires: Grupo de Trabajo Juventud, CLACSO, ASDI.

Barrera, Paulo. 2001. *Tradição, Transmissão e Emoção religiosa. Sociología do protestantismo contemporáneo na América Latina*. Sao Paulo: Ed. Olho d'Agua.

Berger, Peter L., and Thomas Luckmann. 1966. *The Social Construction of Reality: A Treatise in the Sociology of Knowledge*. Garden City, NY: Anchor Books.

Bourdieu, Pierre. 1971. "Genèse et structure du champ religieux." *Revue Française de Sociologie* 12: 295–334.

Braslavsky, Cecilia. 1995. "La Educación Secundaria en el contexto de los cambios en los sistemas educativos latinoamericanos." *Revista Iberoamericana de Educación* 9 (September–December). Available at http://www.rieoei.org/oeivirt/rie09.htm.

Burbano López, Galo. 1999. "La educación superior en la segunda mitad del siglo XX. Los alcances del cambio en América Latina y el Caribe." *Revista Iberoamericana de Educación* 21 (September–December). Available at http://www.campus-oei.org/revista/rie21.htm.

Canales, Manuel, Samuel Palma, and Hugo Villela. 1991. *En Tierra Extraña*. Santiago: Ed. Amerinda, Sepade.

Carozzi, María Julia, ed. 1999. *A Nova Era no MERCOSUL*. Petrópolis, Brazil: Vozes.

———. 2000. *Nueva Era y Terapias Alternativas*. Buenos Aires: Ed. de la Universidad Católica Argentina.

Castells, Manuel. 1999. *El Poder de la Identidad*. Vol. 2 of *La Era de la Información: Economía, Sociedad, Cultura*. Mexico City: Ed Siglo XXI.

Cleary, Edward L., and Hannah W. Stewart-Gambino, eds. 1992. *Power, Politics, and Pentecostals in Latin America*. Boulder, CO: Westview Press.

CTERA, CNTE, Colegio de Profesores, AFUTU-FENAPES, and LPP. 2005. *Las Reformas Educativas en los países del Cono Sur: Un balance crítico*. Buenos Aires: Ed. CLACSO.

Davie, Grace. 2004. "New Approaches in the Sociology of Religion: A Western Perspective." *Social Compass* 51, no. 1: 73–84.

Debray, Régis. 1996. *El Arcaísmo Postmoderno*. Buenos Aires: Manantial.

De Roux, Rodolfo. 1983. *Una Iglesia en estado de alerta. Funciones sociales y funcionamiento del catolicismo colombiano: 1930–1980*. Bogotá: Servicio Colombiano de Comunicación Social.

Dussel, Enrique. 1972. *Historia de la Iglesia en América Latina*. Barcelona: Ed. Nova Terra.

———. 1985. *Historia General de la Iglesia en América Latina*. Salamanca: Sígueme.

ECLAC (CEPAL). 1999. *Panorama Social de América Latina*. Santiago de Chile: Cepal.

Freston, Paul. 1994. "Popular Protestants in Brazilian Politics: A Novel Turn in Sect-State Relations." *Social Compass* 41, no. 4: 537–70.

———. 1998. "Pentecostalism in Latin America: Characteristics and Controversies." *Social Compass* 45, no. 3: 335–58.

Frigerio, Alejandro. 1999. "El Futuro de las Religiones Mágicas en Latinoamérica." *Revista Ciencias Sociales y Religión* 1, no. 1: 51–88.

González, Pablo. 2002. *Elementos de la regulación de la actividad privada en educación*. Santiago: Programa de Promoción de la Reforma Educativa en América Latina y el Caribe (PREAL).

Guerreiro, Silas. 2003. *A magia existe?* São Paulo: Paulus.

Gutiérrez, Benjamin F., ed. 1995. *En la fuerza del Espíritu. Los pentecostales en América Latina: un desafío a las iglesias históricas*. Guatemala City: AIPRAL/CELEP, FCE.

Gutiérrez, Tomás, ed. 1996. *Protestantismo y Política en América Latina y el Caribe.* Lima: CEHILA.

Inglehart, Ronald, and Wayne E. Baker. 2000. "Modernization, Cultural Change, and the Persistence of Traditional Values." *American Sociological Review* 65 (February): 19–51.

Instituto de Estudios Políticos para América Latina y África (IEPALA). 1982. *Las relaciones entre cristianismo y revolución.* Madrid: IEPALA.

Instituto Nacional de Estadísticas (INE). 2003. *Censo, 2002: Sintesis de Resultados.* Santiago: Instituto Nacional de Estadísticas.

Instituto Nacional de la Juventud (INJUV). 1999. *Segunda encuesta nacional de Juventud. Los jóvenes de los noventa: el rostro de los nuevos ciudadanos.* Santiago: INJUV.

———. 2001. *Tercera Encuesta Nacional de Juventud.* Santiago: INJUV.

———. 2004. *Resultados Preliminares Cuarta Encuesta Nacional de Juventud 2003.* Santiago: INJUV.

Klaiber, Jeffrey, S. J. 1999. "Peru: Evangelization and Religious Freedom." In Paul E. Sigmund, ed., *Religious Freedom and Evangelization in Latin America: The Challenge of Religious Pluralism,* 253–68. Maryknoll, NY: Orbis.

Lagos, Humberto. 1987. *Las Sectas religiosas en Chile.* Santiago: Lar, Presor.

Lalive d'Epinay, Christian. 1975. *Religion, dynamique sociale et dependence.* Paris: Mouton.

Lamanna, Gabriel. 2003. "La juventud argentina y la participación política." *Cambio Cultural, Colaboraciones* (October). Accessed November 3, 2004, from http://www.cambiocultural.com.ar/investigacion/jovenes.htm.

Lambert, Yves. 2003. "Young People Confound the European Religious Exception." Paper presented at the twenty-seventh annual conference of the International Society of Sociology of Religion, Turin, July 21–25.

Landsberger, Henry, ed. 1970. *The Church and Social Change in Latin America.* Notre Dame, IN: University of Notre Dame Press.

Lehmann, Carla. 2001. "Chile: ¿Un País Católico?" *Puntos de Referencia* 249. Available at http://www.cepchile.cl/dms/lang_1/cat_752_pag_1.html.

———. 2002. "¿Cuán Religiosos Somos Los Chilenos? Mapa de Religiosidad en 31 Países." *Estudios Públicos* 85: 21–40.

Levine, Daniel H. 1981a. *Religion and Politics in Latin America: The Catholic Church in Venezuela and Colombia.* Princeton, NJ: Princeton University Press.

———. 1981b. "Religion, Society, and Politics: State of the Art." *Latin American Research Review* 16, no. 3: 185–209.

Loaeza, Soledad. 2003. "The National Action Party (PAN): From the Fringes of the Political System to the Heart of Change." In Scott Mainwaring and Timothy R. Scully, eds., *Christian Democracy in Latin America: Electoral Competition and Regime Conflicts,* 196–246. Stanford: Stanford University Press.

Maduro, Otto. 1987. "La démocratie chrétienne et l'option de libération des opprimés dans le catholicisme latino-américain." *Concilium* 213: 111–25.

Mafra, Clara. 2001. *Os evangélicos.* Rio de Janeiro: Zahar.

Mainwaring, Scott. 1986. *The Catholic Church and Politics in Brazil, 1916–1985.* Stanford, CA: Stanford University Press.

Mariz, Cecilia. 1995. "El Debate en Torno del Pentecostalismo Autónomo en Brasil." *Sociedad y Religión* 13: 21–32.

Marostica, Matt. 1994. "La Iglesia Evangélica en la Argentina como Nuevo Movimiento Social." *Sociedad y Religión* 12: 3–16.

Martin, David. 1978. *A General Theory of Secularization.* Oxford: Blackwell.

———. 1990. *Tongues of Fire: The Explosion of Protestantism in Latin America.* Oxford: Blackwell.

Martínez, Avelino. 1989. *Las Sectas en Nicaragua.* San José, Costa Rica: DEI.

Masferrer Kan, Elio, ed. 2000. *Sectas o Iglesias, Viejas y Nuevas Religiones.* Mexico City: ALER.

McCarthy, John. 1993. "Religion, Democratization, and Market Transition." Paper presented at workshop sponsored by the NSF Sociology Program, December 6–7.

MERCOSUR. 2004. "Indicadores Estadísticos del Sistema Educativo del Mercosur 2004." Available at http://www.sic.inep.gov.br/index.php?option=com_content&task=blogcategory&id=21&Itemid=39&lang=br.

Mignone, Emilio F. 1999. *Iglesia y Dictadura.* Buenos Aires: Universidad Nacional de Quilmas.

Muñoz Izquierdo, Carlos, and Alejandro Márquez Jiménez. 2000. "Indicadores del desarrollo educativo en América Latina y de su impacto en los niveles de vida de la población." *Revista electrónica de investigación educativa* 2, no. 2. Available at http://redie.uabc.mx/vol2no2/contenido-munoz.html.

Muratorio, Blanca. 1982. *Etnicidad, evangelización y protestas en el Ecuador.* Quito: CIESE.

Oro, Ari Pedro. 1999. *Axé MERCOSUL, as religiões afro-brasileiras nos paises do prata.* Petrópolis, Brazil: Vozes.

Oxhorn, Philip D. 1995. *Organizing Civil Society: The Popular Sectors and the Struggle for Democracy in Chile.* University Park: Pennsylvania State University Press.

Pace, Enzo. 1997. "Religião e Globalização." In Ari Pedro Oro and Carlos Alberto Steil, eds., *Globalização e Religião,* 25–42. Petrópolis, Brazil: Vozes.

Parker Gumucio, Cristián. 1996a. *Las Iglesias y su Acción Social en Chile.* Santiago: Ed. UNICEF-Academia.

———. 1996b. *Popular Religion and Modernization in Latin America.* Maryknoll, NY: Orbis.

———. 1998. "Les transformations du champ religieux en Amérique Latine, Introduction." *Social Compass* 45, no. 3: 323–33.

———. 1999. "Chile: Identity and Diversity in Urban Popular Catholicism." In Thomas Bamat and Jean Paul Wiest, eds., *Popular Catholicism in a World Church,* 19–55. Maryknoll, NY: Orbis.

———. 2000. *Los jóvenes chilenos: cambios culturales; perspectivas para el siglo XXI.* Santiago: Mideplan, UEP.

———. 2003. "Abstencionismo, Juventud y Política en Chile actual." *Revista Interactiva* 2, no. 4. Available at http://web.usach.cl/revistaidea/html/revista%204/portada.htm.

———. 2005. "Is Latin America No Longer Catholic? Increasing Cultural and Religious Pluralism." *América Latina Hoy* 41 (December): 35–56.

———. 2007. "Universitarios, Ciencia Tecnología y Conciencia." Informe Final, Proyecto FONDECYT No. 1040261. Unpublished paper. Santiago: Instituto de Estudios Avanzados, Universidad de Santiago de Chile.

Parker, Cristián, and Luis Peña. 2005. "Aceptación en la Población de la Región Metropolitana de medidas alternativas a la reclusión." In *Segundo Simposio Nacional de Investigación sobre Violencia y Delincuencia,* 247–68. Santiago: Fundación Paz Ciudadana and Instituto de Sociología Universidad Católica de Chile.

Parker, Cristián, Luis Peña, and Rodolfo Barría. 2002. "Perfil de los estudiantes de la Universidad de Santiago de Chile y sus valores." Unpublished paper. Santiago: Instituto de Estudios Avanzados, Universidad de Santiago de Chile.

Pecora, Vincent P. 2003. "Religion and Modernity in Current Debate." *Journal for Cultural and Religious Theory* 4, no. 2 (April). Available at http://www.jcrt.org/archives/04.2/pecora.shtml.

Pierucci, Antônio Flavio, and Reginaldo Prandi, eds. 1996. *A realidade social das religiões no Brasil: religião, sociedade e política.* São Paulo: Hucitec.

Prien, Hans Jurgen. 1985. *La historia del cristianismo en América Latina.* Salamanca: Sígueme.

Puiggrós, Adriana. 1999. "Educación y sociedad en América Latina de fin de siglo: del liberalismo al neoliberalismo pedagógico." *Educación y Política en América Latina* 10, no. 1. Available at http://www.tau.ac.il/eial/X_1/puiggros.html.

Rama, Claudio. 2002. "Latin America and the Caribbean's University Massification and Professional Emigration in the Knowledge-Intensive Society: A Few Unanswered Questions." Paper prepared for the International Institute for Higher Education in Latin America and the Caribbean (IESALC/UNESCO). Available at http://www.sela.org/public_html/AA2K2/eng/docs/Coop/migra/spsmirdi15-02/spsmirdi15-02.htm.

Rama, Germán W. 1994. "Educación y cambios en la estructura social en América Latina." *Boletín* 35 (December). Available at http://unesdoc.unesco.org/images/0009/000998/099895s.pdf#99896.

Ricci, Rudá. 2003. "Vinte anos de reformas educacionais." *Revista Iberoamericana de Educación* 31. Available at http://www.campus-oei.org/revista/rie31f.htm.

Richard, Pablo, and Guillermo Meléndez, eds. 1982. *La Iglesia de los pobres en América Central.* San José, Costa Rica: DEI.

Rodríguez Gómez, Roberto. 2001. "Educación, desarrollo y democracia en América Latina." *Perfiles Educativos* 23, no. 94: 6–42. Available at http://www.cesu.unam.mx/iresie/revistas/perfiles/perfiles/94/a01.pdf.

Romero, Catalina. 1989. "The Peruvian Church: Change and Continuity." In Scott Mainwaring and Alexander Wilde, eds., *The Progressive Church in Latin America*, 253–75. Notre Dame, IN: University of Notre Dame Press.

Sanpedro, Francisco. 1986. *Ante las principales sectas o nuevos movimientos religiosos.* Valparaíso, Chile: UCV.

Sigmund, Paul E., ed. 1999. *Religious Freedom and Evangelization in Latin America.* Maryknoll, NY: Orbis.

Smith, Brian. 1982. *The Church and Politics in Chile.* Princeton, NJ: Princeton University Press.

Smith, Dennis A. 2001. "Religion and the Electronic Media in Latin America: A Review." Paper presented at the 2001 meeting of the Latin American Studies Association, Washington, DC, September 6–8.

Sonería, Abelardo Jorge. 1996. "Iglesia Estado y Sociedad en la Argentina: Desde la caída del peronismo hasta la caída del peronismo (1955–1976)." In Abelardo Sonería, ed., *Sociología de la Religión*, 167–83. Buenos Aires: Docencia.

Stoll, David. 1990. *Is Latin America Turning Protestant?* Berkeley: University of California Press.

Tavares Gomes, Fatima Regina. 2000. "O circuito 'Nova Era': Heterogeneidade, Fronteiras e Resignificacoes locais." Paper presented in the colloquium X Jornadas sobre Alternativas Religiosas en América Latina, Universidad de Buenos Aires, Buenos Aires.

Torres, Carlos Alberto, and Daniel Schugurensky. 2004. "The Political Economy of Higher Education in the Era of Neoliberal Globalization: Latin America in Comparative Perspective." In Maria J. Cannino and Silvio Torres-Saillant, eds., *The Challenges of Public Higher Education in the Hispanic Caribbean*, 21–45. Princeton, NJ: Markus Wiener.

Trombetta, Pino Lucá. 2003. "Sincretismo e mercato religioso." *Rivista di scienze sociali della religione* 18: 81–102.

Tünnermann, Carlos. 1997. "La educación superior en América Latina y el Caribe en su contexto económico, político y social." In *Hacia una nueva educación superior.* Caracas: Ediciones CRESALC/UNESCO.

UIS-OECD. 2005. *World Education Indicators.* Available at http://www.uis.unesco.org/ev.php?URL_ID=5263&URL_DO=DO_TOPIC&URL_SECTION=201.

UNESCO. 2005. *EFA Global Monitoring Report 2005*. Available at http://portal. unesco.org/education/en/ev.php-URL_ID=35939&URL_DO=DO_ TOPIC&URL_SECTION=201.html.

UNESCO Institute for Statistics (UIS). 2005. Available at http://stats.uis.unesco .org.

Van Hove, Hildegard. 1999. "New Age: A Debate, Introduction." *Social Compass* 46, no. 2: 115–19.

Weber, Max. 1958. *The Protestant Ethic and the Spirit of Capitalism*. Trans. Talcott Parsons. New York: Charles Scribner.

———. 1963. *The Sociology of Religion*. Trans. Ephraim Fischott. Boston: Beacon.

PART II

Church Responses to Democratic and Religious Pluralism

With or Without the People

The Catholic Church and Land-Related Conflicts in Brazil and Chile

PATRICIA M. RODRIGUEZ

Land is more than land . . . it is soil and symbol. It is, without doubt, the piece of terrain necessary for the subsistence of the family, but it is also the Promised Land, whose conquest only occurs in unity, in organization, in the confrontation against the owners who support themselves through public institutions.

—*Dom Tomás Balduino, founder and president of the Brazilian Pastoral Land Commission*

Land redistribution has been one of the most well-known and controversial popular causes embraced by the progressive wing within the Catholic Church in several Latin American countries since the 1950s.[1] Although struggles over land concentration and rural poverty were muffled by co-optive or repressive state policies during authoritarian periods in many countries of the region, the Catholic Church continued to provide crucial—and sometimes the only—material, legal, and spiritual support to poor rural populations throughout the years. Upon the return to democratic rule in the 1980s and 1990s, the relationship between peasants and the church began to be transformed as poor and indigenous peasants organized more autonomously and less restrictedly. Democracy has opened opportunities for peasant and indigenous groups to seek alliances and receive support from sources other than the church, including political parties, unions, and other nongovernmental organizations (NGOs). Democratic rule has also curbed the possibility of repressive responses from the state, thus enabling more radical activism by peasant groups eager to implement new agrarian policies.

These new political possibilities have not sidelined the church from its central role in agrarian issues, but they have transformed the playing field. As rural grassroots movements intensify their economic, social, and political demands, the stakes for continued church support have increased. To endorse popular land-related demands means to take a position that places the church in the middle of an intense crossfire between powerful elite groups and vociferous popular movements. Rural social movements represent a very dynamic sector of civil society—poor and indigenous peasants—and the church seeks to maintain links of faith to these groups in particular. Therefore, the church increasingly finds itself forced to confront the distinct internal and external challenges that arise as a result of its continued presence in the agrarian policy debate. But how exactly does the Catholic Church position itself in this public realm? What determines whether the church will support the claims of popular movements, and, if it does side with these movements, what kind of support it can offer?

In line with this volume's theme of the embeddedness of the church within its popular bases, this chapter examines the links between the Catholic Church and groups in civil society that act in defense of social justice and equality in Brazil and Chile. While conducting field research on the issue of the political and mobilization strategies of land-related movements in both countries, the differences in the involvement of church actors in each case struck me as worthy of a more in-depth look and interpretation. The distinct church approaches to land-based movements in these two countries are illustrative of the possibilities and limitations of the connections between religion, civil society, and democratic politics; they also speak to the manner with which—and reasons for which—the hierarchy can mobilize for the people, as well as learn from them. Since 1975 an arm of the Brazilian Catholic Church, the Pastoral Land Commission (Comissão Pastoral da Terra, or CPT) has been at the forefront of efforts to implement agrarian reform and curb rural violence. Church activism intensified through the close ties built between progressive priests and the thousands of peasants that form the Brazilian Landless Workers Movement (Movimento dos Trabalhadores Rurais Sem Terra, or MST). Although these ties receded as the MST sought autonomy, the CPT has continued to play a critical role in raising government, church, and public awareness of the land issue. In a similar fashion, Mapuche indigenous organizations in Chile have sought out progressive bishops as allies in the dialogue with the state, beginning in the 1970s, regarding the devolution of ancestral land and constitutional recognition. In this case, however, both the church and Mapuche organizations have taken a much more cautious approach to their process of approximation. In fact, only in 2003 did a handful of local bishops step up efforts to strengthen the relationship between the church and Mapuche communities.

How can we explain the different trajectories in the involvement of the Brazilian and Chilean churches with land-related problems? In this chapter I argue that the explanation lies in the structure of the Brazilian and Chilean church pastoral agencies and their ability to influence the institutional church to prioritize the land-related concerns of rural grassroots groups. While the CPT has established a well-organized and autonomous advocacy structure through which to help rural landless communities and has received the backing of the National Conference of Brazilian Bishops (Conferência Nacional dos Bispos do Brasil, or CNBB), the Chilean church has been sporadic in its institutional and practical efforts to provide support for the demands of Mapuche organizations. It is imperative, therefore, to look *within* the church in order to better understand the church's public stand in each case. Following a brief discussion of the role and significance of church pastoral work, I examine the relation between church pastoral work and the early land struggles in Brazil and Chile. I then turn to the efforts of pastoral agents and bishops to sustain church activism in the tense atmosphere of the 1990s and beyond in both countries, highlighting the transformations in the relationship between religious and civil society actors. In the final section, I turn to an analysis of specific factors that help explain the divergence in religious response to land conflicts in both countries and discuss implications of this work for the church's grassroots strategies into the near future.

Pastoral Action and Church Reaction

The presence of priests in poor urban and rural communities throughout the region has been relatively constant since the late 1960s as a result of the Vatican's emphasis on the "preferential option for the poor." Priests' ties to grassroots groups have taken different forms and have allowed for different degrees of lay leadership and participation. Besides the ecclesial base communities (comunidades eclesiais de base, or CEBs) and their focus on religious discussions in community settings, pastoral agencies have commonly been established by various national Catholic churches as a way to deal with problematic issues affecting society or groups within society in a more focused way. This is illustrated by the names of such commissions, including the Worker's Pastoral, Land Pastoral, Indigenous Pastoral, Children's Pastoral, and so forth. Their basic functions are to provide legal defense of human rights, promote informational and skills training campaigns, and assist in mobilizing particularly marginalized sectors of the population. Perhaps more than any other institution, the church worries about land conflicts, human rights, and a series of other social maladies. As such, pastoral agencies play a critical role in delineating the relationship between the grassroots and the hierarchical church in each country since they represent the main venues through which the concerns of the grassroots reach the top-ranking officials of the church (that is, from the bottom up).

On the other hand, pastorals are a part of the national church's strategy to retain its links with constituents, and thus they are a critical element within the church's mission and vision of faith (Mainwaring 1986; Mainwaring and Levine 1989). Although clergy, religious pastoral agents, and lay religious leaders are generally responsible for the day-to-day activities of the church pastorals, they are under the formal control of the institutional church. The endorsement (or lack thereof) by the institutional church of the social justice activities of these pastorals (that is, from the top down) has been noted as a critical variable that defines the connections between the Catholic Church and its popular organizations. Accordingly, recent scholarly work has focused primarily on the limits imposed by the institutional church on the political activism of church pastorals. In the case of Brazil, the effort of pastoral agents to maintain nonconflictive relationships with the institutional church has been an important factor in the consolidation of a progressive Catholic Church. In other countries, most notably Argentina, the more politicized stance of progressive pastoral agents alienated the institutional church in the 1980s (Mainwaring 1986).

But how do the church's bottom-up efforts impact its top-down concerns, and vice versa? In order to answer this question we need to better understand the reciprocal relationship between the church, its pastorals, and grassroots movements; to do so, it is worth examining the work and influence of pastorals in practice. Do they, or can they, play a role in responding to the problems and demands of grassroots organizations? In what ways can they do so, and how do they operate? Are they able to construct a bridge between the church and its base, or do the political limitations imposed by the hierarchy inhibit pastorals from significantly influencing that relationship? As noted above, under democratic rule grassroots groups have had greater access to allies other than religious organizations. A continued role for religious organizations depends on the willingness of the pastoral agents and grassroots groups to maintain ties, even if they are ties of a different sort than those that existed under authoritarian rule. The dynamism of the pastoral work among grassroots groups plays an important role. I argue that two key elements of this dynamism are (1) the degree of autonomy that pastoral agents have to make decisions and take action on behalf of grassroots groups, and (2) the degree of influence that pastoral agents can exert upon the Catholic Church as an institution. Dynamic pastoral action can bring grassroots groups and the church together, while more constrained pastoral efforts are not likely to generate the same bonds. Before any further discussion of this proposition, I trace the insertion of the church and its pastorals into land-related debates in Brazil and Chile in the past and present.

The Seeds of Land Activism in the Catholic Church

A Grassroots Effort to Bring the Church into Action: The Brazilian Pastoral Land Commission

In Brazil, after decades of social unrest caused by unrestrained land concentration in the hands of a few owners, land reform was a hot political topic leading up to the 1964 military coup d'état.[2] With a few exceptions, the Brazilian Catholic Church had sided with traditional landowning families in offering conservative solutions to rural poverty.[3] Yet, military interference and growing social pressures in rural areas gradually influenced the church to become more closely involved.

For their part, the military government was eager to deter both the growth of organized rural unions and the influence of landlords in government decisions, and with this in mind it enacted the Land Statute in 1964. This statute provided a framework by which unproductive land could be redistributed pending generous compensation by the government. The government's commitment to the land reform program was questionable, however, as it placed great emphasis on the modernization of agricultural production for export purposes and on the colonization of the Amazon Basin. Packaged in the form of a national security project aimed at establishing a definitive claim over the Amazon region, the government's land program sought to provide a peaceful solution to rural social conflict, particularly in the Northeast Region (Fernandes 1999; Alston, Libecap, and Mueller 1999). The mechanisms that enabled expropriations were created but used only sporadically to halt violent land conflicts (Fernandes 1999, 33). Meanwhile, peasants confronted many difficulties in the new territory, including the bureaucratic process of receiving official titles to lands, the unsustainable nature of slash and burn techniques, and harsh climatic and living conditions.

As the problem of land concentration failed to improve, a few church leaders began voicing concern about the half-hearted implementation of the Land Statute and the dire living conditions of laborers, small owners, *posseiros* (peasants who cultivate land without possessing title to the land), and indigenous groups in the Amazon and elsewhere. In 1973 the CNBB produced a series of documents that denounced the neglect and abandonment of rural workers in the Northeast and Center-West Regions, as well as the usurpation of indigenous territory in the Amazon (Poletto and Canuto 2002). This effort by church leaders culminated in a national pastoral meeting to discuss the problems in the Amazon in June 1975. One of the results of this meeting was the creation of a CNBB-linked Pastoral Land Commission (CPT) that would have the mission of providing logistic, material, and spiritual support for peasants caught in land disputes.[4]

In the eyes of the progressive bishops and clergy who had close contact with peasants, it was critical to establish the CPT with CNBB backing. Many members of the clergy felt that their pastoral efforts among the peasants would be imbued with greater legitimacy if they carried the stamp of the institutional church (Poletto and Canuto 2002). Due to its links with the CNBB, for instance, the CPT was for the most part able to organize even in dioceses where bishops were not supportive of its work. Nevertheless, CPT leaders were also mindful of the weight of this stamp of approval and careful not to relinquish too much freedom of action. The creation of a pastoral agency with a certain degree of autonomy from the institutional church structure was perceived by several progressive priests as a chance to "change the form of action, [making the CNBB] less centralized" (Poletto and Canuto 2002, 22).

The proposal for the creation of the CPT sent shockwaves among the conservative bishops, many of whom argued that it was intolerable that the Catholic Church should betray the landowners. Some called for military action against some progressive figures in the church, while others urged an alternative solution that would emphasize the need for peasants to cooperate with President Ernesto Geisel in settling agrarian conflicts (Poletto and Canuto 2002). Yet, the creation of the CPT and other pastoral agencies was seen by other members of the hierarchy as a way to strengthen the church's roots in society, particularly in response to the break in the church's traditional alliance with the state and elite sectors of society in the post-1964 period (Hewitt 1990; Mainwaring 1986). Nevertheless, the CNBB repeatedly emphasized the importance of vesting the CPT with a nonpolitical character, rejecting in particular direct participation of priests and ecclesial agents in the organizing of people into political associations (Mainwaring 1986).

Both the CPT's links to CNBB bishops and the extensive networks constructed by CPT agents and staff among grassroots groups help explain the influence it has acquired in the agrarian public sphere. The work of documenting land conflicts and providing legal assistance and material and spiritual support for poor peasants in their struggle to obtain land established a solid foundation for the CPT's presence in rural society during the years from 1970 to 1985. Although there were several instances of CPT involvement in land-related struggles during this period, the events that took place in Ronda Alta in the southern state of Rio Grande do Sul illustrate the crossroads facing the priests and hierarchy of the Catholic Church as they became involved in the peasants' struggle for land.[5]

The Conflict in Ronda Alta

Since the 1950s the southern region of the country had been the scene of land conflicts. Although attempts at expropriation of large estates had been made in the early 1960s, the efforts were interrupted by the 1964 coup. By the late 1970s, however, hundreds of impoverished, landless peasant families had taken matters into their own hands and settled on lands that officially belonged to the Kaingang Indians. While several families finally accepted the government's offer of land in the Amazon or elsewhere, hundreds of others insisted in pressing the government for settlements in the abandoned lands in the north-central region of Rio Grande do Sul.[6] They took matters into their own hands by occupying unproductive portions of public and private lands and then planting crops. Although some land occupations involved the formation of small encampments alongside public roads, several other settlements were established inside fenced (but idle) lands. These tactics angered landowners and generated tense confrontations, but they also served to call the attention of federal and state government officials to the landless problem.

Armed with words of encouragement and strong bonds with the peasant population (built largely during the process of formation of CEBs in the 1970s), a handful of local parish priests and friars with links to the CPT supported the peasants in their plight. In the initial phase of their relations with landless groups, these priests provided food and clothing donations. As the conflict intensified, the Catholic Church began providing trucks for the transportation of agricultural products to markets, at times even distributing church-owned land to the most needy (Carter 2002; Burdick 2004). Additionally, a network of lawyers and sympathizers was established to help explain the peasants' rights to them, to provide resources to organize peasant meetings at CPT headquarters, and to organize pilgrimages that called public attention to the land problem and the living and working conditions of the landless (Burdick 2004).

Perhaps most importantly, the presence of progressive priests in the occupied encampments provided the spiritual support that peasants needed to understand their struggle and its consequences for their families. Burdick (2004) and Carter (2002) recount the critical role that Father Arnildo Frietzen of Ronda Alta played in inspiring peasants by connecting the stories from the book of Exodus to their daily struggles.[7] The material and symbolic meanings associated with land in the Bible ignited powerful interpretations among the peasants, with land occupations being perceived not solely as a duty protected by law but as a "defense of a 'divine gift'" (Burdick 2004, 113). The *caminhada* (or journey) to obtain land stands at the root of the priests' commitment and connection to the peasants.

By the early 1980s the clergy's involvement in the landless struggle had moved beyond a support role and toward an emphasis on mediating the dialogue between grassroots leaders and the state. This intermediation was at first dispersed, as different wings of the church offered various solutions to impasses. In the Ronda Alta conflict specifically, several conservative bishops urged movement leaders to accept the offers of settlement on the Amazon frontier (Carter 2002). However, the members of the clergy who were most involved with the landless suggested that they maintain their struggle in Ronda Alta. One of the most influential CPT figures and head of the diocese of São Felix do Araguaia in the Amazon region, Dom Pedro Casaldáliga, offered peasants an illuminating, firsthand account of the hardships of life on the frontier during a June 1981 visit to the Ronda Alta encampment. The numerous priests, nuns, and lay workers that lived in encampments with the peasants called for increased support by the church hierarchy, regardless of the personal sacrifices that it entailed (Carter 2002).

As landless workers and the state remained steadfast in their strategies, the church publicly denounced the violent actions of landowners and the state against the landless. In one of the church's strongest endorsements of CPT work, in 1980 the CNBB approved a CPT-drafted document in which the church critiqued the state's endorsement of land accumulation for business instead of living and working purposes (Mainwaring 1986; Chaves 2000). Moreover, several bishops in conflict-ridden areas stood by the CPT in denouncing the increasing violence by landowners and police forces against peasants and priests.[8]

In 1981, at the height of repression by the National Intelligence Service (Serviço Nacional de Informações, or SNI) in areas of rural conflict, the military commander Coronel Curió, who had been issued orders to disperse the Ronda Alta encampments at any cost, requested the intervention of the moderately conservative bishop Dom Sinesio Bohn (Carter 2002).[9] Although many bishops from Rio Grande do Sul had been actively critical of CPT activities, their intervention in favor of the landless was inevitable once it became clear that it was a matter of life and death (Carter 2002). Thirteen state bishops (including the conservative archbishop of Porto Alegre, Dom Vicente Scherer, whose support was deemed indispensable by Coronel Curió himself) drafted a letter to government officials in Brasília requesting a peaceful solution to the conflict. In a bold move, they also issued a public statement calling for an intensification of land reform in Rio Grande do Sul.[10]

In the Ronda Alta large-scale violence was avoided largely due to the unlikely support that a group of conservative southern bishops offered to the peasants and progressive priests (Carter 2002). In 1982 the church organized a fundraiser and subsequently purchased several hectares of land for the settlement of several families near the encampment. In 1983 the government agreed to settle the remaining families on nearly two thousand acres of land in the Ronda Alta region. The participation of several previously reticent CNBB bishops in the negotiations was crucial in persuading all sides to find a solution to the impasse at Ronda Alta. The surprising actions of the CNBB and its southern bishops marked the church's commitment to the defense of social justice, land reform, and human rights issues. As we will see below, such a commitment was also forthcoming from a few Chilean bishops, particularly during the most difficult years of the military dictatorship.

Mapuche Lands in Contention: 1880–1980s

The Mapuche—"people of the land"—live predominantly in the southern region of Chile and are historically known for fiercely resisting conquest by Inca, Spanish, and Chilean military forces until late in the nineteenth century.[11] When the Chilean military finally subdued them in 1881 in a bloody civil war known as the Pacification of the Araucanía, Mapuche territory was reduced to a mere three thousand reservations, which represented less than one-tenth of their original territory.[12] These reservations were placed under the control of the state, which assigned to Christian missionaries the task of evangelizing, educating, and integrating the indigenous population into Chilean society (Degarrod 1998). Much of the reservation territory was further divided and distributed to the nonindigenous population by successive governments in the first half of the twentieth century.

By 1966 nearly three-fifths of Mapuche families lived on poor-quality lands of less than ten hectares, while many others had migrated to urban centers in search of jobs (Saavedra 2002). In 1967 President Frei Montalva announced a land reform that reignited the hope of thousands of Mapuche families that their usurped lands would be restored to them. The church, in the figure of Cardinal Raúl Silva Henriquez, became intensively involved in the land reform program, even to the point of distributing church-owned land to indigenous groups and peasants (Aguilar 2004). However, the program designed by the government was not easy to implement in the Araucanía, since much of the ancestral land was in the hands of small and medium landholders who held legal titles and had kept the lands productive throughout the years (Mallon 2004).[13] Although by 1971 nearly 70,000 hectares of usurped lands had been restored to indigenous ownership, the largest portion could not be legally expropriated by the state. As a result, the land reform process began to take a violent turn that entailed dangerous land occupations (or *tomas*) and armed resistance by landowners. In all, thousands of Mapuche families were able to recuperate at least part of the ancestral land that had been taken by the Chilean state throughout the years. By 1968 the majority of the nearly 3,100 Mapuche communities owned their lands collectively, as they had historically (Sznajder 2003). In the early 1970s agricultural cooperatives thrived and strengthened bonds of solidarity and a sense of pride and optimism among indigenous families (Mallon 2004, 121).

With the military coup d'etat of 1973, the experimentation with Mapuche land devolution came to an abrupt end. In 1979 the government issued Decree 2.568, which ended the communal indigenous land program and effectively placed all lands in private hands. Thousands of Mapuche communities were subdivided into individual plots distributed to people from inside and outside the communities. Indigenous families received no more than six hectares of land each, although this land could not be considered communal (Aylwin 2004). Additionally, the individuals or families that had migrated to urban centers were not included in the final division of land, thus generating tension within families as well as within communities. The military government sold much of the most fertile indigenous lands to forestry companies that would help stimulate its market-oriented economic and developmental policies. In a few years the emphasis on profits from the lumber industry damaged the ecosystem and greatly diminished the quality of land in the Araucanía (Maggio 2007).[14]

The military counter-reform was accompanied by human rights violations; somewhere between 120 and 300 Mapuche leaders were executed or disappeared and several hundred more were imprisoned and tortured, particularly in the early years of the Augusto Pinochet dictatorship (Saavedra 2002, 192). The Catholic Church, particularly through the actions of several bishops from the southern region, began playing a critical role in pressing the government for the release of indigenous leaders and demonstrating solidarity with the prisoners.[15] Furthermore, the church organized popular kitchens that became the sole source of subsistence for indigenous families in many communities (Mallon 2004). The reliance of Mapuche groups on the church in the initial years of the dictatorship is attested to by the Mapuche leaders' constant requests for assistance from the bishop of Temuco, Sergio Contreras. In a letter published in the *Diario Austral* in August 1978, they ask Bishop Contreras to speak on their behalf to convince the government of the need to include indigenous groups in the design of the impending land decree of 1979. The letter highlights the uncertainty and helplessness of the indigenous population in its final claim: "our future as a race is at stake" (Mallon 2004, 168).

The intervention of the Catholic bishops in May 1979 through a pastoral letter calling for the recognition of Mapuche land use rights did not deter the passage of the 1979 land decree.[16] Nevertheless, in the 1980s the Catholic Church, through the actions of several of its southern bishops, played a central role in stimulating cooperative efforts to alleviate poverty and marginalization among indigenous communities. One example is the creation of training initiatives in agricultural and fishing techniques in collaboration with nongovernmental organizations such as the Council of Fishery and Peasantry Development (Consejo de Desarrollo Pesquero Campesino, or CODEPECA) (Mallon 2004). Besides promoting technical workshops, the church constantly intermediated in conflicts between indigenous and nonindigenous peasant groups that had been relocated to the Araucanía in the aftermath of Decree 2.568 (Mallon 2004). The bishop of Temuco also provided support for the creation of Mapuche Cultural Centers of Chile in 1978 and was responsible for restructuring the Indigenous Institute Foundation (Fundación Instituto Indígena) in 1979 toward a primary focus on legal advice and support for rural development projects of Mapuche communities, in place of the evangelizing focus that the Maryknoll priests had given it at its creation in 1962. As centers of discussion of Mapuche cultural, socioeconomic, and political issues, these nonprofit agencies contributed to the reemergence of Mapuche organizations later in the 1980s.

The reemergence of social movements on the political scene of the mid-to-late 1980s in Brazil and Chile contributed to a shift in the relationships between the state and civil society organizations, including the Catholic Church. On the one hand, the democratic governments initiated land redistribution policies in response to popular mobilization. Yet, as these policies fell short of the expectations of grassroots groups, the church strove to find a balance between heeding the calls of pastoral and grassroots organizations for more progressive land policies and endorsing the *government-controlled* efforts to distribute land.

Toward New Relationships in the 1990s: Land Struggles and the Role of the Church

Maintaining a Pastoral Presence Amidst the Land Debate in Brazil

Relations between the church and landless grassroots groups changed considerably during the democratic transition years in Brazil in the mid-1980s. Landless groups quickly gained strength throughout the nation, and by 1984 thousands of peasants decided to form the MST during the First National Encounter of Landless Rural Workers in Paraná. Under the slogan of "Land for Those Who Work It," the MST established itself as an autonomous organization, free from formal links to other religious or political organizations. The decision was embraced by the CPT, particularly because CPT leaders emphasized a "commitment to respect and support the lead role of peasants in their position as subjects, authors and receivers of their own history" (Balduino, qtd. in Poletto and Canuto 2002, 38). This solidified a relationship of respect and consultation between the CPT and the MST. No longer wanted in the role of organizing peasant encampments, the CPT turned to the surprisingly necessary role of monitoring and calling attention to the human rights situation of rural peasants in democratic times.

By 1985 the MST changed its campaign slogan and actions to reflect a more confrontational position that promoted land occupations as the only solution to the landless problems. Although the new democratic government devised a National Program for Agrarian Reform (Programa Nacional de Reforma Agrária, or PNRA) that promised to implement expropriations that would benefit seven million landless rural workers in a span of fifteen years, the MST leadership rejected the effort because it was reminiscent of past failed attempts at reforms and unclear as to what lands could be expropriated (Medeiros 2002).[17] Instead, the MST intensified land occupations nationwide to keep the pressure on the government to implement land reform. In the face of the efforts of the government and the MST to implement one or another version of land reform, the landowners, mostly through their organization, the Ruralist Democratic Union (União Democrática Ruralista, or UDR), organized violent raids on landless camps and ignited serious confrontations. Table 5.1 depicts the intensity of land conflicts in Brazil for the 1990–2003 period.

As conflicts intensified, particularly in the Northeast Region where the UDR maintained a strong presence, the CPT grew concerned. Early efforts by the CPT to organize rural workers in the northeast centered on peaceful demands for better wages and the provision of services such as training in machinery and crop marketing (Harnecker 2002; Branford and Rocha 2002). In 1989 progressive priests with CPT ties worried that the strategy of intensifying land occupations was "insensitive to the people making the occupations" (Burdick 2004, 105). In one emblematic MST occupation in the state of Paraíba, several adults were beaten and one child died during a 1988 confrontation. The CPT had opposed this occupation due to the possibility of violence (Branford and Rocha 2002, 45).

As the Cardoso government stepped up the land redistribution efforts, the MST and other rural organizations continued to press for a more speedy

Table 5.1. Land Conflicts in Brazil, 1990–2003

Year	Number of Conflicts	Number of Workers Killed in Confrontations	Number of People Involved in Conflicts
1990	401	75	191,550
1991	383	49	242,196
1992	361	35	154,223
1993	361	42	252,236
1994	379	36	237,501
1995	440	39	381,086
1996	653	46	481,490
1997	658	29	477,105
1998	751	38	662,590
1999	870	27	536,220
2000	556	20	439,805
2001	681	29	419,165
2002	743	43	425,780
2003	659	73	1,127,205

Source: CPT (1990–2003).

resolution to land impasses. In great part through the strong organizational efforts of the MST at both the national and local levels (as well as several other smaller but well-organized peasant organizations), thousands of families began to receive titles to the unproductive lands that they had occupied. Issues of infrastructure, credit, and education still remained unresolved, however, and thousands of other families were encouraged by the success of the land-claiming process in some regions. Although the CPT frequently disagreed with the radical methods used by MST leaders, there was rarely any public criticism.

Throughout the 1990s the CPT continued to be supportive of the efforts of rural organizations, although now in a manner that focused primarily on the protection of the human rights of rural workers. With rural peasants more self-organized than ever before, the CPT recreated itself by turning to two roles that fit the organization perfectly: documenting and denouncing the thousands of cases of mistreatment, beatings, and assassinations of rural workers by police and landowners, and assisting other groups that had not been able to organize as the landless had, such as rubber tappers, coconut gatherers, and former slave communities (*quilombos*). By focusing on these marginalized groups and compiling rural violence statistics, the CPT renewed its sense of purpose. With regional headquarters spread throughout twenty-two Brazilian states, the CPT established links with a network of individuals and organizations (lawyers, NGOs, international governmental organizations) that provided up-to-date information about rural conflicts and assistance to rural workers. Throughout the years, the CPT has compiled an annual list of rural conflicts that includes information about the number, location, and reasons for the conflicts and about killings and death threats received by rural workers. CPT regional staff members have played a key role in gathering this information from interviews, newspaper searches, and personal experiences in rural locations.

As confirmed in numerous interviews with landless leaders and workers in several regions of Brazil, the CPT has been the first (and at times sole) organization to which workers can turn to denounce an injustice. For instance, in the state of Paraná, where violent conflicts are common, the CPT has been at the forefront of denunciations of police brutality in the dispersion of landless activists. In 1999 the CPT accused the police of torturing six leaders of the MST and demanded the release of more than twenty MST activists who had been detained following a police raid on one encampment. In May 2001 CPT-Paraná played a key role in bringing together a group of politicians, church leaders, scholars, and representatives of international organizations to discuss human rights violations in that state at the Informal Tribunal of Rural Crimes and Government Human Rights Violations. Throughout the country, the CPT regional headquarters have taken similar actions, attesting to the key role that the CPT has played in defending the legal rights of peasants.

For its part, the church as an institution has been steadily supportive of the CPT and its work. As in the 1980s, the severity of the conflicts pitting rural workers against landowners and the state has much to do with the increased involvement of the CNBB hierarchy in pressing the government for a solution to rural violence. Public statements from top members of the CNBB hierarchy certainly give the CPT grassroots efforts greater legitimacy. Following the massacre of nine *posseiros* in Corumbiara, Rondônia, in 1995, the CNBB protested and issued a statement demanding an acceleration of the government's land reform program as a way to curb tensions.

Similarly, following the massacre of nineteen landless workers by police forces in Eldorado dos Carajás in Pará in April 1996, the CNBB criticized the government for not adequately addressing the land concentration problem and for authorizing the use of police force. A year later, during the massive MST-sponsored National March for Agrarian Reform, Employment, and Justice that took thousands of landless activists and sympathizers from around the nation to the capital city of Brasília, the pastoral representative from the CNBB, Dom Demétrio Valentini, lashed out at the Cardoso government's efforts to initiate a popular forum for discussion of agrarian reform that would exclude MST leaders and activists (Chaves 2000, 274).

Criticism of governmental policies continued in later years. Through its yearly sponsorship of the *Grito dos Excluídos* (literally, "shout of the excluded") national marches since 1997, the CNBB highlights the perverse effects of the neoliberal economic policies of the government, including the neglect of rural peasants and communities.[18] In May 2000 the new president of the CNBB, Dom Jayme Chemello, affirmed that the country would not achieve full democracy or growth if it did not realize comprehensive agrarian reform. The attention given by the CPT and CNBB to the issue of rural violence intensified during the first administration of Luiz Inácio "Lula" da Silva, particularly as it failed to live up to its promise of settling 400,000 landless families in 2003–2004.[19] This lack of action on the part of the Lula government led to increased restlessness on the part of landless workers, and in April 2004 the MST initiated a series of waves of occupations throughout the nation that marked the institutional break between the MST and the government. Rural violence in the 1990s did not spare church members and CPT activists. After the violent killings in 2005 of an American missionary, nun Dorothy Stang, and other land activists in Pará, Dom Tomás Balduino harshly criticized the government for ignoring CPT reports of death threats and for failing to punish the perpetrators of crimes against peasants (Teixeira and Correia 2005).

As it pressures the government, however, the CNBB has been careful not to endorse the radicalism of the landless groups' occupation strategy. In several instances the president of the CNBB, Dom Lucas Moreira Neves, condemned land occupations as a source of tension and as a nonlegitimate way to pressure the government. Additionally, some of the most conservative bishops have maintained their opposition to CPT and MST activism in their dioceses. For instance, the CPT had great difficulty in organizing in the city of Presidente Prudente, in the heart of one of the most conflict-ridden regions of São Paulo state, as a result of the hostility of the local bishop. The CPT was only able to install a headquarters in that region in 2002 when the bishop presented his resignation at age seventy-five. The new bishop, Dom José Liborio, was more supportive of the landless and publicly affirmed that "God gives land to all people, not just the landowners."[20]

Other diocesan bishops have demonstrated concern with the actions of the CPT, but their objections have not impeded CPT activism. In recent years the regional representation of the CPT in the Northeast has stepped up its opposition to the bureaucratic nature of the government's land reform by organizing and leading land occupations itself. In 2003, after the government ordered the eviction of three hundred families from a CPT-led encampment in the state of Pernambuco, CPT leaders mounted a radical campaign to halt the eviction. After burning several tractors during the attempted eviction, the landless quickly reconstructed the encampment. The CPT then organized a protest in Brasília and demanded a judicially mandated inspection by the National Institute of Colonization and Agrarian Reform (Instituto Nacional de Colonização e Reforma Agrária, or INCRA) before an eviction was ordered. On another occasion, in Alagoas, the CPT protested the delays in government food assistance to several encampments by supporting supermarket raids by landless workers. Although this CPT activism in the Northeast may be exceptional, one CPT staff member noted that due to the circumstances in the region (that is, the violence and influence of landowners in politics) such radicalism was considered the only solution to the local landless problem.[21] In addition, another pastoral organization, the Rural Pastoral, had organized land occupations in several states in the region until 1988, when it was disbanded by the bishop of Recife, Dom José Sobrinho, who had succeeded the progressive bishop Dom Helder Câmara in 1985. Several of the pastoral agents from the Pastoral Rural then joined the Northeastern CPT, where they continued direct participation in land occupations, although not without the criticism of CPT activists in other regions.[22]

Although its concerted focus on human rights issues in rural areas has not eradicated violence, the CPT has undoubtedly succeeded in influencing the church to take a position in favor of land reform and peasant issues despite some reticence with respect to occupations. Progressive clergy and CPT activists constantly invoke the church to participate in a more effective manner, such that the "social, ethical and political influence of the episcopate [can be] felt concretely in such a way as to favor those devoted to the cause and force authorities to legislate and administer in favor of the majority of the population" (Poletto 2003, 342). Although the institutional church has at times criticized the methods used by the MST, it has not ignored the work of the CPT, one of its most recognized pastorals. While the CPT could easily have lost its direction once politicians and social movements began the real process of land redistribution, its ability to adapt to changes and still maintain ties to the peasant population remains one of its most remarkable features. As we will see below, the Chilean Indigenous Pastoral Commission played a more distant role in land conflicts in the 1990s, despite the efforts of some local bishops.

Mapuche-Chilean State Conflicts in the 1990s and the Role of the Church

Struggling against further land usurpations by the Chilean state during the Pinochet dictatorship, Mapuche groups were politically active throughout the 1980s. By 1988, at the height of the mobilization by opposition forces against the dictatorship, they were voicing Mapuche demands for land at a national level. The center-left opposition coalition, the Concertación, took note of indigenous demands in its election platform. The signing of the Nueva Imperial Pact in 1989 by Concertación presidential candidate Patricio Aylwin promised new attention to indigenous issues, particularly land claims and constitutional recognition as "peoples." In exchange, several indigenous organizations joined the Concertación in an effort to increase indigenous participation in the election and in favor of the democratic transition.[23] In 1990 newly elected president Patricio Aylwin created the Special Commission for Indigenous Peoples (Comisión Especial para los Pueblos Indígenas, or CEPI) to stimulate discussion of indigenous policy initiatives among indigenous communities. With extensive participation by indigenous organizations, the negotiations over the mechanisms through which usurped lands would be returned to indigenous hands culminated in the proposal for a Land Fund (*Fondo de Tierras*) that would be dedicated to the buying of lands by the government for transfer to indigenous groups. This Land Fund was to be administered by the National Corporation for Indigenous Development (Corporación Nacional de Desarrollo Indígena, or CONADI), an institution conceived to encourage indigenous participation in promoting the development and cultures of the indigenous peoples of Chile. In an effort to engender closer ties between Chilean society and its indigenous groups, CONADI's council would be composed of equal numbers of indigenous and government representatives.

CONADI and its Land Fund generated great expectations for improved relations between the state and indigenous groups, but several issues contributed to the gradual dissipation of those expectations even before its creation in 1993. In 1991, before the approval of Law 19.253—which was known as the Indigenous Law and that created CONADI and the Land Fund—the Supreme Court ruled in favor of expelling several indigenous families that had lived in the southern city of Quinquén. A forestry company, Sociedad Galletué—which had already received a multimillion-dollar indemnity approved by the military government as compensation for the suspension of logging activities in the Quinquén region—claimed to hold title to the lands occupied by the indigenous families. Although these titles were of dubious origin, the Supreme Court's decision generated an intense conflict that was resolved with a government award to the forestry company in the amount of six million dollars in 1992 (Bengoa 2002).

Moreover, despite the government's espoused commitment to solve indigenous claims, several of the promises made by the new government in 1989 had been nullified by the mid-1990s. The political power of landowners and forestry and hydroelectric companies (and their megaprojects) in Chile ensured a slow and expensive process of finding solutions to land claims. This difficulty was compounded by the demand by various Mapuche organizations for political and territorial autonomy, which to a large part of the Chilean political elite represented a direct challenge to the unity of the Chilean nation (Gundermann, Foerster, and Vergara 2003). As it turned out, the constitutional recognition of indigenous peoples and the establishment of procedures for consultation of indigenous communities in development projects were taken out of the final draft of Law 19.253 in a last-minute maneuver by several right-wing senators (Sznajder 2003; Bengoa 2002).[24]

Without a solid legal foundation for effective participation by indigenous leaders, CONADI began to lose legitimacy as a venue for the resolution of land conflicts. By 1998 two consecutive indigenous national directors of CONADI (Mauricio Huenchulaf and Domingo Namancura) had voiced strong opposition to plans for the construction of the Ralco hydroelectric dam in indigenous territory and the relocation of hundreds of families to other (less fertile) regions of the country. As a result, the government asked for their resignation and the dam project was approved. This led to an intensification of conflict between indigenous groups and the Ralco Hydroelectric Company. Although a majority of families accepted the compensation offered by Ralco, a handful of families still resisted and gained the support of indigenous groups that favored more radical activities such as land occupations, destruction of tractors, fires, and other violent activities. By 1999 land being worked by several forestry companies had been occupied in an effort to call the government's attention to land claims. Several of these occupations led to deadly conflicts in which the police justified the use of force and imprisonments under the antiterrorist Law of National Security (Bengoa 2002). In this tense atmosphere CONADI came under fire from indigenous groups for its inability to bring all players to the negotiating table and to offer legal assistance to indigenous groups.

As the Mapuche conflict spiraled out of control, it fell to the Catholic Church's National Indigenous Pastoral Commission—which was created in 1991 to disseminate and implement a pastoral plan of action with respect to the indigenous population—to play a mediating role, although one that was not devoid of controversy. In search of allies in the tense dialogue with the government, Mapuche leaders staged several occupations of cathedrals in Temuco and Santiago beginning in the early 1990s. The protestors made specific requests of Catholic bishops linked to the Indigenous Pastoral Commission to intercede in the release of indigenous leaders imprisoned for taking part in occupations and to solicit the government's attention toward indigenous land and legal rights. The protestors called upon the bishops to heed Pope John Paul II's words when he announced that ethnic minorities "should continue their fight for a fair distribution of land."[25] Although church occupations were usually peaceful and relatively small, the immediate response of the bishops was defensive. In one instance, Bishop Contreras of Temuco criticized the occupation of his cathedral as a "profound lack of respect [because] if anyone has raised the authentic cause of the Mapuche people, even when no one else dared say anything about the issue, it has been the Catholic Church."[26]

Notwithstanding this position, the bishop interceded to mediate the release of indigenous prisoners in this and other instances. Several of the bishops of the southern regions also declared national prayer days or released pastoral letters that called attention to the demands of the indigenous population. With the intensification of conflict in 1997, the Indigenous Pastoral Commission began assuming a larger role in advocating for the rights of indigenous peoples, particularly by highlighting the dire living conditions of the majority of the Mapuche population. Several bishops asserted that the poor quality of the soil and lack of employment in rural indigenous communities only contributed to their increasing economic and cultural marginalization, which ultimately resulted in the radicalization of conflict areas. In 1998 a southern bishop, Don Sixto Parzinger, called attention to the deteriorating conditions of Mapuche communities that eked out a living on minuscule plots of land.[27] Several bishops called for the government to adopt a real commitment to land reform and the devolution of territory to indigenous owners. These declarations were made at the same time that the Vatican spoke out in support of land reform in a January 1998 document entitled *For a Better Distribution of Land: The Challenge of Agrarian Reform* (Pontificio Consejo de Justicia y Paz 1998).

Largely through the efforts of the southern bishops, the Chilean Church has maintained its support for the Mapuche cause. In May 1999 the Chilean Episcopal Conference (Conferencia Episcopal de Chile, or CECH) issued a statement highlighting the deep significance of land in the lives of the Mapuche people and urging the government to come to a solution to the conflicts between indigenous groups and forestry and Ralco officials (CECH 1999). Moreover, in November 2000 the church acknowledged its own omissions with respect to the indigenous peoples of Chile and asked for forgiveness for the sins committed by Catholic Chileans throughout history as part of a "Liturgy for the Purification of Memory." Among the nine sins mentioned in the liturgy were the lack of respect for Mapuche cultural and religious traditions and the unjustifiable silence of baptized Catholics in the face of the injustices and evictions committed in the late nineteenth and early twentieth centuries.[28]

Such a declaration by the national church might be interpreted as an important endorsement of the indigenous cause. Indeed, the liturgy generated immediate reactions from within the hierarchy of the church. The archbishop of Santiago, Francisco Javier Errázuriz, warned that such a statement should not imply any acknowledgment that the Catholic Church itself had historically mistreated the Mapuche people.[29] This statement represented, at minimum, the cautious approach of the church toward the potentially explosive issue of the Mapuche conflict, on which there was a sharp difference of opinion among the church hierarchy.

Some Mapuche organizations have also expressed concern about the liturgy. One of the most radical groups, Meli Wixan Mapu, voiced its outrage in a letter made public shortly after the declarations of church representatives:

> We repudiate the new attempt by the Catholic Church to establish a biased and false version of the historic truth, in its recognition of certain "sins of omission" . . . This attempt to distort reality achieves two basic objectives: to establish a historic truth that hides the genocidal character of the conquest and creation of the Chilean state, making some believe that the relationship between Chilean society and the Church with the Mapuche nations is one of equality and harmony, thus not acknowledging its racist and oppressive character; and to create the social and cultural conditions for a greater impulse to the new process of evangelization, a process that in practice is racist and oppressive since it considers our people as an object of evangelization, and does not recognize our own Mapuche philosophy and religion.[30]

The letter also calls for the Catholic church to assume direct responsibility for the sins committed during the conquest and formation of the Chilean state. Meli Wixan Mapu represents only one of the several Mapuche organizations that have sprouted up throughout southern Chile, but this sentiment is certainly shared among other groups. In April 1999, for example, the Coordinadora Mapuche (Mapuche Coordination) interrupted an Easter homily by the archbishop of Santiago, Javier Errázuriz, to protest the church's silence concerning the violent confrontation between police forces and indigenous representatives in southern Chile.[31] In another instance, the indigenous community of Juan Currín pursued legal action against Temuco's Bishop Contreras (as a representative of the Catholic Church) and the municipality of Temuco for the seizure of Mapuche lands.[32]

Notwithstanding this criticism from within and outside the church, southern bishops have continued their advocacy for the Mapuche. Although it has been hard to unify the church behind an official position, the southern bishops have brought the institutional church into the public discussion of the Mapuche conflict. Several bishops have individually issued statements calling attention to the urgent need for Chilean society as a whole to come to terms with the historical antecedents of the Mapuche conflict and to adopt a new posture of respect toward the Mapuche population. Moreover, in September 2001 a committee of eleven southern bishops met to discuss a project that would call upon society to bring dignity to the Mapuche people. In that forum the bishops praised the efforts of politicians to open channels of dialogue with Mapuches through the creation of the Historical Truth and New Treatment Commission headed by former president Patricio Aylwin.[33] For two years the southern bishops continued their discussions, which culminated in the publication in January 2003 of the working document "Toward a New Treatment of the Mapuche People" (National Indigenous Pastoral Commission 2003). The bishops explicitly requested that the state recognize the historical usurpation of indigenous territory by the Chilean state during the pacification of the Araucania.[34] This would be, as the bishops announced, the initial step toward the achievement of social justice for indigenous peoples.[35]

Besides explicitly stating that the Indigenous Law has not effectively protected the rights of indigenous Chileans, the working document prepared by the bishops highlighted the cultural and religious traditions of the Mapuche and challenged the church to develop the "inculturated evangelization" that was called for in the 1992 Latin American Bishops' Assembly in Santo Domingo, Dominican Republic. According to the document, pastoral efforts with indigenous populations should be constructed in "dialogue with the culture of each people, [thus] strengthening its value and denouncing the powers of sin and injustice that threaten [them]" (National Indigenous Pastoral Commission 2003). Although the document calls for the support of the entire church in the struggle for the recovery of seized lands, the eradication of unjust poverty, and the creation of greater opportunities for education and training, its main purpose, according to Bishop Contreras, was to generate discussions within the church (particularly in ecclesial base communities, parishes, and church-sponsored movements) about how best to go about constructing an evangelizing strategy that would incorporate native religious and cultural values.[36] In an effort to strengthen their pastoral effort, the southern bishops created the Indigenous Pastoral Commission of Southern Chile in March 2003, with the very specific mission of bringing the church closer to the Mapuche population by promoting a new understanding of Mapuche culture. Notwithstanding its lofty goals, the creation and mission of the Indigenous Pastoral Commission exposed the difficulties that the Chilean church has had in consolidating its presence among the indigenous population. A significant part of this difficulty derives from the manner in which the indigenous pastorals have been organized in Chile, particularly their subordination to the Permanent Commission of the CECH. Sympathetic southern bishops have had to balance their pro-indigenous actions with their larger role within the Chilean church as an institution.

The Structure and Impact of Pastorals

Pastoral agents have been present in the lives of peasants and indigenous groups in both Chile and Brazil during dictatorial and democratic times. During the authoritarian years, the Chilean and Brazilian churches each opposed government repression of rural and indigenous peasants. But since the transitions to democracy in each country, the church's pastoral responses to pressure from governments and grassroots groups have varied. The work of pastoral agents has been greatly influenced by the manner in which the pastoral agencies have been structured within the Catholic Church in each country. The most striking difference between the CPT in Brazil and the Indigenous Pastoral Commission of Chile is the degree of autonomy with which they operate and the freedom of action that this autonomy entails. Amidst a climate of intense and at times radical mobilization in the countryside, the CPT has been able to forge an identity as an organization of its own, and as such provide legitimation for its presence among the people and its influence within the church. The Chilean Indigenous Pastoral Commission, on the other hand, has not amassed the status of an independent entity, and, therefore, it holds a fragile link to the indigenous and their land-related struggles.

It is plausible to think that the different responses of these pastorals to agrarian issues has more to do with the elaborate level of organization of the landless in Brazil (particularly in the case of the MST) versus the more fragmented indigenous organizations in Chile, which impede a unified call to the Chilean pastoral. However, if that were the case, the CPT would have an organic tie to the MST. Instead, what we notice is that the CPT and the MST are distinct organizations and that the CPT has sought to carve out its own arenas of action, particularly ones where it can play a parallel, but distinctive, role: systematically documenting and denouncing rural problems and injustices. It is more likely that the possibility for a pastoral to hold this role hinges on its ability to do so, rather than on the organizational strength of the grassroots movements.

The Brazilian Experience

Although the CPT was initially cast in 1975 as an institution with close ties to the leading ecclesial authorities within the CNBB, it quickly acquired an ecumenical nature with the endorsement of the Lutheran Church. At the time, the Brazilian Lutheran Church was composed largely of subsistence farmers struggling against the encroachment of large landholdings, particularly in southern Brazil. By 1982 the Lutheran Church had embraced a campaign entitled "Land of God, Land for All," which early on helped to spread the word about the work of the CPT on agrarian issues. Most importantly, it helped to cast the CPT as an entity that was involved in the life and struggle of peasants without denominational limitations. This ecumenical focus in turn enabled the CPT to strengthen its autonomous character and, thus, to become less dependent on the Catholic Church for support. At the same time, the CPT maintained a presence in the lives of peasants in general, not just Catholic peasants.[37]

This flexibility greatly facilitated the CPT's ability to recast itself beyond its initial role of organizing and defending peasants and into a more dynamic organization that was accessible to all types of rural workers and provided assistance for different types of land-related injustices. To cite one example, the CPT recently called attention to the problem of access to water in rural areas. Although water access has been a constant problem for many years, the CPT brought this issue to light by organizing regional and national conferences as well as the CNBB Fraternity Campaign about Water in 2004. Moreover, the CPT's role in bringing attention to violations of labor and human rights of peasants throughout the nation casts it as the premier organization to which peasants can appeal for assistance, without necessarily having to hear loaded religious messages. Although the CPT has been constantly criticized by some of the most conservative bishops for acting in an exceedingly social and politicized (and, therefore, less religious) manner, the organization is also praised by other bishops for the seriousness of its efforts to defend the cause of rural workers (Poletto and Canuto 2002). Its ability to insert itself into the popular struggles on its own terms, while still being part and parcel of the conglomerate of social movements that struggle for greater social justice, attests to the potential of pastoral organizations to build strong ties to the poor.

Moreover, CPT activists undoubtedly place an important premium on their ability to make decisions and act autonomously of the church. According to one of the CPT founders, decisions are made during assemblies without interference by the CNBB.[38] One of the only moments in which the church did intervene was at the end of the 1980s, when a few conservative bishops accused the CPT of misusing international Catholic relief funds for the promotion of radical social movements.[39] In this instance, the CNBB signed an agreement with the CPT in which it was stipulated that both the president and vice-president of that organization had to be Catholic bishops. Although this decision was designed to appease the conservative bishops who wanted to exert more control over the CPT, it has arguably not produced a significant change in the way the CPT functions or in the way CPT activists perceive their autonomy.[40] For instance, when asked about the response of the institutional church to the more direct forms of action that local CPT activists in the Northeast have adopted, one CPT activist gave the following reply: "There is little that the church could or should say about it, since we have our autonomy of action. In any case, how can the church turn its back on its people? [The CNBB bishops] have to be with the people, and that is the CPT mission."[41]

Within the church, the presence of priests, nuns, and lay workers in encampments (or in the network of action created by the CPT) allows the more progressive priests to act upon their commitment to stand *with* the people, or to seek a "deep rapprochement with those perceived as victims of social injustice" (Carter 2002, 255). Yet, in the process of becoming more intensely involved in publicly denouncing the dire socioeconomic conditions of the rural poor and the violence perpetrated by landowners, the progressive clergy has also convinced the Catholic Church as an institution to do what it can to improve the plight of peasants. If the CPT had not established its systematic approach to the recording of land conflicts, it would certainly not be possible to envision the church as an institution pressing the government for more effective agrarian reform policies. The work of the CPT alongside the peasantry transformed the church and its bishops in ways that would not have been possible otherwise. The words of Dom Moacyr Grechi, the first president of the CPT, reveal the impact that the actions of the CPT had on the more moderate and conservative bishops:

> I was forced . . . to assume in a concrete manner the preferential option for the poor in the case of rubber tappers, small farmers, poor settlers . . . I was grabbed and taken (by the people from the first CPT, by many bishops, priests, religious people, union leaders, and above all by the poor) to where I did not want to go, and thought with great conviction that no bishop should ever go. In this manner, God was converting me and filling me with such profound happiness, peace, and courage that, even nowadays, surprise me. (qtd. in Poletto and Canuto 2002, 53)

Besides persuading a number of CNBB bishops to support the landless struggle, the CPT has also undoubtedly influenced the church as an institution to embrace the land cause as its own. While the CNBB voted at its Thirty-Fifth General Assembly in April 1997 to veto the idea of sending a commission of bishops to the MST's National March for Agrarian Reform in Brasília, the president of social pastorals for the CNBB, Dom Demétrio

Valentini, refused to abide by the decision and confirmed his presence and the support of the church for the MST.[42] While scolded by the CNBB for his rebelliousness, his actions contributed to bringing the church as an institution and the MST closer together. In fact, institutional backing for Dom Demétrio's position came directly from the Vatican's Pontifical Justice and Peace Council in January 1998 in the document *For a Better Distribution of Land: The Challenge of Agrarian Reform*. In this document the Vatican Council rejects the process of land concentration in developing countries and defends land occupations as a tactic to promote agrarian reform (Pontificio Consejo de Justicia y Paz 1998). Merely a year after its refusal to stand alongside the MST in its most important demonstration, at its Thirty-Sixth General Assembly in April 1998, the CNBB urged the federal government to increase its efforts to provide agrarian reform settlements with better access to health, education, and markets.[43]

The CNBB has also elevated the land cause in its campaigns. Its adoption of the theme of access to land in its annual Fraternity Campaign in 1986 was symbolic of the institutional shift toward greater acceptance of grassroots efforts to implement land redistribution. By 1997 the CNBB had taken the lead in organizing the *Grito dos Excluídos,* an annual march that occurs in several cities across the nation to protest the governments' lack of attention to social problems, including agrarian reform. In the previous two years, the *Grito dos Excluídos* had been considered an isolated initiative of a few progressive bishops. In 2004, as noted above, the CNBB's Fraternity Campaign was centered on the problem of access to water in rural areas. The CPT has helped mount nearly all of these church campaigns, which bring national and international attention to the plight of the landless.

The heightened role of the CNBB in pressing for increased governmental attention to rural violence and poverty and in mediating conflicts between the government and the landless has cast it as a significant player within the land debate. The intense criticism from the Brazilian church has certainly been noted by government officials. For instance, in a 1997 meeting with the pope, President Cardoso allegedly complained about the attitude of a few priests and bishops who were active defenders of agrarian reform in Brazil but then publicly retracted the complaint in an effort to make amends with the president of the CNBB, Dom Lucas Moreira Neves.[44] In October 2000 the CNBB announced that because of the government's intransigence, CNBB representatives were withdrawing in protest from the eight-month-long negotiations between the government and the MST regarding access to agricultural credit for 110,000 families that had already been settled on expropriated lands.[45] In 2002 the CNBB became the principal mediator in the impasse surrounding the MST occupation of lands owned by President Cardoso's relatives, after the opposition Workers' Party (Partido dos Trabalhadores, or PT) withdrew its support for the MST.[46] As these examples show, political elites in general have increasingly counted on the presence of the church as a conflict mediator. Now that the PT government of President Lula has adopted a middle-of-the-road-approach to agrarian issues (that is, land redistribution at a slow pace while also supporting agribusiness ventures), the key role of the CPT and the CNBB in activism and mediation will continue to evolve.

Just as the CPT would not be the same without its CNBB links, the CNBB would not have taken the stands it has taken with respect to agrarian reform were it not for the actions of the CPT. That the Brazilian Catholic Church speaks with one voice on the land issue certainly makes it an important actor in policy debates. Without doubt, the decision to establish the CPT in 1975 was an important step in the establishment of links between the episcopate, its pastoral agents, and peasants.

The Chilean Experience

In contrast to the bottom-up pastoral experience in the Brazilian case, the Chilean Church's efforts to support indigenous land and rights claims have been organized in a markedly top-down fashion, with bishops taking the lead in the National Indigenous Pastoral Commission and other initiatives. The bishops' efforts have focused on the implementation of educational and developmental projects within indigenous communities. Since the pastoral efforts are primarily coordinated by bishops, the CECH has a significant say in the decisions taken by the pastoral agencies. This lack of autonomous decision making has limited the freedom of action of southern bishops, particularly in matters concerning conflictive situations. The defensive reaction of Bishop Contreras to church occupations in Temuco is indicative of the fact that the bishop is first and foremost a high-ranking representative of the church as an institution. Likewise, during the tense negotiations between eight indigenous families and Ralco Hydroelectric Company in August 1998, the bishop of Los Angeles in the region of Alto Biobío stressed in an interview that his participation as a mediator in the conflict would have to be approved first by the Permanent Committee of the CECH.[47] In both of these examples, indigenous groups had to specifically request the intervention of the church—or more precisely, of the local bishop—as an ally in the land struggles with the state: this help was not automatically forthcoming. The participation of the church in land disputes has had to be approved by top church leaders, a reflection of the control exerted by the CECH on its Social Action Pastorals (to which the Indigenous Pastoral Commission is linked). In contrast to the Brazilian pastoral initiative, the Chilean case reflects a lack of accessibility by indigenous groups to a local- or regional-level church institution that is prepared to denounce violence and abuse of power by state forces or landowners.

Moreover, the church has notably refrained from publicly criticizing the state's handling of the Mapuche protests. According to one indigenous news source, there were more than seventy instances of violent conflict between indigenous groups and police forces between 1998 and 2003, and the police resorted to the use of force and imprisonments in a substantial number of these conflicts.[48] Furthermore, the state applied its antiterrorist and national security laws (dating from the Pinochet years) against thirty-one Mapuches between 2001 and 2003 (Informe del Programa de Derechos Indígenas 2003, 429). Yet, surprisingly, the church has not played the role of public advocate for the human rights of indigenous groups in Chile. Although complaints by priests have been made at the local level—as when the priest in Tirúa launched a public complaint charging the police with favoring forestry companies in that town's violent confrontations in June 2001—the Indigenous Pastoral has not pursued a concerted effort to call attention to human rights violations.

Instead, the church has preferred to highlight the historical social injustices committed against the indigenous population. In the words of Bishop Contreras, it is important for Chileans to understand the "deep roots of [Mapuche] problems, and not just the conflictive episodes of the present situation."[49] With this in mind, in 2003 the southern bishops prepared the document "Toward a New Treatment of the Mapuche People," which presents a broad overview of the historical antecedents of the current conflicts, a description of key religious and cultural aspects of Mapuche society, and suggestions for pastoral actions that the church can take in its evangelizing mission (National Indigenous Pastoral Commission 2003). Although the document contributes to a less biased understanding of Mapuche society, it bypasses the theme of violence and radicalism by indigenous groups. As Bishop Contreras has put it, "we, [southern] bishops, lament the acts of violence and do not support such acts, but we cannot reduce the Mapuche problem to certain acts of violence."[50]

Throughout the 1990s the southern bishops have undoubtedly sought to bring the Chilean hierarchy and church as a whole toward a position of understanding and advocating for the Mapuche. For instance, in July 1999 the southern bishops convened with several CECH bishops at a seminar on "Indigenous Peoples and Pastoral Action" with the explicit purpose of having CECH incorporate this theme into its Plenary Assembly in November 1999 (Fundación Instituto Indígena 2000). The southern bishops recognized that the National Indigenous Pastoral was in a weak position to confront the current challenges, in terms of both economic and human resources.[51] The creation of the Indigenous Pastoral Commission of Southern Chile reflects the desire of the southern bishops to boost the church's ability to maintain a more visible presence in regions where indigenous groups stake their claims to land and legal recognition. From its endorsement of the working document developed by the southern bishops, it appears that CECH has willingly accepted the creation of the new regional pastoral. Whether the head of the National Indigenous Pastoral, Bishop Sixto Parzinger of Villarica, and the southern bishops will be able to transcend the limitations imposed from above by CECH in their quest to reach out to the indigenous population is still questionable. The bishops' autonomy in making decisions on the ground may continue to be undercut by the church's strong declarations on the specific directions that pastoral organizations may take.

The advocacy of the bishops has certainly raised eyebrows among political elites already weary of the church's constant intervention in public policy matters such as divorce, the death penalty, and abortion. In February 1998 one senator from the Progressive Center Center Union (Unión de Centro Centro Progresista, or UCCP) publicly stated that the church should avoid the ridiculous position of entering political debates not having to do with matters of faith.[52] Yet, the participation of Bishop Contreras in the government-created Historical Truth and New Treatment Commission demonstrates that the church is seen, at least by a portion of the political elite that belongs to the Concertación coalition, as a legitimate advocate for Mapuche concerns. Nevertheless, it has been extremely difficult to enact legislation favoring indigenous rights, despite the Concertación's favorable position with respect to some of the legislative proposals. While the Concertación governments have taken important steps toward indigenous recognition—for example, the passing of the Indigenous Law of 1993—they have also taken a defensive position toward the radical activism of some Mapuche organizations, at times applying antiterrorist legislation to deal with violent episodes. Moreover, legislators from right-wing parties have repeatedly blocked legislation regarding the constitutional recognition for indigenous people and the ratification of the International Labor Organization's (ILO) Convention No. 169 concerning Indigenous and Tribal Peoples in Independent Countries.

The position of the main figures within the National Indigenous Pastoral in Chile as both national bishops and pastoral representatives has limited the pastoral's ability to reach out to its indigenous grassroots constituents in the way that the CPT has in Brazil. Mapuche leaders who want the church to intervene in land conflicts have to get the attention of the top figure in the local hierarchy in their regions, sometimes in a confrontational manner. Because the bishops of southern Chile do not have the same autonomy of action as their counterparts in the CPT, their activism has predominantly been confined to institutional channels. The Chilean clergy have at times played a distant role, acting only when called upon to do so. Nevertheless, the southern bishops have succeeded in placing indigenous matters on the agenda of the Chilean church.

Conclusion

The work of Brazilian and Chilean pastoral agents in land-related issues highlights the important presence of the Catholic Church in social justice advocacy. This work points to two different trajectories of church support for the land demands of civil society groups. The Brazilian case has shown that to side with the people—with the peasants—means almost literally becoming one with them: pastoral agents need to unite, to organize, and to confront. The autonomy with which the CPT has been able to act plays a major part in its ability to sustain the church's role in agrarian issues, even as grassroots movements transform their visions and strategies. Undoubtedly, the perseverance and adaptability with which leaders of the CPT have managed their position as mediators between grassroots movements, the hierarchy within the church, and the democratic political actors play a key role in the sustained presence of the church in rural areas. New democratic governments in the region have had to deal with the outspokenness of the church in conflictive situations and with the injustices they produce. This has sometimes exacerbated the tensions between government and religious authorities, but the relationship has for the most part remained cordial.

On the other hand, the institutional action plan that the Indigenous Pastoral has adopted in Chile makes it difficult to imagine a broad embrace by the Chilean church of the social justice efforts of its southern bishops. The symbolic steps that the Chilean church has taken in recognizing the mistreatments that indigenous groups have endured throughout Chile's history certainly represent a step toward becoming real participants in the day-to-day struggle of indigenous peasants with landlessness, poverty, marginalization, and discrimination. However, the relationship that will most likely continue to prevail is one of cautious linkages between the church and indigenous movements that take radical action in their attempt to address these problems. This relationship is in itself a victory for the bishops and clergy members that work more closely with the grassroots organizations, considering that the Chilean church has notably leaned toward conservatism in its public policy positions on moral issues such as abortion and divorce. Yet, as long as unresolved land, ethnic, and cultural issues continued to place the government, landowners, forestry companies, and indigenous groups in confrontation with one another, the members of the clergy that are closest to the indigenous cause will maintain a watchful eye.

In the democratic game of push and pull between social forces involved in land conflicts, the church as a whole certainly has the capability to be very influential. This influence is largely contingent on the dynamism of the church and its pastoral agencies at the grassroots level. Whether vested in hands-on efforts to document land conflicts or in attempts to instill institutional change within the church so as to bring it closer to the people, the spirit of grassroots connectedness inspired by liberation theology remains very much alive.

Notes

Field research for this chapter was funded by an NSF Dissertation Improvement Grant (Sociology Program).

1. All passages originally in Portuguese or Spanish quoted in this chapter, including the epigraph, have been translated into English by the author. The epigraph is from Poletto and Canuto (2002, 39).

2. Although the agrarian issue was certainly not the sole motive for military intervention, some scholars mention it as a key contributing factor. For an analysis of the pre-1964 pressures for land reform, see Martins (2000).

3. One of these solutions was the strengthening of the family unit of production in order to stem the rural exodus that was leading the rural poor into the hands of communist organizations in the cities (Martins 2000). Some of the exceptions to this type of church response included efforts to start educational and rural unionization campaigns in the Northeast Region.

4. The Indian Missionary Council (Conselho Indigenista Missionário, or CIMI), created in 1973 by the CNBB with the purpose of providing pastoral guidance and self-help assistance to Amazonian indigenous groups, offered a model for the organization of the CPT.

5. Other important conflicts involving the CPT and peasants include the conflict over the creation of the Itaipú hydroelectric dam, which displaced hundreds of families in Paraná in the late 1970s, and the confrontation with police and landowners in the Araguaia/Tocantins region in 1980. These are discussed in Souza (2001), Mazzarollo (2003), and Mainwaring (1986).

6. Interestingly, one state official who raised the peasants' awareness of the thousands of acres of uncultivated land in Rio Grande do Sul was João Pedro Stedile, who later became one of the founders and national coordinators of the Brazilian Rural Landless Movement (MST). For details, see Branford and Rocha (2002).

7. A passage of great impact in the book of Exodus consists of God's acknowledgment of the suffering of the people of Egypt and His assurance to Moses of the need for liberation. For more details on the use of religious messages, see Carter (2002).

8. Throughout the country several clergy members were kidnapped, tortured, and/or killed as a result of their alliance with peasants in the late 1970s and early 1980s.

9. Although this type of request was uncommon, especially coming from an astute and highly successful military commander like Coronel Curió, Carter (2002) suggests that the very real possibility of a massacre of hundreds of landless men, women, and children who were camped at Ronda Alta, as well as career-related interests, led Coronel Curió to issue such a request.

10. According to Carter (2002), this statement triggered an immense response from other groups and politicians who visited the encampment and urged a solution to the impasse between the landless and the state.

11. There are several indigenous groups besides the Mapuche in Chile, including the Aymara, Colla, Quechua, Rapa Nui, Yamana, and Atacameños. The Mapuche comprise the vast majority (98 percent) of the indigenous population in the country. In the 2002 census, 604,000 people were counted as Mapuche (4 percent of the national population). In this chapter I use the terms *indigenous* and *Mapuche* interchangeably since the Mapuche have been the most vociferous indigenous group in conflicts with the state and land entrepreneurs.

12. Much of the rest of the conquered territory was allocated to European settler families who were encouraged to migrate by the Chilean state.

13. Expropriations required lands to be at least eighty hectares and unproductive, and many holdings met neither threshold. Although the land reform program did reach Mapuche communities, it was taken up by the Frei and Allende governments largely as a class issue and not specifically as an ethnic or cultural issue. In 1972 an indigenous law was promulgated that limited the legal division of Mapuche lands and stimulated the economic, social, and cultural development of indigenous communities.

14. Saavedra (2002, 195) notes that the land area occupied by pine plantations was far superior to the land area destined for indigenous groups in the southern regions of Chile. When some of the land bought by forestry companies was legally returned to Mapuche families in the 1990s, most of it proved to be unusable for subsistence farming because of the techniques used by forestry companies over the span of several decades. Pine and eucalyptus plantations dry out even surrounding fields since they absorb large amounts of water and pesticides (Maggio 2007).

15. Bishop Sergio Contreras formed the Human Rights/Solidarity Committee when he took office as bishop of Temuco in 1978.

16. Cited in National Indigenous Pastoral Commission (2003). The document is titled "Evangelización del pueblo mapuche," Carta Pastoral de los Obispos de Concepción, Temuco, Los Ángeles, Araucania, Valdivia, Osorno (May 4, 1979).

17. The failure of the PNRA soon became evident, as only 6 percent of the families that the program proposed to settle by 1989 had received land. The efforts of several civil society organizations, including the MST, to implement the

program and revise constitutional stipulations regarding agrarian reform were thwarted by the conservative landowners' lobby in Congress. The Constitutional Assembly of 1988 enshrined the landowners' right to keep productive lands and was vague about how to deal with unproductive lands because it failed to provide a definition of what constituted the fulfillment of the social function of land.

18. "Igreja Católica comanda protesto," *Correio Braziliense* (Brasília), September 7, 1999.

19. By March 2004 only 14,000 families had been settled, putting the program far behind the MST targeted settlement of one million families in the 2003–2006 period.

20. "MST provoca estragos na própria imagem," *Correio Braziliense* (Brasília), March 26, 2002, 26.

21. Interview with CPT staff member, October 23, 2004.

22. Personal communication with Antonio Canuto, from the National Secretariat of the CPT in Goiânia, September 9, 2005.

23. According to Saavedra (2002), there was interest among Concertación politicians to control indigenous demands so as to avoid large-scale occupations and mobilization by indigenous groups similar to those that occurred in the early 1970s.

24. Incidentally, while the Chilean church played a consultative role within CEPI and in the delineation of the Indigenous Law, the Permanent Committee of the Chilean Episcopal Conference issued a statement in 1993 calling for the constitutional recognition of Chilean indigenous people, which in the bishops' opinion would not constitute a recognition of their right to independence or a threat to Chilean sovereignty, as some politicians argued. See CECH (1993).

25. "Mapuches ocuparon la Catedral de Temuco," *La Tercera* (Santiago), October 22, 1991.

26. "Mapuches abandonaron la Catedral de Temuco," *Diario Austral* (Temuco), July 14, 1992.

27. "Mapuches necesitan más tierras," *Diario Austral* (Temuco), February 20, 1998.

28. "Liturgia de Purificación de la Memoria," *La Tercera* (Santiago), November 25, 2000.

29. "Es mentira que la Iglesia no hizo nada por los mapuches," *Diario Austral* (Temuco), November 26, 2000.

30. "Los mapuches y el perdón de la Iglesia," *El Siglo* (Santiago), December 1, 2000.

31. "Mapuches reclamaron omisión de la Iglesia," *Diario Austral* (Temuco), April 3, 1999.

32. "Querella contra Iglesia Católica y el Estado," *Diario Austral* (Temuco), November 22, 2000. The community promised to pursue its demand at the International Court of Justice in The Hague if the national tribunals did not act.

33. "Mapuches perdieron tierras y libertad," *Diario Austral* (Temuco), September 9, 2001.

34. The bishops of Temuco, Concepción, Osorno, Valdivia, Los Ángeles, Ancud, and Aisén (as well as the Apostolic Vicariate of the Araucania) have signed this document.

35. "Obispos llaman al Estado a reconocer que usurpó tierras a mapuches," *La Tercera* (Santiago), January 22, 2003.

36. "Tenemos la obligación de fortalecer la Pastoral Indígena," *Diario Austral* (Temuco), March 26, 2003.

37. This point was brought to my attention by Antonio Canuto, one of the founders of the CPT and currently the head of the CPT executive secretariat, in a personal communication.

38. Personal communication with Antonio Canuto.

39. Ibid.

40. This may be even more true since August 1997, when Dom Tomás Balduino, bishop of Goiás Velho, was elected president of the CPT. Balduino is commonly referred to as the "red bishop" (*bispo vermelho*) due to his progressive views and early involvement in CPT conflict-mediation efforts.

41. Interview with CPT activist in Curitiba, Paraná, October 23, 2004.

42. "Bispo contraria CNBB e vem a Brasília," *Correio Braziliense* (Brasília), April 11, 1997.

43. "CNBB exige atenção para o campo," *Correio Braziliense* (Brasília), April 27, 1998.

44. "CNBB faz as pazes com o governo," *Correio Braziliense* (Brasília), February 28, 1997.

45. "Difícil reforma agraria," *Correio Braziliense* (Brasília), January 1, 2001.

46. "PT rejeita mediar negociação entre o MST e o governo," *Folha de São Paulo,* March 7, 2002.

47. "Obispo no descarta enfrentamiento en Ralco," *La Tercera* (Santiago), August 18, 1998.

48. A report published by *MapuExpress,* an online publication organized by Mapuche leaders, lists seventy-eight instances of violence by state and police officials and/or by security personnel of the lumber companies that occurred between 1998 and 2003. See http://www.mapuexpress.net.

49. Boletín Informativo, Fundación Instituto Indígena, April 2003. See http://www.institutoindigena.cl/boletin01.htm.

50. Bishop Sergio Contreras press conference, January 21, 2003. See http://www.mapuche.info/docs/ObispoTemuco030124.html.

51. "Tenemos la obligación de fortalecer la Pastoral Indígena," *Diario Austral* (Temuco), March 26, 2003.

52. "Nuncio: Es Errázuriz quien hace el soberano ridículo," *La Tercera* (Santiago), February 12, 1998.

References

Aguilar, Mario. 2004. *A Social History of the Catholic Church in Chile*. Lewiston, NY: Edwin Mellen Press.

Alston, Lee, Gary Libecap, and Bernardo Mueller. 1999. *Titles, Conflict and Land Use: The Development of Property Rights and Land Reform on the Brazilian Amazon Frontier*. Ann Arbor: University of Michigan Press.

Aylwin, José. 2004. "Los mapuche o esa parte de la realidad que no queremos ver." In Richard Vera, et al., eds., *El despertar del pueblo mapuche: nuevos conflictos, viejas demandas*. Temuco, Chile: Instituto de Estudios Indígenas/Universidad de la Frontera.

Bengoa, José. 2002. *Historia de un conflicto: el estado y los mapuches en el siglo XX*. Santiago: Editorial Planeta.

Branford, Sue, and Jan Rocha. 2002. *Cutting the Wire: The Story of the Landless Movement in Brazil*. London: Latin American Bureau.

Burdick, John. 2004. *Legacies of Liberation: The Progressive Catholic Church in Brazil*. Hampshire, UK: Ashgate.

Carter, Miguel. 2002. "Ideal Interest Mobilization: Explaining the Formation of Brazil's Landless Social Movement." Ph.D. diss., Columbia University.

Chaves, Christine Alencar. 2000. *A Marcha Nacional dos Sem-Terra: Um Estudo Sobre a Fabricação do Social*. Rio de Janeiro: Relume/Dumará.

Comissão Pastoral da Terra (CPT). 1990–2003. *Conflitos no Campo*. Goiania, Brazil: Setor de Documentação da CPT.

Conferencia Episcopal de Chile (CECH). 1993. "Por la dignidad de los pueblos indígenas." Available at http://www.iglesia.cl.

————. 1999. "Resolvamos los conflictos con los pueblos indígenas." May 7, Doc 258/99. Available at http://www.iglesia.cl.

Degarrod, Lydia. 1998. "Female Shamanism and the Mapuche Transformation into Christian Chilean Farmers." *Religion* 28: 339–50.

Fernandes, Bernardo M. 1999. *MST: Formação e territorialização*. São Paulo: Hucitec.

Fundación Instituto Indígena. 2000. *La pastoral indígena nacional*. Internal bulletin.

Gundermann, Hans, Rolf Foerster, and Jorge Vergara. 2003. *Mapuches y aymaras: el debate en torno al reconocimiento y los derechos ciudadanos*. Santiago: Universidad de Chile.

Harnecker, Marta. 2002. *Sin Tierra: Construyendo Movimiento Social*. Madrid: Siglo Veintiuno.

Hewitt, W. E. 1990. "Catholicism, Social Justice, and the Brazilian Corporativist State Since 1930." *Journal of Church and State* 32: 831–51.

Informe del Programa de Derechos Indígenas. 2003. *Los derechos de los pueblos indígenas en Chile*. Santiago: LOM/Universidad de la Frontera.

Maggio, Marcelo. 2007. "El conflicto con las empresas forestales en territorio mapuche." http://www.biodiversidadla.org/content/view/full/29521.

Mainwaring, Scott. 1986. *The Catholic Church and Politics in Brazil, 1916–1985*. Stanford, CA: Stanford University Press.

Mainwaring, Scott, and Daniel Levine. 1989. "Religion and Popular Protest in Latin America: Contrasting Experiences." In Susan Eckstein, ed., *Power and Popular Protest*, 203–40. Berkeley: University of California Press.

Mallon, Florencia. 2004. *La sangre del copihue: La comunidad Mapuche de Nicolás Ailío y el Estado chileno 1906–2001*. Santiago: LOM Ediciones.

Martins, José de Souza. 2000. *Reforma agrária: o impossível diálogo*. São Paulo: Edusp.

Mazzarollo, Juvêncio. 2003. *A Taipa da Injustiça*. São Paulo: Edições Loyola.

Medeiros, Leonilde. 2002. *Movimentos sociais, disputas políticas e reforma agrária de Mercado no Brasil*. Rio de Janeiro: CPDA/UFRRJ and UNRISD.

National Indigenous Pastoral Commission. 2003. "Al servicio de un nuevo trato con el pueblo mapuche." Working document. Available at http://www.iglesia.cl/portal_recursos/social/pastoral_indigena/documentos.html.

Poletto, Ivo. 2003. "A CNBB e a Luta pela Terra no Brasil." In Instituto Nacional de Pastoral, *Presença Pública da Igreja no Brasil*. São Paulo: Paulinas.

Poletto, Ivo, and Antonio Canuto. 2002. *Nas pegadas do povo da terra: 25 anos da Comissão Pastoral da Terra*. São Paulo: Edições Loyola.

Pontificio Consejo Justicia y Paz. 1998. "Para Una Mejor Distribución de la Tierra: El Reto de la Reforma Agraria." *Boletín CELAM* 279 (March).

Saavedra, Alejandro. 2002. *Los Mapuche en la sociedad chilena actual*. Santiago: LOM/Universidad Austral.

Souza, Cimone R. 2001. "A Cooperação como Estratégia Organizacional do Movimento dos Trabalhadores Rurais Sem Terra no Paraná." Master's thesis, Universidade Federal do Paraná.

Sznajder, Mario. 2003. "Ethnodevelopment and Democratic Consolidation in Chile: The Mapuche Question." In Erick Langer, ed., *Contemporary Indigenous Movements in Latin America*, 17–36. Wilmington, DE: Scholarly Resources.

Teixeira, Gisele, and Karla Correia. 2005. "Pastoral exige reação rápida de Lula." *JB Online*, February 17. Available at http://www.jb.com.br/jb/papel/brasil/2005/02/16/jorbra20050216001.html.

6 | The Changing Face of Religion in the Democratization of Mexico

The Case of Catholicism

ROBERTO J. BLANCARTE

What is the role of different religions, churches, and individual believers in the long process of democratization in Mexico? How have relatively recent events changed the relationship between the secular state and religious institutions? In what manner has the process of democratization in the country had an impact on the internal life of churches? What has been the role of such liberties as the freedom of individual conscience and of the secular state in shaping the religious landscape in Mexico? How have the particular Mexican processes of democratization and secularization[1] contributed to citizenship building and expanding religious and civil rights?

The role of religion in the democratization process of Mexico has preoccupied scholars since it became evident in the late 1980s that the authoritarian political system was crumbling. In 1995 I edited a book entitled *Religión, Iglesias y Democracia*. What my colleagues and I wanted to understand was how religions perceived democracy, how churches and religious communities experienced democracy internally, and how, eventually, they contributed to a more democratic political system. The results were complex and somewhat surprising. We found that for Protestants democracy meant primarily equal rights. Thus, Protestant or evangelical churches have historically demanded guarantees of respect for religious plurality and fair and equal juridical treatment, and, until recently, they did not intend to influence the sociopolitical arena. The Jewish community has demanded freedom to develop its own culture at the same time that it unquestionably adheres to national values.[2] Finally, the Catholic Church has responded in multiple ways to the question of democracy. Bishops have oscillated between establishing a privileged relationship with the government—hoping to shape state policies—and advocating a kind of prophetism that questions the model of medieval Christianity in an attempt to defend the poor and human rights. Lay Catholics, on the other hand, have worked within a secular framework and demanded more freedoms, questioning not only political institutions but their own church as well.

Of course, religion is about more than religious institutions, and the influence of Christianity extends beyond churches. At the national level, approximately two-thirds of the nongovernmental organizations (NGOs) in Mexico are of religious origin or are influenced by religion in some way. The role of these organizations has been and will continue to be crucial to defining how religion matters in both the democratic life of the country and areas of social life that are particularly sensitive, such as the defense of human rights. This is particularly true since the church all but expelled many priests and lay people from religious institutions, to the benefit of civil society. Liberation theologians now working for NGOs in defense of human rights are a case in point.

If we want to understand the role of religion in general and religious actors in particular in the democratization process of Mexico, we must examine the relationship among religion, culture, and national identity. The national debate on the role of religion—and particularly of Catholicism—in the national culture is especially relevant because important decisions on key public policies concerning education, social justice, and public health depend on it. Political events have changed the relationship between the government and the religious associations in Mexico, although not between church and state. The victory in 2000 of the National Action Party's (PAN) presidential candidate, Vicente Fox, and the formation of a government heavily influenced by conservative Catholic thought resulted in confrontations concerning social policy, especially in such key areas as reproductive health, sexual rights, and public secular education. Religion resurfaced during Fox's presidency, becoming one of the main social debates in the country. The victory of Felipe Calderón of PAN in the 2006 presidential elections and the introduction of religious references of all sorts into the arena of political debate has fueled hopes and fears (depending on one's political position) of a return of the pervasive influence of the Catholic Church in public policy. Mexico is facing a relatively new situation in which the role of religion in the life of the nation is being redefined.

The objective of this chapter is to show how the different and changing faces of religions, churches, and individual believers have influenced the democratization process in Mexico. Although I focus on the case of the Catholic Church, all religions and organized Christians at different ends of the political spectrum have played important roles in the construction of democracy. I also argue that the relation between religion and democracy in Mexico cannot be understood without reference to the historically central role of the secular or lay state (*estado laico*)[3] and its protection of freedom of conscience. In other words, it is important to acknowledge that Mexico is a very religious country but at the same time a very secular one. The democratic process and the process of secularization are intimately related: at the heart of both is an evolving freedom of conscience. That is why public debates concerning the role of religion in politics and in national identity define and shape public policy and why freedom of conscience—as part of the building of citizenship and growing religious and civil rights—is key to understanding the relatively recent transformation of democratic culture in Mexico. In other words, religions and particularly Catholicism have certainly contributed to democracy in Mexico, but they have done so in the context of a secular social and political framework.

Religious and Secular Mexico

Mexico is considered a deeply religious country; most Mexicans are Catholic, or even more specifically, Marian or *guadalupano*—that is, devoted to the Virgin of Guadalupe. Nonetheless, Mexico is experiencing a growing evangelical presence and an increasing religious plurality. At the same time, history and recent surveys suggest that Mexico also has deeply rooted laicism and an increasingly secularized society. Mexicans emphasize the importance of the separation of church and state, of the public and the private. Freedom of conscience is painfully but persistently making headway, and democratization is closely related to this growth.

The road that has led to the present situation has been long, arduous, and winding, although the pace of change has accelerated in the last decade. In 1991, for example, churches and religious groups did not exist from a juridical standpoint, which meant, among other things, that the Mexican state only recognized and guaranteed the individual liberties of believers. Mexico had no diplomatic relations with the Holy See, and churches and minority religious groups had virtually no formal public presence. The government did not have an entity in charge of making policy in matters of religion, except for a small agency within the State Department that was responsible for "firearms, explosives, and cults." Neither the separation of church and state nor the laicism of the state was included in the national juridical framework. Paradoxically, although religion was omnipresent and churches never ceased their activities, religion was not a matter of public interest or a sociojuridical reality. In other words, churches did not legally exist.

Fifteen years later, this panorama has changed significantly. There are more than six thousand juridically recognized "religious associations,"[4] more than half of which (about 52 percent) are Protestant or evangelical. A little more than 47 percent belong to the Roman Catholic Church, and various religious denominations, including the Church of Jesus Christ of Latter-day Saints (Mormons), Jews, Muslims, Hindus, Jehovah's Witnesses, Orthodox Christians, and Buddhists, among others, constitute the remaining 1 percent. This panorama has enhanced the public presence and social activity of various denominations, particularly minority cults. In September 1992 Mexico established diplomatic relations with the Holy See. That same year the constitution clearly established the "historical principle of separation of church and state." Its third article, the Law on Religious Associations and Public Worship (Ley de Asociaciones Religiosas y Culto Público), passed in July, established "the laicity (secularity) of the Mexican state" (Secretaría de Gobernación 1992). Additionally, the Ministry of the Interior created the General Direction for Religious Affairs, recognizing not only the new status of religious associations but also the need to have a formal relationship with them.

One of the consequences of these changes is that at present it is no longer taboo for religious associations to have a relationship with the state. The same holds true for politicians' religious ascription; under the strict division between the public and private, politicians were driven to the shameful extreme of concealing their personal beliefs. This produced widespread confusion in establishing the difference between the public and the private, the legal and the illegal, and that which was socially accepted and politically condemned. In any case, currently only a few Mexicans are surprised or scandalized to hear that the president professes Catholicism. This does not mean, however, that people approve of politicians basing public policies on personal beliefs. For a country that is mostly Catholic, it is increasingly clear that the Catholic majority prefers to maintain a strict separation of politics and religion, of public and private. Individual conscience, with its implicit freedom, rules in this matter. However, the fact that some government officials or governors, such as Pablo Salazar Mendiguchía in Chiapas, are Protestant or evangelical is no longer regarded with fear or concern. Furthermore, PAN, the right-wing, quasi-Catholic political party, participated in the coalition that elected Salazar the governor of Chiapas.

Since World War II Mexico has begun to perceive itself as an increasingly religiously plural country. Although efforts to equate "Guadalupanism" with the national identity persist, the truth is that a growing number of Mexicans no longer identify themselves with that symbol, and when they do, they use it more as a cultural reference than as a religious one. In 1950 more than 98 percent of the Mexican population self-identified as Catholic. Half a century later, Mexico is genuinely religiously diverse, and in the last three decades of the twentieth century, the trend toward religious plurality increased. Although the number of Catholics has grown significantly in terms of absolute numbers—making Mexico the second largest Catholic country in the world after Brazil—in relative terms such growth has actually slowed when compared to that of other religions. In other words, the number of Mexican Catholics increased from 70 to 85 million (an increase of approximately 20 percent), whereas the number of mainline Protestants, evangelicals, and members of the "non-evangelical biblical churches" (which include Mormons, Adventists, and Jehovah's Witnesses) increased from 3.5 to more than 6 million (a roughly 70 percent increase). If the pace of that growth remains steady, the proportion of Protestant and evangelical Mexicans will increase significantly in the decades to come.

The Constitutional and Legal Reforms of 1992: A Step in the Democratization Process

Religious freedom in Mexico was introduced in the 1857 Constitution and enshrined in the Reform Laws (1859–1860). The 1992 constitutional reforms discarded most of the revolution's anticlerical norms and returned to the liberal spirit of the 1857 Constitution and the Reform Laws. These 1992 reforms also responded to two parallel phenomena: Mexico's growing religious pluralism, which had become evident in the 1950s (when non-Catholics represented less than 2 percent of the population), and the impossibility of keeping religious beliefs in the private sphere without acknowledging their social role. It became increasingly obvious that religion shapes attitudes toward specific public problems, such as health, education, or social justice, and that it was important to acknowledge that role. Additionally, the growing plurality of religion and the acknowledgement of its new social role made it necessary to establish public liberties (such as family planning, educational, and reproductive health policies) that could transcend belief-specific moral norms, which some churches attempted to impose on the population as a whole through legislation or public policy. Consequently, for most Mexicans the secular state and public education were widely regarded in those decades as the best guarantors of public freedoms, including religious freedom.

The 1992 reforms that modified the 1917 Constitution neither fully satisfied the churches, particularly the Catholic Church, nor did it please the large anticlerical sectors of society, which were not convinced that the changes were positive due to possible church interference in state affairs. Nevertheless, the constitutional reforms (approved in December 1991 and officially enforced in January 1992) and the new Law on Religious Associations and Public Worship, passed in July 1992, eliminated the most anticlerical constitutional provisions, which had been the most annoying to religious leaders.[5]

The objective of the reforms was to eliminate the anticlerical character of the 1917 Constitution, particularly with respect to the juridical recognition of churches and religious associations. The main reforms consisted of eliminating from Article 3 of the 1917 Constitution the prohibitions against private schools imparting religious instruction and religious congregations or ministers opening or running primary schools. In practice, these prohibitions had not been enforced since the 1940s. For decades the state tolerated numerous religiously run schools, where even the children of politicians were educated. Nevertheless, there had always been a possibility that the law would come down hard on these schools. Consequently, the reform was welcomed as a step toward eliminating cases of false compliance.

Additionally, the prohibition against establishing monastic orders was eliminated from Article 5. This prohibition had been established by the 1917 Constitution and based on the nineteenth-century argument that the state could not allow the creation of a contract, pact, or agreement whose purpose was to "jeopardize, take away or irrevocably sacrifice man's freedom, for reasons related to labor, education, or religious vows" (Blancarte 1992, 429–33). Evidently, the Catholic Church had been the most affected by that prohibition and had regarded Article 5 as a constraint on the right to freedom of association. Priests and members of religious orders of the Catholic Church had never considered joining a monastic order an act that could jeopardize, take away, or "irrevocably sacrifice man's freedom"; they believed quite the opposite, in fact.

Article 24 of the 1992 reforms eliminated the requirement that believers attend religious ceremonies, pray, or do other religious acts only in churches or at home. It created the possibility that while "ordinary public religious acts will be celebrated in churches," "extraordinary religious acts" could be "celebrated outside them," provided they did not violate regulatory law. This article and its interpretation continue to cause conflicts between the Catholic Church and the state.

Article 27 of 1917 Constitution forbade any "religious association known as a church" of any denomination to purchase, possess, or administer real estate or capital. The 1992 reform modified that article to allow religious associations to "have the capacity to purchase, possess, or administer exclusively the assets that are essential to accomplish their purposes, in accordance with the requirements and limitations set forth by regulatory law." This confirmed that religious associations were legally allowed to own primary and secondary schools, which also meant that any building erected by religious associations from that date would be church-owned, whereas those predating the 1992 reform would remain the property of the nation. Despite the vagueness of the definition of assets "that are essential to accomplish their purposes," it became evident that this reform represented an important step toward the liberalization of norms concerning religious associations.

Finally, Article 130 of the 1917 Constitution, which governed political matters, was completely reformed. Although the main change consisted of recognizing the legal status of churches and religious groupings (which had been expressly denied between 1917 and 1992), there were other important modifications as well. The reform eliminated the prohibition on religious ministers criticizing government authorities or the nation's laws during a public "or a private meeting." The reformed version of the article only states that "ministers of religion will not oppose the laws of the country or its institutions during public meetings, religious ceremonies, or through religious propaganda and publications." Additionally, ministers were granted the right to vote (though still not the right to stand for office), but the prohibition on political parties having religious affiliations was not removed. Lastly, concerning freedom of speech, before 1992 religious periodicals were not allowed to "comment on national political affairs or give information concerning activities of government officials or individuals directly associated with the operations of public institutions." The reform lifted this prohibition as well as that against foreigners becoming ministers of any religion.

The political involvement of religious ministers is specified in detail in various legal provisions, including the constitution itself, the Law on Religious Associations and Public Worship, and the Federal Electoral Code. Article 130 of the constitution prohibits ministers from proselytizing in favor of or against a political candidate, party, or association and from engaging in activities that oppose the laws of the country or its institutions during public meetings, religious acts, or acts of religious propaganda.

Article 29 of the Law on Religious Associations and Public Worship re-states that prohibition. Moreover, Article 268 of the Federal Electoral Code also instructs the Federal Electoral Institute to inform the Ministry of the Interior whenever religious ministers, associations, churches, or groupings of any denomination violate the law by attempting to "persuade the electorate to vote for or against any political candidate or party, or to abstain from voting, inside places of public worship or at any other venue."[6]

Despite these restrictions, which can be explained by the strict Mexican tradition of separation of religion and politics established by the liberal-era reform laws and followed by the anticlerical measures of the revolution, the 1992 constitutional reforms were tremendously important. Although they reasserted the principle of the separation of church and state, they also recognized many rights that had been formerly denied to churches and their ministers, namely, the freedoms of instruction, association, expression, and public worship and the right to own property. Above all, these reforms conferred juridical status on "religious associations," thus granting them the legal recourse to claim their rights.

For all intents and purposes, a new relationship between church and state was established in 1992. After July 2, 2000, some conservative groups, encouraged by PAN's electoral victory, began to advocate for a new relationship between the Mexican state and the churches. For at least some sectors in Fox's government—and most, if not all, of the Catholic episcopate—the 1992 reforms did not go far enough. Under the banner of religious freedom, these groups wanted religious instruction in public schools, the right of the church to own electronic media, and greater involvement of the Catholic Church in public policy, particularly in the health sector (in order to slow or halt the availability of contraception and abortion).

Religion, of course, is not limited to ecclesiastical matters. There is a third actor in the church-state relationship—the individual. In Mexico individuals have established a link with the state to defend themselves against any infringement on their liberty from churches, including the Catholic Church, just as in the past churches have occasionally protected individuals from the excessive meddling of and even persecution by the state. In the twenty-first century Mexicans are looking to churches to act as agents to find a formula that guarantees the individual and social freedoms of all citizens, believers and nonbelievers alike, and helps to strengthen public and private liberties. The democratization process undertaken by Mexican society in recent years has become an appropriate framework for a new kind of participation by churches and believers.

A Secular Society and a Lay State

The exercise of greater religious freedom does not necessarily imply that society has become less secular. In a recent study of the impact of religious beliefs on the mestizo youth of Puebla, Gabriela Rodríguez argues that "structural transformations are removing the burden of religious regulations and the foundations of a patriarchal system in rural Mexico" (2002, 3). She adds, "the selective appropriation of urban symbols and lifestyles, of foreign and domestic cultural offers has led peasants to reflect upon religious regulations, while clinging to the need for the saints' indulgence and to magical-religious beliefs" (6). Indeed, she found that more than 53 percent of rural women today use contraception and one in five women has had an abortion (6). Additionally, according to Rodríguez, more than half of the youth who claimed not to be Catholic in responding to the 2000 National Youth Survey also reported that they do not practice any religion. They said they trust physicians and teachers more than priests. The vast majority (almost 80 percent) of all youth reported that religious beliefs do not influence their sexuality. Moreover, only 1 percent of adolescents said that the church is an important resource for information on sexual issues. For the rest, schools have supplanted the church as their main source of information on sexuality (Rodríguez 2002, 12).

This example vividly illustrates the rapid secularization of Mexican customs, a product of the demands of Catholics (who constitute the vast majority of Mexicans) to strengthen secular education, separate the political and religious spheres, and maintain a clear distinction between the public and the private. According to recent surveys, roughly two-thirds of the population believes that the Catholic Church has considerable power or too much; although they trust the church as an institution—more than other social and political institutions, which lack legitimacy in their view—they do not trust priests (Blancarte forthcoming). In Guadalajara, widely regarded as the center of Mexican Catholicism, two-thirds of the population believes that the family (not the church or the schools) is the ideal institution to transmit values that are deemed fundamental in their children's upbringing, whereas only 7.2 percent regard the church as the prime source of education on values (De la Torre Castellanos 1999, 122).

Furthermore, most Mexicans, Catholics and non-Catholics alike, believe that public policy should be clearly separated from personal convictions. According to a 2000 public opinion survey on abortion (Population Council 2000), the vast majority (69 percent) of Mexicans believe that abortion should be legal under certain circumstances. Ten percent think it should be legal in all circumstances, but only 21 percent of respondents believe that abortion should not be legal under any circumstances (Population Council 2000).[7] Interestingly, the percentage of Mexicans who were aware that abortion is legal under some circumstances in most Mexican states was fewer (45 percent) than those who approved it under some circumstances.[8]

This survey suggests that Mexicans do not want to mix abortion with religious issues; rather, they want public officials in the executive branch and legislatures to separate their personal beliefs from their decisions on the issue of abortion and the government to design nonreligious public policy (in health care and other areas). Nearly half (48 percent) of respondents expressed the view that the group that legislators should listen to most carefully when crafting abortion-related laws was women, followed by "the society" (29 percent) and physicians (14 percent); only 7 percent cited the church. In other words, Mexicans think that on the issue of abortion the opinions of women and society should weigh most heavily. Moreover, the overwhelming majority (95 percent) think that policy makers should consult the public before passing new laws (Population Council 2000). That they express such views in a country where legislators are not accustomed to consulting their constituents should be regarded as a major step in democratic thinking. The most illuminating result of this survey is that 80 percent of respondents expressed the view that "in matters of abortion" it was wrong for legislators to "pass laws according to their religious beliefs." (Population Council 2000). Mexicans are not opposed to legislators professing the belief of their choosing, but they want personal convictions to be kept separate from public decisions in the design of public health policy. To underscore this point, they believe legislators should regard abortion as a public health problem, not a moral issue.

Another survey commissioned by Católicas por el Derecho a Decidir (CDD, or Catholics for the Right to Choose), an organization linked to Catholics for a Free Choice, was the first specifically designed to tap the opinion of Mexican Catholics on social and political matters, particularly those related to sexual and reproductive rights. The results of the survey, conducted in July 2003, are astonishing for those who are not aware of how secular Mexico has become, but they indeed confirm other studies. The survey shows that a silent revolution has taken place among Mexican Catholics. A secularized Catholic population now differentiates politics and religion, the public and private spheres, as well as the affairs of church and state. Mexican Catholics defend by a wide margin the lay state (*estado laico*), the separation of spheres (82 percent), and reproductive rights (96 percent). They would like to see a church devoted to the poor and to protecting human rights and less involved in party politics. Above all, Mexican Catholics want a more tolerant institution that is much more sensitive to the needs of worshipers and their rights as citizens and members of the church. According to this survey, Catholics in Mexico would like their church to promote human rights (92 percent), denounce domestic violence (88 percent), allow the use of condoms in order to prevent the spread of HIV/AIDS (85 percent), allow Catholics to use artificial contraceptive methods (72 percent), accept the right of homosexuals to express openly their sexual preferences (65 percent), and allow Catholics to use emergency contraception (58 percent) (CDD/Population Council 2003).[9]

These examples plainly illustrate that in twenty-first-century Mexico, the separation of the political and the religious spheres and the distinction between public management and personal beliefs are essential principles of social life. From this perspective, freedom of conscience has emerged as a fundamental value that Mexican Catholics want political institutions to guarantee. This framework also helps to explain the increase in the strength of the secular Mexican state, despite the change of government and the new political aggressiveness of the religious right unleashed by Fox's victory.[10] Against this backdrop, the contribution that religious organizations will make to democracy will depend, in a sense, on the definition of the culture and the identity of the nation, as well as the answer to this question: "Is

Mexico primarily a Catholic or Christian nation, or is it a religiously plural nation with a secular state?" For the Catholic hierarchy, the answer demands a new project of nation building and a new relationship between church and state.

The Nation-Building Project of the Mexican Catholic Hierarchy

On March 25, 2000, in the midst of the Catholic Church's Jubilee and, coincidentally, Vicente Fox's presidential campaign, the Mexican Conference of Catholic Bishops published a pastoral letter entitled "From the Encounter with Jesus Christ to Solidarity with All: The Encounter with Jesus Christ, the Path to Conversion, Communion, Solidarity, and Mission in Mexico on the Threshold of the Third Millennium" (CEM 2000).[11] In the pastoral letter's introduction, the bishops stated their intention to review the history, ecclesiastical life, and current situation of the country, with an emphasis on reinforcing the identity and unity of the nation. They underscored that which unites Mexicans and highlighted common referents to the kind of country all Mexicans want to have (CEM 2000, 10). In short, the pastoral letter proposed a new project of nation building based on the Catholic-Guadalupean identity of the country.

The letter belongs to a school of thought that emerged in Latin America's Southern Cone in the 1970s. This school consists of Catholic thinkers who are critics of rationalist modernity and labeled "essentialists" by their detractors.[12] In handing the bishops a model of the region's identity that conforms to the bishops' social and political expectations, these thinkers have gained influence in the Latin American Bishops' Conference. They contend that there are two alternative cultural models for the region: the "illustrated rational" model, which originated in Europe, and the essentially Latin American baroque or "symbolic-dramatic" model. Whereas the former is based on belief in instrumental reason—that is, in reason as a means to dominate nature and achieve material progress—the latter constitutes a religious aesthetic approach to reality through what could be called "sapiential rationality." The illustrated rational model "underscores the abstract and conceptual discourse and appeals to reason; the symbolic-dramatic model underlines the images, dramatic representations and rites, and appeals to sensitivity" (Larraín n.d., 4). Seen in this light, Catholic essentialism can be viewed as "a Catholic sociological discourse that seeks to prove that the Latin American cultural identity has an inherently Catholic substrate compatible only with baroque modernity; an alternative to illustrated modernity" (Larraín n.d., 5). Drawing on the interpretative current of Catholic essentialism, the March 2000 pastoral letter reveals the bishops' commitment to democracy as mediated by their idea of the country's cultural identity and the role of the state.

"From the Encounter with Jesus Christ to Solidarity with All" (CEM 2000) is indeed an extraordinary example of Mexican Catholic essentialism: it may be the most ambitious text written by the episcopate since 1968, when the Mexican bishops voiced their feelings about what was happening in the country (CEM 1968). At that time, after presenting a thorough analysis (moderate but critical) of the social situation, they proposed a Christian vision for the development and integration of the country based on the social doctrine of the church and the conclusions of the Second Vatican Council. For the more than three decades from 1968 to 2000, not one of the episcopal documents issued by specific dioceses, pastoral regions, and the plenary of the Mexican Episcopate Conference (Conferencia del Episcopado Mexicano, or CEM) revisited the historical and social circumstances of the country. It was not until the end of the century, in the midst of the Jubilee celebrations and in the context of growing political and electoral agitation, that the bishops decided to publish a major document that also constituted an essential element of the project to build a new relationship between church and state.

The purpose of the 2000 pastoral letter was to show that "the subjectivity of the nation" is essentially Catholic. It presents the history of the country as schizophrenic—that is, as a Catholic people living with a liberal, anticlerical regime. The document does not recognize that modernity and liberalism were important in strengthening individual conscience, which in turn led to the secularization of society and public institutions. Catholics themselves (which in the nineteenth century were virtually the entire population) separated politics (understood in the institutional sense) and religion (at the level of individual conscience). For Mexicans, being Catholic was and still is compatible with being anticlerical. The same phenomenon can explain the anticlericalism of the Mexican Revolution. Most rank-and-file revolutionaries (with the exception of the Zapatistas) were anticlerical and promoted a clear separation of church and state and radical measures to diminish—and even to eliminate—the political power of the church. Without an understanding of this historical anticlericalism, which was nursed by a long tradition of popular religion, it is difficult to explain the Liberal movement of the nineteenth century, the Mexican Revolution, and the anticlerical articles of the 1917 Constitution. The Catholic hierarchy denies that the secular state that separated the church from the public sphere emerged because it was no longer possible to identify the nation with one single church or religion, and that Mexican Catholics themselves chose that kind of political organization because it conformed to their historical circumstances. In declaring that Mexican liberalism was alien to the cultural reality of the nation, the bishops presented liberalism as something foreign to Mexican history and Catholicism as something intrinsic to Mexican culture.

The bishops stated that Mexican Catholics "have a wounded heart" because they have to be faithful to two different entities (CEM 2000, 25). Actually, Mexican Catholics were able to differentiate between their political loyalty and their religious conviction, which they embraced according to their conscience. Indeed, this behavior was not what the Catholic hierarchy had expected. They strove and are still struggling to persuade Mexican believers to adopt an integrated vision of their reality, one that could unite religion and politics. However, the Mexican people, like many others who went through this process of secularization, understand that they can be Catholic according to their individual consciences rather than to ecclesiastical precepts.

The letter also states that the church was marginalized to the private sphere because it was regarded as the main obstacle to constructing Mexican identity. In actuality, the process of secularization and laicization of religious institutions, which paralleled the creation of a national conscience, gave way to a search for civic elements that could allow the construction of a new national identity and a common project. The relative marginalization of religious institutions was a consequence of the separation of church and state, the freedom of worship, and the growing incompatibility between professing a single religion and the national identity. The church was not deemed a hindrance to the construction of the Mexican identity but rather an obstacle to the construction of a state free of religious interference.

The bishops developed their own definition of national identity, one that was linked to Catholicism. They argued that the encounter with Catholicism endowed Mexico with "a reality that has marked us as a nation and . . . the main features that define us and give us an identity." Viewed this way, the Mexican nation would essentially be Catholic. The episcopate defines the nation as "a plural reality based on the many ethnic groups, languages, traditions, and customs that compose it," leaving out, significantly, religious plurality. The bishops affirm that in the case of Mexico, the nation precedes the state and "the nation's sovereignty precedes the state's political sovereignty." They conclude that "the state's priority calling is to serve the nation" and, quoting John Paul II, that "the state is solidly sovereign when it rules society while providing for its common good and when it allows the nation to realize itself within its own subjectivity, within its own identity." If, as stated earlier in this letter, "the sovereignty of a people lies in the subjectivity of its society and nation," and in Mexico "faith in Jesus Christ, announced by the Church and the miracle of the Virgin of Guadalupe . . . is a historical and cultural component that configures the identity of the nation" (CEM 2000, 103–5), the only possible conclusion of the episcopal letter is that the Mexican state must serve the Catholic nation. From this perspective, the Mexican secular state becomes an artificial entity that is foreign to the national culture and identity.

There is another view concerning the church and national identity, of course. In the eyes of historians, Mexico, like many other countries, constructed its national identity gradually, based on the growing awareness of its ethnic, economic, political, social, cultural, and religious pluralism. Seen from this perspective, the state is not something alien but rather the sort of political organization that best promotes social coexistence. Furthermore, the secular state is not alien to the social subjectivity of the Mexican nation; rather, it is a direct product of such subjectivity. Therefore, organizations that represent the Mexican people—not Catholic subjectivity—guard the nation's sovereignty. The Catholic bishops' arguments rest on the erroneous assumption that Catholicism constitutes the main element of national identity. Even if this was once true, the nation and its identity are dynamic, not static, and the referents of Mexico's identity have changed and continue to change in the present. Logically, the bishops believe it necessary and urgent to "update the Constitution of the Republic" based on "the history of our nation" (CEM 2000, 106), as if the present constitution were not precisely the result of that history. In other words, the church's historical revisionism seeks to delegitimize the liberal and social character of the current constitution, thus implying that a truly respectful charter should take into account the Catholic character of the nation.

A consequence of the position of the Catholic prelates is the dissemination of intolerance toward ideological pluralism. This intolerance is particularly evident in the following statement: "although indeed, tolerance constitutes an essential element of a free, plural society, it is also true that indiscriminating tolerance is bound to turn against itself." Although the bishops agree that Mexicans "experience and face" a growing pluralism that is not only technical, political, and economic but also cultural "and even religious," they also warn against the "dangers . . . [that threaten] the very existence of society"—namely, other religious offers—thus displaying a genuine lack of tolerance for what they call the "proliferation of unhealthy forms of religiosity." The Catholic hierarchy also seeks to persuade the state not to treat all religious associations equally, as illustrated by the following statement: "we consider it legitimate to state that not all [religious associations] have the same representativeness and that therefore, not all of them contribute in the same manner and to the same extent to the common good. The law demands that different contributions to the nation be fairly recognized" (CEM 2000, 113–15). The Catholic hierarchy, it is clear, still longs for those times when it had special privileges and power that other religious associations did not enjoy. The position also explains why the existence of a truly democratic and secular state is important for the maintenance of civil and religious liberties in Mexico.

This review of the Catholic bishops' position on the essential core of the nation and the character and role of the state and pluralism in Mexican society underscores the Catholic hierarchy's view that in a democratic Mexico, the Catholic Church should maintain its privileges over all other religious options and the state should be an institution that preserves the nation's supposedly Catholic character. This position rejects a priori the principle of equality of all churches and believers. Paradoxically, the

Mexican Conference of Catholic Bishops advocates the democratization of the political system and, at the same time, demands a legally privileged position in society. In the liberal view, the idea of a state that would preserve the Catholic essence of the nation violates the rights of individual Catholics who would oppose the social and moral rulings of the bishops. Thus, the idea of a Catholic state that "allows the nation to realize itself within its own subjectivity, within its own identity" would be in practice antidemocratic. Church attacks on the secular state that describe it as an entity that promotes antireligious or areligious ideologies do not recognize the possibility that Mexicans continue to favor a secular state because it guarantees respect for freedom of conscience, expression, belief, and worship. In fact, when the bishops assert "we should lay a solid foundation that allows us to achieve unity within the legitimate diversity of our great nation" (CEM 2000, 103–5), they are ignoring that this is precisely the function of the Mexican secular state.

According to surveys, most Mexicans in fact attach great importance to what is called the "lay state" and its intimate relationship to a more democratic society. In the above-mentioned survey of Catholic opinion, only 18 percent of respondents believe that the Catholic Church should be permitted to influence politics or public policy, while 82 percent of Catholics think that the Mexican government "should be protected from the influence of the Catholic Church, preserving the secular character of the state" (CDD/Population Council 2003, 20). A similar percentage of Mexican Catholics (80 percent) think that the church should not have any influence in the design of Mexican public policy. Even a higher percentage (92 percent) disapproves of the Catholic Church promoting or denigrating candidates or political parties during religious services. Only 8 percent of Catholics think that a Catholic president should govern based on the teachings of the Catholic Church, as opposed to 92 percent who affirm that a president should follow the diversity of existing opinions in the country (CDD/Population Council 2003, 24, 27, 29). It is logical to assume that these percentages would grow if the opinion of non-Catholic believers and nonbelievers were taken into account.

The Mexican Catholic episcopate's view of the modern, secular world and the lay state puts it at odds with its own flock. Its vision of the lay state is limited to and rooted in the difficult historical experience of the revolutionary period, which was associated with anticlericalism and persecution of the church. "The 'laicity of the state,'" according to the Catholic bishops, "cannot be used as a pretext to promote antireligious or areligious ideologies that violate the right to religious freedom" (CEM 1968, 114). The church's perception of the state as antireligious (or rather, anticlerical) originates in nineteenth-century struggles in Latin America to define the newly independent nations politically.

From a liberal perspective, it is just the opposite. For liberals, the state managed, despite the hostility of the Catholic Church, to establish religious freedoms, including freedom of belief and of worship. Beginning in the 1940s the Mexican secular state shed the antireligiosity and anticlericalism of a combative laicity (see Blancarte 1992). The 1992 constitutional and legal reforms did not completely eliminate all restrictions against the activities of religious groups, but they do show the state's recent openness to a kind of laicity linked to democratic values. The Mexican secular state is in theory impartial but not value neutral, inasmuch as it defends a series of values closely linked to laicity: tolerance, respect for diversity and minorities, separation of church and state (that is, separation of the political and religious spheres), religious plurality, democracy, and popular sovereignty. Thus, laicity is closely linked to democracy when democratization is understood, as it is in Mexico, not merely as an electoral but also as a social process.

These very different worldviews come into conflict over issues such as public education and public health, which are at the center of the current political debate. From the perspective of the bishops, religious education should be permitted in public schools. Because "the respect due by the state to the churches, religious associations, and each and every one of their members excludes any tacit or explicit promotion of irreligiosity or indifference," and because the religious dimension "is never foreign to the people's existence," the episcopate strongly believes that "the state is obliged to provide the necessary (and fair) mechanisms that allow those who want to give their children religious education to obtain such education *freely* from either public or private schools" (CEM 1968, 115). They decry that religious education is allowed only at private schools and is not included in the syllabi of public elementary education: "The right of parents to choose the type of education they wish to give their children is of capital importance. It is contrary to justice that only those who are well off can exercise this fundamental right. Educational 'laicism,' supposedly 'neutral' in moral and religious matters, becomes in practice a 'laicist religion' that is imposed and intolerant" (CEM 1968, 143).

From the perspective of the lay state, the episcopate's defensive attitude toward laicity is based on an incomplete understanding of it. Liberals take the bishops' view that the state somehow promotes, tacitly or explicitly, irreligiosity or indifference, and that laicist education imposes an intolerant "laicist religion," as clear evidence of episcopal intransigence and the inability of prelates to accept the perspective of the Catholic majority. The Mexican bishops propose reviewing Mexican national history in search of a common project with which all Mexicans can identify. Their vision, as expounded in their pastoral letter, however, remains anchored to their past relationship with laicity and the secular world, which they continue to identify with atheism and the promotion of irreligiosity and indifference. In their nation-building project they attempt to recover the Catholic substrate of culture while denying the value and historical presence of the secular world, hence inverting roles and doing precisely that which they criticize. Under these circumstances, the likelihood of the bishops understanding the dynamics of a democratic, secular system and consequently of any improvement in relations between the Catholic Church and the state seems quite remote even under conservative governments, unless they abandon the principle of democratic rule.

Religion and Authoritarianism

Thus, the role of religion can be ambivalent, paradoxical, and even contradictory. The religious message can represent a form of individual or collective liberation from civic or ecclesiastical power or from social restrictions, as when it inspires the faithful to participate in struggles for democratic liberation or to advance the cause of human rights. Alternatively, this same message can be coercive and used to restrain liberties, as when it mobilizes the faithful against the most elemental rights.

In the struggle for a more democratic political system in Mexico in the second half of the twentieth century, efforts by the Catholic hierarchy and laity did not always move in the same direction. Bishops prioritized obtaining more privileges for the ecclesiastical institution and influencing legislation and public policies directly, while lay Catholics pushed for democratic reforms in the context of a secular political system favorable to their own freedoms not only as believers but also as simple citizens. Only on rare occasions did bishops and their flock converge on objectives and methods. As we will see below, that was the case in Chihuahua in 1986.

The Catholic bishops endorsed the creation of a civic culture. They fought against abstentionism and promoted responsible voting. Not infrequently, however, their recommendations were thinly veiled endorsements for PAN and its candidates. Such partisanship was not only prohibited by the constitution but also seen by many Mexicans, particularly members and followers of the other parties, as unfair and inappropriate. Many bishops assumed (and continue to assume) that the problem was that Catholics did not participate as such in the political life of the country, thereby allowing an anticlerical, liberal elite to rule the country against the wishes of the Catholic majority. With what amounted to one-party rule, political statements of this sort by the Catholic hierarchy did not have a significant impact on the regime and official reactions were minimal. Politicians from the Institutional Revolutionary Party (Partido Revolucionario Institucional, or PRI), which had ruled the country since 1929, pointed out that it was erroneous to think that Catholics voted only for PAN, when in fact many of them voted for the majority PRI. Later, as the political system rooted in the hegemonic party began to decay, the clergy's criticism and interventions in political matters aroused much suspicion and distrust, not only within political ranks but also among common people.

When a member of the hierarchy came out against voting for opposition parties, as was the case in the late 1970s when Cardinal Ernesto Corripio distributed brochures in his archdiocese discouraging parishioners from voting for the Mexican Communist Party, government reaction was relatively mild. When the bishops denounced electoral fraud and the injured party turned out to be the ruling party (the PRI), however, the government's position was much more intense. The situation became critical during Chihuahua's local elections in 1986, when local bishops openly declared themselves against electoral fraud and threatened to close the churches, a reaction reminiscent of the Cristero War.[13] At any rate, up until

2000 citizen opinion differed with respect to church intervention in electoral matters. On the one hand, some considered the clergy's involvement to be a contribution to the democratic process, mainly to prevent electoral fraud. On the other hand, others rejected any form of intervention by ministers of (any) religion as harmful to the political life of the country. Many regarded this position as a thinly veiled defense of the political order that emerged after the revolution and, more specifically, the obsolete PRI regime. Few on the left understood that opposition to clerical intervention in the political life of the country should not be confused with gross anticlericalism (designed to uphold the old order) or with permissiveness (aimed at opening the doors to the "clericalization" of Mexican politics). Only some understood that not all religious expressions meant a return to religious fundamentalism or an attempt by the churches to exert their influence on the country's public affairs.

In any event, throughout the country's slow democratization process—symbolically triggered by the student revolt of 1968—the participation of lay Christians was remarkable. Clearly alluding to the repeated cases of electoral fraud committed by the then-ruling party, the Mexican episcopate, in its May 1968 pastoral letter "Development and Integration of the Country," maintained that systems were in place "to discourage the free exercise of citizen life" (CEM 1968, 402). The impact of this letter was immediate; only a few months later a congress made up of the main nonreligious organizations of the country stated the need to create "authentic, free, and operating unions" and that Catholics were obliged to participate actively in politics, "as Mexicans and as Christians" (see Blancarte 1995, 48).

This democratizing drive would also affect the church itself because authoritarian ecclesiastical structures, traditional Catholic social doctrine, and what some thought to be the episcopate's lack of social commitment or "critical prophetism" came into question. Most critics were lay members of the church, but there were also many priests and some bishops, immediately and not always justly, targeted as leftist, revolutionary, or liberationist. As a result, the Catholic hierarchy was forced to address the problem from two perspectives: On the one hand, the church was demanding more freedom and democracy for Mexican society. On the other hand, the church was facing the demands of many of its members, priests and laymen alike, to reform itself. Critics urged it to "create free opinion forums" as well as to "democratize" or eliminate ecclesiastical structures, which were too rigid or authoritarian according to the conclusions of the Second Vatican Council. Progressive sectors of the church organized themselves in associations such as "Christians for Socialism" and "Priests for the People." Catholic Action (Acción Católica Mexicana), traditionally submissive to the hierarchy, continued its organic, disciplined participation in the hierarchical apostolate, and the episcopate, while seeking to restore discipline and impose hierarchical authority, continued to insist on the need to revitalize Catholics' civic spirit in order to achieve constitutional reforms in ecclesiastical matters.

By the mid-1980s the episcopate as a whole, encouraged by John Paul II and his visit to Mexico in 1979, began to insist not only on the responsible exercise of the right to vote but also on combating electoral fraud. In Chihuahua in 1986, as mentioned above, the bishops warned against the possibility of such fraud during the campaign. After the elections took place in July, the archbishop of Chihuahua and diocesan priests denounced electoral fraud in their homilies and announced that they would close churches the following Sunday as a protest. Only the intervention of papal nuncio Girolamo Prigione stopped the threat from being carried out.[14] The immediate reaction of President Miguel De la Madrid was to introduce into the electoral code an article imposing a fine and jail sentence (of up to seven years) for religious authorities who for any reason exhorted the electorate to vote for or against a political party or candidate, promoted abstentionism, or pressured voters. At the end of that year, however, the government itself had to relax these sanctions by eliminating the threat of imprisonment, which had the effect of weakening the article because it could no longer be enforced. De la Madrid's policy was in fact the prelude to the constitutional changes announced by Carlos Salinas de Gortari when he assumed the presidency in December 1988.

Conclusion: Civil Society, Religion, and Democracy in Mexico

In the early 1990s more than half and perhaps up to two-thirds of the NGOs involved in electoral transparency and watchdog activities in Mexico were affiliated with Christian denominations. During the decade that witnessed the PRI's downfall, the bishops promoted "democracy workshops" and fought the state's authoritarianism. Nonetheless, through nongovernmental and extra-ecclesiastical organizations, lay Catholics— acting mostly in accordance with their own consciences as Christians and independently of the bishops—adopted political positions that promoted political change. Notably, and in contrast to the situation in Poland or the Philippines, this was not a social, political protest led by the Catholic hierarchy or clergy; rather, it was a case of civic participation by committed Christians and lay nonbelievers who worked jointly to democratize the political system. The Catholic bishops accompanied this effort with their traditional criticism of the state's authoritarianism, but they were not at the center of this political protest.

The formal democratization of Mexican political structures was the result of a secularized process, in which committed Christians participated as citizens. In that sense, paradoxically, the condemnation of liberation theology by John Paul II in the early 1980s helped to democratize Latin America. By "expelling" the followers of this kind of church organization to civil society, the pope helped "de-clericalize" Catholicism. In the past two decades many liberation theologians and their supporters have worked in NGOs defending civil and religious rights, democratic advances, and civic freedoms. Gustavo Verduzco Igartúa, who studies NGOs, affirms that Jesuits were pioneers in this kind of work, with the closing of the Instituto Patria (a school for Mexican elites) in 1971 and the founding of Fomento Cultural y Educativo, A. C. (a civic association). The creation of other organizations would follow, including the Mexican Institute of Social Studies (Instituto Mexicano de Estudios Sociales), the Mexican Institute of Political Studies (Instituto Mexicano de Estudios Políticos), and the Center of Educational Studies (Centro de Estudios Educativos). Civic Alliance (Alianza Cívica), an electoral watchdog organization, was comprised of many Christian-inspired social organizations and leaders (Verduzco Igartúa 2003, 84). Verduzco confirms that, in many cases, the roots of the NGO leaders could be traced to the organizations of the Catholic Church that socialized them. He maintains that "although some of them preferred not to talk much about those times, they saw it as an important period in their lives" in which they received "a solid formation." Apart from their common past, there were generational differences: "the older had been formed in a period in which memories of the ancient church-state conflict had been kept alive in different activities in youth ecclesiastical organizations" (Verduzco Igartúa 2003, 11). Some of these new organizations exerted their influence in the process of democratization that was gaining space in Mexican society. According to Verduzco Igartúa, while "the sentiment of distrust toward the government also reinforced independent trade unionism . . . a process of secularization created a distance between the clergy as authority and the groups and organizations in which Christian ideology prevailed" (2003, 84–85).

The Catholic hierarchy has been more reluctant to advocate or grant freedoms. Women's rights, for instance, a particularly prickly subject, have tested the ability of churches to satisfy the needs of more than half of the population and, indeed, of their own faithful. In general, religious institutions have made little headway in matters of sexual and reproductive rights. With few exceptions, most advocates of reproductive rights regard mainstream religious leaders as the main obstacles to the legal recognition of those rights. For example, the complex relationship among religion, freedoms, and rights (along with ethnic issues) in Mexico has been played out in Chiapas. In the early 1990s the governor attempted to modify the state penal code to include abortion as a legal family planning method. The immediate reaction of Samuel Ruiz, bishop of San Cristóbal de las Casas, sparked a conflict between the Catholic Church and the state government that would have severe future consequences. The bishop opposed decriminalizing abortion—which proponents saw as a sexual and reproductive right—under any circumstances because he identified abortion with the secular state. He argued that this initiative—if passed—would violate the rights of indigenous women, who would be forced to interrupt their pregnancies in order to control population growth in indigenous communities. Whether or not this assertion was true, the bishop subordinated the right of women to control their own bodies to the defense of indigenous rights against the alleged intervention of an authoritarian state. Undoubtedly, there was an assumption here that indigenous populations needed paternalistic protection against the state's authoritarian intervention. This conflict led the Catholic Church to distance itself from the civil government and to limit its informal role in curbing the growing social agitation in indigenous communities, which undoubtedly contributed to the indigenous uprising that broke out in Chiapas on January 1, 1994. As the case of

Chiapas shows, the issue of democratization in Mexico is a complex one that certainly goes well beyond features of the electoral system.

The bishops' position regarding indigenous rights should be viewed in a broader context of doctrine. In Mexico the Catholic Church's permanent opposition to sexual and reproductive rights has influenced the debate on the subject. In the 1970s some of these rights were recognized, but only because they served government goals to lower the birth rate and reinforce family planning campaigns. The January 1974 General Law on Population and the creation of the National Population Council generated distrust among the bishops, who criticized the Planned Parenthood Program of the Mexican government because they viewed it as bordering on "becoming a pro-contraception campaign." They accused the government of going along with the dictates of world powers and multinationals that manufactured contraceptives. The episcopate went as far as to declare that demographic policies, contraceptive campaigns, and sterilization and abortion campaigns were all part of a "smoke screen that hides the maneuvers of dominant countries whose political and economic interests are unmasked in times of crisis" (CEM 1975, 7). They espoused similar positions regarding sex education, which was being disseminated through new textbooks.

The Mexican episcopate's opposition to birth control and sex education programs became their leitmotif in the decades that followed. The ascent of John Paul II to the papacy in October 1978 and his visit to Mexico (his first to a foreign country as pope) in January 1979 reinforced the trend toward conservatism of the Mexican episcopate. The struggle in Mexico to construct and strengthen sexual and reproductive rights would involve a direct confrontation with the position of the Holy See, which became increasingly conservative in the 1990s. Such a confrontation can be illustrated with the above-mentioned crisis in Chiapas (which nonetheless involved one of the most progressive bishops in the country) and the heated polemics surrounding the government delegation and participation in the Cairo and Beijing conferences. The composition of the Mexican delegation, which included many of the most progressive women involved in official family planning programs, was contested by the conservative right. Catholic groups were also very active in putting pressure on the Mexican delegation in Beijing and forcing the Mexican government to second guess its position.

The conservative influence of the pontiff allowed the Catholic hierarchy in Mexico to step up pressure on the federal, state, and municipal governments and on political institutions in general to modify public policy through the increasingly broad spectrum of political parties. According to numerous testimonies, the confusion regarding the role and importance of the secular state in Mexico has hindered the progress of programs that advocate sexual and reproductive rights and has promoted, within centrist, left- and right-wing governments, the dissemination of openly conservative political positions that adhere to the doctrinal guidelines of the Catholic hierarchy (see Blancarte 2004).

In this context, it became clear to advocates of sexual and reproductive rights in Mexico that the official position of the church had become an obstacle to women's liberties. Not surprisingly, the struggle for those liberties and rights has been construed as a struggle against the doctrinal intransigence of the Catholic hierarchy. Within this context, it is also understandable that Vicente Fox's promises and victory in the 2000 presidential elections created high expectations among conservative groups and the Mexican Catholic episcopate. They hoped that the new government would put an end to what they saw as the laicist, liberal trend that had opened the door to women's demands and to the gradual introduction of sexual and reproductive rights. Here again, however, the social relevance and political preeminence of the secular state became clear. Not only was the Catholic hierarchy unable to promote any major changes in the constitution or in laws regarding religious affairs, but even Fox's conservative government officially introduced emergency contraception (or the morning-after pill) into the public health system. This outcome can only be explained as part of the larger process of democratization of Mexican society, in which Catholics and other believers have made clear their disagreement with the bishops' doctrinal positions. As the polls and surveys showed, a very large proportion of the Mexican population and of Catholics approved of the introduction of the new contraceptive method in spite of the opposition of Catholic bishops, who even threatened all those involved with excommunication. In the Population Council survey on abortion, 67 percent of the Mexican population "totally agreed" with the idea that emergency contraceptive pills should be included in the government's National Program of Family Planning. Another 19 percent "partially agreed," whereas only 4 percent "partly disagreed" and 7 percent "totally disagreed" (Population Council 2000, Q. 38). In other words, the democratization process had produced, inevitably, mature citizens who maintained their distance from church authorities.

The growing role of freedom of conscience in Mexico has had an effect not only on the electoral system but also on building a democratic political culture broadly speaking. The democratization of society has meant that Mexicans increasingly embrace the maxim that no one and nothing should be above the law. There is an increasing demand for public scrutiny of all persons and institutions. Mexicans—including Catholic Mexicans—are asking that resources be used responsibly and legitimately and that all actors be held accountable for their actions. Churches in Mexico have not escaped from this demand; democracy is not limited to electoral ballots. In that sense, it seems clear that secularized worshipers, exercising freedom of conscience in the context of a lay state—by working in NGOs concerned with democracy or other civil society organizations, for example—have done more to help build democracy in Mexico than the Catholic Church and its hierarchy.

Notes

1. The concept of *secularization* is probably the most discussed and controversial in the sociology of religion. In a recent work, I have revised the concepts of secularization and "laicity" (from the French *laïcité*), arguing that theory construction should be based on the different experiences of Western, semi-Western, and non-Western societies. As scholars have noted, there is a difference between understanding secularization as privatization and as social differentiation. With respect to the former, religion has reappeared in public life not only in the South but also in Western countries to some extent. Although privatization of religion has clearly taken place since the sixteenth century, this has not necessarily obstructed the social role of religion. With respect to social differentiation, the reappraisal of the role of religion in the public sphere does not mean that religion is still the main framework for the daily life of ordinary people in those countries. My point here is that secular thinking—in developed and underdeveloped countries alike—is predominant due to the differentiation process, where religion is only one aspect of society and certainly not a comprehensive frame of meaning. Nevertheless, in countries where the Catholic Church has been a dominant force (such as Mexico and Latin America in general), the secularization or "laicization"

of public institutions does not always follow the social process of secularization, which creates gaps between the legal and political structures of a state and the daily life of most believers and citizens. On this subject see Blancarte (2007).

2. In every country of the world, including Mexico, Judaism has undergone transformations that have altered the traditional way in which Jews participate in society and politics. For most Mexican Jews, democracy provides security in their lives and allows them to preserve their culture.

3. The word *laico* or lay, comes from the Greek *laos* and was used in the Catholic Church to differentiate common believers from the clergy. In the nineteenth century, *laico* was used to signal someone or something that was separated from religious or ecclesiastical influence. In 1870 the French invented the neologism *laïcité* and used it to refer to nonreligious public instruction and schools. *Laicism* was later used as a combative term against the influence of the church in public affairs. We understand *laïcité* or *laicity* (which is different from secularism) as a social system in which political institutions are no longer legitimated by the sacred or religious institutions but through popular will. In an *estado laico* (lay or secular state) political institutions enjoy autonomy from religious and ecclesiastical power.

4. Churches and religious groups achieved legal status as "religious associations" in 1992.

5. This section is based on the analysis of the *Political Constitution of the United Mexican States* (Secretaría de Gobernación 1997) and the "Ley de Asociaciones Religiosas y Culto Público" (Secretaría de Gobernación 1992, 38–44).

6. All changes to the code made during the 1990s can be found at http://www.ife.org.mx.

7. The Population Council is an NGO founded in 1952. The national survey was conducted in September–October 2000 by the Market Research and Consulting Services firm IDM (Investigación de Mercado y Asesoría, S. A. de C. V.) in the private homes of three thousand people between fifteen and sixty-five years of age. Participants were selected randomly, and the sample is representative of the Mexican population. The margin of error is +/- 1.82 percent.

8. Mexico is a federal republic. Most states have decriminalized abortion under certain circumstances, such as rape, danger to the mother's life, fetal malformation, etc. Only one state (Yucatán) allows abortion for economic and social reasons.

9. This survey of public opinion, which took place from June 15 to July 13, 2003, was based on a national representative sample in urban and rural areas of Mexico. The 2,328 interviews were based on a probabilistic selection in seventeen of thirty-two Mexican states and conducted only with those persons who self-identified as Catholic. Some of the conclusions can be found in Blancarte (2004, 323–30).

10. The Christian right in Mexico has always existed but never had significant influence due to the anticlerical and secular ideology of the Mexican Revolution. Some of these more moderate groups formed part of PAN and other parties, such as the Partido Demócrata Mexicano (Mexican Democratic Party, or PDM). Others created more integrist, extreme-right, or fundamentalist groups such as "Los Conejos," "la Base," Sinarquismo, "el Muro," or "el Yunque," some of which have resurfaced with the crumbling of the PRI regime. There is not much information on the subject due to the secrecy of these movements, but Delgado (2003, 2004) has documented the increasing participation of the extreme right in Fox's government.

11. At the time, some observers interpreted this pastoral letter as an open endorsement by most of the episcopate of the PAN candidate in the 2000 presidential race, Vicente Fox. Even if that had not been the intention of the bishops, Fox did everything in his power to persuade the citizenry it was the case by underscoring the paragraphs in the letter that mentioned the possibility of political alternation in the presidency approvingly. The other candidates were not able or willing to quote passages that could be viewed as supportive of their proposals; they were ambivalent because it was not clear whether citizens in general or even Catholics would welcome or reject endorsements by religious leaders.

12. Among their most renowned exponents are Alberto Methol Ferré (1981), Pedro Morandé (1984), Carlos Cousiño (1990), and Bernardino Bravo Lira (1981).

13. The Cristero War was a counterrevolutionary peasant rebellion that surged in 1926 in the Bajío region in the center-west, the most Catholic region of Mexico, when the bishops ordered that churches be closed in reaction to anticlerical government measures. The war ended in 1929, after the bishops reached an agreement with the Mexican government, something that most rebel leaders considered a betrayal of their movement. See Meyer (1971–1974).

14. Girolamo Prigione became papal nuncio when Mexico established diplomatic relations with the Holy See in September 1992.

References

Blancarte, Roberto. 1992. *Historia de la Iglesia Católica en México 1929–1982*. Mexico City: El Colegio Mexiquense-Fondo de Cultura Económica.

———, ed. 1995. *Religión, iglesias y democracia*. Mexico City: La Jornada-UNAM.

———. 2004. *Entre la fe y el pode: Política y religión en México*. Mexico City: Grijalbo-Random House-Mondadori.

———. 2007. "Mexico: A Mirror for the Sociology of Religion." In James A. Beckford and N. J. Demerath III, eds., *The Sage Handbook of the Sociology of Religion*, 710–27. London: Sage Publications, 2007.

———. Forthcoming. "El factor religioso." *Tercera encuesta nacional de valores.* Banamex.

Bravo Lira, Bernardino. 1981. "El Barroco hispanoamericano." In Bernardino Bravo Lira, ed., *El Barroco en Hispanoamérica, manifestaciones y significación.* Santiago: Fondo Histórico y Bibliográfico José Toribio Medina.

Católicas por el Derecho a Decidir (CDD)/Population Council. 2003. "Estadística Aplicada, Encuesta de Opinión Católica en México." Mexico City (July). Available on CD-Rom from CDD.

Conferencia del Episcopado Mexicano (CEM). 1968. "Carta Pastoral del Episcopado Mexicano sobre el Desarrollo e Integración del País." *Christus* 33, no. 390 (May): 394–439.

———. 1975. "Declaración del Episcopado Mexicano sobre el respeto a la vida humana." *Documentación e Información Católica* 3, no. 38: 1–10.

———. 2000. "Carta Pastoral del Encuentro con Jesucristo a la Solidaridad con Todos: El Encuentro con Jesucristo, Camino de Conversión, Comunión, Solidaridad y Misión en México en el Umbral del Tercer Milenio." Mexico City: CEM.

Cousiño, Carlos. 1990. *Razón y ofrenda: Ensayo en torno a los límites y perspectivas de la sociología en América Latina.* Santiago: Cuadernos del Instituto de Sociología, Pontificia Universidad Católica de Chile.

De la Torre Castellanos, Renée. 1999. "El Catolicismo: ¿un Templo en el que Habitan Muchos Dioses? In Patricia Fortuny Loret de Mola, ed., *Creyentes y Creencias en Guadalajara,* 101–31. Mexico City: CONACULTA, CIESAS, INAH.

Delgado, Álvaro. 2003. *El Yunque: la Ultraderecha en el Poder.* Mexico City: Plaza and Janes.

———. 2004. *El Ejército de Dios: Nuevas Revelaciones sobre la Extrema Derecha en México.* Mexico City: Plaza and Janes.

Larraín, Jorge. n.d. "Razón y modernidad en América Latina: crítica del discurso esencialista católico." Unpublished paper, Department of Social Sciences, Alberto Hurtado University.

Methol Ferré, Alberto. 1981. "El resurgimiento católico latinoamericano." In Consejo Episcopal Latinoamericano, ed., *Religión y Cultura.* Bogotá: CELAM.

Meyer, Jean. 1971–1974. *La cristiada.* 3 vols. Mexico City: Siglo XXI.

Morandé, Pedro. 1984. *Cultura y Modernización en América Latina: Ensayo Sociológico acerca de la Crisis del Desarrollismo y su Superación.* Santiago: Cuadernos del Instituto de Sociología, Pontificia Universidad Católica de Chile.

Population Council. 2000. *Encuesta nacional sobre aborto en México*. Available at http://www.popcouncil.org/projects/RH_MexicoPrevalenceInducedAbort .html.

Rodríguez, Gabriela. 2002. "Jóvenes, Cristianismo y Cultura Laica." Lecture presented at the seminar Los retos de la laicidad y la secularización en el mundo contemporáneo, El Colegio de México, February 26–27.

Secretaría de Gobernación. 1992. "Ley de Asociaciones Religiosas y Culto Público." Diario Oficial de la Federación; Órgano del Gobierno Constitucional de los Estados Unidos Mexicanos (July 15).

———. 1997. *Political Constitution of the United Mexican States*. 3rd ed. Mexico City: Secretaría de Gobernación.

Verduzco Igartúa, Gustavo. 2003. *Organizaciones no Lucrativas: Visión de su Trayectoria en México*. Mexico City: El Colegio de México/Centro de Estudios Sociológicos-Centro Mexicano para la Filantropía.

7 | Social Justice, Moral Values, or Institutional Interests?

Church Responses to the Democratic Challenge in Latin America

FRANCES HAGOPIAN

This chapter returns to the question posed in chapter 1: How is the Latin American Roman Catholic Church responding to the challenges of secularism and eroding religious hegemony in a context of democratic politics? Its aim is to propose a framework for understanding the responses of national episcopates to what can be understood as the church's contemporary strategic dilemma and flag the consequences of their decisions for electoral politics, public policy, and the church itself.

I begin from the premise that church responses to government proposals to make available emergency contraception, license media outlets, or reform national educational curricula, and to the demands of the faithful for land or justice, are not well understood in the customary dichotomous terms of left or right, traditional or modern, or progressive or conservative. This is because the church's positions on these and related policies cannot be collapsed along a single issue dimension. Ideally, the Catholic Church would simultaneously pursue multiple goals—to evangelize, guard institutional interests, promote public morality, and ground public policy in

Catholic social teaching. But because its positions on socioeconomic policies and public morality crosscut the existing cleavage structures of party
systems in most contemporary democracies in Latin America and elsewhere, the church's stance on social justice might suggest one set of political allies on an issue such as wage and employment policy, while those
same allies might be opponents on another issue, such as abortion rights.
Thus, church leaders entering national policy debates face a dilemma:
forced to emphasize one agenda or another, they must choose which of
these two dimensions—the socioeconomic or the rights/morality—to prioritize; how far they should move away from a national consensus, if one
exists; and how intensely they should advocate their positions; the farther
they travel along one dimension, the less capable they will be of intervening
on the other. Moreover, the need to protect its institutional interests may
compromise the church's ability to advance the various strands of its policy
agenda. In the United States, to cite one example, the Catholic Church once
decried the nuclear arms race and poverty, but it has fallen silent on a range
of issues—the war in Iraq, widening inequality, inadequate health care, and
environmental degradation, all of which the Vatican has condemned—in
favor of promoting a pro-life political agenda, which is also backed by the
political party that has expressed an openness to providing public subsidies
for religious schools and faith-based charities.

Not all Latin American bishops respond to this dilemma in the same
way. While many national episcopates are falling into step with a more conservative Vatican leadership, imposing greater control over the grassroots,
defending their institutional interests, and seeking special protection from
secular state authorities to enforce the policy outcomes that they cannot induce through moral persuasion, others have maintained progressive positions, invited more popular participation, devoted more pastoral care to
the poor and excluded, and championed the church's social doctrine. The
Argentine and Chilean bishops, who diverged sharply in their responses to
military governments (the Argentine hierarchy supported an authoritarian
regime while the Chilean opposed one), have converged in recent years on
a strategic option to emphasize public morality more vigorously than the
church's social justice message. In contrast, the Brazilian church, which like
the Chilean opposed authoritarianism, has devoted considerably more attention to mobilizing the poor to use democracy to achieve social justice.

The Salvadoran church has focused on the themes of unemployment, social exclusion, violence, and hopelessness, while its Peruvian counterpart has maintained relative silence on these questions despite similarly devastating poverty levels.

Why this should be the case has not been well explained by the principal frameworks that have guided the study of religion and politics in Latin America. The institutionalist paradigm is hard-pressed to explain diverse episcopal responses to the democratic dilemma given that national churches operate in the same institutional milieu, and the rational choice paradigm is similarly unable to account for this diversity given its expectation that the logic of religious competition and resource scarcity under democracy (Gill 2002) should produce a uniform pattern of retrenchment from popular causes. The fact that scores of like-minded leaders were appointed by the same "conservative" pontiff, moreover, undermines the ideational paradigm's emphasis on competing visions of mission. We also cannot explain the diverse responses of national churches to prioritize institutional interests, moral issues, or socioeconomic principles as mere reactions to different public policy agendas. As we shall see in this chapter, bishops from different countries vary their responses to similar policy proposals, ranging from the public provision of condoms to wealth-concentrating policies, and it is this variation that must be explained.

To explain why religious hierarchies make the choices they do, I propose a framework that, following the "embedded church" approach laid out in chapter 1, privileges the nature of church connections to civil society. The central contention of this chapter is that given a common order of priorities and preferred positions, each national episcopate will respond to its own strategic dilemma arising from religious and political pluralism according to three factors: (1) its capacity to mobilize the faithful for its goals of protecting its institutional interests and influencing the public policy agenda; (2) the directions in which the faithful pull it; and (3) the nature of the political risk it faces. Its capacity to mobilize the faithful depends on religious hegemony (the size of the flock in relation to its degree of observance) and its connections to an organized civil society. If the church never had or has lost the capacity to mobilize the faithful—that is, if religious competition and/or secularization have eroded the church's religious dominance and the institutional reach of the church and the vitality of its subcultural organizations are weak—then the faithful have little influence. But if, on the other hand, religious pluralism is high and the church must be attentive to the possibility of defection, and if Catholic religious and lay activists lead a dense network of civic and political associations that are reasonably autonomous from the control of religious authorities, then its base has more potential leverage. Now the political and ideological orientation of the laity matters more and may push the hierarchy to deviate from its preferred positions and priorities.

This calculus is tempered by another set of considerations, however: the nature of the political risk the church faces. "Political risk" may take the form of institutional attacks or government proposals and state policies that violate church teaching. The latter may be partly endogenous to the political orientation of Catholics in that if Catholics as voters were to overwhelmingly support the availability of emergency contraception, then governments might become emboldened to offer it to them. But the highest form of risk—the loss of privilege, autonomy, and support for church institutions and church-sponsored schools and media outlets—is more readily analytically separable. If the church faces political risk, it may modify its responses to its strategic dilemma. Whatever choices bishops make will have profound consequences for the nature of politics and policy, society, and religion itself.

In the sections that follow, I first lay out the theory behind the framework proposed here in greater detail. Next, I examine the authoritarian antecedents to the church's capacity to mobilize civil society in the last quarter of the twentieth century by examining the impact of the actions of dictators and religious hierarchies on religious associations and civil society organizations. The third section introduces measures of the church's religious hegemony and its capacity to mobilize the faithful, and the fourth reviews the political and policy orientations of lay Catholics and provides a preliminary assessment of the degree of political risk that the church faces. These sections lay the foundation for a preliminary classification, according to the variables proposed, of the Catholic Church in seven Latin American countries—Argentina, Brazil, Chile, El Salvador, Mexico, Peru, and Venezuela—each with very different levels of religious hegemony, mobilizational capacity, ideological orientation of mass electorates, and political risk. In the next section I sketch out episcopal responses, drawing from pastoral letters, messages, declarations, and reports issued or publicized by bishops since 2000 in these countries; finally, I offer some concluding thoughts.

Framing the Church's Strategic Options in Plural Democracies

The Roman Catholic Church has multiple goals. The first, defending its institutional interests—which includes maintaining the status of Catholicism as the dominant religion; keeping the flock; gaining public support for the web of schools, hospitals, and charitable organizations that educate and socialize Catholics; and staying financially solvent—is of paramount concern to the hierarchy. Church influence and institutional interests have been threatened in several Latin American countries. The 1980 Peruvian constitution disestablished the Catholic Church, and the 1991 constitution in Colombia put a formal end to the 1973 concordat.[1] Across the region, congresses have debated laws governing television licenses to religious bodies, the religious identity of elected officials, public subsidies for any or all religiously denominated schools, and the tax-exempt status of religious institutions (Sigmund 1999).

But the church has other core interests in addition to this single dimension of institutional survival. A second, crucial goal that is closely related to the first is to evangelize—to bring the Gospel to the far corners of the continent. Another, as we saw in chapter 1, is to maintain morality in the public sphere, to protect human rights and dignity, and to influence public policy on the family and on issues of life and death. Yet another is to advance its social doctrine—to reduce material poverty and achieve social justice and peace. All of these interests are important to the church. Access to voluntary sterilization, condoms publicly distributed to combat the spread of HIV/AIDS, and legal abortions, while typical of plural democracies, threaten the church's moral agenda. At the same time, causes of economic justice such as fair compensation for labor, the recognition of access to health and education as social rights, and the guarantee of social peace go to the core of the church's social doctrine.

The strategic dilemma for the church arises from the fact that in democratic regimes, these goals cannot easily be pursued simultaneously. The church's strong leanings toward income equality and social welfare and justice—which often means contesting neoliberal or even market-oriented economic reforms for generating higher rates of unemployment, depressing wages, and exacerbating inequality while championing demands for land by the landless—place it on the left on a traditional left-right continuum on state intervention in the economy, income redistribution, and the social safety net. But on a second, rights/morality axis, the church opposes any public provision of sex education and contraception, as well as any liberalization of legislation governing matters of life and death that contradict the church's moral doctrine. Church positions favoring state protection for the poor and life and public morality do not map easily onto existing political space and do not comfortably match most partisan options (Figure 7.1). Most parties that are willing to defend the church's institutional interests and preferred moral policies are not open to defending the church's economic agenda, and vice versa, leaving the church relatively isolated in the lower-left quadrant of Figure 7.1. Thus, the church's social doctrine may bring the institution into direct conflict both with governments that promote neoliberal economic reform and fail to mount adequate safety nets to cushion the most vulnerable strata of society from the shocks of the rapid capital mobility of today's international financial markets, as well as with those that do protect the poor but also promote morally permissive social policies.

Because its strategic options to advance its positions do not necessarily all point in the same direction, the church must choose not *what* its position will be on the social issues of the day—on which all episcopates agree—but rather *which aspects* of Catholic social doctrine and moral teachings it will prioritize. Church leaders could choose to defend institutional interests or denounce poverty. Also, how intensely a church hierarchy holds these positions and how far along one axis a church moves may take it farther away from finding common cause with any political actor that could represent it on another axis. In game theoretic terms, the church may choose to hedge its risks against a turn of the political tide at election time by straddling the center of issue space, or it may opt for the riskier course of heavily privileging one goal—and issue dimension—over another. There is not a compelling theoretical reason to believe that each country's bishops will make the same choice. We need to develop a framework to understand

Figure 7.1. The Ideological Axes of Political-Religious Competition and the Church's Strategic Dilemma

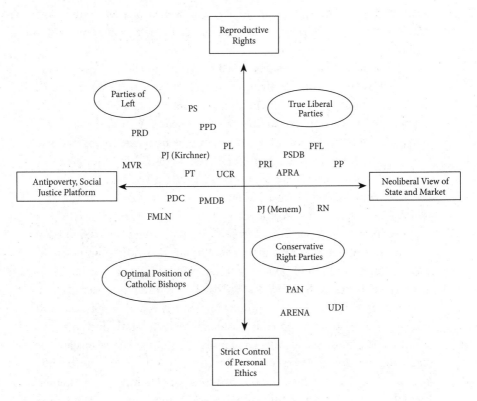

Party Key:

APRA: American Popular Revolutionary Alliance (Peru)
ARENA: Nationalist Republican Alliance (El Salvador)
FMLN: Farabundo Marti National Liberation Front (El Salvador)
MVR: Movement of the Fifth Republic (Venezuela)
PAN: National Action Party (Mexico)
PDC: Christian Democratic Party (Chile)
PFL: Party of the Liberal Front (Brazil)
PJ: Peronist Party (Argentina)
PL: Liberal Party (Brazil)
PMDB: Party of the Brazilian Democratic Movement

PP: Progress Party (Brazil)
PPD: Party for Democracy (Chile)
PRD: Party of the Democratic Revolution (Mexico)
PRI: Institutional Revolutionary Party (Mexico)
PS: Socialist Party (Chile)
PSDB: Party of Brazilian Social Democracy (Brazil)
PT: Workers' Party (Brazil)
RN: National Renovation (Chile)
UCR: Radical Civil Union (Argentina)
UDI: Independent Democratic Union (Chile)

whether church leaders will choose primarily to defend institutional interests, advocate for a moral public sphere, or promote peace and denounce
social and economic injustice, even at a cost to their own institution, and
whether they will ally with political actors of the left, center, or right—
and why.

In the theoretical model developed here, I begin with the assumption
that there is an implied hierarchy of church interests that each episcopal
conference would pursue if it could implement its agenda with full state
support and it were not constrained by other actors. Within these simpli-
fied parameters, the church's top priority will be to defend its institutional
interests—to keep the flock, gain public support for the institutions that
constitute its social web and means of penetrating civil society (schools,
hospitals, and charitable organizations), maintain influence over the education and socialization of Catholics, and stay financially solvent. This is so
because in order to evangelize, the church must survive. Its second most
important goal will be to maintain morality in the public sphere—to influence family and moral policy (such as sex education and divorce), especially on issues of life and death (that is, contraception, sterilization,
abortion, and euthanasia), and protect human rights and dignity. Its third
goal will be to advance the church's social doctrine—to reduce material
poverty and achieve social justice and peace. There are two reasons for this
implied hierarchy of interests. First, the church professes to prioritize life
over all else (although it would be hard to argue that introducing knowledge about sexuality and artificial contraception to young people is a more
egregious violation of church teaching than launching an unjust war). The
second, more important factor is that the third goal is the hardest to pursue
at the same time the church defends its institutional interests. That is to say,
fighting for social justice brings the church into conflict not only with those
who usually do not share the church's goals on moral issues but also those
who typically defend the church's institutional prerogatives.

These priorities can be reordered when the church operates under severe constraints. The first of these constraints comes from a decline in religious hegemony. As I argued in chapter 1, religious pluralism involves more
than religious competition; a concept of religious hegemony must also take
into account the degree of secularization of society and the strength of
the church's institutional reach into society. Churches that enjoy uncon-

tested religious hegemony may not need to move far from their preferred option. But those that operate in more plural environments—either due to competition with other religious faiths and Christian denominations, secularization, or even internal pluralism—may not have that luxury. Where the base has leverage, it can pull and tug the church in another direction and onto another dimension—for example, from morals to pocketbook issues, about which, at least in Latin America, the base cares more deeply. For the church to be effective, moreover, it must be able to mobilize its grassroots. The church's ability to mobilize its rank and file varies inversely with the degree of secularization and the intensity of religious competition, but it also depends positively on the density of voluntary associations and the degree to which memberships in secular civic and religious associations overlap. A church that is embedded in its own civil society and can mobilize its base will be more effective in shaping social and economic policy, ethical debates, legislation on public morality, and even election outcomes than one that cannot.

Following from this insight, once the calculus moves to political space, how forcefully the church intervenes, in what arenas, and whether it addresses its exhortations and critiques to voters or politicians will be further influenced by the ideological orientation of the mass public and the Catholic grassroots as well as the nature and degree of political risk the church faces. In taking mass ideological orientations into account, I do not mean to argue that church leaders are necessarily won over by the visions of faith of their parishioners but rather that in calculating their interventions in the public debate, they take into consideration how much support they have or opposition they will face. Political risk begins with state proposals and the specific policies that public officials place on the political agenda. In religiously and politically plural societies, the church faces two types of risk: challenges to its institutional interests, and policy proposals that contradict its moral agenda. The latter are partly endogenous to the orientation of the electorate but not entirely; it is theoretically possible that political elites might suppress an issue on which the majority might prefer policy change or, alternatively, that one political party or faction might place such an item on the policy agenda in response to a narrow but intense constituency. A proposal to deprive the Catholic Church of its privileged status will be regarded as more ominous than one to distribute condoms or make available emergency contraception, but the church takes both threats seriously. Political risk is also measured by the church's perception that such proposals might pass. Part of this calculation can be assessed by prior public opinion polls, but an honest judgment would admit that "political risk" as such is a moving target, as the church attempts to sway public opinion on such issues precisely in order to prevail. A complete risk assessment would also take into account not merely the orientation of the incumbent government but also the policy positions and electoral viability of various partisan options in the political opposition, some of which might be more threatening than those of the incumbents. In some cases, these opponents might be on the brink of national power or even already the party of government at the state or provincial level and, thus, possess considerable capacity to implement policy in federal systems of government. Three important implications follow:

1. The base of the church has more leverage over the hierarchy in religiously plural settings at moderately high levels of organization and mobilizational capacity than in countries where the church enjoys a high degree of religious hegemony and civil society is not well organized.
2. A mobilized civil society with overlapping religious and civic memberships is an asset to church leaders, but a mobilized civil society without overlapping religious and civic memberships can pose a political risk to the church.
3. Where the church's capacity to mobilize civil society is low, the ideological self-placement of Catholics matters less in determining church positions and influence than levels of religious hegemony and whether parties in power are friends or foes of the church.

These conditions suggest various church responses:

1. Where civil society is only weakly organized, religious—and more specifically, Catholic—decline continues, and there is little hope of mobilizing the faithful, church leaders who cannot restore moral authority and the principles of faith to the public sphere on their own will move strategically to the right, rely on conservative political elites to protect

the church's institutional interests and its moral agenda, and if necessary forfeit or deemphasize their own social justice agenda. Since the church can, by definition, offer little political gain, its position is weak and its leaders are only likely to be successful if its interests and agenda will not cause its political patrons to lose support; otherwise, the church will see its influence diminish altogether. In such circumstances, when Catholicism is at best the plurality religion, we should expect church leaders to submerge the church's social doctrine. Depending upon the degree of sympathy the church can expect from political authorities, two different outcomes are possible:

- If incumbent politicians and parties are sympathetic to church interests and conservative on moral issues, church leaders will refrain from attacking these politicians and parties that are willing to defend church privilege, a position I call *defensive moralism*.

- If political elites are not sympathetic and the church faces political risk, however, church leaders will more aggressively defend their moral positions and institutional interests, even if they must clash with the government in office to do so, in one manifestation of what I call *proactive moralism*.

2. Where, on the other hand, the Catholic Church enjoys higher levels of religious hegemony and fewer potential votes might be lost by catering to church demands, then even though religious hierarchies may have little capacity to mobilize the faithful, their position is stronger. In this environment, the church may also assume a stance of *proactive moralism*. The form of its intervention may vary, however, depending upon the political orientation of incumbent politicians:

- Church leaders may vocally support incumbent conservative politicians.

- If incumbent politicians are located on the center-left and are permissive on moral issues, church leaders may attack them, hoping either to raise the electoral costs to those politicians of defying the church or to dislodge them from office.

3. If civil society is more densely organized and accessible to the church and if religious hegemony is low, then the leverage of the grassroots is greater, and where the Catholic electorate is located matters more. When the Catholic grassroots lean in a more progressive direction and

enjoy some autonomy from church leaders due to religious competition, the chances are greatest that they can pull the church along with them toward a *moderate pluralism*. In this case, the church may respond in one of two different ways:

- Church leaders may eschew strategic alliances with elites, moderate their stances on issues that the grassroots identifies as salient and on which it has strong opinions, and generally be constrained by the preferences of the faithful on questions of public morality and social and economic justice. With a mobilized effort on the ground, the hierarchy may be effective in a different way and in the longer term. This is true at lower levels of political risk.
- As political risk increases, the religious hierarchy may move to defend its institutional interests as well as its moral agenda, but it will not abandon its social justice agenda.

4. Where, on the other hand, religious hegemony is high *and* the church's networks crisscross a robust associational life, the church has the greatest capacity to mobilize its civil society. In this scenario, the ideological orientations of the Catholic grassroots are typically more conservative on moral issues and conform more closely to those of ecclesiastical authorities. Where the base is thus compliant, the church may hedge its bets, aligning with politically progressive parties on the impact of market reform and with social conservatives on moral issues. The intuition here is that a vibrant church with good connections to civil society, sufficient resources from private sources, minimal constraints from a progressive laity, and little to fear from religious competitors and secularism can afford to reject political alliances with conservative elites in which the church plays the role of junior partner. It is unlikely to face substantial political risk and has a greater opportunity to provide what I call *evangelizing leadership* in society. It may press its own ambitious programmatic agenda and straddle the difficult political space of ethical doctrines and social teaching.

Each of these strategies carries consequences for the church's relationship with its followers, its influence over public policy, and itself. If the church is disconnected from its grassroots and it chooses to ally with conservative elites that can independently mobilize voters in order to defend its institutional interests and promote its moral agenda, these alliances will accelerate the trend toward religious defection, shrink the church's base in society, and ultimately further erode its potential influence. Such a church, which has only a weak bargaining position, will subsume or even forfeit its social justice agenda, and its privileges and influence may not be safe if conservative political leaders fear that protecting the Catholic Church may alienate more numerous secular and Protestant voters. If, on the other hand, the church maintains strong links with well-organized grassroots groups, its influence will be greater. That influence is maximized where it faces less competition and its base fully accepts all aspects of church doctrine. If the church's political alliances are more varied and it is embedded in a plural civil society, the church—and democracy—will reflect that pluralism.

Political Change, the Church, and Civil Society

If Catholic churches across the region face common dilemmas, their responses not only differ markedly from one another but they also deviate from the courses on which these churches appeared headed during recent authoritarian regimes. In a classic metaphor Max Weber ([1922–23] 1946, 280) identified a force—in his example, the "world images" created by ideas—that, like "switchmen," determine the tracks along which action is pushed by some other force—which for him consisted of material interests. For the Roman Catholic Church in Latin America, military dictatorships in country after country acted like Weber's switchmen to push the church's integralist projects of the postwar period along a different set of tracks than originally intended.

In Brazil, Argentina, Chile, and Uruguay in the Southern Cone, and in El Salvador and Guatemala in Central America, notoriously brutal authoritarian regimes took power in the 1960s and early 1970s, joining such longer-running dictatorships as that of Alfredo Stroessner in Paraguay. Truly horrific military repression drove the death tolls under dictatorship to unimaginable levels—an estimated 70,000 in El Salvador and 180,000 in Guatemala. Milder authoritarian regimes also governed in Peru, Ecuador, Panama, Nicaragua, and, for a period, Bolivia (until the dictatorship there, too, turned more repressive in 1971). When authoritarian regimes bore down on the faithful in Brazil, Chile, and El Salvador, the church—in a departure from its past behavior—became a forceful advocate for human rights, economic justice, and the transition to democracy.[2] In El Salvador the outspoken archbishop Óscar Romero, assassinated by death squad leader Roberto D'Aubuisson's hitmen, heads a long list of martyrs that also includes prominent Jesuit academicians who did not live to see the culmination of the peace process they set in motion. But, as Mainwaring and Wilde put it, "dictatorship was a necessary but not sufficient condition to bring the progressive church into being" (1989, 14). In Argentina, Paraguay, Uruguay, and, until 1983, Guatemala, the church either continued to support dictators or equivocated. At the extreme, the Argentine church in the 1970s staunchly defended the grim repression of a military regime that left 30,000 dead. The church also opposed the moderate populist and self-styled revolutionary regimes in Ecuador, Panama, and Nicaragua.

Military dictatorships and the responses of national churches to them had a profound if ambiguous impact on civil society and the capacity of grassroots organizations to sustain initiatives, both within and outside of religious organizations. Many dictators that set out to squash autonomous trade associations and community groups and remand people to their private lives were remarkably successful in destroying social capital. In some of these cases, Catholic networks in particular felt the brunt of military repression, and mere association with the Catholic Church placed the faithful at grave risk. This was especially so where the popular church had been effective in organizing the poor for political action. In Guatemala the church's developmental and liberationist projects crumbled when grassroots church communities were brutally suppressed and their leaders singled out for elimination. Fifteen priests and thousands of catechists and other lay workers—teachers, community health workers, and volunteers in charitable organizations—were reported to have been murdered between 1978 and 1985, as were many Mayan activists associated with the Christian Democratic party (Calder 2004, 107–8). In El Salvador, where the military also killed many clergy and lay catechists (Stein 1999a, 123), civic associations survived only in guerrilla-controlled zones (Wood 2003). Religious communities suffered a secondary blow when regime repression drove the imperiled toward safer, Protestant churches. In retaliation for the Catholic hierarchy's condemnation of large-scale human rights abuses by military authorities and state-sponsored paramilitary organizations, state actors made overtures to, and in some cases even abetted, the growth of evangelical and Pentecostal sects. Whether regimes were of the left, as in Nicaragua (Stein 1999b), or right, as in El Salvador and Guatemala, did not matter.

Elsewhere, however, military dictatorship provided an impetus to civic association—if for no other reason than self-defense. Women organized soup kitchens to feed the unemployed and hungry, and frantic mothers seeking information about their disappeared children coalesced in proto–human rights organizations (Navarro 1989; Alvarez 1990; Baldez 2002). Where military regimes allowed the church to provide safe haven and sanctuary to inchoate civic, human rights, and religious associations, as was the case in Brazil and Chile, this gave an advantage to religious networks but did not a guarantee that once the veil of repression was lifted religious leadership of civil society organizations would continue. In Chile the hierarchy's heroic opposition to the notorious abuses of human rights under the Pinochet dictatorship did not produce lasting effects, and civil society eventually became estranged from the church that had sheltered it. This was the case because, first, once political space was opened after 1989, activists who were not really tied to the church left the religious orbit to participate in secular associations, an option that of course had been foreclosed during the years of dictatorship. Second, in the 1990s the church also disengaged from civil society, closing the pastoral commission that had served as a refuge for victims of repression and their families (Vicaria de la Solidaridad) and discouraging its members from pressing ahead with claims against the military for human rights abuses during the dictatorship (Cruz 2004). Instead it raised its voice to oppose the legalization of divorce.

In Brazil, by contrast, where the church also led civil society's opposition to an authoritarian regime, religious networks survived and flourished, and the church has maintained a reasonable degree of capacity to reach civil society, even amid vigorous competition from Pentecostal denominations and a tenuous reach into the educational system. What distinguishes the Brazilian church from the Chilean is not merely the former's sustained support for popular causes after the transition to democracy but also its encouragement of grassroots participation in religious communities. Left-leaning Catholics who participated intensively in a decentralized web of these grassroots communities and pastoral commissions during the dictatorship did not separate themselves from the church or its moral concerns after redemocratization, perhaps because their activism had a religious foundation and their alliance with church leaders who shared their aspirations and visions was not merely one of political convenience. In fact, we might hypothesize that the grassroots did not stay within the fold because the hierarchy supported its causes but rather that the Brazilian hierarchy supported the grassroots' causes and pleas for social justice because a space for religiously motivated action was preserved within the church. The spillover effects were palpable; in a country in which the state historically had monopolized social organization through corporatist networks, in 1993 two-thirds of Brazilians reported belonging to at least one voluntary association, twice the rate in Spain (McDonough, Shin, and Moisés 1998). Today, Brazil is seen as having one of the most vigorous civil societies in Latin America, spearheaded by a vibrant and plural church.

Peru, Ecuador, and Mexico represent intermediate cases of authoritarian regimes that did not close off opportunities to associate. The Peruvian military that came to power in 1968 with an agenda to reform land tenure relations, settle unresolved claims with foreign-owned natural resource concessions, and even organize the poor and tie them to the state's corporatist project, the National System of Support for Social Mobilization (Sistema Nacional del Apoyo a la Movilización Social, or SINAMOS), closed some political space but left other political opportunities open. Christian communities in Peru did not play the formally political role they did in other countries where opportunities to associate were restricted; rather, they offered a "complementary space" for association and critical reflection, and committed Christians were "careful to act on their own, and not in the name of their particular church, Catholic or Evangelical" (Levine and Romero 2006, 247–48). Civic organizations remained relatively weak on the whole, though as Stokes (1995) has shown, some activists socialized in military-era unions, schools, and community associations did assume leadership of more radicalized civic associations after military rule ended. Tragically, during the first dozen years after the transition to democracy from 1980 to 1992, civil society was targeted by members of the Shining Path guerrilla movement, who attacked the union and community leaders they saw as their closest competitors. Many civil society groups were also victims of state repression, and as a result of suffering the aggression of both sides, they became seriously imperiled as organizations. As civil society began to recover in the late 1990s and the first decade of the twenty-first century, the church's prominent role in the struggle against poverty and later in the promotion of the defense of human rights opened new areas for common action with other organizations in Peruvian civil society and international agencies (Levine and Romero 2006, 248).

In Ecuador a populist military also governed in the 1970s. Like its Brazilian counterpart, the Ecuadorian military allowed church-sponsored schools and religious communities to function unimpeded. Catholic educational missions and social networks were crucially important both for creating social capital and for keeping the church firmly planted in rural, indigenous communities in both the Andean and Amazonian regions of the country. Yashar (2005, 100) credits churches with helping to create the mobilizational networks among previously dispersed communities that coalesced as a powerful indigenous movement spanning the Andean highlands and Amazonian regions of the country. In a description reminiscent of accounts of the impact of the liberationist church in poor communities in Brazil and even El Salvador before the brunt of the repression, Yashar writes: "In most interviews with indigenous leaders, the church was described as a kind of catalyst for them—either because a progressive priest encouraged them and supported them in educational pursuits, or because churches organized schools where they developed skills and contacts" (2005, 104). In supporting rural indigenous catechists, sponsoring seminars and meetings, and encouraging indigenous organizations, the church contributed to Ecuadoran civil society in ways that clearly outlasted the original religious missions that inspired them. As in Brazil, religious communities encouraged grassroots participation.

In Mexico, where for decades an inclusionary authoritarian regime applied only limited and targeted repression, however comfortable working relations were between the church and state in the decades following the Cristero rebellion and especially the Ávila Camacho presidency (1940–1946), the church perceived that it operated under the watch of a hostile state (Camp 1997). For much of the twentieth century, until its official rapprochement with Mexican secular authorities in 1992 during the Salinas presidency, the Mexican Catholic Church could not cozy up to a regime that was at least formally anticlerical, as its Central and South American counterparts had been able to do, and so it hunkered down close to its own grassroots.

Where dictatorship did not intrude, religious projects in civil society continued along their original tracks. In Costa Rica, Venezuela, and Colombia the relationship between the Catholic Church and its ranks was not disturbed, and the percentage of Protestants was among the lowest in the region. In Venezuela, where associational life exhibited a dynamic quality for decades (Levine 1973) and grassroots religious communities were afforded a reasonable degree of autonomy from church officials (Levine 1993), regime continuity left intact the church's bridges to civil society organizations. In Colombia, where the church had long enjoyed the perquisites of establishment and maintained tight control over its grassroots communities, civic associations did not exhibit the same strength and certainly not the degree of autonomy that they did in Venezuela or even in Mexico. Wilde (1984, 1987) and Levine (1981, 1993) have written in remarkably similar terms about the response of the hierarchy of the Colombian church to liberationist groups. Wilde went so far as to assert that by squelching independent initiative and backing oligarchical democracy, the church missed an opportunity both to democratize the regime and augment church influence, consigning itself instead to a more marginal role.

It is often observed that church officials paid a high price in lost institutional privileges and influence over policy for boldly opposing authoritarian projects. Even right-wing dictatorships exalting God, family, and fatherland moved ahead on policies, such as the legalization of divorce, that contradicted church positions after church leaders badly embarrassed them over human rights violations (Htun 2003). One lesson of this cursory examination of church responses to its grassroots during political regimes of the left and right is that if heroic opposition to dictators turned out to be costly, *not* opposing dictators was—in the longer run—costlier still. Religious networks were dealt a severe blow when national episcopates abandoned civil society to an authoritarian onslaught. In Argentina and Uruguay complicity with brutal dictators accelerated the exit of the faithful from the church and a life of faith altogether. A second lesson is that what happened during transitional moments and immediately after the restoration of democracy mattered too. Whereas the Chilean and Peruvian churches disassociated themselves from religious activists in the 1990s, in Brazil the sustained support of the hierarchy for the rights of landless peasants and striking workers paid dividends in strong church membership. Third, it was important not merely that the hierarchy took forceful positions in defense of their own societies but also that they permitted religious pluralism and religiously motivated political action within their own houses. Thus, the decisions of the episcopates to stand with their faithful or not were hugely consequential for their future capacity to keep them in the fold and, as we shall see next, to mobilize them in defense of church interests in democratic polities.

Religious Hegemony and the Capacity to Mobilize

The cumulative effects of dictatorship, religious competition, secularization, and the creation or destruction of civic and religious social capital have profoundly shaped the church's capacity to mobilize the faithful. Following the framework discussed earlier in this chapter, a determination of this capacity depends first on a working understanding of how to measure religious hegemony and the extent to which civil society is organized, socialized, and reachable by the Roman Catholic Church.

Table 7.1 provides two measures of religious hegemony—the percentage of the population that self-identify as Roman Catholics and of those that participate in religious services at least once a week. Religious hegemony is a fairly straightforward concept to interpret. At one extreme, self-identified Catholics represent about three-quarters or more of the population in Colombia, Peru, Argentina, and Mexico, and at the other, fewer than 60 percent in El Salvador, the Dominican Republic, Chile, and Uruguay. But the intensity of commitment also matters, and this can vary from checking a box on a census form to ordering one's life according to a religious identity. I include the frequency of religious practice—specifically the percentage of the population that meets the benchmark of attending religious services at least once a week—as a proxy for religious intensity. To arrive at a composite measure of religious hegemony, I simply multiply the two measures. The results at least mimic the conventional wisdom. The Mexican Catholic Church emerges as enjoying the highest levels of religious hegemony and the church in highly secular Uruguay the lowest.

Table 7.1. The Religious Hegemony of the Catholic Church in Latin America, 2000

	Percent Self-Identified Roman Catholics[a]	Percent Who Practice at Least Once a Week[b]		Religious Hegemony[c]
Mexico	74	62.3	46.1	High
Colombia	84	47.5	40.0	High
Peru	84	45.9	38.6	High
El Salvador	59	61.1	36.0	High
Dominican Republic	59	50.0	29.5	Moderate
Brazil	70	36.2	25.3	Moderate
Venezuela	66	35.2	23.2	Moderate
Chile	54	38.3	20.7	Moderate
Argentina	79	23.9	18.9	Low
Uruguay	41	17.6	7.2	Low

Sources: World Values Survey (Inglehart et al. 2004); see also Tables 1.3, 1.4, and 1.6 in this volume.
[a]Percent responding "Roman Catholic" to the question, "Do you belong to a religious denomination? If so, which one?"
[b]Percent responding "once a week or more often" to the question, "How often do you attend religious services?"
[c]Classification scheme based on multiplying percentage of self-identified Roman Catholics by the percentage who report practicing at least once a week.

Measuring the capacity to mobilize is harder. Such a measure depends on reliably counting civic organizations, and, as Levine and Romero (2006, 241) explicitly caution, those numbers may be unreliable. We would ideally want to know not merely how many associations actually exist and how many members they have but also something about how committed their members really are to those organizations, how strong the ties are between secular and religious associations and their members, and how tightly controlled the organizations are by religious authorities. But even given their limitations, the available comparative data on associational memberships provide important comparative benchmarks that we cannot afford to forego.

We begin by examining participation in a number of civic, trade, and political associations, as reported by respondents to the 2000 round of the

World Values Survey in five countries—Argentina, Chile, Mexico, Peru, and Venezuela. Comparative research suggests that members of churches are generally far more likely to belong to other civic and especially political associations than people who are not, and that religiosity "dramatically conditions levels of political participation" and has a "powerfully positive effect" on formal associational memberships in postauthoritarian regimes (McDonough, Shin, and Moisés 1998, 925, 938–40). The data in Table 7.2, which report membership in 2000 in civic, trade, political, and cultural associations for those who claim membership in a church organization and for those who do not, as well as the ratio between the two, confirm this finding, albeit to different degrees in the countries in our sample.

At one end of the spectrum members of church groups in Mexico joined civic, trade, and professional associations across the board at much higher rates than nonmembers. Members of religious organizations were from four to seven times more likely than nonmembers to belong to environmental groups, perform service in civic health care organizations, participate in peace movements, and belong to women's groups, local community action groups, and human rights groups, respectively.

The contribution of spiritual capital to social capital is more ambiguous in the other cases. In Venezuela rates of participation of members of religious organizations were quite high in most civic and political associations, but the impact of that participation was not as dramatic as in Mexico due to high overall levels of civic participation. In Peru, although members of religious organizations were also more likely than nonmembers to join civic and political associations, the difference in the two groups was not nearly as significant as it was in the other countries in the sample. Membership in religious organizations boosted participation in human rights, women's groups, elderly social services, and environmental associations by roughly a factor of two, but church membership had only a slight impact on participation in local community action groups, the peace movement, and professional associations, and it actually depressed participation in health care associations, labor unions, and political parties. In Chile and Argentina participation in religious groups provided a selective impetus to joining other groups; the most significant impact was on women's groups and heath care associations in both countries, the peace movement in Chile, and local community action and human rights groups in Argentina.

Table 7.2. Social Capital, Spiritual Capital: The Effects of Religious Membership on Civic and Political Participation in Five Latin American Countries, 2000

	Argentina			Chile			Mexico			Peru			Venezuela		
	Members of Church Organizations		Member/ Non member	Members of Church Organizations		Member/ Non member	Members of Church Organizations		Member/ Non member	Members of Church Organizations		Member/ Non member	Members of Church Organizations		Member/ Non member
	Yes	No	Ratio[a]	Yes	No	Ratio	Yes	No	Ratio	Yes	No	Ratio	Yes	No	Ratio
Civic Associations															
Social welfare for elderly	8.5	4.1	2.1	11.6	5.4	2.1	15.7	4.7	3.3	6.8	3.2	2.1	14.9	4.1	3.6
Youth work	5.0	2.4	2.1	7.6	3.8	2.0	8.1	3.1	2.6	7.9	5.1	1.5	14.2	6.7	2.1
Health	6.0	1.8	3.3	8.4	2.0	4.2	15.4	3.4	4.5	4.0	5.0	0.8	7.6	10.0	2.3
Trade/Professional															
Labor unions	2.5	2.5	1.0	2.8	3.0	0.9	8.7	4.9	1.8	4.2	4.6	0.9	4.4	2.6	1.7
Professional associations	1.0	1.9	0.5	3.6	3.5	1.0	5.0	2.0	2.5	6.8	5.5	1.2	15.3	7.5	2.0
Political Associations															
Political parties	6.0	4.3	1.4	3.2	2.2	1.5	6.4	3.1	2.1	3.9	4.9	0.8	6.5	3.1	2.1
Local community action	10.4	2.0	5.2	8.0	3.8	2.1	14.0	2.2	6.4	9.2	5.6	1.6	18.2	7.9	2.3
Human rights	1.5	0.4	3.8	1.6	1.9	0.8	7.3	1.0	7.3	4.7	1.6	2.9	16.4	6.7	2.4
Environmental	2.0	2.2	0.9	4.0	2.6	1.5	10.4	2.7	3.9	4.7	2.5	1.9	16.7	10.5	1.6
Women's groups	3.0	0.5	6.0	14.1	3.0	4.7	8.1	1.5	5.4	9.9	4.6	2.2	9.5	3.8	2.5
Peace movement	n.d.	n.d.	n.d.	3.6	1.2	3.0	7.6	1.6	4.8	1.0	0.8	1.3	13.1	3.7	3.5
Culture/Recreation															
Cultural activities	9.5	9.1	1.0	9.6	8.9	1.1	12.0	6.4	1.9	18.1	11.0	1.6	28.0	14.8	1.9
Sports club	5.5	8.0	0.7	12.1	15.7	0.8	11.5	7.9	1.5	10.7	11.6	0.9	22.9	20.5	1.1
Other	6.0	3.6	1.7	1.2	1.5	0.8	2.0	0.8	2.5	0.3	0.1	3.0	1.1	0.5	2.2

Source: 2000 World Values Survey (Inglehart et al. 2004).

Note: Some data not available (n.d.) for Argentina.

[a] Ratio of members of religious associations to nonmembers.

These data are illuminating, but to determine the church's capacity to mobilize, socialize, and influence those who call themselves Catholic, we need to know more about overall levels of civil society organization and the degree to which membership in religious organizations overlaps with membership in civic associations. I build such a measure in Table 7.3. The table takes as a baseline the percentage of all respondents in the World Values Survey who belong to any voluntary associations, including religious organizations (this information is provided in the first column under each country). Membership in religious groups is by and large higher than in any other category of organization, ranging from a low of 16 percent in Argentina to a high of 25 percent in Peru, with 21 percent in Chile, 23 percent in Mexico and Venezuela, and 22 percent in Brazil. The second column under the first five countries provides the percentages of members of each of the civic, trade, and political associations who also belong to church organizations; the average for each category of association is weighted by the size of the associations that comprise it (as indicated by the percentage of the entire sample claiming membership in them). The intuition is that if lay and religious Catholic activists are present in human rights groups, women's groups, political parties, youth groups, and community organizations, they will infuse Catholic principles into the organizations they join and spread church influence beyond the orbit of regular churchgoers. This information allows us to determine the percent of the sample whose memberships in both religious and civic, trade, and political associations overlap, which is reported in the third column under the first five countries. The classification of the church's capacity to mobilize civil society in each country is based on a final composite measure that totals overall participation by members of religious organizations in civic, professional, and political associations.

Venezuela has the highest rates of self-reported associational activity of any country included in the World Values Survey, followed by Mexico. Around 10 percent of all Venezuelan respondents belonged to a health, professional, local community, human rights, or environmental association. More than six times as many Venezuelans as Argentines belonged to environmental groups, and five times as many participated in health-related civic associations and women's groups. Overall, Chile and Peru represent intermediate levels of association and Argentina a low level. Fewer

Table 7.3. Overlapping Memberships: Bridges between Religious Association and Civil Society in Select Latin American Countries, 2000

	Argentina			Chile			Mexico			Peru			Venezuela			Brazil
	Percent of Total Sample[a]	Percent Overlap with Church Orgs.[b]	Percent of Sample in Both Orgs.	Percent of Total Sample	Percent Overlap with Church Orgs.	Percent of Sample in Both Orgs.	Percent of Total Sample	Percent Overlap with Church Orgs.	Percent of Sample in Both Orgs.	Percent of Total Sample	Percent Overlap with Church Orgs.	Percent of Sample in Both Orgs.	Percent of Total Sample	Percent Overlap with Church Orgs.	Percent of Sample in Both Orgs.	Percent[d] of Total Sample
Church Organizations	16			21			23			25			23			22
Civic Assns																
Social welfare for elderly	5	27.9	1.4	7	36.3	2.5	7	50.5	3.5	4	41.9	1.7	7	51.9	3.6	10
Youth work	3	27.8	0.8	5	34.5	1.7	4	44.6	1.8	6	34.5	2.1	8	38.6	3.1	4
Health	2	38.7	0.8	3	52.5	1.6	6	57.9	3.5	5	37.5	1.9	10	40.7	4.1	3
Average (weighted)		30			39			52			37			43		
Subtotal			3.0			5.8			8.8			5.7			10.8	
Trade/Professional																
Labor unions	3	15.6	0.5	3	19.4	0.6	6	34.8	2.1	5	23.9	1.2	3	33.3	1.0	6
Professional associations	2	9.1	0.2	4	21.4	0.9	3	42.9	1.3	6	29.9	1.8	9	37.8	3.4	5
Average (weighted)		13			21			38			27			37		
Subtotal			0.7			1.5			3.4			3.0			4.4	
Political																
Political parties	5	20.7	1.0	8	27.6	2.2	4	38.3	1.5	5	21.4	1.1	4	38.3	1.5	5

Local community action	3	48.8	1.5	5	35.7	1.8	5	65.8	3.3	7	35.7	2.5	10	40.7	4.1	8
Human rights	1	42.9	0.4	2	18.2	0.4	3	68.4	2.1	2	50.0	1.0	9	42.1	3.8	1
Environmental	2	14.3	0.3	3	28.6	0.9	5	53.6	2.7	3	39.1	1.2	12	32.2	3.9	3
Women's groups	1	54.5	0.6	5	54.7	2.7	3	61.7	1.9	6	42.2	2.5	5	42.6	2.1	2
Peace movement	n.d.	n.d.		2	45.0	0.9	3	58.7	1.8	1	30.8	0.3	6	51.4	3.1	2
Average (weighted)	*31*			*35*			*57*			*36*			*40*			
Subtotal			3.8			8.9			13.3			8.6			18.5	
Total Overlapping Memberships[e]	7.5			16.2			25.5			17.3			33.7			
Church Capacity to Mobilize Society	Low			Medium			High			Medium			High			

Source: 2000 World Values Survey (Inglehart et al. 2004).
Note: Some data not available (n.d.) for Argentina.

[a] Percentage of all respondents who are members of civic, trade, and political associations.

[b] Percentage of members of civic, trade, or political associations who also belong to church organizations.

[c] Percentage of all respondents with overlapping memberships in civic, trade, or political associations and religious organizations (that is, percentage of association members who belong to religious organizations).

[d] Brazilian figures are derived from the 1990 World Values Survey, as these questions were not asked in Brazil in the 2000 round.

[e] Percentage could theoretically exceed 100 because it is a sum of potentially multiple memberships.

Argentines belong to *any* civil society organization than Chileans, Peruvians, Mexicans, and especially Venezuelans, including unions and professional associations, civic associations, groups and movements with a political character, and even cultural groups and sports clubs that require only the loosest of commitments from their members.

Members of religious organizations play a huge role in all associations, but especially in political and civic associations and less so in trade and professional organizations. They also play significantly larger roles in these associations in some countries than in others. On average, 52 percent of members of civic associations and 57 percent of members of political associations in Mexico are members of religious organizations; for particular associations (local community action and human rights groups), the numbers can be as high as two-thirds. Also impressively in Venezuela, more than 50 percent of members of social work associations for the elderly, 43 percent of members of civic associations, and 40 percent of participants in groups and movements with an explicitly political orientation also belong to religious organizations.

These figures make sense against the backdrop of what we know about these countries. That Argentine civil society should emerge as the least densely organized of five Latin American countries for which there were data is not surprising. Argentina was hard hit by the effects of trade liberalization and other market reforms on aging and unprofitable industries, which would naturally cut into union membership. Ordinary Argentines are more likely to receive patronage from the neighborhood networks of the Peronist Party than actively participate in running economic activities and debating political futures (Levitsky 2003). In Venezuela there are high levels of civic association, particularly since the collapse of the traditional political parties, Democratic Action (Acción Democrática, or AD) and COPEI (the Christian Democratic party). In the 1990s there may have been 15,000 neighborhood associations and, by 2004 between 25,000 and 54,000 civil associations (including neighborhood associations, the cooperative movement, and human rights groups), according to one estimate (Levine and Romero 2006, 246).

In Peru civil society is moderately organized, but there is not the same degree of overlapping membership between religious and civic and political organizations as in Mexico and even Venezuela. This result is consistent with the separation from the church of the civic associations, which, at various points in the 1980s and 1990s, were more closely connected either to the United Left (Izquierda Unida, or IU, a party of the left with strong roots especially in the poor neighborhoods of Lima) or eventually even to the Fujimori government, as was the case with 2,000 soup kitchens (*comedores*), 3,000 Mothers' Clubs, and 7,000 "Glass of Milk" committees in Lima (Levine and Romero 2006, 243). Chilean civil society is also only moderately well organized, and it bears little resemblance to the highly polarized and hypermobilized society of the late 1960s and early 1970s. Two decades of demobilization by both military rulers and political parties eager to calm jittery supporters of the former authoritarian regime apparently depressed levels of civic and political association in the 1990s even relative to other postauthoritarian regimes (Oxhorn 1995). Today there is less overlap of memberships in secular and religious civic associations than in any other country in the sample except Argentina. That today's Chilean civil society is not as connected to the church as it was in the past is consistent with our analysis of the nature of this relationship during the period immediately following the dictatorship, as discussed earlier in this chapter. This conclusion is also buttressed by the fact that in a sweeping study of social movements in the late 1990s, not a single mention was made of any church linkages to labor unions, professional guilds, student organizations, and environmental movements (De la Maza E. 1999).

To arrive at a composite measure of the church's capacity to mobilize, I determined the percentage of members of religious organizations in each civic, trade, and political association about which membership was asked in the World Values Survey and totaled them. These figures should be taken with a grain of salt, however, since they do not account for multiple memberships. Nonetheless, especially when taken together with the overlapping memberships, they provide some benchmarks that will enable us to make meaningful comparisons across these five cases. On this basis, I classify Venezuela and Mexico as cases of high mobilizational capacity, Peru and Chile as intermediate cases in which the church has a moderate degree of mobilizational capacity, and Argentina as a case of low mobilizational capacity (see Table 7.3).

The same questions about associational membership were not asked in two other countries that are examined in this chapter—Brazil and El

Salvador—in the 2000 round of the World Values Survey. These countries are nonetheless included to provide crucial variation on the other variables in our model—religious hegemony, political orientation, and political risk. Of the two, we know more about civic association in Brazil. There, in 1993, 40 percent of women and 31 percent of men responding to a survey claimed membership in a grassroots church community (McDonough, Shin, and Moisés 1998, 925); in another survey conducted in 2002, 27 percent reported participating in religious charitable associations (ESEB 2002). In the 1993 survey, 28 percent belonged to at least one voluntary association, 18 percent to two, and 20 percent to three or more. A quarter reported very close relations with their neighbors, a result the authors of the survey attributed to religiosity: "religiosity has a very strong, practically uniform, and probably reciprocal connection with neighborhood ties. . . . the more numerous such ties, the more religious the community, and vice versa" (McDonough, Shin, and Moisés 1998, 925, 938). Case studies and anecdotal evidence confirm the survey evidence. Social movements linked to the Workers' Party (Partido dos Trabalhadores, or PT) are reported to have close, interlocking ties to grassroots church communities (Hunter 2006). Mainwaring (1986) referred to the youth Catholic Action movements of the 1960s as recruiting grounds for future social movement leaders, a trend that appears to have continued: based on data gathered at meetings, Gomez de Souza observed that a "significant part of the leadership of the Movimento dos Trabalhadores Rurais sem Terra—MST (Landless Workers Movement)—have stemmed from the youth pastorals of the Catholic Church" (2005, 8). I classify Brazil, like Venezuela and Mexico, as a case of high mobilizational capacity.

There are fewer surveys and studies of social organizations available for El Salvador. What little we know suggests that civil society is not well organized. A 2004 survey reported that Salvadorans participate more frequently in religious organizations than in any other activity but that overall rates of civic participation in El Salvador are "very low," the lowest in Central America, Mexico, and Colombia (Córdova Macías, Cruz, and Seligson 2004, 164–66). Assuming that there may be some overlap of organizations but that levels of civic and political association are low, I tentatively classify El Salvador as a case of low to moderate capacity to mobilize.

These measures of religious hegemony and mobilizational capacity should open a theoretical window for us on how influential the base of the church can be in modifying the responses of religious hierarchies to a complex set of calculations about advancing the church's institutional interests, moral agenda, and social doctrine. Our expectations are depicted in Figure 7.2. The leverage of the base is anticipated to be highest in cases where civil society is extensively mobilized but the church does not enjoy uncontested religious hegemony—that is, Brazil and Venezuela. In these cases, civic and religious organizations overlap, but neither is dominated by church leaders. At higher levels of religious hegemony and a more limited capacity to mobilize the grassroots, religious authorities face fewer constraints.

Political Orientation and Political Risk

Religious hegemony and the church's capacity to mobilize explain when a church may need to adjust its positions and whether or not it may

Figure 7.2. Religious Hegemony, Capacity to Mobilize, and Leverage of the Base

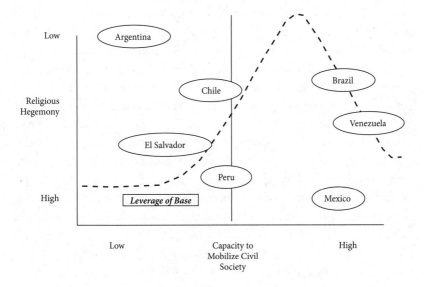

be motivated to forego comfortable alliances for institutional self-protection. They do not tell us, however, in what direction and how far religious hierarchies may stray from their otherwise preferred positions. That calculation is influenced, where the base has leverage, by the beliefs and motivations of ordinary Catholics—about social doctrine, economic justice, moral dilemmas, and politics itself. It is also tempered by the amount of political risk the church hierarchy perceives it faces—from government leaders, political representatives, opposition actors, and even public opinion—to its moral agenda and its institutional integrity and survival.

Political Orientation

In democratic times Catholic politicians respond to constituents, often to a greater degree than to bishops. In such a context, the ideological and political orientation of Catholic (and other) voters can influence the church's strategic options, especially in those countries where the church's capacity to mobilize is moderate to high. In all ten countries included in the 2000 round of the World Values Survey, Catholic respondents expressed high rates of unconditional opposition to abortion—ranging from 53 percent in Uruguay and 60 percent in the Dominican Republic to 92 percent in El Salvador (the unweighted mean across the ten countries was 70 percent)—and moderate rates of unconditional opposition (on average 54 and 53 percent across cases, respectively) to homosexuality and euthanasia (Table 7.4). But Catholics are less persuaded about the moral perils of divorce (only roughly one-third of the respondents to the World Values Survey in these ten countries were unconditionally opposed to divorce), sex education, and contraception, which the church also opposes. In Argentina over four-fifths of respondents in one poll thought it was an important priority to teach sex education in the schools—and most did not think the church should speak up on the issue.[3] In Chile the legalization of divorce was supported by three-fourths of the population and nearly half of Catholics (Centro de Estudios Públicos 1995). In Brazil in 2007, 94 percent of Catholics favored the use of condoms. Brazilian Catholics also evinced a moderation of opinion on homosexuality and even abortion: 49 percent favored same-sex civil unions and 46 percent believed homosexual couples should be allowed to adopt children; and whereas 65 percent favored re-

Table 7.4. Catholic Views on Moral Issues in Ten Latin American Countries, 2000

Question: *Please tell me for each of the following statements whether you think it can always be justified, never be justified, or something in between*[a]

	Homosexuality		Abortion		Divorce		Euthanasia		Index of Moral Values[b]
	Never Justifiable (%)	Mean	Never Justifiable (%)	Mean	Never Justifiable (%)	Mean	Never Justifiable (%)	Mean	
El Salvador[c]	78	2.15	92	1.50	55	3.94	83	2.13	2.43
Peru[d]	54	2.74	73	1.80	40	3.92	n.d.	n.d.	2.82
Venezuela	63	2.34	71	1.98	29	4.77	55	3.09	3.05
Brazil	55	3.11	76	1.95	30	4.85	61	2.95	3.22
Colombia	61	2.63	75	1.89	33	4.77	45	4.14	3.36
Mexico	53	3.57	70	2.59	41	4.43	40	3.37	3.49
Chile	38	3.71	71	2.14	31	5.13	49	3.37	3.59
Dominican Republic	48	3.31	60	2.82	23	5.18	53	3.29	3.65
Argentina	39	4.32	67	2.43	24	5.41	49	3.97	4.03
Uruguay	48	3.74	53	3.29	26	5.74	42	4.40	4.29

Source: 2000 World Values Surveys (Inglehart et al. 2004).

[a]Responses were on a ten-point scale, with 1 indicating never justifiable, and 10 indicating always justifiable.

[b]Average of "never justifiable" responses to all four questions.

[c]In El Salvador, respondents were given the opportunity to self-identify as "Roman Catholic" and as "Catholic who doesn't follow rules." Reported here are the combined percentages and means. Means for the two populations separately are the following:
Catholic who doesn't follow rules (*n* = 332): 2.3 (homosexuality), 1.62 (abortion), 4.18 (divorce), and 2.3 (euthanasia)
Roman Catholics (*n* = 406): 2.04 (homosexuality), 1.39 (abortion), 3.74 (divorce), and 2.0 (euthanasia).

[d]The question on euthanasia not asked in Peruvian survey, so the Peruvian case is averaged across the three available issue areas.

taining the nation's abortion laws to allow abortion only in cases of rape or risk to the mother's life, 16 percent favored allowing abortion in more circumstances and only 10 percent were in favor of making abortion a crime in all circumstances (DataFolha 2007).

Catholics also tend to be socially progressive. Although opinions are mixed on whether or not incomes should be made more equal or greater income differentials should be permitted as an incentive for individual effort, on the whole they favor greater government (over private) ownership of business and industry; the state taking more responsibility to provide for people (rather than leaving people to provide for themselves); and radically changing or gradually reforming society rather than valiantly defending the status quo (Table 7.5). These views on questions of fundamental social justice are important because Latin American voters identify economic and social issues as more salient than moral ones. From 2001 to 2004, in twelve major Latin American countries, unemployment, poverty, economic crisis, personal security, and access to health and education topped the list of survey responses to the question "What are the most important problem(s) facing the country?" Moral issues were not among the five most salient in a single country (Hagopian 2005, 346). In these circumstances it is hard to imagine the church could motivate Catholics to vote against their perceived economic interests to advance their moral views, especially when the latter are not intensely held.

Within this general picture national differences do emerge. The percentage of Salvadorans who were unconditionally opposed to homosexuality and divorce was *twice or more* as high as that of Argentines. Chilean Catholics were situated much farther to the left on social justice issues than Salvadorans, Dominicans, and Peruvians. Some of these differences may be explained by each country's starting point. The views of respondents on income inequality and private ownership may more accurately reflect actual levels of wealth distribution and the efficiency of government-provided services, which differ across countries, than their ideal levels of both. Thus, citizens of a country with gross inequality may on average respond that incomes need to be made more equal to a greater degree than those living in a country of relative equality. Residents who might pay exorbitant rates to private suppliers of public utilities may favor more government ownership than people who suffer from lengthy delays and poor provision of

Table 7.5. Catholic Views of Issues of Social Justice in Ten Latin American Countries, 2000

| | Basic Attitudes Toward Social Change "Society must be"ᵃ (in percent) | | | Attitudes Toward Equality, Market, and State (mean)ᵇ | | | |
	Radically Changed	Gradually Improved by Reform	Valiantly Defended	Income Differentials	Private Ownershipᶜ	Government Take on More Responsibilityᶜ	Social Justice Index
Dominican Republic	14.6	70.4	15.0	7.74	3.65	4.52	5.30
Peru	5.7	75.1	19.1	7.49	3.54	4.76	5.26
El Salvador	6.4	79.0	14.9	6.85	3.87	5.05	5.26
Brazil	18.0	61.5	20.5	5.75	4.78	4.72	5.08
Venezuela	11.8	58.2	29.9	5.57	4.54	4.63	4.91
Colombia	6.5	74.7	18.8	6.19	3.41	4.08	4.56
Mexico	16.4	57.5	26.1	4.79	4.44	4.10	4.44
Argentina	3.2	82.5	14.3	4.97	4.53	3.38	4.29
Uruguay	5.0	76.8	18.2	5.12	4.54	2.99	4.22
Chile	6.8	80.1	13.1	4.12	4.21	3.12	3.81

Source: 2000 World Values Survey (Inglehart et al. 2004).
Note: Subsamples of national samples were created from self-identified Roman Catholics. Sample sizes are 1,003 for Argentina; 803 for Brazil; 645 for Chile; 5,053 for Colombia; 245 for Dominican Republic; 738 for El Salvador; 1,129 for Mexico; 1,236 for Peru; 397 for Uruguay; and 787 for Venezuela.
ᵃRespondents were asked, "On this card are three basic kinds of attitudes concerning the society we live in. Please choose the one which best describes your own opinion." Options were, "Our society must be radically changed by revolutionary action"; "Our society must be gradually improved by reform"; and "Our present society must be valiantly defended against all subversive forces." Figures represent percentages of self-identified Roman Catholics who chose each option.
ᵇResponses were based on a ten-point scale, with 1 equaling "incomes should be made more equal," "private ownership of business should be increased," and "people should take more responsibility"; and 10 equaling "We need larger differences as incentives," "government ownership of business should be increased," and "the government should take more responsibility."
ᶜMeans subtracted from 10 (the maximum value) in order to normalize direction of means.

state-owned enterprises. In that vein, it is perhaps not surprising that the highest percentages of those that would "valiantly defend" society "as it is" were recorded in Venezuela—not the country with the most conservative electorate but the one in which society "as it is" is arguably the most threatened. But even given different starting points, genuine differences in orientation remain, especially on moral issues.

How, then, can we translate these views about social justice and moral issues to politics? Ordinarily, political scientists take self-identification on the ideological scale as a reasonable shortcut, especially in one-dimensional space. But in the sample under examination in this chapter, there are theoretically at least two dimensions to consider, and electorates may not always exhibit ideological consistency in their responses across issues. To determine the degree of ideological consistency between respondents' views on social justice and moral questions and their self-placement on the traditional left-right political scale, I examine whether or not the correlations between views on each of eight issue items and the self-placement score are statistically significant (for issue items see Table 7.A1 in the appendix to this chapter). Where they are, the interpretation of the political orientation of the Catholic electorate is fairly straightforward. Where voters are not ideologically consistent, we need to determine whether they are oriented by moral or pocketbook issues.

In fact, there was a fair amount of ideological consistency on only two issues—basic attitudes toward societal change (which correlated with ideological position in seven of ten country cases) and attitudes toward abortion (which did so in four). There was a great deal of ideological consistency in only two countries in our sample—Uruguay and Colombia. In Uruguay, where the mean ideological score of 5.67 was significantly correlated with all eight issue positions on the socioeconomic and rights/morals dimensions of politics, Catholics are consistently progressive on social justice and moral issues. In Colombia, where there was ideological consistency on five of eight issues, the Catholic electorate was more conservative, though perhaps not as much as the Colombian church itself. In Venezuela and Peru, on the other hand, there was not a single statistically significant correlation between ideological self-positioning and any of the eight issue areas, suggesting that the overall mean ideological position in these cases is meaningless. In these cases I take the indexed positions on both social justice and moral questions as the more accurate indicator of the orientation of respondents. Where correlations are partial, I interpret the issue on which there was greatest ideological consistency as the more accurately indicative, on average, of that population. Figure 7.3 maps the location of national samples of Catholic opinion on these two dimensions (the full results of the statistical correlations can be found in Table 7.A1).

On the traditional left-right scale, Chileans, who reported a mean ideological self-placement score of 5.23, are the most radical of the ten Latin American countries for which World Values Survey data for the 2000 round exist. Additionally, 25 percent of Chilean Catholics identified on the political left (scoring themselves between one and four on the left-right scale; see Table 7.6). These scores more closely match the positions of respondents on social justice questions than they do on moral questions, although by this measure Chileans are not the most socially conservative in South America, as is often alleged, and restrictive policies on divorce and abortion do not necessarily reflect grassroots opinion. Mexicans, Colombians,

Figure 7.3. Political Orientation of Catholics in Ten Latin American Countries, 2000

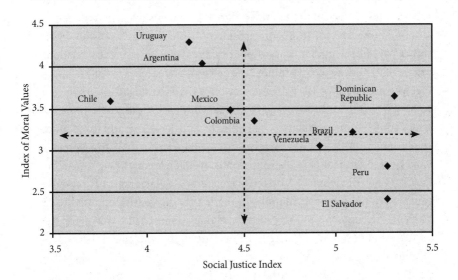

Sources: Tables 7.4 and 7.5.

and Dominicans, with mean scores of 6.65, 6.63, and 6.63, respectively, were located farthest to the right, but respondents in these countries were not the most morally conservative. Dominicans, in fact, who are highly integrated via migration into northeastern U.S. cities, were more open to liberalizing reproductive rights than most Latin Americans. On the other hand, Peruvians, with a mean score of 5.69 and 20 percent of Catholic respondents located on the political left, are far more conservative on moral issues. On both sets of issues, Salvadorans are the most conservative of all Latin Americans in the sample.

The issue positions of Brazilian and Venezuelan Catholics are more difficult to interpret. With ideological scores of 5.94 and 6.32, respectively, these appear to be relatively conservative electorates. Yet, 18 percent of Brazilians were open to changing society radically through revolutionary action, and 27 percent identified themselves on the political left (the highest percentage of Catholics in any Latin American country), compared to 3 and 12 percent, respectively, in Argentina, a country with a more progressive electorate on both indexes. In Venezuela ideological orientation is uncorrelated with views on social and moral issues, and in Brazil responses are correlated only with basic attitudes about social change.

To confirm the validity of these issue correlations as a way of determining how the orientation of the Catholic grassroots maps onto issue positions, and to provide more information on which issue dimension determines overall orientation toward politics in cases where such correlations are weak to nonexistent, I examine the partisan preferences of Catholic voters, who are not as conservative as they once were (or at least were believed to have been) in Latin America. In several countries these partisan preferences confirm our summary judgments. In El Salvador nearly three times the number of self-identified Catholics favored ARENA (Alianza Republicana Nacionalista, or Nationalist Republican Alliance) on the right than the FMLN (Frente Farabundo Martí para la Liberación Nacional, or Farabundo Marti National Liberation Front) on the left (37 percent as opposed to 13 percent), though the proportion is less than double (18 percent for the FMLN as opposed to 31 for ARENA) among those who called themselves "Catholics who don't follow the rules."[4] Partisan preferences help us to see that social justice and moral orientations are more illuminating in this case than mean ideological score. Likewise, in Mexico more respondents

Table 7.6. The Political Orientation of Catholics in Ten Latin American Countries, 2000

	Mean Score on Left-Right Scale	Percent Left (1–4)	Social Justice Index	Index of Moral Values	Partisan Preferences	Summary Measure and Basis (dimension, orientation)
Argentina	5.99	12	4.44	4.03	Alianza (39); PJ (38)	Socially and morally progressive
Brazil	5.94	27	5.08	3.22	PT (28); PMDB (23)[a]	Socially polarized, morally moderate
Chile	5.23	25	3.81	3.59	Concertación (48); Right (22)[b]	Socially progressive, morally moderate
Colombia	6.63	9	4.56	3.36	Liberal (41); None (24)[c]	Socially and morally moderate
Dominican Republic	6.63	17	5.30	3.65	PLD (44); PRD (35)[d]	Socially conservative, morally moderate to progressive
El Salvador	6.30	18	5.37	2.43	No party (39); ARENA (37)[e]	Socially and morally conservative
Mexico	6.65	15	4.44	3.49	PRI (48); PAN (26)[f]	Socially progressive, morally moderate
Peru	5.69	20	5.26	2.82	Perú Posible (50); APRA (19)[g]	Socially and morally conservative
Uruguay	5.67	20	4.23	4.29	Colorado (31); PN (24); FA (24)	Socially and morally progressive
Venezuela	6.32	18	4.91	3.05	MVR (39); None (36)[h]	Socially polarized, morally moderate

Source: 2000 World Values Survey (Inglehart et al. 2004).

[a] In third place was the Party of Brazilian Social Democracy (PSDB) with 12 percent, and in fourth the PFL with 10 percent.

[b] Separate preferences for Concertación parties were PDC (24), PPD (15), and PS (9); separate preferences for parties of the Rightist coalition were UDI (12) and RN (10).

[c] Conservative was cited by 17 percent of respondents, and 14 percent identified themselves as Independents.

[d] The Social Christian Reform Party (PRSC) was named by 10 percent of respondents.

[e] Scores for self-identified Roman Catholics. Thirteen percent of Roman Catholic respondents named the FMLN. Among "Catholics who don't follow the rules," preferences were 31 percent for ARENA and 18 percent for the FMLN.

[f] The Democratic Revolutionary Party (PRD) was a distant third with 8.5 percent.

[g] Unidad Nacional was cited by 11 percent of respondents.

[h] The second place party, Democratic Action (AD), was named by only 8 percent of respondents.

identified in the survey with the PRI (Partido Revolucionario Institucional, or Institutional Revolutionary Party) than the prochurch National Action Party (Partido Acción Nacional, or PAN), and in 2000 Catholic voters evenly divided between the two parties in an election in which a vote for PAN's presidential candidate was widely perceived as a vote for democracy (Magaloni and Moreno 2003). This political orientation is more consistent with the views of Mexicans on economic and moral issues than their ideological score, which was the farthest to the right of any country in our sample. In Chile, where the parties of the right have courted the religious vote on moral issues, Catholics still identify overwhelmingly with the centrist Christian Democratic Party (Partido Demócrata Cristiano, or PDC) and its coalition partners in the Concertación—24 percent favored the Christian Democrats, 15 percent the Party for Democracy (Partido por la Democracia, or PPD), and 9 percent the Socialist Party (Partido Socialista, or PS), as opposed to 12 percent for the Independent Democratic Union (Unión Demócrata Independiente, or UDI) and 10 percent for the National Renovation (Renovación Nacional, or RN). In addition, religiosity, which was so important in the 1960s, no longer predicts party preference between the PDC and the left (Torcal and Mainwaring 2003, 65–66, 74). In Argentina Catholics evenly split their partisan allegiances among two parties—the Peronists (Partido Justicialista, or PJ), which was favored by 38 percent of respondents, and the Alianza (Alliance of Radicals and FREPASO), chosen by 39 percent—with which they were more closely in line on moral issues than they were with religious authorities.

In other countries the political orientation of Catholics may illuminate the contradictory results of their ideological, moral, and social orientations. In Brazil 27 percent of Catholics expressed an affinity with the Workers' Party; we may assume many are members of the CEBs (comunidades eclesiais de base, or ecclesial base communities), who vote in greater numbers for Lula and the PT and with lower rates of blank and null voting than other Catholics (Pierucci and Prandi 1994, 25). In Venezuela, despite their fairly conservative ideological orientation, with oil prices soaring nearly two-fifths of respondents identified with the Movement of the Fifth Republic (Movimiento Quinta República, or MVR) of Hugo Chávez (a figure that climbed further before falling in late 2008). These results suggest that the mean ideological responses and views on social justice questions obscure more than they illuminate, and it may be more accurate to classify Catholic grassroots opinion in both countries as "polarized" on social justice issues rather than as "conservative." It is harder to provide an up-to-date characterization of the political orientation of Peruvians, given that in 2000, when one half (50 percent) identified with Perú Posible (Possible Peru) and about a fifth with APRA (Alianza Popular Revolucionaria Americana, or American Popular Revolutionary Alliance), the leftist-leaning Partido Nacionalista Peruano (Peruvian Nationalist Party, or PNP) led by Ollanta Humala had not yet formed.

In sum, the most conservative electorates, on both moral and socioeconomic issues, are located in Peru and El Salvador, though both have a leftist constituency consisting of roughly one-fifth of Catholics. Brazil and Venezuela constitute intermediate cases, with Brazil registering the highest percentage of "left" respondents of any country in the sample. Mexicans self-identify on the political right but maintain moderate views on moral issues and moderately progressive views on social justice. The most progressive Catholic electorate on economic issues is in Chile and on moral issues in Uruguay. Progressive views on moral issues can themselves constitute an element of political risk, as we see next.

Public Projects, Political Risk

Earlier in this chapter I identified the two forms that political risk for the Catholic Church may assume: a threat to the position and privileges of the institutional church, and a threat to the policy agenda on which the church places priority. A clear example of the former is the threats by the Venezuelan government to Catholic Church institutions (especially its schools and media outlets). Twenty years ago a summary assessment of risk to the church's moral agenda in Latin America would have focused on proposals to legalize divorce and provide access to contraception. Today, the moral issues that tend to provoke reactions from religious authorities range from the public provision of sex education for youth to proposals to permit same-sex civil unions and to decriminalize abortion or liberalize the circumstances under which the procedure may be performed. Though the church's position on sexual ethics is clear and consistent across our cases and bishops could in principle lash out at public health programs promoting the use of condoms among youth (and some do), the most contentious issues and those around which the emerging fault lines of moral hazard are being drawn across countries are homosexual rights, including the right to marry and adopt children, emergency contraception, and, especially, abortion. In country after country, the lid is being lifted that had heretofore silenced debate on these issues. A summary of such proposals is provided in Table 7.7.

The risks to the church policy agenda vary to a considerable extent in Latin America today. At one extreme, El Salvador has one of the most restrictive abortion laws in the world: the criminal code makes no exception for rape, incest, fetal deformity, or risk to the life of the mother; imposes serious prison sentences on providers (including physicians) and women who undergo the procedure clandestinely; and mandates full investigations of possible infractions of the law. At the other extreme, with a majority of seats in the state legislature of the Federal District, representatives of the Mexican PRD (Partido de la Revolución Democrática, or Party of the Democratic Revolution) passed a measure in 2007 in Mexico City to legalize abortion in the first trimester of a pregnancy, the most liberal provision in Central and South America outside of Cuba and Guyana. The Mexican Catholic Church has promised to contest the measure in the courts as a violation of the constitutional protection of the right to life. In Chile, though the Bachelet government has instructed public hospitals and health clinics to make available emergency contraception, the Christian Democratic Party, which forms a key part of the governing coalition, has constrained its partners in the Socialist Party from even raising the issue of loosening the country's abortion laws, which forbid abortion in all cases, including if there is a risk to the life of the mother.

A full assessment of risk on the part of religious hierarchies and a calculation of whether the church is in a sufficiently strong position to engage in a public policy debate—or if it should instead surrender to an alliance of expedience—would involve more than an examination of the content of government proposals. Another element of political risk that may influence church hierarchies to hedge bets or to risk an alliance with government or the opposition has to do with the viability of the opposition and the issue positions of all competitors. Chilean bishops, for example, who would have little to fear were the opposition to win a future election given that the rightist alliance of the UDI and the RN is closer to the church's positions than the incumbent Concertación alliance, may choose to confront the government over emergency contraception. Similarly, the Mexican Catholic Church may contest the PRD's position on abortion since it lived comfortably with the PRI for decades and the PAN, the party of current president Felipe Calderón, has always attended to the institutional interests of the church and aligned itself even more closely on democracy and moral issues to the positions of the hierarchy and Catholic voters (Loaeza 2003). (Calderón's predecessor, Vicente Fox, also of the PAN, was the first Mexican president in nearly a century to attend church services openly.) On the other hand, the Argentine church is more isolated politically, as neither of the two major political parties appears willing to advance church interests.

If churches do decide to fight, they may contest government proposals that threaten their moral agenda in different ways. They may attempt to influence the implementation of national programs through government ministries, national and state government bureaucracies, and the delivery of social services through decentralized local governments. Or, they may attempt to influence political legislation and even bring popular pressure to bear on court decisions, as the hierarchy pledged to do in Colombia following a court ruling loosening a total ban on abortion in 2006. They may lose a battle temporarily in a health ministry or even the national Congress but rally provincial-level or even local public officials to their side. Some conservative mayors in Chile, for instance, claimed their religious beliefs would not allow the morning-after pill to be distributed at public clinics in their municipalities, in contravention of a 2005 Ministry of Health order to make the morning-after pill available free at state-run hospitals to all women, including girls as young as fourteen (the age of consent in Chile) without any requirement of parental notification.[5] In this and related cases, church arguments have hinged on the right of individuals to exercise their conscience against state mandates, as well as what religious authorities claim are constitutional rights of parents to educate their children as they see fit and to protect life from the moment of conception.

A complicating factor in assessing risk is that once relations harden between the church and government, a tit-for-tat dynamic takes hold. Opposition is an inherently risky business. The Venezuelan bishops, who are locked in a tense conflict with the Chávez government, have reacted to

Table 7.7. Political Risk to the Roman Catholic Church in Seven Latin American Countries

Government Proposals	Argentina (Kirchner)	Brazil (Lula)	Chile (Bachelet)	El Salvador (Saca)	Mexico (Fox, Calderón)	Peru (Toledo, García)	Venezuela (Chávez)
Moral Agenda							
Introduce sex education in public and private schools	Yes, in 2004–05	Yes, above age 10	Yes	Abstinence only	Yes, new textbooks introduced in 2006	Yes	n.d.
Distribute condoms	Yes, in 2004–05	In public schools to youth over 13	Yes, in 2007 to poor youth in Santiago	No	Yes, but retraction in 2007[a]	No	Yes
Permit embryonic stem cell research	Yes; cloning banned	No	Not prohibited; cloning banned	No	Yes, since 2004 cloning banned	Not prohibited; cloning banned	n.d.
Make available emergency contraception	Yes	Yes, 2005	Yes, 2002 (private) 2005 (public)	On market	Yes, 2005	Yes, 2004	On market
Abortion: Current[b] Proposed liberalization	L, PH, R[c]	L, R F	None	None	L, R, F Federal District (first trimester)	L, PH	L 2004, R, I
Same-sex marriage/ Civil unions	Yes, in Buenos Aires & Rio Negro	Yes, in Rio Grande do Sul[d]	No	No	Yes, in Federal District (2006)	No	In Merida; national referendum proposed[e]

Public Policy Risk	Moderate-High	Moderate	Moderate-Low	Low	Moderate	Moderate-Low	High
Institutional Interests							
Catholic media	No	No	No	No	No	No	Yes[f]
Religious education	No	No	No	No	No	No	Yes
Privileged status of church	Yes	No	No	No	No[g]	No[h]	Yes
Institutional Risk	**Moderate**	**Low**	**Low**	**Low**	**Low**	**Low**	**High**

Sources: Campbell (2006); Center for Reproductive Rights (2007); Wheat and Matthews (2006).

Note: Some data not available (n.d.) for Venezuela.

[a]The health minister in the Calderón government, José Córdova, expressed his opposition to government promotion of condom use during the Fox government.

[b]L = threat to life of mother; R = rape; I = incest; F = fetal deformity; PH = physical health of mother.

[c]In Argentina, abortion is permitted in cases of rape of a woman with a mental disability.

[d]Brazil allows homosexual couples the right to inherit pension and social security benefits. In 2005, a São Paulo judge ruled that same-sex couples may adopt children.

[e]Also, the attorney-general's office created a Department of Information for the Gay, Lesbian, Bisexual, and Transgender Community.

[f]In April 2006 the Venezuelan government's telecommunications regulator reassigned the frequencies that had been used since 1999 by a Catholic-operated station, Vale TV.

[g]A 1992 reform reversed discriminatory measures against the Catholic Church.

[h]A 2003 constitutional amendment recognizing all faiths also acknowledged the historical, cultural, and moral importance of the Catholic Church to the nation.

threats to their institution, to Catholic schools, and to the country's abortion code. But it is not clear whether the Chávez government proposals constituted an *inherent* risk to the church or whether the government floated these proposals as retaliation for the hierarchy's opposition to government infringement on civil liberties and freedom. A similar dynamic is evident in Argentina, though the risk to the church is not nearly as grave. A sober assessment of political risk would require a contextual examination of each case. In sum, only in Venezuela can the threat to the church as an institution be considered high. But in several South American countries, notably Uruguay, Colombia, Argentina, and recently Brazil, national debates on abortion are beginning. In Chile, Peru, and El Salvador the issue of abortion is not on the political agenda.

The Bishops' Dilemma

We are now ready to predict responses to the bishops' dilemma. Figure 7.4 maps the church's religious hegemony and capacity to mobilize the faithful, the degree of political risk it faces, and the political orientation of Catholics toward moral and social justice issues in the seven countries under study onto the predicted responses of the church to its strategic dilemma.

To summarize these predictions, where religious hegemony is high, the church's capacity to mobilize is limited, and the orientation of the Catholic electorate is morally and socially conservative—as we have characterized Peru and El Salvador—we expect national episcopates to adopt a position of proactive moralism. When religious hegemony erodes and the church has limited capacity to mobilize its grassroots, which is the case in Argentina, bishops may move from a position of defensive to proactive moralism. Where religious hegemony and the capacity to mobilize are moderate at best and the orientation of the electorate carries a moderate degree of risk, as is the case in Chile, the church may succumb to a position of defensive moralism. Where religious hegemony is moderate but the capacity to mobilize is high, as is true in Brazil and Venezuela, the leverage of the base is greatest. In Brazil, where the grassroots are polarized on social justice issues and their orientation is moderate and nonthreatening on moral issues,

Figure 7.4. The Bishops' Dilemma

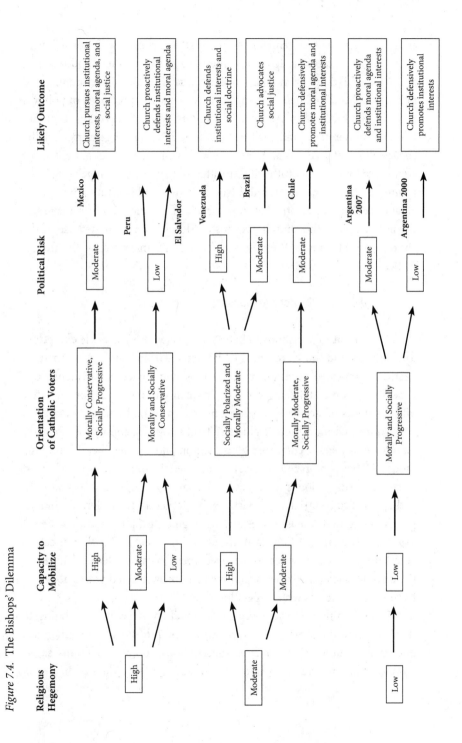

church leaders will be reluctant to identify too closely with conservative elites, causes, and parties to achieve their goals; instead, they support minimum wage hikes, peasant land struggles, and the cultural, economic, and political rights of indigenous peoples. In Venezuela a high level of political risk tilts the hierarchy's response in a highly political direction. Both are cases of moderate pluralism. Finally, where religious hegemony and the capacity to mobilize are high, as they are in Mexico, the climate is most conducive for religious authorities to attempt to exercise evangelizing leadership and defend public morality, social justice, and institutional interests all at once. The moderation of the Catholic electorate, however, may raise the policy risk to the church and push bishops toward the defense of the church's moral agenda. We now turn to a preliminary test of the framework.

Assessing Church Responses

All Catholic bishops in Latin America, without a single exception, forcefully uphold church teaching on human life from conception to natural death. On repeated occasions each bishops' conference has stridently opposed embryonic stem cell research, human cloning, the morning-after pill, assisted suicide, and abortion under any and all circumstances. All have supported indigenous rights and land struggles, condemned poverty and inequality, and denounced globalization and the neoliberal economic model. All have embraced democracy, affirmed the importance of informed electoral participation and honest politicians who govern transparently, and claimed to be strictly nonpartisan. Nonetheless, the difference in emphasis placed on these issues, especially in guiding Catholic voters at election time, is glaring. Whereas Brazilian bishops sounded a clarion call to voters not to sell their votes but to invest them in candidates committed to the church's social doctrine, Argentine bishops instructed voters above all to vote for politicians who respect life.

To determine the orientation of national churches in responding to their strategic dilemma, I analyzed a total of 726 official and unofficial documents, studies, pastoral letters, declarations, communiqués, messages, homilies, and interviews of bishops publicized on the websites of their episcopal conferences from 2000 to 2007 on the subjects of institutional interests, moral issues, and Catholic social doctrine (see Table 7.A2 in the appendix).[6] The universe of these documents is not entirely comparable. Chilean and Argentine bishops post Independence Day homilies and brief messages by individual bishops on religious holidays, while Salvadoran and Peruvian bishops do not. Mexican and Brazilian bishops tend to publicize not only official documents but also studies and reflections by lay experts on salient public issues, something other conferences do not do. Venezuelan bishops speak collectively as a conference, or are represented by their four officers. Though these differences in postings are interesting in and of themselves and signal something important about the way bishops view their communication with the faithful, they do introduce a bias that needs to be corrected, and thus it makes sense to privilege some documents over others. Official pastoral letters and declarations voted upon at biannual plenary sessions of conference meetings on the state of the economy, democracy, and protection of human life are generally far weightier tomes than Christmas and Easter greetings. It also makes sense, when considering messages issued by individual bishops, to determine whether they conform to, or dissent from, the "center of gravity" of the episcopate (see Mainwaring and Wilde 1989, 5; Gill 1998, 104–5).

In order to classify these messages according to the axis on which they may be placed, I separated traditional religious messages and routine personnel appointments from those directed explicitly to the defense of institutional interests, and pronouncements on social and economic justice from those extolling the virtues of democratic participation and world peace. A simple summary of the proportion of documents of each national episcopal conference addressed to one theme or the other is presented in Table 7.8. It is difficult, however, to draw meaningful inferences from this summary because these messages are in significant part endogenous responses to the political context in which the Catholic hierarchy finds itself. Bishops do not always set their own agenda but tend to react to public policy issues of the day. Thus, Chilean bishops issued a number of documents on marriage when a national divorce law was being debated in 2004 and on the government's anti-AIDS campaign in 2005; the Argentine bishops reacted to proposals to introduce sex education in public and private schools and loosen restrictions on abortion; and the Brazilian conference condemned court decisions and proposed legislation to permit embryonic stem cell research and to decriminalize abortion in cases of anencephalic fetuses. Even the number and type of elections and opportunities to speak out on democratic participation during national election campaigns vary in a fairly narrow range of years. It also stands to reason that religious leaders of countries that send large numbers of migrants to the United States, such as Mexico and El Salvador, may be more apt to address messages to migrants than bishops in countries that have not experienced such high rates of out-migration.

While readers should approach these data with caution, they do nonetheless tell us more than might at first appear. Though the content of particular moral messages may differ according to which issues are salient, bishops nonetheless choose to focus on these themes or they do not. Moreover, even if Salvadoran bishops "should" speak out more on poverty and

Table 7.8. Bishops' Messages, 2000–2007
(in percent)

| | Document Themes | | | | | |
| | Institutional | | Catholic Social Doctrine | | Moral Issues | |
Episcopal Conference	Traditional Religious Messages	Institutional Interests	Political (Domestic and International)	Social Justice	Life, Family	Cultural
Argentina	15	10	31	24	13	6
Brazil	0	12	14	30	44	0
Chile	13	48	6	11	11	11
El Salvador	28	10	11	49	1	0
Mexico	16	11	22	27	15	0
Peru[a]	0	16	26	16	29	0
Venezuela	11	14	65	5	6	0

Source: Author's compilation. See Table 7.A2 for original sources.
Note: Only official church documents were considered here.
[a]For Peru, the remaining 13 percent of the bishops' messages were general in nature.

hopelessness than Chilean bishops given the grinding poverty of El Salvador and Chile's recent prosperity, Peruvian bishops who should also be concerned about their poor are by comparison surprisingly mute—at least officially—on the subject. Each conference also had the same opportunities to comment on several common events and developments within their borders and on issues of international scope that were not on their national agendas, but not all seized them. Most denounced *The Da Vinci Code,* but the Peruvian bishops alone of the seven Latin American cases under examination denounced—stridently—the Spanish legalization of same-sex unions. In the sections that follow, I highlight the distinctive responses of the national episcopal conferences according to the theoretical framework elaborated earlier in this chapter.

Defending Institutional Interests and the Moral Agenda

This section examines three cases: Argentina, where the church is shifting from defensive to proactive moralism; Peru, where it has moved in the direction of greater proactive moralism; and Chile, where the church enjoys less hegemony and has defensively promoted its moral agenda.

From Proactive to Defensive Moralism: Argentina

The hegemony of the Roman Catholic Church in Argentina is declining not because of robust competition from Protestant denominations but because of the rapid secularization of Argentine society. Sensing the church's declining influence over the faithful—recall that three-quarters of Argentines felt that religious leaders should not attempt to influence how people vote in elections and nearly two-thirds that they should not influence government (see Table 1.9)—the government and women's movements have pressed an agenda that brings them into conflict with the nation's bishops. Political risk in the Argentine case, in other words, is rising, and it is endogenous to the church's declining hegemony and its own first moves against the Kirchner government. When the Peronist health minister advanced a plan to introduce sex education in the public and private schools and distribute contraceptives to minors in 2004–2005, Military Chaplain General Bishop Antonio Baseotto ominously declared that the minister should be thrown into the sea with a millstone around his neck—a reference to a biblical passage that for many Argentines evoked strong memories of the dictatorship's practice of throwing the bodies of drugged prisoners into the sea. In the ensuing firestorm between church and government officials, President Kirchner cut off the salary of the army chaplain and failed to attend the Te Deum Mass at the Plaza Mayor Cathedral in Buenos Aires for Argentina's Revolution Day. One bishop of retirement age famously mounted a successful electoral challenge against the Peronist governor (and Kirchner ally) of the province of Misiones by heading a slate of candidates in the elections for the provincial assembly.

My framework predicts that in cases of low religious hegemony and a low to moderate capacity to mobilize, the political orientation of the electorate will not constrain the hierarchy, which will defend the church's institutional interests and moral agenda—either quietly and in a nonconfrontational manner if it is allied with the government of the day or vocally if it is not. In the case of Argentina, which fits the first two criteria, the hierarchy in fact did speak out on moral issues and to protect church subsidies and privileges. In the wake of the collapse in 2001 of Menem's signature convertibility program, the economy, and even the Radical government, and the concomitant rise of the anti-neoliberal, Kirchner wing of the Peronist party, the church might have plausibly aligned with an angry civil society around issues of unemployment and inequality and an antiglobalization agenda. The church did participate—although "not without apprehension"—in the national Roundtable of Argentine Dialogue in 2002, but its advocacy of social justice was muted, as was its criticism of potential allies in the effort to protect church subsidies and privileges.

But then, as the electorate veered leftward on moral and economic issues and the level of political risk rose, the church's position shifted from the days when it relied on state support to maintain its institution and to fulfill its pastoral tasks. In response to an increasingly secular landscape and a center-left government's proposals to extend liberal rights, the church has clung more tightly to its traditionally conservative positions and promoted them even more aggressively. Church leaders have gone so far as to advocate a "balanced" approach to the history of the *Proceso* (as that period of military rule is known) and controversially endorsed the positions of the Memoria Completa (Complete Memory) group, which stresses the violence committed by leftist guerrillas as well as that by the military.[7]

In the 142 documents issued in the two-year cycle from 2004 to 2005, Argentine bishops spoke out frequently on the issue of abortion, and they uniformly condemned the *piqueteros,* a social movement of unemployed workers that resorted at times to violent protests. While the bishops repeatedly denounced economic neoliberalism, they did so for the deleterious impact that the laws of the market and profit incentives had on undermining the value of work, encouraging tax evasion, and corrupting political leaders. Economic liberalism was equated with an equally pernicious cultural liberalism. Poverty and exclusion were viewed as symptoms of a moral crisis, which two key pastoral documents identified as rooted in a "secularist cultural dimension" that carries ideologies of moral relativism with respect to "the concepts of marriage and the family, certain perceptions of gender, and new models of relationship between the sexes" (CEA 2003, 2004). The bishops had harsh words for "anti-birth" and "pro-divorce" legislation (CEA 2003). They condemned the media, in particular, for publicizing violence and destroying the family. Though they decried social exclusion and upheld the rights to shelter, employment, education, health, and of indigenous peoples, they issued the pastoral letter "Una Luz para Reconstruir la Nación" ("A Light to Rebuild the Nation"), which condemned the government and its role in rising inequality, only after the Kirchner administration proposed introducing sex education in public and private schools (CEA 2005). Most episcopal messages promoted evangelization, warned of a crisis of values, and specifically opposed the legalization of assisted reproduction and abortion in cases of rape. In 2004 and 2005, of two dozen bishops making pronouncements, only one, Juan Rubén Martínez of Posadas, spoke out in his homilies against clientelism, and only the retired bishop of Viedma, Miguel Hesayne, favorably mentioned the base communities and spoke out on what could be construed as a social justice agenda.

Proactive Moralism in Peru

The theoretical framework proposed in this chapter suggests that in cases of medium to high religious hegemony, a low to moderate capacity to mobilize, a conservative to moderate electorate, and low political risk, Roman Catholic bishops will stress moral issues. Peru shares with Argentina a similar percentage of self-identified Catholics but is a less secular society—people claim to worship at almost double the rate in Argentina—and apparently a more densely organized one. Nonetheless, the church no longer enjoys the links to society it once had. Its activists were the victims of violence, and the Peruvian hierarchy jettisoned its liberationist wing, which was born in Peru with the publication of *A Theology of Liberation* (Gutiérrez 1973). As Catalina Romero's contribution to this volume reveals, that church may have disappeared from view but it has not disappeared.

With a limited capacity to mobilize the grassroots civic and religious communities that exist and undoubtedly account for the 20 percent of Peruvian Catholics favoring radical social change, the Peruvian hierarchy has adopted a posture of proactive moralism, but since the political risk to its institution and policy agenda is low, it has not clashed with the government to the same extent as in Argentina. The political orientation of the electorate matters less, except indirectly, causing the episcopate to seek elite allies and state support.

The Peruvian episcopate has issued relatively few documents. Of the thirty-one documents issued between 2003 and 2006, nine (29 percent) highlighted moral issues, five (16 percent) defended institutional interests, and another five (16 percent) addressed issues of social justice (the four remaining documents were broad-ranging and covered a gamut of themes). Of the five addressing social justice themes, four (one each year) were addressed to migrants on the occasion of the Day of the Migrant. Only one document in the four-year period for which documents were available mentioned the church's social doctrine (this was in 2003). Among the eight messages (26 percent) with explicitly political themes, three condemned strikes and violent protests, and one expressed solidarity with the victims of the Madrid train bombings of 2004. Of the remaining four, one spoke of Peruvian national institutions' loss of credibility, one issued faint praise and a warning against high expectations for the about-to-be-published Truth and Reconciliation Commission Report in 2003 (CEP 2003), and two urged Peruvians to vote in elections but offered little guidance for whom they should vote. Two were issued in 2006 to denounce as affronts to believers *The Da Vinci Code* and apocryphal reports about the Gospel of Judas, which called into question the divinity of Jesus. One decried that Holy Week in Peru was not being observed in a sufficiently pious manner, and, more significantly, one issued in 2003 spoke out in favor of a proposed amendment to the 1993 constitution recognizing the special place of the Catholic Church in Peru, an amendment that ultimately passed but in a form that also advanced the religious liberty of other denominations.

The Peruvian bishops issued a series of forceful messages on moral affairs. It is not surprising that Peru's Roman Catholic bishops would oppose abortion and emergency contraception—as they do in every country—but in 2004 when the minister of health proposed making the morning-after pill available the Peruvian conference went beyond customary condemnations of the pill as an abortifacient; bishops warned that the government's campaign would open the path toward the fracture of Peruvian society and essentially declared the campaign unconstitutional for its violation of the right to life (CEP 2004). Every conference issued statements in favor of life and against abortion on the "Day of the Unborn Child" (celebrated on March 25, the presumed date of the conception of Christ), but the Peruvian conference took the additional step of pointing out that "many NGOs with a lot of economic resources have as one of their principal objectives to legalize abortion in our country" (CEP 2006a). Moreover, the Peruvian episcopate, alone among the seven Latin American national episcopal conferences under study here, condemned the July 2005 reform to the Civil Code in Spain that allowed same-sex marriages and same-sex couples to adopt children. In a particularly aggressive statement, the CEP wrote, "To transgress natural law is not a cry of liberty, but an irresponsible outrage against human nature and society; above all, against children and the future of society. It constitutes a new form of abuse of the right of children to grow up in a natural environment" (CEP 2005). The Peruvian bishops also used the occasion of International Women's Day to impart the message that "in the area of education, she [a woman] is the transmitter of family values and traditions par excellence. A good part of education in a crucial period of the life of persons depends on women. . . . today we confront a hazard of devaluing her role as mother and educator and an attempt to replace that role with models foreign to what is essential to her vocation" (CEP 2006b).

Since the church was not really under attack from state authorities, it is not surprising that such a small percentage of the hierarchy's messages were classified as of primary interest to the institution. But its adoption of a series of positions so virulent in defense of morality, in a country in which by its own admission more than half the population lives in poverty and another fifth in dire poverty, is evidence that the Peruvian church has adopted a stance of proactive moralism.

Defensive Moralism in Chile

Church leaders in Chile—who bravely opposed military authorities when Catholic politicians were exiled, bishops insulted, the faithful tortured, and the poor defected to Pentecostal competitors—like their Argentine and Peruvian counterparts, have emphasized moral issues. When authoritarian enclaves remaining in the new democracy and inequality inherited from the dictatorship were highly salient in the public eye in the 1990s, church leaders waged a lengthy and ultimately losing campaign against the legalization of divorce. Since 2000 they have also prominently opposed sex education in schools, the government provision of condoms to combat the spread of AIDS, any liberalization of the country's abortion laws, and the removal of religious instruction from the public schools. Church leaders condemned President Lagos, the Concertación, and Catholic politicians who made possible the 2004 Marriage (divorce) Law as well as the morning-after pill, and they were especially critical of the Lagos government's distribution of condoms as part of its anti-AIDS campaign, which they decried as expensive, potentially ineffective, encouraging of sexual promiscuity, and aimed at undermining church moral authority by suggesting that Catholics do not follow church teaching on birth control. They even opposed a Ministry of Education regulation requiring all schools to provide access and services to pregnant girls on the grounds that it constituted state interference in religious education. The most significant pastoral letter of this period, "Matrimonio y Familia, una Buena Noticia para la Humanidad" (Marriage and Family: Good News for Humanity) (CECH 2005a), celebrates the family and warns of the potential burden that falling birth rates will place on the nation's pension system.

These moral and institutional concerns were not matched by a similar level of concern about economic justice questions. In a set of coordinated Independence Day messages in 2004 and 2005, bishops gave thanks for economic prosperity, good copper prices, and a new health law. Only 11 percent of messages in 2004 focused on social justice issues (compared with 22 percent that addressed moral and cultural issues), and those that spoke about equality focused on equality of opportunity. Most (60 percent) addressed institutional issues, not the least because the Chilean church was wracked by its own sexual abuse scandal. On the relatively few occasions they spoke out on politics, Chilean bishops stressed that democratic pluralism could not fail to recognize natural, moral principles. Along with human rights for ethnic and religious minorities, opportunities for youth, fair wages, and the reduction of inequality, they identified as issues of overriding importance the dignity of life from conception, the benefit of families founded in the union of a man and a woman, and support for biological maternity (CECH 2005b). The hierarchy's predominant message to Catholics in a context of official nonpartisanship was to vote for candidates that upheld the dignity of life from conception to natural death.

The consistent priority assigned to the church's institutional interests and moral agenda amid high inequality and authoritarian vestiges is consistent with the theoretical framework advanced in this chapter. With at best moderate levels of religious hegemony and a middling capacity to mobilize the faithful, Chilean bishops have been able to resist pluralist pressures from their base and defend their moral agenda. The difference between proactive and defensive moralism in the Chilean case may be subtle, but it is important nonetheless. Although Chile's bishops enjoy cordial relations with the Socialist Party of President Michelle Bachelet, their even stronger alliances with other political actors across the spectrum from the Christian Democrats to the UDI have allowed them to tone down their criticism of government officials. Despite the fact that Chile has been governed by two consecutive agnostic Socialist presidents, the risk to the church's institutional interests and even its policy agenda is fairly low in comparative Latin American terms.

Moderate Pluralism, Social Justice, and Political Engagement

My theory predicts that in densely organized civil societies, amid low to moderate religious hegemony, with moderate to left-leaning Catholic electorates, national episcopates will be constrained from moving too far to the right. Moreover, if they have friends in political parties that lie to the left on social justice issues, the risk to the institution and public policy agenda will be lower, and they should not feel the need to defend their moral agenda. On the other hand, where the risk to the institution is greater, the church's emphasis will be on defending its institutional interests, even ahead of its moral agenda.

Moderate Pluralism in Brazil

Historically, the Brazilian church did not penetrate society as deeply as its counterparts elsewhere in Latin America, and it faced competition not merely from evangelical Protestants but also from African Diaspora and Spiritist religions among Brazil's sizeable population of color. Like in Chile, when the military trampled on Brazilian society, the Catholic hierarchy spoke up forcefully for the defense of human rights and a range of popular causes such as a fair minimum wage and land for the landless. But unlike in Chile, the Brazilian episcopate maintained a progressive posture during the transition to a fully democratic regime and beyond: it has sustained its Workers' Pastoral (Pastoral Operária, or PO) for more than thirty years; created other pastoral commissions on the landless, AIDS, "marginalized women," "street people," and migrants; and launched highly visible campaigns to educate voters about political parties' electoral programs and commitments to the poor. Bishops have kept social justice issues such as corruption, the external debt, and participation in free trade agreements at the forefront of the public debate (Wanderley 2003); issued harsh pastoral letters on indigenous rights, agrarian reform, and rural enslavement (CNBB/Instituto Nacional de Pastoral 2003); and spoken out on poverty, inequality, and other social issues.

The Brazilian bishops' conference has criticized proposed legislation on abortion of anencephalic fetuses, birth control, and same-sex marriage (Brazil now grants same-sex partners the same rights as married couples with respect to pensions, social security benefits, and taxation). Yet, in sharp contrast with Argentina, the bishops' statement "respectfully disagreeing" with the government's distribution of condoms to stop the spread of HIV applauds the government's intent while voicing concern that any policy to stop the AIDS epidemic should embrace Christian principles and values. It does not condemn such a policy outright, however.

In 2002 the church laid out a blueprint for its involvement in the electoral campaign that could be read as an endorsement of the change promised by the PT, though it urged parish priests and lay workers to observe the guidelines established by the Vatican document "Catholics in Politics" (Congregation for the Doctrine of the Faith 2002). From 2003 to 2005 Brazilian bishops issued twenty-four documents on the theme of the church and politics. Those released at the time of the 2004 municipal elections instructed voters on the functions of mayors and city councilors, admonished voters not to sell their votes or vote for anyone who offered them a benefit in exchange for their support, and identified the type of issues on which voters should seek the positions of the candidates. Voters were explicitly urged not to vote for politicians who did not uphold Catholic teaching on human life in only two messages, but even in these cases the bishops did not focus exclusively or even primarily on this issue. Church leaders clearly emphasized to a far greater degree a politician's honesty, competence, and commitment to the poor. In the late 1990s the CNBB's Pastoral Commission on Justice and Peace launched a petition drive to sponsor citizen's legislation to prohibit the practice of clientelism. The church mobilized sixty organizations in fifteen months to collect the requisite one million signatures, a campaign that successfully culminated in the passage of Law 9840/99, which made buying votes by a candidate to public office a crime punishable by loss of mandate. The church followed up this initiative with public campaigns such as "Your vote does not have a price, it has consequences" (Voto não tem preço, tem consequências) and the formation of "Faith and Politics" groups to monitor and hold accountable public officials. The objective of these campaigns was broader than to elect candidates that might defend the church's institutional interests or even its moral agenda; rather, they aimed to mobilize civil society and raise public awareness to promote programmatic political parties, make government transparent and accountable, and foster pro-poor public policies. Moreover, the range of social and economic topics on which Brazilian bishops pronounced contrasts sharply with every other country under discussion, including Mexico. These include the message of Dom Luciano Mendes on the privatization of the Rio Doce Valley Mining Company, land reform, and May Day. One bishop even favorably mentioned the CEBs.

Moderate Pluralism in Venezuela

Like Brazil, the Venezuelan church enjoys moderate levels of religious hegemony, although for different reasons: it faces less competition but a more secular society. It also enjoys a moderate to high capacity to mobilize civil society. As we saw earlier in this chapter, Venezuelan civil society is highly organized, and Catholics straddle both religious and civic organizations. Even the political orientation of Catholics is very similar in the two countries. But there the similarities end, as the Venezuelan church is operating in a radically different political climate.

The church in Venezuela is facing the highest degree of political risk of any church in Latin America today. At stake is its institutional survival as well as the passage of public policies it stridently opposes. The government has threatened to withhold the appointment of bishops, declare that education should be of a secular nature, and silence the Catholic media (all media in Venezuela face harassment and ever more restrictive press freedoms). Proposals have also been floated to loosen the nation's ban on abortion to allow termination of pregnancy in case of incest or rape, which the hierarchy has resisted vigorously. Relations with the government are tense. While President Hugo Chávez claims to be a devout Christian—at his inauguration beginning his third presidential term in January 2007, he declared Christ was "one of the greatest socialist revolutionaries ever born on the Earth"—he has forsaken the Roman Catholic Church, in which he served as an altar boy, for the Christian Evangelical Church and has famously called the nation's Roman Catholic bishops a "tumor" in Venezuelan society. Before hundreds of thousands of the faithful on the occasion of the procession of the Divine Shepherdess, the eighty-three-year-old retired Cardinal Rosalio Castillo Lara accused Chávez of being paranoid and his administration of having "lost its democratic course" and presenting "the semblance of a dictatorship." Speaking in the name of the Venezuelan Episcopal Conference (Conferencia Episcopal Venezolana, or CEV), Archbishop Jorge Urosa Sabino of Caracas attempted to smooth over the conflict by urging Catholic priests to refrain from voicing political opinions during religious functions.

Since 2002, in messages, communiqués, and exhortations to the Catholic faithful and to men and women of good will, Venezuelan bishops have accorded the highest priority to politics and the escalating national crisis, which they have referred to as the "deepest in recent years" (CEV 2002). Sixty-five percent of all messages were classified as pertaining to political themes, and another 25 percent to the church's institutional self-defense (14 percent) and traditional religious themes (11 percent). However, the balance of these messages tells us more about the state of Venezuelan society and church-state relations than what the bishops independently chose to emphasize and in what way. More than in any other case discussed in this chapter, we need to focus on the content of these messages.

During the years in which the nation's Roman Catholic bishops and the Chávez government have had a difficult relationship, the CEV has spoken out consistently and forcefully on a series of recurring themes: the integrity of national political institutions, especially the National Electoral Commission (Comisión Nacional Electoral, or CNE); violence and the militarization of Venezuelan society; the growing polarization of the country between government supporters and their "enemies," that is, those in the "opposition camp"; and increasing threats to liberty, freedom, and rights— above all the right to hold dissenting opinions without fear of persecution and retaliation, especially dismissal from public-sector jobs. In 2002, the year of the coup attempt against Chávez, the bishops issued numerous documents about national events, calling for national dialogue, reconciliation, and respect for human rights, as well as for the CNE to act impartially and transparently. In their campaign for a national recall referendum, Chávez's opponents lamented the deterioration of the nation's institutions and warned of national collapse. But while relations between Venezuela's bishops and the government are obviously strained, they have not fractured entirely. Rather, the bishops have on occasion accepted the government's invitation to dialogue and even met with the president and vice president to keep open the channels of communication.

The Venezuelan hierarchy has also spoken out on behalf of institutional interests. Bishops mounted a forceful defense of religious education in response to the government's proposed education reform, which would have declared education secular, and supported the freedom of the Catholic media. But church leaders also used pastoral letters to address such traditional religious themes as the year of the Eucharist and the institutional crisis of vocations (CEV 2005a, 2005b). Messages concerning moral issues were few but uncompromising; bishops unsurprisingly opposed government proposals to liberalize abortion in cases of rape and incest (CEV 2004), and while they preached a message of love and solidarity with those suffering from AIDS, they asserted that the spread of HIV was essentially the result of irresponsible sexual behavior (CEV n.d.). The Venezuelan bishops also stressed the importance of social justice within their carefully worded statements about transparency in the electoral process and the threat to civil liberties. They have distanced themselves from economic and social policies pursued by Venezuela's two dominant parties in the late 1980s and 1990s; like other Latin American bishops' conferences they opposed laissez-faire capitalism along with statism but, unlike many others, reaffirmed the church's preferential option for the poor and even invoked the martyrdom of Salvadoran archbishop Óscar Romero (CEV 2005c).

Evangelizing Leadership, Social Doctrine, and a Moral Public Sphere

It is rare that Latin American episcopal conferences are able to straddle the two dimensions of political space that we have discussed—the socioeconomic and the public morality/individual rights. Yet this is what they must do if they are to make the attempt to exercise evangelizing leadership. Evangelizing leadership does not automatically follow from high levels of religious hegemony. As I have argued, the church must exercise a sufficient degree of religious hegemony in a society in which citizens are mobilized for political action and where, as voters, their issue stances essentially conform to that of the Catholic hierarchy. Thus, for example, in Colombia, where the church exercises a great deal of hegemony in society but does not necessarily share orientations toward politics and policy or enjoy deep connections with its grassroots, the church is not assured of the capacity to lead on both moral and material policy issues. The claim here is not that a church with the requisite hegemony, capacity to mobilize civil society, and pliant grassroots will necessarily succeed in providing such leadership—only that it will make the attempt.

Hegemonic Leadership and Hedging Bets: Mexico

Compared to Brazil, the Mexican hierarchy places more emphasis on the church's moral agenda, but unlike its counterparts in Peru, Argentina, and Chile, it also criticizes the government when it betrays Catholic social doctrine. Independence from the state and the incumbent government elites has allowed the church to speak with moral authority on a range of public issues. For decades, the Mexican church consistently maintained the position that the greatest state threat to its flock was the excessive concentration of authority in the federal executive branch, party/government control of the electoral process, and the sixty-year reign of a single party due to the organizational corporatism that reduced pluralism and civic responsibility and led to abuses of power (Camp 1997, 292).

Catholic leaders in Mexico have staked out a distinctive position, which could not be readily predicted by its twentieth-century history. The Mexican Catholic Church, of course, was the victim of a revolution that established a fundamentally anticlerical order, one with a sharper separation of church and state than in any other country in the hemisphere except Cuba. The church could own no property, priests could not vote, and church authorities could not speak about politics. Though tensions with the state eased in the 1940s, the church operated under what it perceived to be the hostile watch of the state for another half century (Camp 1997, 32). In 1992 President Carlos Salinas initiated a series of historic constitutional reforms that removed the prohibition against the church owning property "indispensable" to its tasks and granted voting rights to priests but left in force bans on the clergy proselytizing for or against any political party or candidates (Camp 1997, 31–34; Soberanes Fernández 1999). In the decade since then, the church's positions on such moral issues as human cloning, euthanasia, in vitro fertilization, and the national abortion law have been clear and uncompromising. But bishops have also defended social justice and democracy, indigenous rights and culture, and the plight of Mexican migrants in the United States, and they have denounced the application by the pro-Catholic Fox administration of the value-added tax to food and medicine, increases in the minimum wage as too small, and proposals to legalize gambling as injurious to the poor. The church has assumed a more assertive tone on public policy than at any time in nearly a century.

Of fifty-five episcopal documents issued between 2000 and 2005, eight (15 percent) pertained to moral themes, fifteen (27 percent) to themes related to the church's social doctrine, another twelve (22 percent) to explicitly political themes extolling peace and democratic elections and values, and fifteen (27 percent) to themes related either to institutional interests or traditional religious messages. A substantial pastoral letter, a papal message for Mexico, and four closing messages from plenary sessions of episcopal conferences covered multiple themes. As in Brazil, the Mexican hierarchy not only exhorted Mexicans to vote and not to sell their votes, but it also instructed them to be well informed about the positions of candidates and parties on various economic, social, and moral questions of the day. It reminded them that Christian faith obligated them to work for a just society, and that, in conscience, Catholic citizens should not vote for politicians who do not respect the dignity of human life, marriage, the family, and the true common good. In July 2005 Cardinal Norberto Rivera of Mexico City threatened legal action over the Health Ministry's decision to recommend making the morning-after pill available; he once even called for condoms to carry warning labels similar to tobacco products. In contravention of nearly a century of custom and law, the church is also "pushing to be allowed to teach religion in schools and to own broadcasting licenses" (*Latin American Regional Report* 2005). Far from adopting a position of defensive moralism, the Mexican Catholic Church is confidently reaching for a new church-state relationship and a broader role in Mexican politics and society.

Social Justice without Pluralism: The Salvadoran Anomaly

The theoretical framework advanced in this chapter would predict that a church that enjoys high levels of religious hegemony (even with stiff religious competition), a low capacity to mobilize its grassroots (in El Salvador not so much because the church lacks connections to the faithful or has expelled its liberationist elements as it did in Peru but merely because of the devastating effects of military repression and death squad activity), and little risk from either its own base (Catholic opinion is as far to the right in El Salvador as in any country for which we have data in Latin America) or the political establishment would promote moral and institutional interests above all else. We would also expect religious authorities to ally with political actors on the right who do not share the church's social justice agenda. In fact, contrary to expectations, the Salvadoran episcopate has emphasized social justice and peace, almost to the exclusion of every other concern.

The statements of the Salvadoran hierarchy are truly impressive for their poignant emphasis on social justice. A mere two messages of twenty-two posted for the period from 2000 to early 2007 (10 percent) focused on institutional interests—one denounced the book and movie *The Da Vinci Code* and the other decried the heckling of the archbishop who was the president of the conference by a group of radical protestors. A little more than one quarter of the messages were focused on traditional religious messages. Even more surprising, there was only brief mention of moral issues (the family and sex education) in one pastoral letter in the entire period. Nearly half of all messages were devoted to social justice themes. Even more impressive than the quantity of messages was their content. Time and again, the Salvadoran episcopate invoked the church's social doctrine to put itself on the side of the poor, the unemployed, and the victims of violence.

Indeed, the Salvadoran bishops explicitly reference the church's social doctrine in highlighting several key themes: peace and reconciliation after the country's bloody civil war, the right of all citizens to adequate health care, the indignity and hopelessness of poverty and unemployment, and the climate of violence and violent crime that engulfed the nation. Three pastoral letters in this six-year period focused particularly on bringing about an end to all violence in the country. One called for peace by remembering Pope John Paul II's messages during his two papal visits to El Salvador (which took place in 1982, at the height of the conflict, and in 1996, four years after the peace accords had been signed) (CEDES 2003). In another, the Salvadoran bishops enjoined the Salvador laity to embrace the new evangelization and bring Christian principles into the public sphere and political life (CEDES 2004). What is striking is not that Roman Catholic bishops would call for a climate of peace—after all, they played a major role in mediating the cessation of hostilities and an end to a civil war that had spanned decades—but that they would urge the government to abandon its iron-fist policies of harassing youth gang members in favor of overcoming the nation's economic problems and investing in prevention programs instead (CEDES 2005). A major pastoral letter in 2004 praises the growing role of the laity in numerous parishes, associations, and movements but expresses concern about globalization, the advance of the "sects," unemployment, and public and private corruption (CEDES 2004, 17–18).

The stunning emphasis in the Salvadoran case on social justice, which was not predicted by our theoretical framework, may be explained in part by an utter lack of political risk to the church's moral agenda, which makes speaking out on moral issues a moot exercise. Though a sizeable number of "Catholics who don't follow the rules" self-identify with the political left, Catholic opinion as a whole is decidedly morally conservative—to an extreme extent in comparative Latin American terms. But it is also likely the case that the legacy of the martyred Archbishop Óscar Romero lives on in the hierarchy and, especially, among the faithful—still in the fold, unlike in Peru—whose appetite for social justice has not waned.

Conclusions: Bishops, Politics, and Policy

As we have seen, the church's strategic dilemma is considerably more complex than merely maximizing membership. A new "bishops' dilemma" has superseded the dilemma of authoritarian times when debate on moral issues was not raised, either by dictatorships that exalted "traditional" values or by their opponents who, seeking not much more than to survive, were grateful for the church's help in doing so. In that era bishops faced the Hobson's choice of privileging institutional survival or championing social justice and human dignity. Where the church relied on the rich, its decision was obvious; where it faced competition, the argument goes, its calculus shifted. Today, the updated version of the bishops' dilemma moves to two-dimensional space. Moral issues have been placed on the agenda of politics not merely by democratically elected governments and representatives but also by profound social change, and institutional defense becomes ever more salient as religious pluralism has increased and demands for religious liberty, and evenhanded treatment by state authorities, has grown. Political alliances have become more complex, and bishops must establish priorities.

National episcopal conferences have responded to the challenges of religious and political pluralism by establishing different priorities, conveying different messages, and forming different alliances. Attributing the national economic crisis to the globalization of markets and culture and to a crisis of moral values, the Argentine episcopate has reacted to proposals to offer sex education in public and private schools and to legalize abortion in some circumstances with sharp fire. The Chilean hierarchy, which has been uncritical of a more successful version of market-oriented economic policy but in pursuit of similar goals for the national moral agenda, has enlisted elite allies from among politicians of the center and right in the fight to infuse religious, moral, and ethical values into popular culture and the public sphere. Peruvian bishops, too, have placed little emphasis on the church's social doctrine in relation to its moral agenda, on which it has been uncompromising.

But not all churches did or must follow the same path. The Brazilian Conference of Catholic Bishops maintains pastoral commissions to defend aggressively the economic and social rights of the poor, and it has denounced economic injustice and public-sector corruption as vocally as it has any steps to legalize abortion and embryonic stem cell research. In much the same circumstances but facing far greater risk to their institution, Venezuelan bishops have repeatedly called for national dialogue, consensus, and an end to the intimidation of opponents. In Mexico, where the church enjoys greater religious hegemony, bishops have also spoken out on behalf of the poor, but, at the same time, they have more aggressively reminded Catholic voters and politicians of their duties to protect life above all else.

This chapter has attempted to lay out a theoretical framework that would ideally predict but at minimum make sense of the surprisingly divergent responses by national episcopates to similar, though not identical, policy challenges in a universal church that prescribes uniform positions on the great moral and social issues of the day. I began by pointing out what should be a relatively obvious truism of democratic regimes: in order to advance public policy agendas that compete in political space in democracies, churches need to be able to mobilize their bases. Consequently, this framework accords primary importance to the organization of civil society, the church's relationship to its grassroots, and the orientation of voters in the context of the political risks the church faces. This framework explained reasonably well the responses of national episcopates to the strategic dilemma raised by religious and political pluralism in six of seven cases. Bishops upheld institutional interests and the church's moral agenda primarily where Catholic churches are essentially unable to mobilize a Catholic civil society, either amid intensifying secularization, as in Argentina; secularization coupled with religious competition, as in Chile; or where they enjoy a high degree of religious hegemony, as in Peru. On the other hand, where the church enjoys some connection to a highly mobilized civil society but only moderate levels of religious hegemony, as we saw is the case in Brazil and Venezuela, the hierarchy has been more responsive to the social and political needs of that society. In the case of El Salvador, contrary to expectations, bishops have spoken out forcefully on behalf of the needs of the poor for employment, justice, and an end to violence. While more systematic research is clearly needed in order to account for the Salvadoran anomaly, our tentative conclusion is that given robust hegemony and minimal risk, the Salvador hierarchy has been able to act virtually without constraint on its own beliefs, which were conditioned to a greater extent by civil strife and social injustice than by Rome.

This preliminary analysis undoubtedly raises more questions than it answers. Measuring the variables on which the theoretical framework depends is no easy task, in part because of the inherent difficulty in determining the size and strength of voluntary associations but also because of the challenge of interpreting different kinds of strength and capacity. Even the seemingly straightforward task of drawing from survey research to determine the political orientation of Catholics raised the question of how to determine the intensity of those positions. Which should be weighted more heavily in an effort to gauge grassroots influence on religious and political elites: the *average* position of Catholic voters, or the position of a sizable, but very committed, minority of Catholic activists? As we have seen in Brazil and Venezuela, where Catholics were polarized on a variety of social and moral questions, the grassroots may not even project a coherent set of beliefs. Religious hierarchies must take these divergent views into account not only if they wish to respond to them but also in order to assess their advantage, if any, in influencing the outcome of public debates on moral, cultural, and social issues. Because, as any student of public policy knows, there is not an automatic correspondence between public opinion and policy outcomes (as we saw in Chile), bishops must also take into account factors other than the political orientation of the median voter that might influence any public policy outcome. These include the ideological positions of legislators, mayors, judges, and other political elites; the nature of coalitional politics; and even the legislative rules for bringing forth committee reports for floor voting. Finally, we have barely scratched the surface of understanding the implications for the extent to which bishops are influenced by their grassroots and how much influence their intervention may have in cases in which churches have maintained their *internal* pluralism or in cases where dissident clergy and activists have been expelled and religious authorities have successfully imposed doctrinal purity.

My argument also has several important implications for electoral politics, public policy, and the church itself. Future electoral cleavages may be influenced by whether politics is defined by two separate axes of social justice and moral issues or if these collapse into one issue dimension. Given sufficient risk to the institution or its moral agenda, unless constrained by its own base, the church could ally with parties of the right—such as ARENA in El Salvador, PAN in Mexico, and UDI in Chile—that promote the church's moral agenda but not its social doctrine. In that event, national religious authorities could realign their economic ideology to conform to those parties and precipitate an electoral realignment reinforcing, not crosscutting, socioeconomic and political cleavages. Such a scenario is not the church's only option, of course. The Brazilian church has mobilized a congressional Catholic Caucus (*bancada católica*) comprised of representatives drawn from different parties to serve as an informal forum to discuss and lobby for pro-Catholic legislation (Oro 2003), including religious instruction in public schools and a religious presence in public hospitals, as well as stands against embryonic stem cell research, cloning, and the liberalization of abortion in cases of fetal deformity. Where the church can bargain with more than one party and one end of the political spectrum, not only may the church's position itself be stronger but political space may also retain more than one dimension and social justice need not be sacrificed to public morality.

Table 7.A1. Mapping Ideological Space: Correlations between Self-Positioning on Political Scale and Issue Positions (expected signs in parentheses)

	Political Scale Self-Position	Social Justice Issues				Moral Issues			
	Mean	Basic Attitudes Concerning Society (+)	Incomes More Equal (+)	Private Ownership of Business (−)	Government Take on More Responsibility (−)	Homosexuality Never Justified (−)	Abortion Never Justified (−)	Divorce Never Justified (−)	Euthanasia Never Justified (−)
Argentina	5.99	0.100*	-0.074	-0.16	-0.013	-0.025	-0.079*	-0.081*	-0.040
Brazil	5.90	0.105**	0.011	0.035	-0.073	-0.071	-0.050	-0.021	-0.015
Chile	5.23	0.108*	0.077	-0.183**	-0.031	-0.131**	-0.072	-0.039	-0.035
Colombia	6.63	0.079**	0.025	0.070++	-0.046*	-0.072**	-0.075**	-0.034	-0.101**
Dominican Republic	6.63	0.009	0.102	0.113	-0.167**	0.015	-0.024	-0.066	-0.060
El Salvador	6.30	0.117**	0.040	-0.074	0.098*	-0.023	-0.033	-0.006	-0.071
Mexico	6.65	0.077*	-0.008	0.104++	0.063	-0.071	-0.129**	-0.049	-0.085*
Peru	5.69	0.030	0.044	0.005	-0.052	0.025	0.012	-0.025	n.d.^a
Uruguay	5.67	0.136**	0.107*	-0.160**	-0.119**	-0.225**	-0.194**	-0.151**	-0.112*
Venezuela	6.32	0.062	0.014	-0.063	-0.010	-0.030	0.005	0.026	0.011

Source: Author's calculation from 2000 World Values Survey (Inglehart et al. 2004).

[a]The question concerning euthanasia was not asked in Peru.

*Correlation is significant at the 0.05 level (2-tailed).

**Correlation is significant at the 0.01 level (2-tailed).

++ Correlation is significant at the 0.01 level (2-tailed), but sign is in wrong direction.

Table 7.A2. Summary of Documents Issued by Catholic Bishops

	Official Documents (2000–2007)	Bishops' Homilies and Messages[a]	Other	Total
Argentina	39	103		142
Brazil	25		128[b]	153
Chile	56[c]	148	67[d]	271
El Salvador	22			22
Mexico	55			55
Peru	31[f]			31
Venezuela	52[g]			52
Total	280	251	195	726

Sources: Argentina, all documents: http://www.cea.org/ar/. Brazil, official declarations: http://www.cnbb.org.br/index.php?op=pagina&subop=154; analyses, messages, and reports on politics and bioethics, http://www.cnbb.org.br/index.php?op=menu&subop=11&sublinha=01. Chile, all documents: http://www.episcopado.cl/. El Salvador, all documents: http://www.iglesia.org.sv/content/category. Mexico, official documents: http://www.cem.org.mx/doctos/cem/index.htm. Peru, all documents: http://www.iglesiacatolica.org.pe/. Venezuela, all documents: http://www.cev.org.ve/.

[a]For the years 2004–2005.

[b]Includes 24 documents on the theme of "Church and politics" and 61 on "Church and bioethics" from the Vatican and other conferences; working documents of pastoral commissions; unofficial reports by medical, educational, and legal professionals; and 43 general "analyses of the current situation" by lay authors, written in 2000–2005, which carry implicit endorsements of the bishops.

[c]Includes 25 collective statements, 24 messages issued by the conference president, and 7 messages by the secretary-general in 2004 and 2005.

[d]Includes documents from press offices, pastoral commissions, diocesan departments, and religious groups and lay movements, issued in 2004–2005.

[f]Includes 20 messages, 10 communiqués, and 1 working document issued in 2003–2006.

[g]Includes 6 documents from 2006, 11 from 2005, 14 from 2004, 6 from 2003, 13 from 2002, and 2 with no date.

To date, national bishops' conferences have had very different capacities to influence the public debate and public policy. Some have courted sympathetic state officials to protect the church's institutional interests to compensate for a lack of connection to their own grassroots. Such a strategy may succeed to a point in semi-democratic contexts and in the absence of genuine pluralism, but as political participation and electoral competition expand and as religious pluralism grows, these churches may find themselves with an ever-smaller base, politically weaker and more isolated, and exercising less influence in shaping the terms of the public debate and the outcomes of public policy. At the other extreme, I have argued that churches that enjoy religious hegemony as well as a capacity to mobilize civil society have an opportunity to exercise evangelizing leadership and defend the church's institutional interests and moral and social doctrines. But the Mexican case raises the question of how stable such arrangements ultimately are as pluralism continues its relentless advance. If the Mexican church were to witness a slippage of its comfortable margin of hegemony, the leverage of its mobilized base might increase. In that event, the church may find that, like its counterparts in Brazil and Venezuela, though it is constrained by an unwieldy base and perhaps unable to dictate the outcomes of public policy in the short term, it may ultimately be able to influence policy more deeply and permanently and at the same time retain a flock.

Notes

1. Though the Peruvian Catholic Church still enjoys tax-exempt status and government payments for the salaries of the clergy, a 2003 amendment to the 1993 constitution obliges the state to collaborate with other religious institutions on an equitable basis, which legal scholars view as a genuine step toward more religious liberty (García-Montúfar, Solis, and Isaacson 2004).

2. In the rural districts of Tenancingo and Usulután in El Salvador, new pastoral practices of catechists, seminarians, and nuns and priests associated with the liberationist church are reported to have played a "significant role" in the emergence of *campesino* insurgent political mobilization in the 1970s (Wood 2003, 99, 119–20).

3. In the poll, conducted by Enrique Zuleta Puceiro, 34 percent thought the clergy should refrain from voicing an opinion altogether and 31 percent felt it should speak out only about such instruction in religious schools. See "De Eso Sí Se Habla," *Página/12*, November 13, 2005.

4. The Salvadoran Christian Democratic Party, which received 43 percent of the vote in congressional elections in 1968 and 52 percent in 1985, received only 7.2 percent in the 2000 elections for the Chamber (Mainwaring and Scully 2003, 57; Williams and Seri 2003, 315–16), and is in disarray.

5. Larry Rohter, "Policy on Morning-After Pill Upsets Chile." *New York Times,* December 17, 2006.

6. Because documents are added and removed from the websites of each episcopal conference, not all documents were necessarily available at the time each website was accessed, and hence the documents examined do not cover the full time period for each country. The URLs for all websites consulted appear in Table 7.A2. Cited documents appear in the reference list.

7. In a major pastoral letter (CEA 2005), the Argentine bishops warned of the danger of "partial truths" about the 1970s in Argentina and urged that the youth be told the "true history of this chapter" of the country's recent history, which would "balance" accounts of state terror against the crimes of the guerrillas who also, in their words, terrorized the population.

References

Alvarez. Sonia E. 1990. *Engendering Democracy in Brazil: Women's Movements in Politics.* Princeton, NJ: Princeton University Press.

Baldez, Lisa. 2002. *Why Women Protest: Women's Movements in Chile.* Cambridge: Cambridge University Press.

Calder, Bruce J. 2004. "Interwoven Histories: The Catholic Church and the Maya, 1940 to the Present." In Edward L. Cleary and Timothy J. Steigenga, eds., *Resurgent Voices in Latin America: Indigenous Peoples, Political Mobilization, and Religious Change,* 93–124. New Brunswick, NJ: Rutgers University Press.

Camp, Roderic Ai. 1997. *Crossing Swords: Politics and Religion in Mexico.* New York: Oxford University Press.

Campbell, Monica. 2006. "Activists Hail Mexico City's New Same-Sex Civil Union Law." *San Francisco Chronicle,* November 23.

Center for Reproductive Rights. 2007. "The World's Abortion Laws" (May). Accessed June 12, 2007, from http://www.reproductiverights.org.

Centro de Estudios Públicos. 1995. "Tema Especial: La Mujer Chilena Hoy: Trabajo, Familia, y Valores." Documento de Trabajo No. 237 (August).

Conferencia Episcopal Argentina (CEA). 2003. "Navega Mar Adentro" (May 31).

———. 2004. "Necesitamos ser Nación" (May 15).

———. 2005. "Una Luza para Reconstruir la Nación" (November 11).

Conferencia Episcopal de Chile (CECH). 2005a. "Matrimonio y Familia, una Buena Noticia para la Humanidad" (November 25).

———. 2005b. "Una Democracia con Valores" (December 14).

Conferencia Episcopal de El Salvador (CEDES). 2003. "Rema Mar Adentro." Carta Pastoral de los Obispos de El Salvador (November 21).

———. 2004. "Testigos de Cristo en la Iglesia y en el Mundo: Carta Pastoral de la Conferencia Episcopal de El Salvador" (February 8).

———. 2005. "No Te Dejes Vencer por el Mal" (November 21).

Conferencia Episcopal Peruana (CEP). 2003. "Mensaje 'La Verdad y la Reconciliación. Compromiso de Todos' con Motivo de la Próxima Presentación del Informe de la Comisión de la Verdad y la Reconciliación" (21 August).

———. 2004. "Comunicado del Consejo de Presidencia de la Conferencia Episcopal Peruana ante la iniciativa de distribuir la 'Píldora del día siguiente'" (April 2).

———. 2005. "Comunicado de la Presidencia de la Conferencia Episcopal Peruana ante la aprobación y publicación de la reforma del Código Civil de España para autorizar (como matrimonio) las uniones homosexuales" (July 7).

———. 2006a. "Mensaje "Día del Niño por Nacer" (March 25).

———. 2006b. "Mensaje por el Día Internacional de la Mujer" (March 8).

Conferencia Episcopal Venezolana (CEV). 2002. "Comunicado de la Conferencia Episcopal Venezolana" (April 11).

———. 2004. "Comunicado No Al Aborto" (September 24).

———. 2005a. "Carta Pastoral en el Año de la Eucaristía" (January 11).

———. 2005b. "Carta Pastoral con Motivo del Año de las Vocaciones" (January 25).

———. 2005c. "Exhortación Diálogo y Perdón para la Paz" (January 11).

———. n.d. "La Iglesia Católica Venezolana ante la Epidemia del VIH/SIDA."

Conferencia Nacional dos Bispos do Brasil (CNBB)/Instituto Nacional de Pastoral. 2003. *Presença Pública da Igreja*. São Paulo: Paulinas.

Congregation for the Doctrine of the Faith. 2002. "Doctrinal Note on Some Questions Regarding the Participation of Catholics in Political Life." November 24. Available at http://www.vatican.va/roman_curia/congregations/cfaith/documents/rc_con_cfaith_doc_20021124_politica_en.html.

Córdova Macías, Ricardo, José Miguel Cruz, and Mitchell A. Seligson. 2004. *The Political Culture of Democracy in El Salvador, 2004: Perceptions and Realities of the Salvadoran Population*. Latin American Public Opinion Project, Vanderbilt University. Available at http://sitemason.vanderbilt.edu/lapop/home.

Cruz, Maria Angélica. 2004. *Iglesia, represión y memoria: El caso Chileno*. Madrid: Siglo Veintiuno.

DataFolha. 2007. "Especial Religião" (March). Available at http://datafolha.folha.uol.com.br.

De la Maza E., Gonzalo. 1999. "Los movimientos sociales en la democratización de Chile." In Paul Drake and Iván Jaksic, eds., *El Modelo Chile: Democracia y desarrollo en los noventa*, 377–406. Santiago: LOM.

Estudo Eleitoral Brasileiro (ESEB). 2002. CESOP-FGV/Brasil02. Dez-1838. In "Banco de Dados do Centro de Estudos de Opinião Pública—CESOP-UNI-

CAMP." Available at http://www.cesop.unicamp.br/site/htm/busca./CESOP/pesquisa_usuario.

García-Montúfar, Guillermo, Moisés Arata Solis, and Scott E. Isaacson. 2004. "Advances in Religious Liberty in Peru." *Brigham Young University Law Review* (Summer): 385–417.

Gill, Anthony. 1998. *Rendering Unto Caesar: The Catholic Church and the State in Latin America.* Chicago: University of Chicago Press.

———. 2002. "Religion and Democracy in South America: Challenges and Opportunities." In Ted Gerard Jelen and Clyde Wilcox, eds., *Religion and Politics in Comparative Perspective,* 195–221. Cambridge: Cambridge University Press.

Gomez de Souza, Luiz Alberto. 2005. "The Roman Catholic Church and the Experience of Democracy in Latin America." Paper presented to the conference Contemporary Catholicism, Religious Pluralism, and Democracy in Latin America, Kellogg Institute, University of Notre Dame, March 31–April 1.

Gutiérrez, Gustavo. 1973. *A Theology of Liberation: History, Politics, and Salvation.* Maryknoll, NY: Orbis.

Hagopian, Frances. 2005. "Conclusions: Government Performance, Political Representation, and Public Perceptions of the Quality of Democracy in Latin America in the 1990s and Beyond." In Frances Hagopian and Scott Mainwaring, eds., *The Third Wave of Democratization in Latin America: Advances and Setbacks,* 319–62. Cambridge: Cambridge University Press.

Htun, Mala. 2003. *Sex and the State: Abortion, Divorce, and the Family under Latin American Dictatorships and Democracy.* Cambridge: Cambridge University Press.

Hunter, Wendy. 2006. "Growth and Transformation of the Workers' Party in Brazil, 1989–2002." Working Paper #326, Kellogg Institute for International Studies, University of Notre Dame (August).

Inglehart, Ronald, Miguel Basáñez, Jaime Díez-Medrano, Loek Halman, and Ruud Luijkx. 2004. *Human Beliefs and Values: A Cross-Cultural Sourcebook Based on the 1999–2002 Values Surveys.* Mexico City: Siglo XXI.

Latin American Regional Report: Mexico and NAFTA. 2005. "Cardinal Threatens Legal Action over Pill" (August 6).

Levine, Daniel H. 1973. *Conflict and Political Change in Venezuela.* Princeton, NJ: Princeton University Press.

———. 1981. *Religion and Politics in Latin America: The Catholic Church in Venezuela and Colombia.* Princeton, NJ: Princeton University Press.

———. 1993. "Popular Groups, Popular Culture, and Popular Religion." In Daniel H. Levine, ed., *Constructing Culture and Power in Latin America,* 171–225. Ann Arbor: University of Michigan Press.

Levine, Daniel H., and Catalina Romero. 2006. "Urban Citizen Movements and Disempowerment in Peru and Venezuela." In Scott Mainwaring, Ana María

Bejarano, and Eduardo Pizarro Leongómez, eds., *The Crisis of Democratic Representation in the Andes*, 227–56. Stanford, CA: Stanford University Press.

Levitsky, Steven. 2003. *Transforming Labor-Based Parties in Latin America: Argentine Peronism in Comparative Perspective*. Cambridge: Cambridge University Press.

Loaeza, Soledad. 2003. "The National Action Party (PAN): From the Fringes of the Political System to the Heart of Change." In Scott Mainwaring and Timothy R. Scully, eds., *Christian Democracy in Latin America: Electoral Competition and Regime Conflict*, 194–246. Stanford, CA: Stanford University Press.

Magaloni, Beatriz, and Alejandro Moreno. 2003. "Catching All Souls: The Partido Acción Nacional and the Politics of Religion in Mexico." In Scott Mainwaring and Timothy R. Scully, eds., *Christian Democracy in Latin America: Electoral Competition and Regime Conflict*, 247–72. Stanford, CA: Stanford University Press.

Mainwaring, Scott. 1986. *The Catholic Church and Politics in Brazil, 1916–1985*. Stanford, CA: Stanford University Press.

Mainwaring, Scott, and Timothy R. Scully. 2003. "The Diversity of Christian Democracy in Latin America." In Scott Mainwaring and Timothy R. Scully, eds., *Christian Democracy in Latin America: Electoral Competition and Regime Conflicts*, 30–63. Stanford, CA: Stanford University Press.

Mainwaring, Scott, and Alexander Wilde. 1989. "The Progressive Church in Latin America: An Interpretation." In Scott Mainwaring and Alexander Wilde, eds., *The Progressive Church in Latin America*, 1–37. Notre Dame, IN: University of Notre Dame Press.

McDonough, Peter J., Doh C. Shin, and José Alvaro Moisés. 1998. "Democratization and Participation: Comparing Spain, Brazil, and Korea." *Journal of Politics* 60, no. 4: 919–53.

Navarro, Marysa. 1989. "The Personal Is Political: Las Madres de Plaza de Mayo." In Susan Eckstein, ed., *Power and Popular Protest: Latin American Social Movements*, 241–58. Berkeley: University of California Press.

Oro, Ari Pedro. 2003. "A Política da Igreja Universal e Seus Reflexos nos Campos Religioso e Político Brasileiros." *Revista Brasileira de Ciências Sociais* 18: 53–69.

Oxhorn, Philip D. 1995. *Organizing Civil Society: The Popular Sectors and the Struggle for Democracy in Chile*. University Park: Pennsylvania State University Press.

Pierucci, Antônio Flávio, and Reginaldo Prandi. 1994. "Religiões e Voto: A Eleição Presidencial de 1994." *Opinião Pública* 3, no. 1: 20–44.

Sigmund, Paul E., ed. 1999. *Religious Freedom and Evangelization in Latin America: The Challenge of Religious Pluralism*. Maryknoll, NY: Orbis Books.

Soberanes Fernández, José Luis. 1999. "The New Legislation on Religious Freedom in Mexico." In Paul Sigmund, ed., *Religious Freedom and Evangelization in Latin America: The Challenge of Religious Pluralism*, 129–38. Maryknoll, NY: Orbis Books.

Stein, Andrew. 1999a. "El Salvador." In Paul E. Sigmund, ed., *Religious Freedom and Evangelization in Latin America*, 113–28. Maryknoll, NY: Orbis Books.

———. 1999b. "Nicaragua." In Paul E. Sigmund, ed., *Religious Freedom and Evangelization in Latin America*, 175–86. Maryknoll, NY: Orbis Books.

Stokes, Susan C. 1995. *Cultures in Conflict: Social Movements and the State in Peru*. Berkeley: University of California Press.

Torcal, Mariano, and Scott Mainwaring. 2003. "The Political Recrafting of Social Bases of Party Competition: Chile, 1973–95. *British Journal of Political Science* 33: 55–84.

Wanderley, Luiz Eduardo. 2003. "Desafios da Igreja Católica e Política no Brasil." In CNBB/Instituto Nacional de Pastoral, *Presença Pública da Igreja*, 459–79. São Paulo: Paulinas.

Weber, Max. [1922–23] 1946. "The Social Psychology of the World Religions." In H. H. Gerth and C. Wright Mills, eds., *From Max Weber: Essays in Sociology*, 267–301. New York: Oxford University Press.

Wheat, Kathryn, and Kirstin Matthews. 2006. "World Human Cloning Policies." Accessed February 26, 2006, from http://www.ruf.rice.edu/~neal/stemcell/World.pdf.

Wilde, Alexander. 1984. "Redemocratization, the Church, and Democracy in Colombia." Kellogg Institute Working Paper #22, Kellogg Institute for International Studies, University of Notre Dame (June).

———. 1987. "Creating Neo-Christendom in Colombia." Kellogg Institute Working Paper #92, Kellogg Institute for International Studies, University of Notre Dame (March).

Williams, Philip J., and Guillermina Seri. 2003. "The Limits of Reformism: The Rise and Fall of Christian Democracy in El Salvador and Guatemala." In Scott Mainwaring and Timothy R. Scully, eds., *Christian Democracy in Latin America: Electoral Competition and Regime Conflicts*, 301–29. Stanford, CA: Stanford University Press.

Wood, Elisabeth Jean. 2003. *Insurgent Collective Action and Civil War in El Salvador*. Cambridge: Cambridge University Press.

Yashar, Deborah J. 2005. *Contesting Citizenship in Latin America: The Rise of Indigenous Movements and the Postliberal Challenge*. Cambridge: Cambridge University Press.

PART III

The Church, Public Policy, and Democracy

8 | Life, Liberty, and Family Values

Church and State in the Struggle over
Latin America's Social Agenda

MALA HTUN

Abortion, contraception, homosexuality, and HIV/AIDS pose challenges to the Roman Catholic Church and to the efforts of Latin American democracies to protect citizen rights. Ecclesiastical doctrine on these issues is strict, but social behavior is not. Though the church hierarchy condemns abortion, for example, it is widely practiced. As a result, tens of thousands of women are hospitalized for botched abortions. A leading cause of maternal mortality, illegal abortions drain the public health system and endanger women's health. Catholic doctrine opposes contraception, yet unmet public demand for contraceptives and poor education about available methods raise the rate of unwanted pregnancy, contributing to the abortion rate as well as the spread of HIV/AIDS. Homosexual partnerships are reviled by the ecclesiastical hierarchy, thwarting efforts to legislate gay rights. As a result, the region's gays and lesbians lack legal protections for their unions, not to mention redress against discrimination and protection from violence.

As more civic groups demand liberal policy solutions to problems of illegal abortion, the spread of HIV/AIDS, and discrimination against gays and lesbians, officials of the Roman Catholic Church find themselves on the defensive. Acting to defend church views, they have prevailed in almost all of the resulting policy conflicts. Most proposals to legalize abortion and same sex unions, for example, have received only tepid support from national governments, and almost no country has changed laws to oppose Catholic doctrine. But the bishops are less and less able to control public debates and the tide of opinion is shifting. In 2007 the Catholic hierarchy suffered a spectacular defeat when the legislature of Mexico City voted to legalize abortion on demand in the first trimester of pregnancy.[1] What does the future portend? Will democratic governments be able to deal with these pressing policy issues? What is the role of the Roman Catholic Church in public debates about contentious moral questions?

In a previous work (Htun 2003a) I attempted to explain when and why countries in Latin America reformed restrictive laws on abortion, divorce, and the family. With a particular focus on Argentina, Brazil, and Chile, that volume considered the era of military rule, political transition, and the early period of democratic governance. Given the policy focus, the church was a crucial player in the story I told. Its doctrine inspired the content of civil and criminal laws on family and reproductive issues. Though secular, these laws conformed closely to the vision of the church. As society changed, and regimes emerged and died, the moral doctrine embedded in the institutions of the civil and criminal codes remained unchanged. This was in part due to institutional inertia but was also attributable to the political and social power of the Roman Catholic bishops. I showed, however, that the ability of bishops to defend their principles regarding morality and sexuality declined under dictatorships and when bishops clashed with governing elites over human rights and economic policy. When church-state relations soured, the government had less to lose by endorsing policies opposed by the church and could even adopt such measures to undercut ecclesiastical influence. In Brazil, for example, the military government that ruled between 1964 and 1985 clashed with bishops over human rights, the persecution of clerics, and economic development. To strike at the church, the government permitted divorce to be legalized in 1977.[2]

I also predicted that the bishops' influence could grow as democracy became consolidated and politicians vied for ecclesiastical support. The church is the most respected institution in society and exercises tremendous moral authority. According to the 2004 Latinobarómetro poll, for example, fully 71 percent of citizens expressed confidence in the church compared to 40 percent in the armed forces, 37 percent in the president,

32 percent in the judiciary, and a mere 18 percent in political parties. In only one year between 1996 and 2004 did the church's confidence rating dip below 70 percent (Latinobarómetro 2004, 34). The bishops' good favor can translate into substantial political capital. Antagonizing the bishops, on the other hand, can tarnish a politician's public image and reputation, compromising his or her ability to seek votes.

It is now time to revisit these claims and assess the extent of religious influence over the most contentious elements of Latin America's social agenda. What are the main factors influencing policy change, or lack thereof, and what is the weight of the Roman Catholic Church among these factors? Is the policy stalemate on abortion, for example, attributable to religious power? How has the consolidation of democratic politics affected the church's role in policy debates? The experience of almost two decades of democratic governance provides evidence for some tentative answers to these questions. In countries where civil society is strong, there is considerable support for and discussion of liberal policy solutions to contentious social issues. The church hierarchy's worldview is but one opinion informing policy choices. In spite of this more open debate, almost no country has changed its laws on moral issues over the objections of the church hierarchy. Even in Uruguay, where polls showed that 63 percent of the population favored decriminalizing abortion, the law has not changed. A bill to legalize the measure was narrowly defeated in the senate in 2005 after having been approved in the lower house.

As this suggests, we need to distinguish between two outcomes: the scope and shape of public debate, on the one hand, and actual legal reforms on the other. As I show in this chapter, which focuses mostly on the question of abortion, bishops often have little power to shape the scope of public debates. Proposals that violate church principles—such as the decriminalization of abortion—are under consideration in several countries and have received significant support from the public. Yet the church can still exercise an indirect veto over legislative reforms. Bishops act to ensure that little electoral benefit will be gained by violating their principles. Fear of church wrath prevents many politicians from acting on the basis of their increasingly liberal views. The risk of being labeled by the church as an immoral politician deters legislators from advocating change on contentious issues.

Historically, many Latin American presidents and party leaders have refused to enforce a party line on contentious moral issues such as divorce, abortion, and gay rights. Instead, they have declared that each party member is free to vote according to their conscience on the issue. This principle of *voto de conciencia* encourages democratic debate but also slows the rate of change. Yet there are several instances of presidents and party leaders supporting restrictions on abortion, among other matters. This convergence between the highest levels of government and the position of the church tends to stifle the voices of those who favor liberalizing reforms. The bishops are most effective at blocking reform and curtailing debate when senior politicians abandon *voto de conciencia* and endorse ecclesiastical views.

Public Contestation

Outside observers, particularly in the United States, tend to stereotype Latin America as Catholic, conservative, and male-dominated. As this volume shows, many of these stereotypes are wrong. Religious pluralism is well established, though the doctrines of major churches, at least on moral and sexual issues, often (but not always) coincide. Women have made significant inroads into public life (Htun 2003b; Schwindt-Bayer 2007), and significant public contestation has emerged over the previously taboo issues of abortion and gay rights. An unprecedented number of proposals to reform strict abortion laws and to recognize same-sex unions have emerged on public agendas in several Latin American countries. What is more, there is scattered evidence that this broader agenda has helped to shape the views of policy makers and the general public.

These changes are primarily attributable to the growth of national and transnational civil society under democratic governance. During dictatorship and in the period immediately following transitions to democracy, the range of actors shaping the public agenda was limited. When parties were banned, civil society organizations repressed, and the media censored, the contours of public debate reflected official views more than the plurality of citizen interests.[3] In some countries public debate remained circumscribed even in the first few years after the transition to democracy. In Chile, for example, liberal politicians decided to put contentious social issues on the back burner in order to focus on consolidating the transition and defending human rights. They felt that introducing divorce and abortion to the policy agenda would antagonize the military and the political right, potentially putting democracy in jeopardy (Htun 2003a).

Over the past two decades national and transnational civil society has witnessed the proliferation of social movements, interest groups, and watchdog and advocacy organizations in Latin America. These groups represent the interests of feminism, the indigenous, homosexuals, the environment, human rights, workers, the handicapped, and so forth. They have advocated the expansion of women's rights and gay rights and supported policy changes that conflict with traditional church doctrine. Importantly, some liberal advocacy has emerged from within the church itself. Católicas por el Derecho a Decidir (Catholics for a Free Choice), a transnational movement with national organizations in many Latin American countries, endorses liberal abortion laws from an ethical perspective based on Catholic theology. When I interviewed the then-president of Católicas in Brazil, Maria José Rosaldo Nunes (a former nun), in São Paulo ten years ago, she explained to me that her objective was to offer women the moral and conceptual resources to make reproductive choices while remaining good Catholics.[4]

The rights and freedoms offered by the region's new democracies help explain the growth of these organizations. Increasing sophistication and access to the global telecommunications network—particularly the Internet—is another important factor. Meanwhile, the United Nations (UN) has come to emphasize social issues such as human rights, the environment, women's rights, and population growth. Global conferences organized by the UN have inspired domestic and transnational advocacy networks and created an opportunity for them to learn media skills, circulate information, acquire resources, and exert leverage on governments (Keck and Sikkink 1998; Friedman 2003, 2005). Finally, we must take into account changes within the Roman Catholic Church in the wake of the Second Vatican Council. Church doctrine became more liberal—it no longer endorsed the patriarchal family and supported women's rights—and its internal structures became more participatory and inclusive.

It would be a mistake, however, to think that only the liberal or reformist elements of civil society—or of the church—have prospered under democratic governance. Socially conservative and church-affiliated transnational and domestic groups have also grown. Many of these groups emerged defensively in order to reverse the decline in moral values triggered, they argued, by the loosening of abortion laws in North America and Europe and the codification of reproductive rights in UN documents. Parallel to feminist and liberal groups, conservative groups have used UN conferences as an opportunity to organize transnationally. In the early and mid-1990s, Latin American countries such as Argentina and El Salvador as well as some Arab governments allied with the Vatican to oppose the way that UN documents seemed to undermine the traditional family structure, depict sexual freedom as a human right, and conceptualize abortion as a public health problem (Friedman 2003).

The growth of an international conservative movement has helped domestic movements frame debates on women's rights and reproductive health in new ways and to acquire additional resources. Their arguments against abortion tend to be pitched not as a defense of traditional values but as a question of human rights: any country committed to human rights must defend all life, especially the weakest and most innocent. These pro-life arguments may resonate more sharply in new democracies trying to distance themselves from the abuses perpetrated by their authoritarian predecessors (Htun 2003a). With resources supplied by transnational networks, conservative movements cooperate with local allies, including Roman Catholic bishops and officials of other Christian denominations. Human Life International (HLI), for example, is a transnational network headquartered in Miami with affiliates in many Latin American countries. HLI and conservative groups like it oppose not just abortion reform but also civil unions for same-sex couples, sex education in public schools, and emergency contraception, and they have objected to use of the word "gender" in governmental discourse (Shepard 2000; Baldez 2001).

The feminist and liberal groups uphold a worldview dramatically different from the church hierarchy. Yet on some issues these citizen groups have agreed and even cooperated with Roman Catholic bishops. Bishops have served as peace brokers in civil conflicts, they denounce violations of civil liberties, and they call on citizens to exercise their democratic rights in clean elections. Bishops conferences, clerics, and lay Catholic groups have united with social movements to advocate the rights of landless people, afrodescendents, slum dwellers, the poor, migrants, indigenous people, and the displaced (Mainwaring 1986; Fleet and Smith 1997; Levine 1992).

As a result there has always been tension within "progressive" movements over how much to muzzle the more controversial elements of their social agenda. In the 1970s and 1980s many movements censored themselves in order to maintain close ties to the bishops. Left-wing parties and human rights groups opted not to endorse reproductive rights, leaving feminist groups to champion this issue on their own (Alvarez 1990). This tendency persisted in some circles through the 1990s: the Brazilian Workers' Party, for example, initially endorsed abortion reform in its campaign platform but later backed down under church pressure.

By 2006, however, the number of civic groups had grown so much that the church could not possibly keep track of all of them, much less pressure them or use its alliance potential as incentive to limit their agendas. The range of allies available to each individual social movement, and each movement's sources of legitimacy, is greater than it was in the past. What is more, the availability of financing from foreign aid organizations and private foundations has increased the viability of single-issue advocacy organizations. A group seeking to increase public awareness of women's reproductive health or the problems encountered by homosexuals, for example, can exist and even thrive without the support of local political parties or other organizations, much less the church. Proliferation of these groups has generated greater public debate about controversial issues, including abortion.

Abortion

Before the 1980s in Latin America, abortion rarely entered public debate. For the first several decades of the twentieth century, debate on abortion policy occurred primarily among criminologists and medical practitioners. Rather than the right of women to choose, these professionals were concerned with eugenics, medicine, and the enforceability of the law. Technical discourse among middle-class men, not emotional exchanges between clerics and women, characterized discussions about abortion (Htun 2003a, chap. 6). The same was true in the United States before the 1970s. California's abortion reform of 1967 was the work of middle-class lawyers and doctors, not feminist reproductive rights advocates (Luker 1984).

The growth of the feminist movement and the wave of abortion reforms in Western Europe and North America, combined with the more open climate created by democratic transitions, inspired some efforts to get Latin American countries to reconsider their restrictive abortion laws. Between the 1980s and the year 2000, proposals for abortion reform came primarily from feminist reproductive rights activists and members of the medical community. Framing the issue in terms of public health, not liberal rights, they attempted to educate the public about the social consequences of clandestine abortions. One central argument was that abortion's illegality did not deter the practice but merely pushed it underground. Abortion rates were high—in some countries around one-third of pregnancies ended in abortion (Alan Guttmacher Institute 1994)—and poor women suffered the most. Whereas wealthy women could go to safe clinics for the procedure, poor women resorted to clandestine abortions in dangerous and unregulated circumstances. The black market in illegal abortions contributed to corruption and a lack of respect for the rule of law. In this context, activists and public health practitioners argued that liberalizing access to abortion would make it less dangerous for women's health and less socially pernicious. They emphasized a woman's right to health, not the right to abortion (Corrêa 1994). What is more, liberal policies would facilitate solutions to related problems such as unwanted pregnancy, teenage pregnancy, and infanticide.

Not surprisingly, the bishops reject the effort to frame abortion as an issue of public health. The Brazilian Bishops' Council, for example, has declared that "such a serious issue cannot be seen simply as a technical question, or one related to health, in complete disregard of its ethical, legal, and cultural aspects. [Abortion] is, above all, an ethical and legal issue because it involves decisions and attitudes that will determine the life and death of another human being" (CNBB 2005). The solution to clandestine abortion is not to legalize it, the bishops argue, but rather to value women, prevent pregnancy, and/or to support childbirth. Good ends (reducing abortion) can never justify poor means (legalizing it), just as "one would not justify teaching how to rob without killing in order to reduce the number of murders coming from future crimes" (CNBB 2005).

Some observers may wonder whether activists should prioritize changing abortion laws in a region notorious for disrespecting the law and where many constitutions are lovely in theory but not enforced and not implemented in practice. Since the law is not enforced anyway, this view points out, why go through the hassle of changing it? What is more, plenty of nice laws sit on the books but remain completely ineffective. Wouldn't a well-intentioned abortion law join their ranks? Shouldn't reproductive rights movements focus on something else besides law, which is elitist and rarely connected to the lives of ordinary people? Concerns about the gap between law and practice are legitimate, but they do not invalidate activists' concern to change punitive abortion laws. Laws, even when they are imperfectly enforced, have normative and symbolic power. They tell society what is right and wrong. They craft social identities and reinforce social hierarchies. By codifying cultural ideals, the law "tells stories about the culture that helped to shape it and which it in turn helps to shape: stories about who we are, where we came from, and where we are going" (Glendon 1987, 8). In addition, abortion laws, as part of the criminal code, lie in the domain of negative liberties. These rights circumscribe a realm of freedom from societal and state interference; they limit the power of the state and protect the autonomy of citizens. Negative liberties are jeopardized in countries where, for example, the police violate citizen rights to privacy and due process with impunity. Yet they may be easier to enforce than the positive liberties contained in many of the region's late twentieth- and early twenty-first-century constitutions. These positive liberties, including rights to education, health, housing, and the like, require massive budgetary outlays and institutional changes to be effective. The gap between the law and practice varies across types of rights. Unlike the right to health care, the removal of punitive abortion statutes (even in a limited number of circumstances, such as fetal anomaly and a threat to the mother's health) would not require state action to be effective. It would simply forbid state agents from punishing doctors and pregnant women. This would reduce the climate of fear surrounding the provision of abortion and make the practice safer and more accessible for poor women.

When I conducted research for my book in the mid-1990s, few politicians were willing to touch the issue of abortion, even on the grounds of public health. A small number of bills to reform restricted laws had been presented in national congresses, but almost none had come up for debate. One Argentine senator I interviewed, who had authored a bill to legalize abortion, said that "no one has demonstrated interest in considering this bill. It is an impolitic issue for the political environment of our country. To speak publicly in favor of abortion is impolitic" (qtd. in Htun 2003a, 152). In neighboring Chile Congresswoman Adriana Muñoz suffered electoral defeat in the early 1990s because, she suspected, she authored a bill to restore permission for therapeutic abortion (performed to save the mother's life) to the country's Health Code. (One of the final acts of the Pinochet government was to revoke permission for therapeutic abortion.) With the partial exception of Brazil, where proposals to require the public health system to attend to legal abortions were widely discussed in the 1990s, the movement to liberalize abortion was fairly isolated, politically and socially.

By the mid-2000s, however, proposals to liberalize abortion had moved into the political mainstream in several countries, including Brazil, Argentina, Colombia, Mexico, and Uruguay. Articles about abortion appear in the media, nonfeminist politicians have embraced the cause, and political parties have been called on by the press to explain their positions on the issue. Debates about liberalizing abortion have become prominent enough that the *New York Times* and the *Economist* have taken note, each publishing articles about a potential regional trend toward reform. All five of the above-mentioned countries have relatively strong and independent feminist reproductive rights movements, including nongovernmental organizations (NGOs), lobbying organizations, and groups that provide health services to women. But that is not the only reason for the growth of the debate. The positions of the president and other senior leaders matter greatly, as illustrated in Argentina. During the presidency of Carlos Menem (1989–1999), there was almost no discussion about changing laws on abortion. In fact, Menem actively campaigned against it. In 1994 he tried to modify the constitution to protect life from the moment of conception, and in 1998 he issued a presidential decree declaring March 25 as the "Day of the Unborn Child" (Htun 2003a, 161–62). Meanwhile, Argentina spearheaded opposition to abortion at United Nations conferences. Though opposition political parties and reproductive rights groups succeeded in resisting many of Menem's efforts (he failed to change the constitution, for example), the president's position created a climate hostile to abortion rights advocacy.

When Menem left office and Fernando de la Rúa assumed the presidency in 1999, the climate changed. De la Rúa opposed abortion but did not actively work against it. As a result, Argentina stopped allying with the Vatican at United Nations conferences; it publicly recognized the connection between women's reproductive rights and human rights; and it incorporated some of the feminist arguments about abortion as a public health problem (Htun 2003a, 164). This more open climate was reflected in a remarkable sentence issued by the Supreme Court in 2001 during the middle of the summer recess. Overturning the rulings of two lower courts, the sentence authorized an abortion in the seventh month of pregnancy for a fetus suffering from anencephaly. As a result, abortion rights advocacy also grew. In 2003 and 2004 several bills to loosen the restrictions on legal abortion were presented to Congress.

Subsequent Argentine presidents, notably Néstor Kirchner, demonstrated willingness to confront the Roman Catholic bishops more openly. In 2004 Kirchner's health minister, Ginés Gonzáles García, declared to the press that abortion should be decriminalized in the interest of improving public health, reducing unwanted pregnancies, and preventing the spread of HIV/AIDS. The church was horrified, and Bishop Antonio Baseotto, the military chaplain, wrote Gonzáles García a letter saying that he deserved to have a stone tied around his neck and be thrown into the sea. The metaphor was unfortunate for its resemblance to the methods of torture and disappearance used during the *Proceso* military regime of 1976–1983. The government was furious and President Kirchner issued a formal request to the Vatican to remove the bishop from his post.[5]

Presidents can open the lid on debate about abortion, but they can also close it. In El Salvador presidential power had the opposite effect as in Kirchner's Argentina: it curtailed debate and elevated the prominence of the church hierarchy's views. Similar to Argentina under Menem, El Salvador joined the international coalition against abortion at United Nations conferences in 1994 and 1995. It objected to the consensus statement issued by delegates for endorsing reproductive rights (and therefore abortion) and insisted on the sanctity of life at conception. Unlike Argentina, however, the country's anti-abortion movement did not confront a well-organized liberal opposition at home. When a bill to eliminate all exceptions to abortion's criminalization was introduced in Congress in 1997, President Armando Calderón Sol and his health minister both publicly declared their opposition to abortion. Pro-life views dominated the subsequent debate in the press, in the streets, and in Congress. Right-wing religious groups organized thousands of Catholic school students to demonstrate in favor of the bill. The archbishop of San Salvador made numerous statements that were reported in the press, and newspaper editorials tended to take his side. Only two female FMLN (Frente Farabundo Martí para la Liberación Nacional, or Farabundo Marti National Liberation Front) deputies defended the previous criminal code in lower house discussions, and almost no one, save the feminist organizations CEMUJER and Las Dignas, defended the feminist reproductive rights position. In 1998 Congress approved modifications to the criminal code to eliminate any exception to abortion (Center for Reproductive Rights and Policy 2001).[6] Thus did El Salvador become the first democracy in Latin America to further restrict abortion.

Sometimes national debates on abortion can be triggered virtually by accident, throwing the church hierarchy off guard and creating possibilities for change. Since 2004 Colombia has been consumed by an abortion debate. In April of that year, lawyer Monica Roa filed a suit with the country's constitutional court alleging that the ban on abortion violates the health and human rights that women are guaranteed under the country's constitution and international treaties it has ratified. She called on the court to admit exceptions to the ban for women who had been raped or whose health was threatened by the pregnancy. Organizations from Harvard and Yale law schools, the New York–based Center for Reproductive Law and Policy, Human Rights Watch, and Planned Parenthood contributed to the some four hundred amicus briefs submitted to support Roa's suit. She also received backing from the editorial staffs of national newspapers and the wife of President Alvaro Uribe, known as a conservative Catholic. Abortion activists rallied eight times in as many months on the steps of the courthouse.

Contention over abortion drowned out debate on presidential reelection, the upcoming legislative elections, and a peace agreement to end the civil war. Catholic groups led by the rector of the national university collected 200,000 signatures on a document to oppose the suit. In December the court ruled on the basis of technicalities that it would not consider Roa's petition. She revised the suit, calling on the court to throw out the abortion ban altogether rather than admit only some exceptions (Karsin 2005).[7] Church opposition and the pending court decision, however, were unable to prevent the abortion issue from entering into the 2006 legislative elections, held in March. And rather than prove a liability, the elections generated opportunities for politicians to express liberal views. A poll of the strongest candidates running for Senate, conducted by the newspaper *El Tiempo*, found that the majority would vote in favor of a law to loosen restrictions on abortion (57 said yes; 38 said no). The names of candidates were printed in the paper,[8] and the press called on parties to clarify their positions on abortion. On an informative election website run by the media conglomerate TERRA, for example, a party's position on abortion was listed alongside its views on the peace process, free trade, and so forth.[9] Juan Manuel Santos, leader of the largest party in Congress, declared himself to be against the ban on abortion, though he also insisted that members of his party were free to vote according to their conscience on the issue. These are striking trends for a country that had not witnessed much public contestation over abortion and had been considered one of the more conservative in the region.

Same-Sex Unions

Another example of the church's inability to stifle public debate is the movement to legalize same-sex unions. Several civic groups around the region are striving to promote gay rights, including the right to marriage. In Panama the New Men and Women's Association of Panama proposed legislation in late 2004 to recognize same-sex unions. The Colombian Senate considered, but neglected to approve, legislation on same-sex unions submitted by Senator Piedad Córdoba in 2001, 2002, and 2003. In the legislative elections held in April 2006, *El Tiempo* asked the strongest candidates running for Senate about their positions on gay marriage and equal rights for homosexuals (as they did for the abortion issue, mentioned above). The vast majority opposed gay marriage (73 against, 23 in favor) but supported equal civil rights for gay couples, such as the right to inheritance (63 in favor, 27 against).[10] In Brazil a bill to recognize same-sex civil unions, submitted by then-congresswoman Marta Suplicy in 1995, has been stalled in Congress despite approval by the Constitutional Commission in 1996. The bill recognized rights to inheritance, succession, welfare benefits, and joint income declarations, as well as the right of foreign partners to acquire citizenship. A similar bill was presented by Rio de Janeiro senator Sergio Cabral in 2003, and in October of that year fifty-three Brazilian deputies and senators launched the Parliamentary Front for Free Sexual Orientation. In the meantime, courts in different states have issued rulings recognizing same-sex unions.

At the time of this writing, however, only two governmental entities in Latin America have approved same-sex civil unions: the city of Buenos Aires and the province of Rio Negro, both in Argentina.[11] The city's law, adopted in 2002 on an initiative from a civic group called the Argentine Homosexual Community, extends to couples of any sex or sexual orientation rights and privileges generally reserved to married couples. It includes the right to receive pensions, take leave to care for a sick partner, receive compensation for wrongful death, make hospital and prison visits, make decisions about major medical procedures, have access to a corpse, and so forth. Deputy Roque Bellomo, who presented the bill, declared that "the formation of a tolerant society founded on the dignity of all people, whatever their sexual orientation, must be the axis of state policy."[12] The bill was approved by a vote of 29 to 10 after a five-hour debate ending in the early hours of the morning. Not surprisingly, the law was vehemently opposed by the church hierarchy. A few days after approval, the archbishop of La Plata said the law "violated the natural order," was "morally irrelevant," and that "citizens had no reason to obey it."[13] Other church organizations argued that the law, rather than set gay and straight marriages on an equal footing, actually privileged the former. The church saw the civil union law as part of a broader crisis of marriage and the family (Argentine Episcopal Conference 2003). Yet in numerical terms, the effects of the new law have been small. In 2003 the city of Buenos Aires ratified only 111 civil unions, 32 of them between same-sex couples. In 2004 the numbers climbed: 161 unions total, 69 of them between members of the same sex.[14]

Changes in Public and Legislator Opinion

The growth of debate on contentious moral issues and the circulation of new bills has not led to actual legal changes. With the exception of Mexico City (discussed below), no Latin American country has loosened its laws on abortion, and no government, save those in two Argentine provinces, has legislated same-sex unions.[15] These policy stalemates are somewhat surprising in light of what we know about public and legislator opinion, particularly with regard to abortion. Though Latin Americans believe the practice is morally wrong, they do not believe it should be criminalized in all circumstances. Unfortunately, most surveys do not distinguish between the morality of abortion and its legality. Surveys assume that moral disapproval of abortion implies support for criminalization and that approval of abortion implies support for legalization. But in fact, the issue of whether abortion is morally wrong is not equivalent to the question of whether some abortions should be legally permitted. People can hold abortion to be morally wrong but still believe that the state should not interfere in the personal decision to bear a child. The ability to distinguish between ethical life on the one hand and legal rights on the other is what characterizes a liberal regime.

Table 8.1. Public Disapproval of Abortion in Latin America: Percent Who Say Abortion Is Never Justifiable

	1995–97	2000
Argentina	48	66
Brazil	66	75
Chile	76	67
Mexico	43	69
Spain	33	28
France	20	14
United States	35	30

Source: World Values Surveys (Inglehart et al. 2004).

Disapproval of the practice can be seen in responses to the World Values Survey (see Table 8.1). A majority of respondents in Argentina, Brazil, Chile, and Mexico say that abortion is "never justifiable." What is more, these views have become more conservative over time (except in Chile). The percentage of those surveyed who object strongly to abortion climbed dramatically in Argentina and Mexico between the mid-1990s and 2000, from 48 to 66 percent, and from 43 to 69 percent, respectively. Latin American public opinion contrasts with Spain, France, and the United States, where policies are more liberal. Though a majority of Latin Americans say that abortion is "never justifiable" (a position that implies abortion should be completely illegal), evidence from other surveys suggests that a majority of citizens believe at least some abortions should be legally permitted. In Brazil a Datafolha poll of São Paulo residents conducted in 1997 revealed that 56 percent felt current abortion laws (which permit the practice in the event of rape or a threat to the mother's life) should stay the same, while 21 percent believed that the law should be more permissive. Nineteen percent thought abortion should be decriminalized.[16] In Chile a poll conducted by a newspaper in 2000 revealed that 78 percent of respondents agreed that abortion should be permitted if the mother's life is in danger, 55 percent agreed in the case of rape, and 54 percent agreed if the fetus is deformed (Blofeld 2001, 19).

Public views supporting legal abortion on some grounds are reflected, and even surpassed, by legislative opinion. In Mexico a 2003 survey of legislators conducted by the newspaper *Reforma* revealed that legislators generally opposed strict abortion laws. When asked their opinion of the statement, "If the woman's life is not at risk, abortion should always be illegal," 54 percent of congressmen surveyed disagreed while only 40 percent agreed. Women tended to disagree more than men—69 percent versus 51 percent. Only 25 percent of women legislators agreed that abortion should be generally illegal, compared to 43 percent of men.[17] Legislators in Brazil have even more liberal views. A 1999 survey conducted by the feminist lobby CFEMEA (Centro Feminista de Estudos e Assessoria, or Feminist Center for Studies and Advisory Services) found that 52 percent of parliamentarians favored increasing the conditions of legally permissible abortion while only 19 percent disagreed. Thirteen percent supported abortion on demand. When the question was phrased slightly differently, 58 percent believed abortion should be considered a crime under certain circumstances while 27 percent opposed any criminalization. Notably, only 6 percent supported the total criminalization of abortion, the position endorsed by the Catholic Church (Rodrigues 2001). In addition, 87 percent agreed that the public health system should perform those abortions already permitted by Brazilian law (in the event of rape and a threat to the mother's life). Only 6 percent disagreed. This makes it genuinely surprising that a bill to oblige the public health system to perform already-legal abortions has been stalled in Congress since 1995. The 6 percent of legislators who claim to oppose the bill—and their civic allies—have succeeded in blocking it from a full plenary vote.

Why, given public and legislator support for loosening restrictions on abortion, have laws not changed in more countries? Is this stalemate attributable to the influence of Roman Catholic bishops? Why were Latin American countries able to legalize divorce, adopt programs to prevent HIV/AIDS, and distribute contraceptives but not liberalize abortion and offer homosexuals greater rights?

Church Power over Policy

It is now time to examine why actual policy outcomes seem to conform to the church hierarchy's views even though the scope and content of public debate is increasingly distant from religious doctrine. The first point to consider is that, though Latin American countries have failed to reform the law concerning abortion and homosexual unions, they have introduced changes on other morally contentious issues. Over the sometimes halfhearted objections of bishops, most countries have administered national family planning programs, distributed contraceptives, promoted sexual education, and even legalized emergency contraception (the morning-after pill). As this suggests, there is something qualitatively different about the nature of abortion and gay marriage that explains policy intransigence.

Indeed, abortion and gay marriage are in many respects unique issues. Few other policies provoke comparable degrees of outrage and inspire positions at absolutist extremes, among both opponents and advocates. For its part, the church cares much more about abortion and marriage than about contraception, sex education, and divorce. The former epitomize the core of Roman Catholic doctrine on the sanctity of human life and the nature of the marriage institution. Since abortion is the murder of innocent human life, it can never be tolerated, even when the life of the mother is at stake.[18] As the Brazilian bishops have proclaimed: "abortion, for the Catholic Church, involves a question of principle. What is at stake is the inviolability of human life, already so cheapened by a contemporary culture that turns human beings into just another disposable market product" (CNBB 2005). In their view, the extent to which the entire society values human life is reflected in its policy on abortion.

Marriage is equally fundamental: as the bedrock of society, it is not a contract between spouses but a public institution of divine inspiration whose sacramental character cannot be altered by human will or public laws. Rooted in the "conjugal covenant of irrevocable personal consent," the existence of the marital bond "no longer depends on human decisions alone" (*Gaudium et spes* 1965/1999, 670–71). Though the church believes that homosexuals should be respected, it holds that the recognition of stable unions between same-sex couples (even when the term *marriage* is not used), undermines the cohesion and stability of all of society. According to the *Compendium of the Social Doctrine of the Church* released in 2004, "laws favoring homosexual unions are contrary to good sense. Given the values at stake, the state cannot legalize these unions without compromising its duty to promote and protect marriage, an essential institution for the common good" (Pontifical Council for Justice and Peace 2004).

The strength of church convictions parallels a deep ambivalence among Latin American publics. In practice, people have abortions. In practice, consenting adults of the same and different sexes cohabit and build lives together. Yet a tradition of hypocrisy has long undermined attempts to compel the law to reflect these de facto situations. This hypocrisy, or "double discourse," refers to the coexistence of morally rigid standards of behavior with considerable personal liberty. Though people tend to do what they want (resort to abortion, have a same-sex partner, live together) in practice, they continue to express support for strict norms (Shepard 2000). What is more, abortions are rarely prosecuted[19] and the law has long accommodated consensual cohabitation without formal marriage. Particularly in

Brazil, Argentina, and Chile, where divorce was not made legal until 1977, 1987, and 2004, respectively, a variety of informal institutions emerged to support couples who were unable to marry (and technically adulterous). The pervasiveness of permissive practices and the informal institutions that support them makes actual reform seem less pressing and allows people to endorse religious values—at least in theory.

Public ambivalence may be one factor working against change; institutional factors may also play a role. Before singling out the church, we should examine executive-legislative relations and the overall rate of legislative action on social issues. In Brazil, for example, where public and legislative support for change is relatively high, institutional deadlock thwarts reform. Since the return to democracy in 1985, 75 percent of bills passed by Congress have originated in the executive branch; the vast majority of bills submitted by legislators are tabled. As a result, most laws reflect executive priorities—that is, economic stabilization and adjustment—and not legislative preferences, such as social concerns (Ames 2001; Figueiredo and Limongi 2000; see also the discussion on abortion in Htun and Power 2006). Even on uncontroversial issues, progress can drag on for years, if not decades. The country's new civil code, first presented to Congress in 1975, was approved by the lower house in 1984 and only sanctioned into law in 2001. Thus, it is not just abortion policy that has been stalemated: Congress has failed to act on a range of pressing issues.

Notwithstanding the uniqueness of these issues, public hypocrisy, and institutional deadlock, church pressure has still been important. Church pressure is exercised both directly, by making public statements and contacting politicians, and indirectly. Indirect pressure—or the implied threat of action—is the main way the bishops influence policy. How does this work? The church is the most respected institution in Latin American societies; its bishops enjoy moral authority and are trusted. Therefore, their views about politics and politicians matter: people will listen and take note. It is in no politician's interest, therefore, to be branded immoral and unethical by the church. Yet the church's ability to tarnish a politician's reputation is not limitless. By comparing the cases of Mexico and Uruguay, we can single out some likely factors shaping when, where, and why the church is likely to be most effective in vetoing policy.

Mexico

In 2000 the northern Mexican state of Guanajuato voted to rescind permission for abortion for women who had been raped. This move, spearheaded by the Partido Acción Nacional (National Action Party, or PAN), which had recently won the presidency, triggered nationwide protests and indignation. Social movements, media outlets, and political parties criticized the change and the party initiating it. People demonstrated in the streets in defense of women's rights. Riding this tide of anti-anti-abortion backlash, then-mayor of Mexico City Rosario Robles introduced a bill to the city legislature to modify the city's criminal code provisions on abortion. The city already permitted the practice in the event of rape and a fatal threat to the mother. The proposal added two additional grounds for legal abortion : if the mother's health (not just her life) was at risk and if the fetus had birth defects. Robles agreed with the feminist movement that abortion is a public health problem posing grave risks for women, but she also sought to use the abortion issue for political advantage. The mayor sought to distinguish her party from the conservative tendencies of PAN and to exploit public fears that the president's party would impose a strict moral order in the country (Htun 2003a). She moved swiftly and the bill was approved in August of the same year through support by her Partido de la Revolución Democrática (Party of the Democratic Revolution, or PRD) and the centrist Partido Revolucionario Institucional (Institutional Revolutionary Party, or PRI). Thus did Mexico City become the only Latin American legislature since the 1930s to loosen restrictions on abortion.

Conservative and church groups protested loudly, opposing the bill through civic and legal channels. They submitted an injunction to the Supreme Court to challenge the law on the grounds that the Mexican constitution protects life at the moment of conception. Yet in 2002 the Supreme Court ruled in favor of the "Ley Robles" (Robles Law), as the measure had become known. In response, the Mexican bishops issued a press release reminding citizens of the church's teaching that "human life must be absolutely respected and protected at the moment of conception" and condemning the decision as a setback for society: "legalizing the assassination of an innocent human life . . . as if it were a right . . . is a regrettable deed that will only lead us to moral decadence" (Mexican Episcopal Conference 2002).

Uruguay

In 2002 the Uruguayan Chamber of Deputies approved, by a vote of 47 to 40 (with 11 abstentions), a bill to decriminalize abortions performed during the first trimester of pregnancy. Called the "Bill to Defend Reproductive Health," it required only that a woman explain to her physician why she felt unable to continue with the pregnancy and that the doctor, in turn, offer her advice about adoption. The bill would also oblige the government to distribute contraceptives free of charge and to introduce sex education. Two years later, however, the same bill was defeated 17 to 13 on the Senate floor. Why? The bill did not fail for lack of public support; indeed, polls found that 63 percent of those surveyed favored the decriminalization of abortion (Coordinación Nacional de Organizaciones por la Defensa de la Salud Reproductiva 2004). In the lower house politicians from all parties voted in its favor (though most of the National Party voted against). Pushed by an alliance of women legislators, medical professionals who contend daily with the problem of illegal abortion, and reproductive rights organizations, the bill also received the support of the deans of the schools of medicine and psychology as well as officials in the health ministry and hospital administrators. Using the slogan *"Educación para prevenir, anticonceptivos para no abortar, legalizar para no morir"* ("education to prevent pregnancy, contraceptives to prevent abortion, legalization to prevent death"), these groups emphasized the importance of reproductive and sexual health, particularly of poor women risking their lives with unsafe abortions.[20]

The church and conservative groups vociferously opposed the bill. The bishop of Montevideo declared that "no legislator who calls himself Christian can vote for this law" (Cariboni 1998). He went further, comparing abortion practitioners with the terrorists who had recently bombed commuter trains in Madrid. Reportedly, anti-abortion organizations mailed to every legislator a video of a grisly late-term abortion procedure. Six U.S. congressmen faxed a letter to Uruguayan senators urging them to avoid the "costly mistake" the United States had made more than thirty years earlier.

Then, President Batlle announced that he would veto the bill were it approved in Congress.

What explains the different outcomes in the two countries? To be sure, the nature of the two bills and political moments varied. The Uruguayan proposal went much further than the "Ley Robles" purported to do, but Uruguay already had a more liberal abortion regime. Though it criminalized abortion, it permitted judges to eliminate criminal penalties for abortions performed due to "economic anguish" or to "recuperate honor." No other Latin American country has offered exceptions for these "social" grounds. In addition, Mexico faced a unique political moment of anti-anti-abortion backlash where advocates of liberalization could portray themselves as defenders of the status quo rather than threats to it.

There are other differences between the two countries. In Mexico City the abortion proposal needed approval of only one legislative chamber (and this was secured relatively quickly). In Uruguay, by contrast, the two-year delay between the Chamber of Deputies and Senate votes put abortion foes, including the church, on the alert and permitted them to mobilize their resources both locally and transnationally. Second, Uruguayan senators ultimately had little incentive to stick their necks out for abortion given the president's threat to veto the bill. In Mexico, by contrast, it fell to the constitutional court, an institution far more isolated from social pressure, to give the abortion measure ultimate approval. Finally, whereas Mexico had just elected Vicente Fox president (Fox was elected in July and the bill was approved in August), Uruguay faced elections several months later: the Senate voted on the bill in May 2004 and elections would be held in October. The imminence of elections made politicians more susceptible to church threats.

A brief analysis of these two cases is suggestive. We could hypothesize that church pressure to block reforms is most effective when brought to bear on the legislature and other elected (as opposed to appointed) officials; when elections are imminent; and on bicameral legislatures. The normal functioning of democratic governance and deliberative decision making in particular offered plentiful opportunities for bishops to remind politicians of their Catholic roots, mobilize the electorate, and threaten their disapproval. In her explanation of why abortion reform went in opposite directions in Colombia and Nicaragua, Eleanor Broh similarly focuses on the power of the church hierarchy over majoritarian institutions like an elected legislature (Broh 2008). By contrast, the bishops exercise less influence over appointed officials (magistrates, health ministers); at the beginning of an electoral cycle (when politicians have plenty of time to recuperate from any reputational blows); and over unicameral legislatures. Finally, the president's position matters. Whether or not a president sides with the church shapes the debate and the structure of incentives governing an individual politician's decision to do likewise.

Conclusion

Democratic politics has produced contradictory effects on the church's ability to enforce its moral agenda. In many respects, the church has lost. People in Latin America use contraceptives with government approval, they receive sex education more often than abstinence counseling, they have access to the morning-after pill, they get divorced, they remarry, they live in same-sex partnerships, they raise children out of wedlock, and they abort unwanted pregnancies at among the highest rates in the world. Ordinary citizens, elected officials, the media, and civic organizations are discussing with greater frequency and intensity the possibility of legalizing these de facto situations. Even Chile, which for decades suffered the greatest gap between the letter of the law and actual social practices, has legalized divorce, distributed the morning-after pill, and entertained debates about liberalizing abortion.

In some instances the church hierarchy has won. In very few cases has the talk led to actual legislative changes. Out of deference to Roman Catholic and other moral doctrines, people remain deeply ambivalent about adjusting the law to conform to how they really live. Citizens have abortions, for example, but since they hold the practice to be morally reprehensible, they believe it should remain largely illegal. This ambivalence helps the church, which, after all, is willing to forgive people for the sins they commit as long as they repent and pledge to adhere to church values. The church's victory, however, arises from a pernicious context: the weakness of public institutions and civil society. Though Latin American civil societies are strong and vibrant enough to put new items on the agenda and to shape public opinion, they have not yet succeeded in consolidating democracy. The regions' institutions in general are discredited by corruption, a history of abuses, and poor performance. Polls evince high levels of distrust in leaders, political parties, and the future of democracy: merely 29 percent of Latin Americans expressed satisfaction with the state of democracy in 2004 (Latinobarómetro 2004). By comparison, the church appears trustworthy and solid. The 2004 Latinobarómetro poll shows that over 70 percent of Latin Americans express high confidence in the church. No other social institution came close: the military, second on the list, lagged the church by a thirty-point gap. In the United States, by contrast, churches occupy sixth place on the Harris Poll's confidence ranking, behind the military, small businesses, institutions of higher education, the Supreme Court, and the medical profession (Harris Poll 2006).

Thus, part of the Catholic Church's strength and influence is attributable to the fact that other institutions are dysfunctional and discredited. This is bad for everyone. To prosper, the region's democracies need to cultivate more public trust. Political parties, courts, legislatures, and other pillars of public life must gain greater legitimacy. The region's economies need to reduce social gaps to foster more confidence in markets and the private sector. When and if democracy becomes more consolidated, the church will become relatively weaker. Yet it need not lose absolutely. Democratic politics presents many opportunities for the church; its challenge is how to make the most of them.

Epilogue

Since this chapter was written, abortion laws in some Latin American countries have changed and Mexico City legalized same-sex unions. These trends reveal a potential split among Latin American countries. In the first group the Catholic Church's influence over policy is growing. Few dare publicly to oppose it and the bishops' authority to speak on public policy issues goes unquestioned. In the second group the church's veto power is diminishing. Politicians confront the bishops without fear for their positions. Rather, it is the bishops who are subject to criticism for meddling in affairs of state.

In Nicaragua bishops succeeded in banning abortion absolutely. Inspired by similar changes in El Salvador in 1998, they demanded that permission for therapeutic abortion (when the pregnancy threatens the woman's life or when the fetus is malformed) in the country's criminal code be revoked. Meanwhile, the November 2006 presidential elections, pitting Sandinista Daniel Ortega against two conservative challengers, were deadlocked. Seizing this window of opportunity, the archbishop of Managua and his predecessor, as well as leaders of evangelical churches, led tens of thousands of people in a march on Congress. In response, legislators fast-tracked a bill to ban abortion and supported it unanimously. Medical associations, women's groups, and international organizations opposed the new law, but almost no politicians dared speak out against it.[21]

Colombia's constitutional court and the government of Mexico City pushed abortion laws in the opposite direction. In a May 2006 ruling, the Colombian court decriminalized abortion under three circumstances: when the pregnancy results from a rape, when the fetus suffers from serious defects, and when the pregnancy endangers the life or health of the woman. Guidelines for its application are permissive. For example, there are no time limits: as long as a doctor certifies that her life or health is in danger, a woman may abort at any stage of her pregnancy. Criteria for what constitutes a threat to life or health are left vague—for example, mental health problems (such as depression) could constitute legal grounds—and there is no minimum age required for a woman seeking an abortion. Finally, the court's sentence went into effect immediately, transforming the country's regime without any intervention by Congress.[22] The court's decision was a response to Monica Roa's petition, and the ruling was preceded by months of public debate and anti-abortion mobilization. After it was announced, Roman Catholic bishops and conservative Catholics were furious. The archbishop of Bogotá declared that women who aborted, doctors performing the procedure, and judges authorizing it would be excommunicated. This move in turn was criticized in the media, as various observers wondered why an institution that pledged to respect life did not threaten excommunication to perpetrators of massacres, pedophiles, or rapists.[23] Unlike in Nicaragua, where the church appeared omnipotent, few Colombians hesitated to disparage the ecclesiastical hierarchy's intervention in state affairs.

In April 2007 Mexico City became the first Latin American jurisdiction outside of Cuba and Puerto Rico to legalize abortion on demand in the first trimester of pregnancy. The city's legislature, dominated by the leftist PRD, easily approved the measure. Mayor Marcelo Ebrard, also of the PRD, supported the reform. Most legislative opposition came from PAN. PAN's leader, Felipe Calderón, had recently assumed the nation's presidency after closely disputed elections, the outcome of which many PRD supporters refused to recognize. It was not the first time that Mexico City had reformed its abortion statute in the wake of a presidential election pitting the PRD against the PAN. As discussed earlier in this chapter, then-mayor Rosario Robles (also of the PRD) responded to the 2000 election of PAN's Vicente Fox, and subsequent changes to abortion law in the northern state of Guanajuato, by pushing the city legislature to loosen its restrictions. In both cases, the PRD was able to portray the PAN as out of touch and aligned with Catholic reactionaries.

During the 2007 debates, the mayor and other government officials urged the Catholic Church and anti-abortion groups not to interfere with the legislative process. (Ecclesiastical participation in politics is banned by Mexico's constitution.) These calls went unheeded. Church leaders spoke out against the bill and called politicians who supported it "killers." Some bishops called for their excommunication, a desire echoed by Pope Benedict during a news conference on the eve of his visit to Brazil. The church was so outspoken that, following the bill's approval, the Interior Ministry announced an investigation into whether the archbishop of Mexico City had lobbied against it illegally.[24]

The conflict in Mexico City continues at the time of this writing. Anti-abortion groups have vowed to challenge the new law in court and to block women from entering hospitals for abortion. Feminist groups, including Catholics for a Free Choice, hope the city's reforms mark the beginning of a region-wide trend. They may be right, since Mexico's experience shows that politicians can defy the bishops and survive. PRD politicians in Mexico City confronted the church over abortion in 2000 and were not punished by voters. In fact, the party became stronger: it took control of the city government again and almost won the 2006 presidential elections. If the church seeks greater success elsewhere, it should refrain from threatening politicians with excommunication and entering the debate with purely religious arguments. Instead, it should focus on educating Catholic voters and making sure they turn out on election day.

Notes

I am indebted to Frances Hagopian, Kenneth Serbin, and Elizabeth Rankin for their comments and help on this chapter.

1. I discuss this in more detail in the epilogue to the chapter.

2. The campaign for divorce had been going on for decades before the government's conflict with the church, however (Htun 2003a, chap. 4).

3. Oddly, however, this repressive climate could sometimes serve the cause of reform with regard to family and reproductive issues. Governments that clashed with the church blocked its influence on divorce legislation. Regimes that wanted to modernize the civil law opened the door to cosmopolitan influences and not conservative ones. In an authoritarian context, policy outcomes reflect regime preferences, which may be surprisingly liberal (see Htun 2003a, chaps. 3 and 4).

4. Interview with the author, São Paulo, Brazil, July 1997. For more information on the positions of Catholics for a Free Choice, see http://www.catholicsforchoice.org, and for the Brazilian chapter, see http://catolicasonline.org.br.

5. See articles in *La Nación* on November 25, 2004; February 15, 2005; February 23, 2005; and February 25, 2005.

6. Before the change, the country had permitted abortions for therapeutic reasons, for women who had been raped, or when the fetus suffered from severe birth defects.

7. The court's eventual decision is discussed in the epilogue to this chapter.

8. *El Tiempo,* February 25, 2006.

9. See http://www.votebien.com.

10. *El Tiempo,* February 25, 2006.

11. Mexico City subsequently legalized same-sex unions, as noted in the epilogue to this chapter.

12. *La Nación,* December 14, 2002.

13. *La Nación,* December 18, 2002.

14. *La Nación,* February 17, 2005.

15. Recent exceptions include Colombia; see the epilogue to this chapter for more information.

16. *Folha de São Paulo,* August 28, 1997.

17. Survey data provided courtesy of Alejandro Moreno, *Reforma* pollster, and in the possession of the author.

18. However, according to church doctrine, if the fetus dies as the indirect consequence of a medical procedure aimed to save the mother's life, such a procedure may be valid since its primary intention is to protect life (Noonan 1970).

19. The sharpest consequence of its illegality is to push the practice underground, with varied effects by social class. Middle-class women have access to safe abortions but poor women do not. Because they tend to be more religious and also because their concerns are for immediate survival, poor women are the least likely to join in movements for abortion reform.

20. *Página 12*, September 27, 2003.

21. N. C. Aizenman, "Nicaragua's Total Ban on Abortion Spurs Critics," *Washington Post*, November 28, 2006, A1.

22. *Semana*, May 13, 2006.

23. Ibid.

24. James McKinley, "Mexico City Legalizes Abortion Early in Term," *New York Times*, April 25, 2007; and Connie Watson, "Mexico City's Abortion Debate," CBC News, April 30, 2007, available at http://www.cbc.ca/news/reportsfromabroad/watson/20070430.html.

References

Alan Guttmacher Institute. 1994. *Aborto clandestino: Uma realidade latinoamericana*. New York: Alan Guttmacher Institute.

Alvarez, Sonia. 1990. *Engendering Democracy in Brazil*. Princeton, NJ: Princeton University Press.

Ames, Barry. 2001. *The Deadlock of Democracy in Brazil*. Ann Arbor: University of Michigan Press.

Argentine Episcopal Conference. 2003. "Navega mar adentro." Declaration from the 85th Plenary, Argentina, May 31. Available at http://www.cea.org.ar/09-Navega/navega_mar_adentro_01.htm.

Baldez, Lisa. 2001. "Coalition Politics and the Limits of State Feminism in Chile." *Women and Politics* 22, no. 4: 1–28.

Blofeld, Merike. 2001. "The Politics of Moral Sin: A Study of Abortion and Divorce in Catholic Chile since 1990." *Nueva Serie FLACSO*. Santiago: FLACSO.

Broh, Eleanor. 2008. "Domestic Implementation of International Human Rights Norms: A Case Study of Therapeutic Abortion in Nicaragua and Colombia." B.A. thesis, Harvard University.

Cariboni, Diana. 1998. "A tres votos de la legalización del aborto." Available at http://www.chasque.apc.org/frontpage/aborto/01noti044.htm.

Center for Reproductive Rights and Policy. 2001. *Persecuted. Political Process and Abortion Legislation in El Salvador: A Human Rights Analysis*. New York: Center for Reproductive Law and Policy.

Conferência Nacional dos Bispos do Brasil (CNBB). 2005. "Pontos para o diálogo da presidência da CNBB com a Ministra Nilcéia Freire, da Secretaria Especial das Políticas Para a Mulher." Brasília, February 23. Available at http://www.cnbb.org.br/index.php?op=pagina&chaveid=253.025.

Coordinación Nacional de Organizaciones por la Defensa de la Salud Reproductiva. 2004. "Encuesta de opinión sobre la Ley de Salud Reproductiva." Carried out by Equipos Mori, April 28–30. Accessed March 10, 2006, from http://www.chasque.net/frontpage/aborto/01noti043.htm.

Corrêa, Sonia. 1994. *Population and Reproductive Rights: Feminist Perspectives from the South*. London: Zed Books.

Figueiredo, Argelina, and Fernando Limongi. 2000. "Presidential Power, Legislative Organization, and Party Behavior in Brazil." *Comparative Politics* 32, no. 2 (January): 151–70.

Fleet, Michael, and Brian Smith. 1997. *The Catholic Church and Democracy in Chile and Peru*. Notre Dame, IN: University of Notre Dame Press.

Friedman, Elisabeth. 2003. "Gendering the Agenda: The Impact of the Transnational Women's Rights Movement at the U.N. Conferences of the 1990s." *Women's Studies International Forum* 26, no. 4: 313–31.

———. 2005. "The Reality of Virtual Reality: The Internet and Gender Equality Advocacy in Latin America." *Latin American Politics and Society* 47, no. 3 (Fall): 1–34.

Gaudium et spes. 1965/1999. In Marianne Lorraine Trouvé, ed., *The Sixteen Documents of Vatican II*, 615–719. Boston: Pauline Books and Media.

Glendon, Mary Ann. 1987. *Abortion and Divorce in Western Law*. Cambridge, MA: Harvard University Press.

Harris Poll. 2006. "Overall Confidence in Leaders of Major Institutions Remains Steady." No. 22, March 2. Accessed April 20, 2006, from http://www.harrisinteractive.com/harris_poll/index.asp?PID=646.

Htun, Mala. 2003a. *Sex and the State: Abortion, Divorce, and the Family under Latin American Dictatorships and Democracies*. New York: Cambridge University Press.

———. 2003b. "Women and Democracy." In Jorge I. Domínguez and Michael Shifter, eds., *Constructing Democratic Governance in Latin America*, 2nd ed. Baltimore, MD: Johns Hopkins University Press.

Htun, Mala, and Timothy Power. 2006. "Gender, Parties, and Support for Equal Rights in the Brazilian Congress." *Latin American Politics and Society* 48, no. 4 (Winter): 83–104.

Inglehart, Ronald, Miguel Basáñez, Jaime Díez-Medrano, Loek Halman, and Ruud Luijkx. 2004. *Human Beliefs and Values: A Cross-Cultural Sourcebook Based on the 1999–2002 Values Surveys*. Mexico: Siglo XXI.

Karsin, Nicole. 2005. "Colombians Push Abortion onto National Agenda." *Women's E News*. December 22. Available at http://www.womensenews.org/article.cfm/dyn/aid/2577/context/archive.

Keck, Margaret, and Kathryn Sikkink. 1998. *Activists Beyond Borders*. Ithaca, NY: Cornell University Press.

Latinobarómetro. 2004. *Informe-Resumen: Latinobarómetro 2004. Una década de mediciones*. Santiago: Corporación Latinobarómetro.

Levine, Daniel. 1992. *Popular Voices in Latin American Catholicism*. Princeton, NJ: Princeton University Press.

Luker, Kristin. 1984. *Abortion and the Politics of Motherhood*. Berkeley: University of California Press.

Mainwaring, Scott. 1986. *The Catholic Church and Politics in Brazil, 1916–1985*. Stanford, CA: Stanford University Press.

Mexican Episcopal Conference. 2002. "Comunicado de la CEM sobre La Ley Robles." January 30. Available at http://www.cem.org.mx/doctos/cem/colectivos/trienio0103/comunicado4.htm.

Noonan, John T. 1970. "An Almost Absolute Value in History." In John T. Noonan, ed., *The Morality of Abortion: Legal and Historical Perspectives*, 1–59. Cambridge, MA: Harvard University Press.

Pontifical Council for Justice and Peace. 2004. *Compendium of the Social Doctrine of the Church*. Vatican City: Vatican Press.

Rodrigues, Almira. 2001. *Direitos das mulheres. O que pensam os parlamentares*. Brasília: CFEMEA.

Schwindt-Bayer, Leslie. 2007. "Women in the Americas: A Report Card." Washington, DC: Inter-American Dialogue. Accessed March 24, 2008, from http://www.thedialogue.org/PublicationFiles/rc_schwindt-bayer.pdf.

Shepard, Bonnie. 2000. "The 'Double Discourse' on Sexual and Reproductive Rights in Latin America: The Chasm between Public Policy and Private Actions." *Health and Human Rights* 4, no. 2: 111–43.

9 | Religion and Public Spaces

Catholicism and Civil Society in Peru

CATALINA ROMERO

This chapter presents some reflections on the influence of religion on politics, and specifically on the process of democratization and the quality of democracy in Latin America—with a focus on Peru—in the context of the new religious pluralism. By *religious pluralism* I mean not only a pluralism *of* religions, or an interreligious pluralism, but also religious diversity *within* religions, or internal pluralism. Of particular interest is how this internal diversity relates to the state, political society, and civil society—that is to say, with public space—during a period of democratization.

Internal pluralism within religion is nothing new. Catholicism and other Christian churches (Troelsch 1960; Weber 1978) are organized in such a way that presupposes a complexity based on the aspiration to be universal and to integrate different groups within a single religious entity. But the interesting question to ask today is how this pluralism within and among religions affects the contemporary quality of democracy. In the case of Catholicism we are not dealing with a traditional church that is trying to relate to a modern, plural, and dynamic society in the sense that Dahl meant when speaking of polyarchy (Dahl 1971). Rather, what we have, on the one hand, is a plural church with different positions on how to act in the distinct public spaces that are opening up with the exercise of democracy and, on the other hand, societies organized on corporatist, vertical, and exclusionary bases that are trying to democratize and build democratic governments while confronting serious challenges in defining democratic public spaces (Mainwaring and Pérez Liñán 2002; Levine and Molina 2007; Romero 2007; UNDP 2006b; Latinobarómetro 2006).

The concept of *civil society*, as applied to Latin America, refers to the new public space for social action that is analytically separable from the state but that is connected to it, thereby forming a complex whole. That is to say, there can be no civil society without the state, nor can there be a state without civil society: they are two sides of the same coin. This new understanding cannot be reduced to the old liberal notion that this space contains society's economic dynamism and social classes seeking to expand the scope of the private in relation to the state. The sense in which I use the concept of civil society corresponds more closely to the way in which de Tocqueville used it to refer to the associational dynamic present in U.S. society in the nineteenth century—a dynamic distinguished by the value citizens placed on associating to resolve problems within an established legal framework. Of course, Latin America does not resemble the American society that de Tocqueville knew and analyzed. In Central and South America, great civilizations that survived the Iberian conquest were reorganized into a colonial society, with new monarchical institutions imposed on them. Today, despite the nearly two centuries that have elapsed since the founding of the new, independent republics, gross inequality—principally economic but also cultural and political—remains a great obstacle to constructing democratic institutions.

Toward a Conceptual Framework

The contemporary meaning of the concept of civil society in Latin America is bound up with the value of personal initiative and the associations that are formed among self-proclaimed equals in order to affirm their rights as human beings and live a decent life, while maintaining their identities and differences. This dynamic is nourished as much with regard to traditional values as it is in the contemporary democratic practices of electing and alternating authorities, participating in assemblies, and making decisions and in the daily interactions among equals. Citizens seeking spaces for dialogue, consensus building, and participation come together in civil society to demand from the state and social institutions a greater integration and recognition of rights.

In this context, the Catholic Church in Latin America has played a crucial and novel role in what has become known as the "third wave of democratization" by stimulating and supporting the formation of a civil society in the region (Casanova 2001; Romero 1989). In observing that Catholicism exercised this same influence in the democratization of countries on other continents where Catholicism was a minority religion, Casanova stresses the importance of internal change within Catholicism itself: "it was a Catholic wave not just because the countries where it occurred happened to be Catholic, but because the transformation of Catholicism was itself an important independent factor in producing the wave" (Casanova 2001, 1043). This chapter picks up this thread, which was more or less dropped in the literature, to ask whether this transformation of Catholicism has continued to shape Latin American society as Casanova and others hypothesized it would. Specifically, is this transformation of Catholicism continuing to influence democratization in this same way, or has this transformation been stalled by the development of neotraditional currents that, with the support of the ecclesiastical hierarchy, tend to reinforce authoritarian church policies that are analogous to similar tendencies in politics?

How does a religion such as Catholicism help break the cycle of poverty that spans the entire continent? In posing this question I am thinking of how Catholicism may contribute to ending the cycle of poverty not only as a heritage of values and culture but also as the way in which people live and relate to one another within the church. The preferential option for the poor raised by the church at the bishops' conference at Medellin in 1968, liberation theology, and the experience of Christian communities' opening of a public religious space had enormous significance during the period in which political society was closed down by the dictatorships. But what is Catholicism's role today in a context of democracy and economic growth? It is significant that the Fifth General Meeting of the Latin American Bishops (V Conferencia General del Episcopado Latinoamericano y del Caribe) in Aparecida, Brazil, had as its principal theme "discipleship in a continent marked by poverty and inequality"; in its final document (CELAM 2007) the conference confirmed the preferential option for the poor as a calling for all in the church and recognized the contribution of ecclesial communities to both the church and society.

I begin this inquiry with three general hypotheses advanced by José Casanova (2001, 1044–48) that will serve as a frame for my analysis of the Peruvian case. The first is that "religions in general and churches especially can serve as autonomous public spaces and as a countervailing power to state power: The more religious institutions have a hierocratic structure, as with the Catholic Church . . . the more this is potentially the case" (1044). The second proposes the conditions necessary for a church to play a role in the constitution of civil society: "to put it bluntly, the church only becomes an institution of civil society when it ceases being a church in the Weberian sense of the term: when it gives up its monopolistic claims and recognizes religious freedom and freedom of conscience as universal and inviolable human rights" (1046). These conditions "imply not only voluntary disestablishment from the state, but also disengagement from political society proper" (1047). Finally, Casanova asserts that "this relocation of the church from the state and from political society to civil society does not necessarily mean the privatization of Catholicism. On the contrary, this relocation is the very condition for the possibility of a modern public religion, for a modern form of public Catholicism" (Casanova 2001, 1047; see also Casanova 1994).

Much was written between 1970 and 1990 about religion and politics in Latin America, and especially about change in the Catholic Church. Scholars noted that the church distanced itself from the dominant classes in some countries (Brazil, Peru, Nicaragua, and El Salvador, among others), but in other countries it remained in permanent alliance with them (Argentina and Colombia). Phenomena such as the ecclesial base communities (*comunidades eclesiales de base,* or CEBs) and the preferential option for the poor were studied as new forms of organization and theological reflection within the Catholic Church. Several scholars (Bruneau, Gabriel, and Mooney 1984; Levine 1980; C. Smith 1995; B. Smith 1998; Williams and Peterson 2001) described and analyzed the relationship of religious associations to social movements and the political dimension of this religious commitment. Later in the 1980s, other phenomena such as the rupture of the Catholic monopoly on the continent and the advance of Protestantism, first in its evangelical form and more recently through Pentecostalism, were also analyzed (Martin 1990; Stoll 1990; López 1995; Bastian 1997; T. Gutiérrez 2000; Ruuth 1995). More specific themes, such as the relationship between religion and ecology, human rights, and sexual and ethnic identities, have been discussed in more recent literature in an attempt to explain the importance of religion in relation to politics. They all, from different perspectives and frameworks, focus on what Casanova refers to as the influence of religion in civil society.

I proceed on the foundation laid by this work and my own work on Peru to analyze the Peruvian case, taking into account the three hypotheses proposed by Casanova. I further develop what it means for a church to transform itself into a modern and public institution that acts from civil society. I also examine the strong resistance to this process, which can lead some bishops and religious movements to seek new alliances with the state when authoritarian tendencies emerge or political regime changes take place, as occurred during the government of Alberto Fujimori.

In order to understand how the relocation of the church to civil society is brought about and the new demands and limits that this space presents for it, we need to go beyond Casanova's reconstruction of the recent historical process to study how the church organizes itself as a modern, public religion. My principal contention is that such a transformation within the church is possible only when a public space is developed within the ecclesial organization itself.[1] This space of internal freedom must be based on interpersonal trust and confidence in the ecclesial institution, respect for internal and external pluralism, and the free expression of ideas and beliefs within it. It also must be possible for members of the church to take political action in society freely, without any implication that they are speaking in the name of the church.[2] In other words, the church's relocation to civil society can happen only when members of the church have a capacity for autonomous and plural action *and* the church transforms itself into a critical community raising ethical questions enlightened by faith—as much for its own faithful as for citizens who do not belong to the church and may not even believe. Following Habermas (1989), I aim to analyze the process of transformation of the public space within a church. A church that meets these conditions would be a modern, public church where, in a context of religious and political pluralism, members' actions are not inspired by fear or institutional constraints.

I propose to analyze the church as a "religious society," using the categories of state and civil society. This way of understanding the church carries the methodological risks inherent in the use of any analogy; therefore, I will begin with a definition of terms and some justification. Many have reached for the analogy of a state to understand the governance structure of the church that goes beyond the Vatican itself, which is limited to a small territory (Ruda 1995). The analogy seems appropriate because the universal church has its own system of government, headed by the pope, with a legal system (canon law) that defines the rights and responsibilities of membership in the church. This formal structure also suggests an analogy between the ecclesiastical hierarchy as a system of religious government and the state as a system of political government. It is on this level that state-to-state relations are established and the power and the legitimacy of the church in each national context can be generally analyzed.

The members of the church are the baptized, who are divided into clergy and laity; nevertheless, the church calls them all "the people of God." Among them are those called to govern the church as well as the faithful called to participate in it and to fulfill their vocation as Christians, giving testimony to their faith in their daily lives. All form part of the religious regime (Bax 1991) and are subject to its laws. All are also members with the rights and obligations of the ecclesial community, an "undifferentiated space" (Habermas 1981) in which each fulfills his or her own distinctive duties and vocations. Proposing to understand the ecclesial community as a civil society in contemporary terms is the first step in recognizing the rights of the faithful (Canon 212)[3] to express themselves and voice opinions, contribute with their own gifts and capabilities to the progress of the church, and fulfill themselves as humans and citizens of this world, which includes the right of association, both inside and outside the church, in the hopes of achieving specific goals.

The incorporation of the poor into the ecclesial community, however, took many forms, ranging from the traditional *cofradias* and brotherhoods put in place during colonial times and still being formed today, to the ecclesial or Christian base communities, which constituted spaces of free and voluntary association within the realm of the parish. CEBs could be short-lived, disappearing when the purpose that gave rise to them had been realized, or they could persist if they built a human community that endured beyond the efforts to achieve their initial goal. The CEBs were not the only associational form that pulled in the poor. A second wave of movements, including the Charismatic Renewal Movement, the *Cursillos de Cristiandad* (Short Courses in Christian Living), the Legion of Mary, and other specialized movements also contributed to building the church as an ecclesial community.

The church also joined with other social organizations to open public space for participation for those marginalized by distance, language, gender, poverty, or, more generally, for victims of all forms of discrimination and oppression. Incorporating the distant and the different into the church through baptism is not the same thing as opening public space to modernization. The latter refers to a transformation in the missionary practice of the church itself that respects and recognizes not only other cultures but also other forms of differences in social life and allows members of the church to speak in different languages and voices.

Developing a public space in its internal life is fundamental to the church being able to successfully transform itself and relocate to secular civil society. It is in this space of civil society where believers encounter citizens in two senses: believers begin to see themselves as citizens, and believers also begin to associate with nonbelievers as citizens. Thus, plural participation in political affairs is made possible where freedom of action, critical reflection, and opinion are exercised and where believers and nonbelievers can come together as citizens, not as defenders of their faith or lack thereof. It is to this modern civil society of citizens, without a distinction between believers and nonbelievers, that the church dedicates itself as a public, modern religion, in Casanova's terms, in order to present citizens with moral criteria as referents for free and conscious action.

In ecclesial society the believer can examine her temporal life in terms of her religious beliefs and from the point of view of faith critically reflect on her human actions. This space can be a space of liberty. Diverse, lay-organized Christian communities, grassroots church communities (such as CEBs), and apostolic movements born of Catholic Action in Latin America were constituted as spaces of association, participation, free expression, and opinion and were joined by clergy and bishops who also

participated in those spaces (Romero 1989). Such spaces were also constructed in other Christian churches, including the Lutheran, Anglican,
and Methodist churches, among others. The validity of these categories of
ecclesiastical state and ecclesial society for analyzing the relationship of the
church to the process of democratization in Latin America will become
clearer in an examination of the Peruvian case.

Religious Pluralism and Catholicism in Peru

For centuries Peru and Latin America resembled Christian Europe before the Protestant Reformation, when there was only one way of
being Christian. In Latin America Catholic religious hegemony began in
the sixteenth century and lasted until the middle of the twentieth century,
when this religious monopoly began to erode. In the late twentieth century
religious pluralism grew most rapidly in such countries as Brazil, Chile,
and Guatemala. In the Andean region the growth of other denominations
was slower, but their presence was generally known. In the twenty-first century the religious-social context has changed in most Latin American countries, including Peru.

Entering the twenty-first century, the Catholic Church in Peru has
forty-five ecclesiastical territories, which are organized in seven archdioceses (Lima, Trujillo, and Piura on the coast, Arequipa, Ayacucho,
Huancayo, and Cusco in the Andes), nineteen dioceses, twelve prelatures[4]
and eight vicariates.[5] Each category corresponds to an administrative level
of what is called a "particular church"[6] and also to levels of economic and
urban development. There was a conceptual shift from "territorial units"
to "particular churches" after the Second Vatican Council, which also acknowledged the separation of church from state. Although it is still organized in territorial units, what defines the church is the relation of the
bishops with the Catholic people and not dominion over territory and the
local population (Ius Canonicum n.d.).

Besides Catholicism there are other religions and nonreligious options
present in Peruvian society that should be considered as well. According to
census data, Catholics in Peru constituted approximately 90 percent of the
population through the early 1990s, but recent sample studies show that the

situation is beginning to change. In the 1981 census evangelicals and other religions (which appeared together in the same, "other" category) constituted 5.2 percent of the Peruvian population. By the time of the 1993 census, that figure (which again included both "other religion" and evangelicals) had risen to 9.7 percent (see Table 9.1).

Because the 2005 census did not include a question about religion, we cannot be sure of the extent of the growth of the evangelical population and those falling into various "other" categories in the period from 1993 to 2005. We can, however, estimate the rate of change of religious affiliation with the use of survey data. Such data indicate that the number of evangelicals increased from 6 percent of the population in 1996 to 7.2 percent in 2001, and again to 11.7 percent in 2006.[7] The percentages of other religions remained stable at a much lower level (around 1 percent), and the Peruvian-born

Table 9.1. Religious Membership in Peru
(in percent)

Religion	1981	1993[a]	1996[b]	2001[c]	2006[d]
Roman Catholic	94.6	88.9	82	82.3	72.1
Evangelical, Pentecostal	n/a	n/a	6	7.2	11.7
Seventh Day Adventist	n/a	n/a	1	1.3	1.5
Jehovah's Witness	n/a	n/a	2	2.7	1.7
Israelites of the New Universal Pact	n/a	n/a	1	0.3	0.1
Believer but Doesn't Belong to Any Religion	n/a	n/a	n/a	n/a	2.9
Indifferent	n/a	n/a	n/a	n/a	4.7
Nonbeliever	0.2	1.4	7	4.7	4.2
Other Religion (includes Evangelicals)	5.2	9.7	n/a	n/a	n/a
Don't Know, No Response	n/a	n/a	n/a	1.5	0.3
Sample Size			1,210	1,500	1,945

Sources: National Census, Peru, 1981–1993, and national surveys as noted below.
Note: n/a indicates categories were not given as a choice to respondents.
[a]Data from 1981 and 1993 are taken from the Peruvian National Census. Census categories are limited to Catholics, nonbelievers, and other religions. For this reason, the figure of 9.7 percent includes an array of other religions, which are specified in the national sample surveys.
[b]Data from the World Values Survey (1996).
[c]Data from the World Values Survey (2001).
[d]Data from the Sociedad Católica en el Perú (2006).

religious group Israelitas del Nuevo Pacto Universal (Israelites of the New Universal Pact) experienced a clear decline after the death of their founder Ezequiel Ataucusi in 2000 (see Table 9.1).

The group that grew most rapidly according to the census was those claiming to be "without religion"; in the most recent surveys this group was broken into two categories: "nonbelievers" and those who are "indifferent." These groups together represented a mere 0.2 percent of the population in 1981 and just a little over 1 percent in 1993, but then their numbers began to increase rapidly. According to the survey data, by 2006 the percentage of nonbelievers had risen to 4.2 and the "indifferent" to 4.7. Two new categories of believers—the "indifferent" and "believer but doesn't belong to a religion" (which represented 2.9 percent of the Peruvian population)—were not offered as options in previous surveys. If we add these two groups to the self-identified Catholics, we arrive at a figure of 79.7 percent, which is the level of Catholics reported in other sample surveys.

According to the 1993 census, in the seven archdioceses with the greatest concentration of diocesan priests and priests from religious orders, evangelicals represented between 1.5 and 4 percent of the local population, while in the departments of Amazonas, Huancavelica, Huánuco, Pasco, and Ucayali evangelicals made up more than 15 percent of the population. This unevenness in the evangelical presence in the country has persisted and still needs to be studied not only in quantitative terms but also in terms of the stability of these communities and their contribution to democracy and politics.

Table 9.2. Number of Priests in Peru, 1969–2002

Type of Priest	1969	1974	1984	2002[a]
Diocesan	958	967	984	n.d.
Religious	1,552	1,492	1,251	n.d.
Total	2,510	2,459	2,265	2,182

Source: CEP (1987, 2002)

[a]The 2002 figure is derived from the total number of names on the list of priests that appears in the 2002 CEP annual report. The 2002 report does not distinguish between diocesan and religious priests.

In terms of intrareligious pluralism, we are also interested in the size of the Catholic clergy (see Table 9.2). While the population has been growing, the number of priests in Peru has fallen to 2,182 (from 2,510 in 1969), and this number has remained stable with a clergy whose average age is approximately forty-five. If we divide 27 million Peruvians by this number, the result is a ratio of 11,842 persons per Roman Catholic priest. Considering that priests are concentrated in the seven archdioceses—that is, the older cities in the country with 25 percent of the population—and in dioceses, rather than in prelatures or vicariates, where the population is disperse, the fact is that the ratio of people to priests is even higher in some portions of the country. With the model of a church in which membership is defined by participating in the Sunday Mass, which can be celebrated only by priests, by definition the deteriorating ratio of parishioners to priests is contributing to a diversification of the religious public space in which people can participate. The expression and exchange of opinions, deliberation, and the formulation of an ethic related to daily life can be achieved in other non-ritual or sacramental contexts and around other practices that broaden the possibilities of sharing information in the ecclesial as well as the ecclesiastical tradition and introduce the believer to a style of life that goes beyond ritualistic behavior to reinforce identity and membership.

In an attempt to understand better participation in the Catholic Church beyond attending Sunday Mass—the typical indicator used to measure religious practice—I asked participants in a 2006 national survey about the type of religious practice with which they most closely and comfortably identified and that was most to their liking. I grouped the options in three sets of three questions: one question in each set corresponded to popular religiosity, a second to institutional practice, and a third to community-building practices (see Table 9.3). In the first set the option that received the highest number of responses was attending Sunday Mass (46.6 percent), followed by working in a religious community or group to resolve a neighborhood or local problem (29.8 percent). Very few respondents (14.2 percent) chose participating in patron saint feasts. In the second group of alternatives, 33.6 percent chose reading the Bible in a community or group, followed closely by attending a religious procession (31.6 percent). Last came reciting the Rosary or participating in a prayer group (22.1 percent). In the third set the majority chose volunteering or service work (59.2

Table 9.3. Religious Practices with Which Catholics Most Closely Identified and Which Were Most to Their Liking
(in percent)

| | | Types of Religious Expression | | |
Options for Religious Practice	Total	Popular Religiosity	Institutional Practice	Community-Building Practices
Responses to Question 1:				
Participate in patron saint festivals	14.2	14.2		
Attend Sunday Mass	46.6		46.6	
Work in a religious community or group to resolve a neighborhood or local problem	29.8			29.8
Responses to Question 2:				
Attend a religious procession	31.6	31.6		
Recite the Rosary or attend prayer groups	22.1		22.1	
Read the Bible in a (religious) community or group	33.6			33.6
Responses to Question 3:				
Take a prominent role in a patron saint festival	3.3	3.3		
Receive the Eucharist	29.7		29.7	
Volunteer or do service work	59.2			59.2

Source: Sociedad Católica en el Perú (2006).
Note: Participants in the survey were asked the following questions:
People practice their religion in different ways. 1. With which of the following religious practices do you feel closer and more comfortable? (choose one) 2. And in the following set? 3. And in the following set? The survey was based on a sample of 1,770 adults (over eighteen years old) nationwide, including urban and rural, men and women.

percent), followed at a distance by receiving the Eucharist (29.7 percent) and taking a prominent role in a patron saint festival (3.3 percent).

The option that was most cited by respondents overall—to volunteer or do service work—is not typically understood as a religious practice that takes place through a church, but it does create a sense of solidarity with others. The second most popular preference was to attend Sunday Mass. (There is a significant correlation between the responses to this question and to the question we later asked all respondents about whether or not they actually attend Mass.) In third place was reading the Bible in a community. The options that correspond to popular religious practices that are very important and widespread in Peru were not the most frequently chosen as the preference of individuals in any of the three questions, but they do form part of the diversity of practices.

Although these results do not point to a common pattern or produce any statistically significant correlations, they support the conclusion that Parker (see chap. 4 in this volume) draws about Chile—namely, that Chilean Catholics believe "in their own way." Peruvian Catholics similarly practice their faith in their own style, combining institutional religious practices with community-building ones. Thus, someone who prefers or is most comfortable going to Mass can also attend a procession, read the Bible in a community, and serve as a volunteer in a neighborhood community service project. Relating religious beliefs to social practices and everyday life enriches the quality of individual participation and produces religious competence in believers who in turn become better integrated into the church.

As in other Latin American countries, religious pluralism is a fact in twenty-first-century Peru. The diversity of religious practices enriches the Catholic Church and allows it to maintain a sense of identity and reach its members in different ways. There is little that is new about such pluralism in organizations that fall within Ernst Troelsch's definition of a church (1960). But to speak of religious pluralism and pluralism in a society presupposes a change in values and political culture that is manifested in the possibility of association among those who are different[8]—in terms of interests, culture, gender, or ethnicity—and in the opening of public spaces that allow free expression and debate. In the next section, we delve more deeply into this dimension.

The Development of a Public Ecclesial Space

There are four ways in which civil society is being constructed within the church—or what we call "ecclesial society"—that can have positive consequences for society and politics. First is the formation of voluntary associations as a space for initiative, solidarity, and expression and for forming opinions and realizing common goals. Second, there are associational spaces where people get together and exchange experiences, thereby opening participation to "the other" and weaving networks that connect different geographic areas, ethnic groups, social classes, and men and women. Third, there is learning from and reflecting about one's experience in light of one's religious beliefs and other forms of knowledge. Finally, there is the possibility of religious expression in religious and nonreligious spaces through publications, arts, the media, and mobilization.

Voluntary Associations

Christian communities that expand the possibilities for joining and participating in the Catholic Church exist everywhere in Latin America. These communities are voluntary associations with specific objectives that allow poorly staffed parishes to function better than they would without the associations' support. Often, they emerge in places where people are seeking to broaden their participation in the church and to improve the quality of that participation. Participation in this type of group is a school for learning responsibility and leadership, as well as a space for personal development, and for this reason many scholars believe that these groups contribute to the democratic development of society and politics (see Bruneau, Gabriel, and Mooney 1984; Romero 2001; and C. Smith 1995, among others). The household survey conducted by the United Nations Development Program (UNDP 2006b),[9] "Democracy in Peru," asked participants about the existence of associations in the localities where the study was conducted. The most frequently cited type of association, consistent with the findings of other studies, were religious groups (cited by 61 percent of respondents). Those responding that they belonged to such a group represented two-thirds of the sample (66.7 percent), and just about one half (50.1 percent) said they attended meetings frequently or always. By comparison, other types of organizations were not as common.[10] Political committees existed in 17.9 percent of respondents' localities; unions in 5.7 percent; producers' associations in 11.5 percent; and associations of parents in the secondary schools in 35 percent. These data confirm that of all groups, religious groups are the most ubiquitous throughout the country and that people participate in them more than in any other type of group. Religious groups can be quite varied. They may include parish groups charged with preparing liturgical celebrations and the catechism, charismatic prayer groups, and Christian communities. Alternatives like the more traditional religious *hermandades* (brotherhoods) and *cofradías* may also be considered here since they have autonomous organizations and regular meetings in addition to their public presence in the festivities of their saints.

One example of the way in which Christian communities have opened new spaces for religious action is their role in carrying out pastoral work in parish-level "chapels." Priests are supposed to be in charge of these chapels, but nuns or lay members of Christian communities have entered this space in order to provide religious services and a variety of pastoral services for people in the absence of priests. In Lurin, a new diocese in the south of Lima, for example, there are 27 parishes, 6 quasi-parishes, and 110 chapels. This organizational pattern is repeated in other dioceses in the vicinity, such as Chosica to the east of Lima, Carabayllo to the north, and others where the high population density makes it impossible for the central parish administration to satisfy the demand for religious services and pastoral care. In many parishes Mass cannot be celebrated because of the lack of priests, but Christian communities or laypeople organize alternative liturgical services that bring together local communities. Assuming responsibility for organizing a celebration of "the Word," having time to discuss their everyday life problems, and presiding over prayers said in common give the community an active role in a religious field previously limited to priests. The priest is not displaced from his sacramental role, but the possibilities for participating in the church are broadened, transforming a ritual moment into a special encounter that places the real life problems of people at the center of the celebration. These associations give a distinctive quality to the social fabric of ecclesial society. In a hierarchical organization such as the Catholic Church, they open spaces for association and internal discussion in which priests and laity can communicate with one another, bringing theological reflection and church doctrine into close contact with the common sense of the believer in a way that reinforces the institutional foundation of the institution.

This heterogeneous and plural activity responds to different objectives and follows from different theological and pastoral orientations. Dioceses

such as Chulucanas on the northern coast of Peru, or Lurin in Lima, organize their pastoral work around the efforts of these communities and the
"New Parish Image"[11] movement. Pucallpa and other dioceses in the Amazon organize their pastoral work in remote villages with the support of *animadores Cristianos* (Christian animators). These animators are elected by
their communities as religious leaders to attend to the needs of the people
in the settlements, including health care, education, and advice to families.
Instead of forming small communities with religious identities, the animators care for the whole village, attending to residents' basic needs and social
concerns and providing opportunities for celebration and self-expression.
Animators need not be well-educated Catholics at the outset; priests, as
part of their mission, visit the villages every three months to supervise the
animators. They receive instruction and are asked to live their lives according to Christian values. This dynamic sets in motion a process of human
development for themselves and their communities. As part of the process
they meet with animators elected in other villages, learning to move around
and network. In the southern Andean region pastoral work also includes
the laity in different forms: they participate as catechists and as *animadores
Cristianos* in local civil communities. The pastoral coordination among the
bishops of the Andean south has been an example of the transformation of
the way in which a significant part of the church addresses its mission
among the indigenous people—respecting their traditions and culture
while at the same time preaching the Gospel.

Catholic Christian communities are somewhat different. They appear
in various forms but share three characteristics: reading of the Bible as a
source for theological reflection, commitment to the option for the poor,
and adherence to the methodology of "to see, to judge and to act" that was
confirmed in the Fifth General Meeting of Latin American Bishops in Aparecida, Brazil, in June 2007 (CELAM 2007). These ecclesial base communities developed following the model of Catholic Action movements and
their specialized branches, such as the university student movements—
National Union of Catholic Students (Unión Nacional de Estudiantes
Católicos, or UNEC) in Peru, Catholic University Youth (Juventude Uni-
versitária Católica, or JUC) in Brazil—the Catholic Youth Workers (Juventud Obrera Católica, or JOC), and those working with peasant youth, and,
later, intellectuals and independent workers. Members of the CEBs are

common rank-and-file Catholics—men and women of different ages who come together to provide religious meaning to their lives. This does not mean that their actions are limited to pastoral work inside the church; on the contrary, the community is open to society. The Fifth General Meeting confirmed the importance of CEBs in the life of the church,[12] saying that "Medellin recognized them as initial cells of ecclesial growth and a focus of evangelization. Puebla reaffirmed that the small communities, above all ecclesial base communities, made it possible for the people to grasp a greater understanding of the Word of God, the social commitment of the Gospel, the rise of new lay services, and the education of adults in the faith" (CELAM 2007, §178).

Through these different forms of association and the construction of new spaces for encounter and interaction, the church has renovated itself and infused religious meaning into life's everyday problems. In the last decade, however, that space has begun to close once again, due to the intervention of a number of bishops who are trying to take back control of public space both in the church itself and in the way the church expresses itself and is represented in civil society, political society, and the state. Cooperating with the bishops in this process are a number of new religious movements whose influence in the structure of the church is growing. These movements have developed within what I call "ecclesial society" as communities of faith, but they have become ecclesiastic movements. They follow different lines of action both within the church and in society. Some examples are the Neocathecumenal Way, founded in 1972 by Kiko Arguello in Spain; the Focolari movement, founded by Chiara Lubich in Trento, Italy, in 1943; and Communion and Liberation, founded by Father Luigi Guissana in Milan, Italy, in 1954. Some of these movements are attempting to increase their power by gaining positions of responsibility in the church's governance structures.

One of these groups, originally from Spain but with a significant presence in Latin America, is Opus Dei; it was promoted to the status of Personal Prelature under Pope John Paul II. There are now around twelve bishops in Peru who are members of or closely related to Opus Dei, including Cardinal Juan Luis Cipriani, archbishop of Lima, and the archbishop of Cusco, as well as those from the Priestly Society of the Holy Cross who are "intrinsically united" with Opus Dei, like the bishop of Juli, in Puno.

A second group is the movement Sodalitium Christianae Vitae (roughly translated as "community of Christian life"), founded in Peru in 1971 by Luis Fernando Figari with the goal of resisting as a lay community the winds of change emerging from the Second Vatican Council as well as the preferential option for the poor.[13] Working among the elites like Opus Dei does, this group has gained positions of power inside the church and in society. John Paul II recognized the movement in 1997, and it has diversified its activities and grown across Latin America and North America. One of the organizations formed by Sodalitium is ACI Press (ACI Prensa), now the largest Catholic news agency in Latin America.[14] Currently, the movement has two bishops in Peru: the archbishop of Piura and the bishop of the Prelature of Ayaviri in Puno. Sodalitium Christianae Vitae was actively opposed to the commitment of the Catholic Church in Latin America to the poor and dispossessed and to the theological reflection that led to the option for the poor, the theology of liberation. Opus Dei members, including laypeople, try to gain positions of power at the local and international levels within the church, and most of them oppose the very notion of a plural and public space inside the church and in society as a whole.

In the rural Andean south, where the Quechua and Aymara peoples, living in extreme poverty, form the largest concentration of indigenous people in Peru, social and cultural concerns have been central to the pastoral work of the local churches. New bishops appointed in the region—such as Ayaviri's bishop, a member of the Sodalitium Christianae Vitae, and the bishop of Juli, a member of the Society of the Holy Cross, which is associated with Opus Dei—are reorganizing the pastoral work of the different prelatures. They are breaking with the pastoral work that former bishops designed for the area, which took into consideration local cultural identities and ecclesial traditions. The new bishops are displacing local laypersons and some priests from functions they had performed prior to their arrival. The bishops' actions sharply contradict the pastoral line set by previous bishops and followed in the prelatures for fifty years: in particular, they do not understand the relation between preaching the Gospel and human promotion. Indeed, some of their actions have been widely criticized.[15]

The traditional fraternities formed around the service to patron saints, the ecclesial base communities in their different forms and orientations, and the religious movements following the Second Vatican Council or those that follow other theologies or perspectives are all part of the ecclesial society under the governance of the Catholic hierarchy. The contribution of the diversity of associations to the sense of belonging to the church is illustrated by data provided by my 2006 survey. Respondents were asked five questions: (1) "In the past twelve months, have you received any information about church activities in your neighborhood?" (2) "In the past twelve months, have you attempted to participate more than the norm in the local church or chapel in your neighborhood or community?" (3) "In the past twelve months, when you have gone to your local church or chapel, have you found people that you know with whom you can talk?" (4) "During the past twelve months, has anyone invited you to go to church?" and, (5) "Do you think the church takes people's interests into account when selecting a parish priest?" Percentage responses to these questions are provided in Table 9.4.

Taking the responses to the first four questions, I constructed an "index of integration." Respondents received a score of 1 for each affirmative response; the minimum score possible, zero, represents no contact whatsoever with the church, and the maximum score of 4 signifies very close

Table 9.4. Ways of Belonging to the Catholic Church in Peru, 2006 (in percent)

Questions Asked Catholic Respondents	Yes	No	Don't Know
Have you received any information about church activities in your neighborhood?	48.8	49.9	1.3
Have you attempted to participate more than the norm in your local church or chapel?	37.3	61.1	1.6
When you go to church do you find people you know to talk to?	74.0	24.4	1.6
Has someone invited you to go to church?	74.4	23.8	1.8
Do you think the church takes people's interests into account when selecting a parish priest?	46.9	46.6	6.5

Source: Sociedad Católica en el Perú (2006).
Note: Respondents were asked to answer each question based on their experience over the previous twelve months.

Table 9.5. Index of Integration into the Church

Values	Frequency	Valid Percent
0	117	33.4
1	230	12.0
2	402	21.0
3	366	18.9
4	286	14.7
N	1,402	

Source: Sociedad Católica en el Perú (2006).
Note: Value scores indicate number of affirmative responses to the first four questions presented in Table 9.4, with a score of zero indicating no contact with the church and 4 indicating high contact between the respondent and the church.

contact between the respondent and the church (Table 9.5). The mean score of all 1,402 respondents is 2.3 (with a standard deviation of 1.2), which means that rank-and-file Catholics feel integrated into the church. A closer analysis of the data suggests that more people are being brought into the church through friends and neighbors than through formal channels of participation. Whereas 74 percent of respondents who attend church activities find people they know and can communicate with, and a similar percentage have been invited to go to church by someone, fewer than half reported receiving information about church activities, and only 37 percent attempted greater participation in their local church. In a question not incorporated into the index, again fewer than half of respondents felt the interests and opinions of the faithful were taken into account when new priests were appointed to the parish. It is one thing to attend Mass and socialize with other church members and another to participate in church life as a public space. The survey also asked respondents the question, "Do you agree or disagree with the following statement? The only way that people like me can participate in the church is by going to Mass." Fifty-five percent disagreed, meaning that they do find different ways of participating in church life, but 42 percent agreed and considered attending Mass to be the only way to integrate themselves into the church.

Spaces for Encounter

The difficult problems on the state's political agenda form a second focus for church participation and encounter. Grappling with the issues facing the nation has allowed church members to interact with each other beyond their own localities—thus acquiring a consciousness of the country—and to confront, articulate, and publicly debate controversial subjects. Three key areas of church participation have been human rights, poverty, and the formation of public policy. In each area the church has been a key actor in the development of institutional spaces that bring together a range of players and constituencies.

Human rights emerged as an issue as a consequence of the internal conflict growing out of the terrorist activities of the Shining Path and the Tupac Amaru Revolutionary Movement (Movimiento Revolucionario Túpac Amaru, or MRTA)[16] between 1980 and 1993. Committees to defend human rights, vicariates of solidarity, and other types of organizations dedicated to the same goal were formed in various parts of the country with distinctive forms of ecclesial participation. Some were formed by pastoral agents or by the church directly; others were formed by civilians who were also lay believers, some of whom were active participants in Catholic Christian communities or other forms of religious associations. The different groups were brought together in the National Coordinating Committee of Human Rights, which was comprised of sixty-seven local organizations, 40 to 60 percent of which were directly related to the Catholic Church. In this umbrella organization people were able to meet with other civic organizations and people of different religious faiths.[17]

The local organizations fulfilled the crucial role of defending human rights during a time of violence and, later, of defending the victims: the families of those "disappeared" by the armed forces and by the Shining Path and the innocent falsely imprisoned. Later, these groups supported victims in the hearings held around the country and organized by the Peruvian Truth and Reconciliation Commission (Comisión de la Verdad y Reconciliación, or CVR) in 2001–2003, and then in the proposals of reconciliation and offers of restitution for the victims, which are still under discussion.[18] These organizations were crucial in forming the *"para que no se repita"* (so that it won't be repeated) network as well as in initiating activities to keep alive *la Memoria*—the memory of what had happened—and reconstructing ties of solidarity among sectors in areas where violence had destroyed the existing social networks.

The public space for encounter that opened in Peruvian society following the internal conflict allowed the members of ecclesial society—laypersons and members of religious orders—to associate with other religious organizations affected by the violence, such as the evangelical churches, as well as with state and civil society institutions. Catholics were also able to network at the national and international levels and express their opinions about public affairs. But the Catholic Church did not speak with one voice on human rights. Members of Opus Dei from both the hierarchy and the laity, for instance, played a prominent role in the movement criticizing the CVR report and the country's human rights organizations. As a result, their opinions have been openly discussed and contested by the media, the intellectual community, and others that understand the importance of human rights for democracy. The possibility of dissent and debate about political and social issues within and outside the church has contributed to a wider opening of political space, including, this time, the participation of ecclesiastical representatives—bishops, priests, pastors—whose opinions now can be publicly discussed.

Another way of opening the public space to religion occurred at the level of interreligious pluralism when evangelical pastors entered politics in Peru. Their entry was highlighted in 1990 when evangelicals ran for public office on Alberto Fujimori's ticket[19] and more recently gained wider exposure with the formation of the National Restoration Party, which was created with the support of evangelical congregations. Intrareligious pluralism is a common feature among evangelical churches and communities; this pluralism generates discussion about how religion relates to politics, including arguments for and against confessional parties. Architect and evangelical minister Humberto Lay, the presidential candidate of the National Restoration Party, came in sixth in the 2006 election; he received well over the minimum number of votes required to keep the National Restoration Party's registration as a political party (T. Gutiérrez 2000; Delgado 2006).

The second area of encounter focuses on issues of poverty, with people from different sectors and points of view brought together in the critically important Roundtable for the Struggle against Poverty (Mesa de Concertación para la Lucha Contra la Pobreza, or MCLCP). This roundtable is an associational space created by the state; it reaches out to civil society with the purpose of setting targets through broad consultation and negotiation for distributing resources from the national budget to the "Struggle against Poverty." Different ecclesial groups with very different kinds of organizations participate in the roundtable as part of civil society. The roundtable is in the portfolio of the president of the Council of Ministers and has a council comprised of representatives from the ministries involved in the Struggle against Poverty—the Ministry of Women and Human Development (Ministerio de la Mujer y Desarrollo Humano, or MIMDES) and the Ministries of Health, Education, and Labor and Social Assistance. The Ministry of the Economy is also represented on this council, which is significant because it advises on the process of drawing up national plans in those areas that relate to development and social promotion policies at the departmental and local levels, as well as in the definition of national budget priorities.[20] Also participating are business associations, labor unions, and nongovernmental, grassroots, and religious organizations. The first president of the Roundtable for the Struggle against Poverty was a Catholic priest, Gastón Garatea SS.CC. He was appointed by President Paniagua—and reappointed by the Toledo and García administrations—in recognition of the work that the ecclesial society has done among the poor and civil society.

In addition to the national roundtable, the MCLCP also includes departmental-, provincial-, and district-level roundtables, as well as roundtables organized around specific subjects. The Interdenominational Roundtable is an example of a very active roundtable that includes people from the evangelical and Catholic churches, the Jewish faith, and the Bahai church, among others. All together, it comprises twenty-two religious organizations that amount to 5.31 percent of the total organizations in the MCLCP (MCLCP 2007). Members of Catholic Church networks, from representatives of diocesan Caritas chapters to laypersons belonging to CEBs, participate in the twenty-four departmental- and provincial-level[21] roundtables on behalf of the levels of government and civil society organizations that are listed in Table 9.6.

Table 9.6. Participation in the Roundtable for the Struggle against Poverty

Sectors	Number of Members	Percent of Total
Central Government	140	33.8
Local Government	24	5.8
Regional Government	30	7.3
Civil Society Organizations	216	52.2
Agencies of International Cooperation	4	1.0
Total	414	

Source: MCLCP (2007).

The struggle against poverty, which was considered a radical commitment in the 1960s, is now a basic practice for citizens and religious believers, and it is the main criteria for the representatives of various branches of government and public-sector agencies as well as representatives from civil society when they present their arguments for funding their projects and establish priorities for assigning resources from the national budget, a process known as participatory budgeting. The association among entrepreneurs, public officials, citizens committed to different projects, and members of the churches has been made possible by a climate of trust and dialogue that they managed to build. Only if the churches participate autonomously, with positions that aim to create agreement among dissenting parts, will they contribute to the efficient functioning of this space.

The third important associational space in which the church has participated is the National Accord, which originated in the political crisis following the fall of the Fujimori regime and has focused on building public policy through a wide-ranging process of consensus building. A year after the election of President Alejandro Toledo in 2001, the government invited opposition political parties and civil society to take part in a systematic and decentralized discussion to determine the government's goals. The goals were understood as public policies to be reached through a process of wide consultation and negotiation, and they would become the subject matter of a National Accord.

The minister in charge of the president's Council of Ministers presided over the accord. Invited to participate were cabinet ministers whose portfolios encompassed the subjects on the agenda; the political party in government, Perú Posible (Possible Peru), and opposition parties: Partido Aprista Peruano (Peruvian Aprista Party), Acción Popular (Popular Action), Somos Perú (We Are Peru), Unión por el Perú (Union for Peru), Unidad Nacional (National Unity), and Frente Independiente Moralizador (Independent Moralizing Front). Also invited to participate as representatives of civil society were entrepreneurs from the National Confederation of Private Entrepreneurial Associations (Confederación Nacional de Instituciones Empresariales Privadas, or CONFIEP) and the National Society of Industry (Sociedad Nacional de Industrias, or SNI); workers from the General Confederation of Peruvian Workers (Confederación General de Trabajadores de Perú, or CGTP); and members of the Regional Defense Fronts (Frentes de Defensa Regionales) made up of local organizations in the provinces. Incorporated as full members early on were the MCLCP and the Catholic and Protestant churches. Clearly, the National Accord was an institutional associational space that required the formal representation of the Catholic Church, as designated by the Peruvian Bishops' Conference (Conferencia Episcopal Peruana, CEP). The accord process permitted broad association, with political and civil representation, but in a transparent space for deliberation and with the aim of building consensus.

The differences in the three types of spaces for encounter that I have outlined are many, but their origins were similar. Civil society, supported by churches, stepped into a void created by the weakness of political actors and institutions; members of ecclesial society took—and continue to take— a major role in promoting dialogue in the spaces that have emerged. These are spaces of transition. The Truth and Reconciliation Commission sought to restore lost rights and rebuild lives, recognize the innocent victims killed by one side or the other in the war and the consequences of those deaths for their survivors, and uncover and keep alive the memory of what happened so that it never happens again. The Roundtable for the Struggle against Poverty sought to establish a public space for various types of associations and the state to formulate together the national budget in a context of decentralization and the constitution of regional governments in 2001. In the absence of actors and representative voices with political power, this round-table can strengthen local actors. And finally, the National Accord continues to be an ethical political space that serves as a reserve of legitimacy given the weakness of political institutions.

Space for Personal Development and Learning

In contrast to the spaces discussed above that bring together civil society actors regardless of religious denomination or even faith, the next space I discuss is one that specifically strengthens the identity of the Catholic Church: the space devoted by the church to personal development and learning. Although it is strictly speaking a "confessional" space, I argue—following the work of Nancy Fraser (1992) on the multiplicity of public spheres and their contributions to democracy—that it nevertheless contributes to broadening public space. This is a space of personal development, reflection, and self-consciousness; it situates the believer as an actor in a reality that she discovers with others. It is a space that includes a dimension of faith.

The church is known around the world for its activity in promoting formal education from elementary and secondary schools to universities. In the Peruvian environment this mission plays a very important role, given the nation's tiny investment in public education and its low quality. Students who pass through these institutions receive more than a religious education; believers and nonbelievers alike who have access to these educational institutions experience personal development across the spectrum. Among these Catholic educational institutions are a consortium of private Catholic schools for upper- and middle-income groups, which have autonomy from church control; the "Faith and Joy" (*Fe y Alegría*) schools, a network of public schools administered by the Jesuits and dedicated to the popular sectors; pedagogical institutes and normal schools for teacher training across a wide array of fields; and the universities. The number of Catholic universities has increased in recent years. The Pontifical Catholic University of Peru (Pontificia Universidad Católica del Peru, or PUCP), the oldest private university in the country, turned ninety years old in 2007. The other principal Catholic universities in the country include the University of Santa Maria; the University of San Pablo, affiliated with the Sodalitium Christianae Vitae; the University of Piura, affiliated with Opus Dei; Sede Sapiens Catholic University, in the recently formed diocese of Carabayllo in Lima; and the Antonio Ruiz de Montoya University, a Jesuit institution.

For adults, an opportunity for personal self-formation can be found in particular in the many schools of catechism and evangelization that are organized at the parish, diocesan, and interdiocesan levels. The adult popular education pedagogy begins from the experiences that participants bring to share with the group and to reflect upon; this social dimension is complemented by information gained through the experiences of the others in the group[22] and from the teaching of experts in different subjects ranging from theology to the family, economics, and politics. At Aparecida the bishops reaffirmed this pedagogy in declaring "in continuity with the former General Conferences of the Latin American Episcopate, this document uses the method to see, to judge and to act" (CELAM 2007, §19). This method is followed by many of these groups in everyday life situations through the integration of the Gospel and the teaching of the Bible in their activities, such as their learning sessions (Romero 2001).

There have been a number of important spaces for personal development that conform to the popular education model. The theology course offered by the Pontifical Catholic University of Peru in August and February each year for thirty years (1970–1999) attracted an average of 2,500 students per year—representing all corners of ecclesial society—from all over the country. Others include the catechism schools in San Juan de Lurigancho and Comas; the seminars and courses of the Andean Pastoral Institute (Instituto de Pastoral Andina) in the southern highlands of the country; the courses for men and women religious organized by the Conference of Religious Orders in Lima and in the dioceses; and the annual seminar organized by the Higher Institute of Theological Studies (Instituto Superior de Estudios Teológicos, or ISET). But it must be borne in mind that almost all parishes and dioceses organize spaces for personal development, many of which are local in scope. This type of training has a strong, theological component, with a rational and critical dimension, permitting students to enter into dialogue with other religions and other fields of knowledge such as politics, the arts, and science. The subject matter of these courses embrace themes like the history of the Catholic Church in Latin America and the documents of the episcopal conferences of Medellín (1968), Puebla (1979), Santo Domingo (1992), and Aparecida (2007); reading and interpreting the Bible; aspects of pastoral work such as human development, work, and youth; and an analysis of the economic, cultural, and political context for action.

These are only some of the formative spaces that adult laypeople find in the Catholic Church—the ones that have been around the longest and have brought together people of origins that transcend local neighborhoods, religious movements, and parishes. They permit participants to articulate a sense of ecclesial institutional membership and a common analysis of problems and situations and to trade in passive attitudes for conscious, committed action. In Latin America feeling the presence of God and experiencing miracles are common in a context of insecurity and poverty. Staying alive, and even improving living conditions as a result of group solidarity and self-initiative, is often experienced as a gift from God. The notion of theology as wisdom, rational knowledge, and critical reflection (G. Gutiérrez 1971) has reached the people, who want more education in this theology. Thus, the Catholic Church contributes in a permanent way to formal education at different levels and to continuous adult education in different fields. But besides this, it transforms the educational experience among adults in a public space of exchange of different experiences and ideas—among intellectuals, politicians, theologians, and citizens—in the context of a Christian community concerned with actual problems in the world.

In Many Voices

Another important task of Catholic ecclesial work has been public expression by bishops, pastoral agents, and Christian communities for the intended audience of common rank-and-file members of the church. The experience of the Catholic Church is full of communiqués and documents that voice opinions and take positions on social affairs as well as on doctrinal themes that relate to the church's teaching. These voices multiplied after Medellin and have continued in a variety of languages and in a multitude of modes—the written word, audiovisual media, the Internet, expressive mobilizations, music, and theater. The church has been and continues to be a space of creativity and aesthetic expression of many types.

Just as the types of expression vary, so too does the scope and the levels of representation of the voices that can be heard. It is clear that there are differences between the texts of the ecclesiastical hierarchy, which speak in the voice of the church and take on a doctrinal character, and the diverse expressions of the faith of believers. This is an important distinction that is part of the organization of the church. Until the mid-1990s documents signed by members of Christian communities, priests, and religious men and women expressing themselves on matters of public interest were published along with official episcopal documents. In the past decade other means of self-expression have appeared, such as newspaper articles, magazines, and radio and television programs. In the field of television the evangelical churches have taken the lead, broadcasting programs over the airwaves on a daily basis. Diverse independent associations of the Catholic Church, in the sense discussed earlier, have radio stations throughout the country that participate in the National Radio Coordinating Committee, which is nondenominational and therefore independent from the Catholic hierarchy. A Catholic television channel, owned by a religious order that serves a parish in Lima, broadcasts on religious themes and is affiliated with the international Catholic Church cable network. This area of public expression is witness to conflicts and exchanges of opinion that are indicative of the existence of a more open public space.

Conclusions

As Casanova made clear in the hypotheses I use to frame this chapter, a church transforming itself from a powerful, universal organization to a modern, public, and global institution is something that even Max Weber could not have imagined, or even conceived of unless it ceased to be a church in the Weberian sense. But the experience of the Catholic Church in Latin America in the second half of the twentieth century, the theological reflections of both theologians and believers who are trying to understand the meaning and consequences of their belief in God, and the organizational plurality inside the church are making possible a slow transformation toward a modern public and dynamic church.

I would like to say a few words here about the Fifth General Meeting in Aparecida, Brazil, because of its transcendent importance in the life of the church on the continent. Religious change is very difficult to understand, perhaps because many see the sacred as immutable and not as an experience of a God who is alive, who has a living project for the world (see CELAM 2007, §129). Since Medellín, according to the final document of the meeting, the Catholic Church in Latin America sees the calling coming from Jesus to become a disciple as great news: "Jesus wants his disciples to come to Him as friends and brothers" (§132). The document continues, "the essential task of evangelization includes the option for the poor, the promotion of the whole person, and genuine human liberation" (§146), and notes that "Jesus came out to encounter persons in very different situations: men and women, rich and poor, Jew and gentile, the righteous and sinners, . . . inviting all of them to follow Him" (§147).

Although we have not considered the contributions made by theologians of the Catholic Church in Peru and Latin America in our analysis, these contributions are very important to understanding the way in which the church sees itself and its mission, as well as to how believers understand their own missions as persons of faith and members of a church and a society and make sense of their actions in the diverse worlds in which they live. The theology of liberation elaborated by the Peruvian theologian Gustavo Gutiérrez (1971) contributed to creating more democratic interpersonal relations, as opposed to the more doctrinaire and dogmatic theologies that tend to undergird more vertical and authoritarian interpersonal relations. The theology of liberation marked one way of being an ecclesial community: its understanding of persons as friends of God was quite different than looking upon them as serfs, in the same way that inviting them to follow God's project was different than ordering them to follow the law. The continuity of this process, which began in the church half a century ago, is particularly critical to the development of the democratic spaces we have explored.

The four complementary and self-reinforcing ways of constructing civil society in and from the church laid out in this chapter—voluntary associations, space for encounter, opportunities for personal development and reflection, and religious expression in many voices—show the transformation of the church and the creation of the conditions that enable it to contribute positively to the construction of a modern civil society in Peru. This includes the development of the church's own public space where laypersons could participate and express themselves independently from their theological perspective and political orientation. Their participation in that public space—and their new ability to reflect upon themselves as human beings and as believers—also allowed them to think about themselves in other roles in other public spaces. Those who participate in this public space in ecclesial civil society feel part of the church, and not as mere passive recipients of the sacraments and lessons. Their religion forms part of their identity; is a source of critical reflection; gives meaning to their lives; and develops their capacity for ethical discernment. And in this sense a modern public space is constituted as Casanova understood it: liberating and pluralistic within the unity of the church but with flexible borders that allow for new ways of connecting with society and politics.

The Catholic Church is capable of transforming itself—on the foundation of Vatican II and its own practice in Latin America—in a way that allows it to break its ties of dependence with the oligarchic state and link itself instead to emerging civil societies that opened spaces of modernity and democracy. But these new conditions of religious pluralism and individual liberties have also produced reactions that might cause the church to close its own internal public space. Such a closure could take many forms, including reducing and controlling the possibility of association; the emergence of religious movements subordinated to ecclesiastical authority; exercising control over religious orders within the territorial organization of the church and the training of traditional clergy; and reducing the voices that can express themselves and the possibilities of internal debate about ethical subjects that affect human development (and thus concern everyone). These new policies may lead the ecclesiastical church to confront those who are different and evade association with "others"—the needy, the forgotten, the poor.

The emergence of an open public space inside the church—and an ecclesial civil society—raises many questions about how this type of religious organization should develop in the future. Hierarchical opposition to change is not unexpected because there is now an open public space where different interests and motivations may interact. What is noteworthy is the way in which some bishops and religious movements may revert to traditional power structures, challenging the new rules of procedure that should be valid for everyone.[23] A public space need not be homogeneous. Rather, what distinguishes a public space is a plurality of opinions and organizations that, within the framework of the law and social rules, adhere to a morality whose tenets are articulated and contested. All religions may be tempted to impose morality from above. But all religions may also issue a call for a type of behavior and practice that is guided by an ethic born in the community's own lifestyle and religious values. Separation from the world or presuming a dichotomy between the sinful world and the purity of the community are also not viable options. They can contribute to reinforcing "invisible spaces" or "spaces of darkness" in which the forces that dominate the weakest take refuge. Most important may not be whether or not people *belong* to a religion but rather the ideological or reflexive *orientation* of the believer and the citizen. More research is needed to understand, according to this frame of analysis, how differences are being reconciled and how Catholics, as well as members of other churches, make meaning of their religious membership.

Notes

1. In order to distinguish religious public space from civil society, we could call it *ecclesial* society. It is different also from *ecclesiastical* society, which refers to the governing regime of the Catholic Church.

2. The question of how legitimate church intervention is in politics has been reopened and is at the center of the debate over the privatization and deprivatization of religion. With evangelical churches entering politics and forming political parties in Latin America, how does the Catholic Church re-enter politics? To do it from civil society is very different than to do it from the church itself.

3. All citations to canon law will be given parenthetically in the text; the specific laws can be found by canon number at http://www.vatican.va/archive/ENG1104/_INDEX.HTM.

4. See Canon 370. A prelature is a local church that does not yet have the elements required to function with autonomy in terms of facilities or number of priests. It is in the process of growing into a diocese and is run by a bishop or prelate.

5. See Canon 371, §1. An apostolic vicariate is a territory—and a group of people—where the church wants to develop its missionary work in order to establish a prelature or a diocese. It is governed by a bishop or apostolic vicar and usually entrusted to a religious order.

6. Particular churches are local churches corresponding to dioceses at different levels: archdiocese, diocese, prelature, vicariate, etc. See Canon 368.

7. The survey on Catholic society is part of a research project by the author at the Instituto Bartolomé de Las Casas, with the support of the Secretariat on Latin America of the U.S. Conference of Catholic Bishops.

8. The issue we are dealing with here is the one of pluralism. The issue of the poor and excluded is a question for everyone in society and therefore for every group, whatever their reason to identify themselves as different.

9. The survey, which was conducted in urban and rural areas in every department of the country, draws a stratified random sample of "5,190 households in 221 districts, yielding 11,215 cases of voting-age citizens" (UNDP 2006b, 292). Investigators conducted the interviews with people of voting age living in each household.

10. The question included neighborhood or tenants' associations, indigenous communities, student organizations, religious groups, sports and social clubs, political committees, workplace unions, producers' associations, parents' associations, and credit unions.

11. The New Parish Image (Nueva Imagen de Parroquia) is an international movement, originating in Spain, that helps parishes to organize their pastoral work. It aims to organize communities on a territorial basis, dividing the parish up into blocks, and promotes the participation of neighbors in different activities following the liturgical calendar of the church.

12. Chapter 5, §178 to §180 (CELAM 2007) of the final version of the conference document is dedicated to CEBs and small communities.

13. The movement has changed from his original position; now they accept the importance of working for the poor, although they do not relate this to social justice or social promotion in the same way the option for the poor does.

14. Through the Vatican radio network Radio Evangelización, the press office of the Bishops' Meeting issued the following statement questioning the veracity of an ACI press release the previous day:

On May 29, 2007, ACI Press put out a press release that does not correspond to the truth. The statement said: "For diverse reasons about thirty voting bishops have left the Fifth Conference and they will not take part in the voting on the Message or the Document that is expected by the participants at some future date.

According to what we have been able to discover, the exact number of the bishops who had to withdraw is nine. Some departed because of health problems and others to attend to strictly personal affairs or to their respective dioceses. We have also been informed that most of them are foreign cardinals and bishops from the Vatican and Canada. Only three bishops are representatives of Latin America, who had emergencies that forced them to return to their countries. (Press office of Fifth General Meeting, CELAM, 048/30-05-07 Oficina de Prensa Desmiente Noticia. Available at http://www.celam.info/content/view/487/356/. Translation mine.)

15. Father Hilario Huanca, a member of the Congregation of the Sacred Heart (SS.CC.) that has been in charge of the Ayaviri prelature for fifty years, wrote a letter to explain the new situation after Father Francisco Fritch was asked to leave the prelature before his contract expired. His letter and one by Father Fritch have circulated on the Internet; they have been read throughout the country and reached the media (Huanca 2006). In addition, Bishop Ortega, recently appointed to the Prelature of Juli, also in the Andean south in Puno, made the news after he expelled a student from the seminary because he had a lesion on his back, which for him was an apparent barrier to being ordained as a priest. Ortega also said in a commemorative Mass for Father Domingo Llanque, a well-known, Aymara-born priest, that because he was Aymara, and the Aymara are pagans, there was no certainty of his salvation.

16. This movement was somewhat different from the Shining Path in its insurrectional strategy. The MRTA became internationally known after it staged the siege of the Japanese Embassy during the summer between 1996 and 1997.

17. Interview with Ernesto Alayza (May 2007); see also the article by Joanna Drzewieniecki (2002).

18. The government of Alejandro Toledo created the CEMAN (Comisión Multisectorial de Alto Nivel, or Multisectoral High-Level Commission) to fulfil the recommendations of the Truth and Reconciliation Commission, and in July 2005 Congress approved Law No. 28592, which created the Integrated Reparations Plan (Plan Integral de Reparaciones, or PIR). To implement this plan, a commission has been created to draw up a "Registro único de víctimas" (unified victims registry). This commission is headed by Sofía Macher, who was a member of the CVR and has started the Program for Collective Reparation, which offered benefits to 440 peasant communities in 2007 (Lora 2007).

19. Carlos García y García, a pastor and representative of the Evangelical Council in Peru, was the second vice-president of Peru during the first government of Alberto Fujimori, between 1990 and 1992.

20. See http://www.mesadeconcertacion.org.pe/contenido.php?pid=148.

21. Peru has 24 departments and the Port Province of Callao. These are divided into 195 provinces and 1,832 districts (UNDP 2006a). The regionalization process that is underway takes the departments as the basis for the constitution of

new regions; it also includes the Port Province of Callao and divides Lima into two regions, bringing the total to 26 regions.

22. The original model was Paulo Freire's pedagogy for liberation.

23. An example of this is the publication by ACI Press of false information, something that happened in Aparecida (see note 14 above).

References

Bastian, Jean Pierre. 1997. *La mutación religiosa de América Latina: Para una sociología del cambio social en la modernidad periférica.* Mexico City: Fondo de Cultura Económica.

Bax, Mart. 1991. "Religious Regimes and State-Formation: Toward a Research Perspective." In Eric Wolf, ed., *Religious Regimes and State Formation: Perspectives from European Ethnology,* 7–27. New York: State University of New York Press.

Bruneau, Thomas, Chester E. Gabriel, and Mary Mooney, eds. 1984. *The Catholic Church and Religions in Latin America.* Montreal: McGill University Centre for Developing-Area Studies.

Casanova, José. 1994. *Public Religions in the Modern World.* Chicago: University of Chicago Press.

———. 2001. "Civil Society and Religion: Retrospective Reflections on Catholicism and Prospective Reflections on Islam." *Social Research* 65, no. 4 (Winter): 1041–80.

Conferencia Episcopal del Perú (CEP). 1987. "Directorio Eclesiástico del Perú." Lima: CEP.

———. 2002. "Directorio Eclesiástico del Perú." Lima: CEP.

Consejo Episcopal Latinoamericano (CELAM). 2007. *V Conferencia General del Episcopado Latinoamericano y del Caribe.* Aparecida, May 13–31. Available at www.celam.org.

Dahl, Robert A. 1971. *Polyarchy: Participation and Opposition.* New Haven, CT: Yale University Press.

Delgado Pugley, Deborah. 2006 "¿Pluralismo y Secularización? Siguiendo la Participación Política de los Evangélicos en el Perú." Licentiate thesis, Pontificia Universidad Católica del Perú.

Drzewieniecki, Joanna. 2002. "La Coordinadora Nacional de Derechos Humanos de Perú: Un estudio de Caso." In Aldo Panfichi, ed., *Sociedad Civil, Esfera Pública y Democratización en América Latina: Andes y Cono Sur,* 516–48. Lima: FCE and Fondo Editorial PUCP.

Fraser, Nancy. 1992. "Rethinking the Public Sphere: A Contribution to the Critique of Actually Existing Democracy." In Craig Calhoun, ed., *Habermas and the Public Sphere*, 99–142. Cambridge, MA: MIT Press.

Gutiérrez, Gustavo. 1971. *Teología de la Liberación. Perspectivas*. Lima: CEP.

Gutiérrez, Tomás. 2000. *El "Hermano" Fujimori: Evangélicos y Poder Político en el Perú del 90*. Lima: Ediciones Archivo Histórico del Protestantismo Latinoamericano.

Habermas, Jürgen. 1981. *Reason and the Rationalization of Society*. Vol. 1 of *The Theory of Communicative Action*. Boston: Beacon Press.

———. 1989. *The Structural Transformation of the Public Sphere*. Cambridge, MA: MIT Press.

Huanca, Hilario. 2006. "Carta sobre los sucesos de la diócesis de Ayaviri." Available at http://www.proconcil.org/document/VCELAM/AYAVIRI.htm.

Ius Canonicum. n.d. "Organización de la Iglesia en circunscripciones eclesiásticas." Available at http://www.iuscanonicum.org.

Latinobarómetro. 2006. *Informe Latino Barómetro*. Available at http://www.latinobarometro.org.

Levine, Daniel, ed. 1980. *Churches and Politics in Latin America*. Beverly Hills, CA: Sage.

Levine, Daniel H., and José Enrique Molina. 2007. "La Calidad de la Democracia en América Latina. Una visión comparada." *América Latina Hoy* 45 (April): 17–46.

López, Darío. 1995. *El Nuevo rostro del Pentecostalismo Latinoamericano*. Lima: CEMAA.

Lora, Carmen. 2007. "Programa de Reparaciones Colectivas. Primeros pasos." In *Pàginas*, no. 206 (June): 96–99.

Mainwaring, Scott, and Aníbal Pérez Liñán. 2002. "Level of Development and Democracy: Latin American Exceptionalism, 1945–1996." Kellogg Institute Working Paper no. 31, Kellogg Institute, University of Notre Dame, IN.

Martin, David. 1990. *Tongues of Fire: The Explosion of Protestantism in Latin America*. Cambridge: Basil Blackwell.

Mesa de Concertación para la Lucha Contra la Pobreza (MCLCP). 2007. *Futuro sin Pobreza: Balance de la Lucha contra la pobreza y propuestas*. Lima: MCLCP.

Romero, Catalina. 1989. "Church, State and Society in Peru, 1968–1988: A Process of Liberation." Ph.D. diss., New School for Social Research.

———. 2001. "Comunidades cristianas entre lo privado y lo público." In Manuel Marzal, José Sánchez, and Catalina Romero, eds., *La religión al filo del Milenio*, 141–70. Lima: Fondo Editorial PUCP.

———. 2007. "¿Existe una sociedad civil en la Iglesia Católica Latinoamericana?" *Religión e Societá, Revista di scienze sociali della religione* 22, no. 57: 41–52.

Ruda, Juan José. 1995. *Los sujetos de Derecho Internacional. El caso de la Iglesia y del Estado del Vaticano.* Lima: Fondo Editorial PUCP.

Ruuth, Anders. 1995. *Igreja Universal do Reino de Deus.* Stockholm: Almquist and Wiksell.

Smith, Brian H. 1998. *Religious Politics in Latin America, Pentecostal vs. Catholic.* Notre Dame, IN: University of Notre Dame Press.

Smith, Christian. 1995. "The Spirit and Democracy: Base Communities, Protestantism, and Democratization in Latin America." In William H. Swatos Jr., ed., *Religion and Democracy in Latin America,* 1–26. New Brunswick, NJ: Transaction.

Sociedad Católica en el Perú. 2006. Survey conducted by IOPPUCP (March).

Stoll, David. 1990. *Is Latin America Turning Protestant? The Politics of Evangelical Growth.* Berkeley: University of California Press.

Troelsch, Ernst. 1960. *The Social Teaching of the Christian Churches.* Vol. 1. New York: Harper Torchbooks.

United Nations Development Program (UNDP). 2006a. *Informe de Desarrollo Humano.* Lima: PNUD.

———. 2006b. *La Democracia en el Perú. El mensaje en cifras.* Lima: PNUD.

Weber, Max. 1978. *Economy and Society: An Outline of Interpretative Sociology.* Berkeley: University of California Press.

Williams, Phillip, and Anna Peterson, eds. 2001. *Christianity, Social Change, and Globalization in the Americas.* New Brunswick, NJ: Rutgers University Press.

World Values Survey. 1996. "World Values Survey, Peru." Available at http://www.worldvaluessurvey.org.

———. 2001. "World Values Survey, Peru." Available at http://www.worldvaluessurvey.org.

PART IV

Conclusions: Looking Back, Looking Ahead

10 | Pluralism as Challenge and Opportunity

DANIEL H. LEVINE

The public face of religion in Latin America, and, in more general terms, the presence of religion in the public sphere and the social and political life of the continent, has changed beyond recognition over the last half century. In the not so distant past, thinking about the public face of religion evoked images and symbols of civic-religious fusion at all levels. The repertoire included Te Deums with the presence of political and ecclesiastical "authorities" at the highest level, along with the infallible presence of politicians, clergy, and military officers at the inauguration of public works, the opening of stores or factories, and a wide range of public events or programs.[1] This joint presence was a public statement of the identification of "the church" (only one was recognized) with political and economic power and social hierarchy. Thinking about the public face of religion in this new century brings very different images to mind. Street preachers fill the scene—men (they are mostly men) carrying a Bible, a loudspeaker, and sometimes a portable platform, preaching and often singing with some small group in a public square, on a street corner, or near a bus or train station. In any city of the continent and in the smallest and most remote towns as well, it is now just about impossible to linger in a public square or get on or off a bus, metro, or train without running into one or more preachers. They no longer represent *the* church but rather speak in the name of many.

The contrast with the traditional face of religion reflects a net of related changes. Where there was monopoly, there is now pluralism; where a limited number of spaces were once officially reserved for religious practice (with a limited number of authorized practitioners), there is now a rich profusion of churches, chapels, and mass media programming, not to mention campaigns and crusades that carry the message to hitherto "profane" spaces: from streets and squares to beaches, sports stadiums, jails, bars, and nightclubs. Instead of a limited number of voices "authorized" to speak in the name of religion, there is now a plurality of voices, not only from among distinct denominations but within churches as well.

The preceding comments suggest that simple references to church and state, much less exclusive attention to the institutional Catholic Church, will no longer suffice as a guide to understanding religion and politics in Latin America. There are too many actors and too much innovation occurring beyond the control of institutions and their official leaders for that kind of approach to yield reliable understanding. Analysis of the public life of religion in Latin America must cast a broader net and pay careful attention to the continuing process whereby religion, politics, and ordinary social life influence one another. Neither religion nor politics can be conceived in static terms. Religion is not the passive reflection of the social order (as Durkheim would have it), nor does society provide a simple and direct medium for the implementation of religious values. There is continuous change—change that is pushed along by the presence of new ideas and new actors and groups who press to claim a voice in public life. This is a dialectical relationship, a continuous process of mutual influence and exchange of ideas, values, and models of organization. Just as growing plurality and pluralism in religion work to transform social and cultural life—creating new actors, voices, and public spaces—in the same way the consolidation of democratic politics, the lowering of barriers to organization, and the gradual development and consolidation of the rules of the game of an autonomous civil society have an impact on religion, facilitating and creating incentives for ever greater pluralism, which is visible in the multiplication of churches, buildings, mass media, new sources of leadership, and so on.

A first step in making sense of the new relation of religion and politics in the twenty-first century in Latin America is to identify and account for the deep transformations in the meaning of both politics and religion and to examine the different ways in which the relations between them are worked out. Understanding this process requires that we look beyond institutions and their leaders. These remain important, to be sure, but much of the dynamic force of change rests on broader social and cultural transformations—including the emergence of a strong civil society—that are only now beginning to consolidate into enduring institutional forms. It is vital, therefore, to identify the new individuals and groups who carry the relation between faith and religious belonging to social and political life and who carry their new capabilities for collective social life into the daily practice of their religion.

Plurality and Pluralism

Before getting into particulars, a brief conceptual clarification is in order. The concept of *plurality* is used here in quantitative terms to denote the growing number of groups, activists, spokespersons, chapels, churches, denominations, communications media, public spaces, and the like in Latin American society. In contrast, the concept of *pluralism* is social, cultural, and political. As used here, *pluralism* points to the construction of rules of the game that incorporate these new actors and voices as legitimate participants in an open social process. Plurality is necessary but not sufficient for pluralism to emerge and be consolidated as a legitimate form of social and political practice.

The new facts of plurality and pluralism are reshaping the public face of religion in Latin America, as they intersect with the equally new facts of pluralism in politics and civil society. A *plurality* of churches, social movements identified with religion, and voices claim the moral authority to speak in the name of religion; a *pluralism* is increasingly evident in civil society and in lower barriers to entry into public spaces. Barriers to organization drop as the rules of the game for a plural religious arena are gradually worked out and put into practice. This is a two-way street—a dialectical relationship to be more precise. Just as religious plurality and pluralism transform social and political life, putting more actors, voices, and options into play, so too the consolidation and expansion of democratic politics, the reduction of barriers to organization and access, and the gradual elaboration of practical rules of the game for a plural civil society have a visible impact on the daily life of religion and change the way religious institutions situate themselves in society and politics.

The emergence and consolidation of plurality and pluralism presents the institutional Catholic Church with a challenge to its traditional role as *the church*—the officially acknowledged wielder of moral and social authority within the boundaries of a defined national territory. The effort to hang on to this unique status and to the privileges that come with it runs counter to the logic of an open and more varied society. Casanova argues that only when religions abandon the status of "church" can they be fully compatible with a modern society. "The conception of modern public religion that is consistent with liberal freedoms and modern structural and cultural differentiations," he writes, "is one that builds on notions of civil society" (Casanova 1994, 217). Social and cultural pluralism, along with emerging democratic rules of the game in politics, also challenge the activist collection of groups, ideas, and practices that emerged within Catholicism in the crucible of the 1970s to 1990s. For those inspired by liberation theology, the global and regional collapse of the left has required wrenching reappraisals of democracy as a goal and of the meaning of politics and political activity. Accommodation, compromise, and alliance building are more the norm in plural societies than revolution and the construction of something utterly new. In many countries activists have been drawn out of religiously inspired groups into ordinary politics, at the same time that the Catholic Church as an institution has opted to move out of the center of political activity and reduce its support for groups and movements.

Plurality and pluralism bring challenges to the growing Protestant community as well. Within all the attention that has been paid to the explosive growth of Protestantism in the region, it is sometimes easy to ignore the process of change embedded in the numbers. New churches grow faster than old ones; Pentecostals grow faster than other groups (including mainline churches and fundamentalists); and churches in urban settings grow faster than those in rural areas (Chesnut 2003; Freston 2001; Garrard-Burnett 1998; Levine 1995; Steigenga 2001; Stoll 1990). The well-established historical tendency to fissiparous growth within Protestantism is fully exemplified in contemporary Latin America. Competition among Protestant churches and alternative national and continental confederations—for members, resources, and public voice—is now as notable as competition between the Protestant and Catholic churches.

This continuing and accelerating growth and competition has produced a shift in the public presence of Protestantism and the elaboration of innovative means of managing its new status in a changed political arena. No longer isolated minorities and weak supplicants for public recognition, Protestant churches have vigorously pressed claims to equal status in the public sphere and a share of the benefits (including subsidies for schools) long allocated to the Catholic Church (B. Smith 1998). In case after case, churches, interchurch alliances, and individual figures have actively engaged in what was once seen as the tainted and corrupting world of politics. At the same time Protestant churches have also engaged broader issues and entered into a wide range of social and political alliances that would have been unimaginable a few decades ago.

To summarize, in less than half a century a securely established routine of mutual support and, indeed, mutual blessing among church, state, and power has been transformed in dramatic fashion. New and sometimes contestatory voices have emerged, ranging from Christian Democratic reformism and liberation theology to Christian-Marxist alliances. At the same time, Protestantism, once a collection of small groups with a public stress on personal salvation, obedience to authority, and a ferocious anticommunism, now constitutes a significant presence on the public stage, incorporating a wide and growing range of views and positions. This is a lot of change in very little time—change that repeatedly caught scholars and observers by surprise. How can we grasp the dynamic of change and look to the future with reasonable confidence of accuracy?

The meaning of the contrast between the old and new face of religion does not end with acknowledging the facts of plurality and pluralism. We must also understand how these developments change the dynamics of religious growth and competition and work in subtle ways to reconfigure the relations between religion (ideas, practices, and institutions) and the ordinary structures of power and identity in society. This occurs as new groups are created and drawn onto the scene, with new voices claiming a legitimate place in public life. The whole process presents both challenge and opportunity for churches as institutions and for their members and activists, who are slowly learning to live in a world that no longer can be defined by *one church* in mutual alliance with *one state*. Reality is now far richer, more complicated, and messier.[2]

Pluralism as Challenge and Opportunity

Pluralism is both a challenge and opportunity for religion. Pluralism presents the challenge of adaptation to new rules of the game and at the same time offers an opportunity to enter the public arena in new ways by supporting openness and a consolidation of democratic institutions, practices, and norms. The challenge of adapting to—or perhaps better, of creating new rules of the game—includes elements that range from the need to create effective means of competing for members or resources in an open market (Chesnut 2003; Gill 1998) to the difficulties of coexisting with hitherto demonized groups or, indeed, of accepting the legitimacy of others as equal partners on the public stage.

Although precursors can be found in every instance, most observers agree that for Catholicism the overall process of change gets underway in the post–World War II period with the emergence of reformist currents within the churches, including a loose network of pastoral centers, journals, and locally based initiatives that in different ways represented a search for ways to create a more effective church presence throughout the region. Related and spin-off organizations soon crystallized into Christian Democratic parties, breaking conventional ties between Catholic groups and conservative politics. These and other similar initiatives were energized and reinforced by the well-known developments in global Catholicism that punctuated the 1960s and 1970s, including the Second Vatican Council, the regional conferences of Medellín and Puebla, and the emergence of liberation theology. The social and political impact of these developments was magnified and extended by the political experiences of the 1970s and 1980s, which drove activists into the churches (often the only space remaining open), where they were met with welcome and shelter. This is a well-known story and I will not go into details here. For present purposes, it is important to underscore that all these movements of change created and legitimized new voices, new agents, and new venues for religious action whose social and political meaning was magnified beyond the original intent of many by political circumstances (Levine 2005, 2006; C. Smith 1991).

The Protestant story begins to consolidate into a visible and public presence of pluralism about twenty years later. With roots in a long, slow process of church "planting" and growth, Protestant groups and spokespersons found their way in growing numbers onto public platforms and into politics starting in the late 1980s. With the end of the cold war and the movement of prominent early figures like Guatemala's Efraín Ríos Montt off center stage, Protestant groups began to consolidate a substantial, varied public presence—building churches, creating schools, acquiring a media presence, and so forth. All this provides an indispensable platform for entering the political arena, while the end of the cold war made it possible for that entry to advance a broad range of interests and positions (Fonseca 2008; Freston 2001; Stoll 1990).

The continuing erosion of Catholicism's monopoly status bears on a host of traditional issues, from censorship and education to subsidies and representation on government commissions, committees, and public platforms. Set in the general political context, pluralization also suggests that building and sustaining a new role will require groups to play the old politics more skillfully and more consistently than in the past. This means working to maintain the presence of groups and hold on to members, sustaining grassroots democracy while working on allies and connections, and assuming a realistic bargaining stance in politics. Groups need to bargain for better terms with everyone and enter into alliances only with great care and caution. Allies, connections, resources, and the shield they provide remain of critical importance; they are required precisely because what ordinary people need in politics and what defines a system as legitimate in their eyes is predictability, accountability, and a sense, however minimal, of being a legitimate part of something larger. Although none of these can be achieved only at the local level, continued work at the local level is the bedrock upon which anything else must be built.

That this still surprises many is a sign of the extent to which many groups representing the grassroots and new religious voices were blinded by faith in their own Gramscian agenda. Many of the groups that appeared and began to consolidate in the conflict-charged circumstances of the 1970s and 1980s in Latin America shared a concept of politics according to which "the people" (defined in terms of social class) constituted a natural majority. In this view of the world, the people would ultimately construct a new counter-hegemony whose eventual victory would obviate the need for ordinary politics. Once a counter-hegemonic understanding could be forged and spread in the population, these people would join together and create a new and different kind of political order.[3] As we shall see, these hopes have been disappointed as the return of democracy brought burnout, demobilization, and division to many of these same groups.

This experience was echoed in the trajectory of newly confident Protestant groups as they entered the political arena in the 1990s. As "children of light" bringing a new ethic and political style, they hoped to moralize politics and the political world. For the Protestant communities in Guatemala, Brazil, or Peru, for example, initial enthusiasm about the prospects for building a new Jerusalem and a new kind of politics yielded to disillusionment and discredit (as in Guatemala or Peru) or to an evangelical pluralism in which utterly new churches (like Brazil's Universal Church of the Reign of God) have emerged as self-confident players of the "old politics" (Fonseca 2008; Freston 2001; Garrard-Burnett 1998; López 2004). As was the case with an earlier generation of Catholic progressives, the old politics proved tenacious—not merely resisting new movements but also effectively incorporating, dividing, and deactivating them. In some cases this demobilization has been accelerated by decisions of the Catholic hierarchy to retreat from the center stage of politics, thereby reducing the material support and ideological cover upon which some groups long relied (Drogus and Stewart-Gambino 2005).

Pluralism offers opportunities as well as challenges. Among the most notable of these opportunities is the chance to acquire new followers, to reach and energize them in new ways, and to exploit new media. There is also the opportunity to develop ways of acting in politics and relating to potential political allies and partners that preserve independence and a moral center to actions while still making it possible for churches and their leaders to pursue goals effectively. This task is complicated by the new fact of a more open, less regulated civil society and by the more open kind of politics that has accompanied transitions to democracy. At the very least, more open politics means the possibility of greater choice, more options for competing for the allegiance and membership of the potential audience, and less regulation of the whole effort. Protestants in many countries have devoted substantial effort to leveling the playing field, above all by sharing in public subsidies hitherto limited to Catholic institutions and by removing or fighting barriers to the ordinary life of their communities, such as laws regulating "noisy churches" (B. Smith 1998).

Analyses of pluralism and plurality often begin from the point of view of groups and leaders: from what those working in a rational-choice vein would term the "supply side." Although this is important, it is clearly incomplete. Ignoring the audience for change is a little like discussions of governability that center attention exclusively on control and order without addressing issues like voice, representation, or access. In religion, as in politics or social life as a whole, we need to ask how such plurality appears to those on the receiving end. From the point of view of the target audience or audiences, the presence of a plurality of options opens possibilities. To be sure, many new churches are exclusive in membership and make extensive demands on new believers. But the choice to assume these demands and obligations is made freely. On the ground level, what we know is that those who belong to new churches are in fact rarely exclusive in group membership. They belong to groups of all kinds at rates closely comparable to other religious groups. This opens possibilities for creating and maintaining ties and relationships across groups, keeping the flow of information open, and undergirding the possibilities of common action.

The challenge that pluralism poses for the Catholic Church in particular is complicated by the multiple and overlapping ways in which religions are present in society, politics, and culture. The emergence of real pluralism reflects and reinforces a reconfiguring of these relationships that is open-ended and out of the control of church hierarchies. For purposes of exposition, it may be helpful to break our consideration of the issues into component parts and treat each aspect separately. To be sure, this is an *analytical* distinction, and, like all such efforts, it presents as separate elements that in reality come together every day in packages and combinations whose variety and speed of formation are subject only to the limitations of resources and creativity.

Plurality and Pluralism in Religion

The most obvious expressions of plurality and pluralism in religion in Latin America are the sheer number of churches, venues, and spokespersons and the visible impact of competition for members, loyalties, and resources. In a very concrete sense, more religion is available in Latin America now than in the past—more churches, more chapels, a greater presence in the mass media, more opportunities for participation, and a greater number of groups of religious origin or inspiration present in social life. All this is evidence of an enormous capacity for sociocultural change and innovation. Pluralism of a kind has of course always been present, whether it be the choice between parish life and *cofradias* or the competition among Catholic religious orders for schools, resources, and territories. But two factors combine to make the present scene qualitatively different. The first is the reorganization and redirection of institutional Catholic resources (with Vatican sanction) away from support of social groups and innovative religious voices and toward a resacralization of its projected message (Drogus and Stewart-Gambino 2005). Such resacralization does not mean not entering new media (such as television) to compete for audiences. But it does connote renewed concern in the Catholic hierarchy with maintaining control and loyalty to the institutional church, elements that hinder action in a fluid environment.[4] There is also a related emphasis on issues defined as moral and a corresponding pressure on groups and individuals to withdraw from what is seen as "undue politicization." With the restoration of democracy throughout the continent, such tasks can and should be left to explicitly political actors such as political parties or trade unions (Drogus and Stewart-Gambino 2005). The second factor is the presence of vigorous competition for members, resources, and public space (Chesnut 2003; Gill 1998) and of what Steigenga (2001) terms the "pentecostalization" of religious belief and practice. Elements once limited to Protestant (and specifically Pentecostal) experience, including stress on the direct experience of charismatic power, divine cure of diseases (faith healing), speaking in tongues (*glossolalia*), certain kinds of music, and patterns of group organization and leadership have been diffused widely in the Christian community.

These new dimensions of pluralism are further reinforced by the reality of another kind of pluralism within Catholicism. Opinion surveys regularly show considerable variation in degrees of commitment to the church. In chapter 4 in this volume Parker suggests that the growing presence of "Catholics in my own way" (*católicos a mi manera*) is as noteworthy as the explosive presence of Pentecostal groups or, indeed, the growth of a sector of nonbelievers.[5] There is nothing new about the gap between leadership expectations and projections and what followers will commit to, but in the context of growing competition from other churches, the matter seems more urgent to Catholic leaders because of the implications for control, as well as, of course, the challenge it raises to the status of the Catholic Church as *the church*. Within the Protestant community pluralism remains the norm, and Protestant churches in Latin America have resisted efforts at regional or even national coordinating bodies that might yield a single authorized voice.

Pluralism in Politics and Civil Society

Over time, the transformations outlined in the previous section have had many and varied impacts on politics. The loosening of long-established ties binding the Catholic Church with established power created a space and opportunity for new movements and alternative positions. In the 1950s Christian Democracy emerged to challenge integralist and conservative parties, and twenty years later liberation theology and associated movements (including human rights groups, neighborhood associations, community kitchens, and associations of the landless, the homeless, and the unemployed) appeared to challenge both the state and the church in the name of a thoroughgoing transformation of politics and culture. The particular form in which the process played out, and the specific career and fate of particular groups, varied from country to country as the political context and opportunity structure created or closed off possibilities. Despite these differences, the basic fact of pluralization and plurality, and the common task of learning to navigate a plural political world, create important shared elements.

The new presence of plurality and pluralism in religion challenges a pattern of public life in which an official or semiofficial *church* (Roman Catholic) customarily had a recognizable authorized spokesperson. For new actors growing pluralism leads to efforts to achieve a legitimate role in public life and a place—alongside the Catholic Church—on public and ceremonial platforms. This has its symbolic side, legitimating new churches as appropriate representatives of religion and morality. It also has a very concrete side in terms of equal access to official subsidies. As noted, Casanova locates this process as part of the shift of the Catholic Church from its status as *church*—that is, a religious institution with an official or semi-official monopoly in a given territory—to one actor among many in an open civil society. He also suggests that in a public sphere open to all, it is in the interest of all to keep it open (Casanova 1994). In the long run the recognition of this self-interest can reinforce the commitment of any group to maintaining an open political life.

Just as the transformation of religion has impacted politics, in the same way political changes have had important and often unexpected effects on religion. With the restoration of democratic politics across the continent, churches and religious leaders have lost (or sometimes abandoned) their openly political roles. To the extent to which political parties and a "normal political life" have regained strength and presence, new social movements, and in general the range of groups in civil society with some link to the churches, have lost resources, members, and effectiveness. It has been common to see activists either withdraw or move into specifically political groups or government positions and for groups to divide on partisan political grounds (Drogus and Stewart-Gambino 2005; Levine and Romero 2004). Explicitly religious political parties or voting blocs have also had limited success. Among evangelicals such parties have not been able to mobilize or guarantee a bloc vote of the faithful, nor have they attracted masses of voters of any kind (Freston 2001). Christian Democrats remain strong only in Chile, and efforts to create explicitly Protestant parties have had only very limited success. The very idea of a confessional state, which resonates strongly in some fundamentalist circles, finds little echo in Latin American Protestantism.

The end of the cold war had a powerful effect on all the churches. Along with the electoral defeat of the Sandinista party in Nicaragua, the global problems of socialism and communism left progressives and liberationists facing a totally new political panorama. Earlier confidence in the power of "the people" to recreate society and politics has given way, slowly, to realization of the need for greater pragmatism. It is ironic that this new awareness should emerge more or less simultaneously with the explosive growth of Protestantism, which has captured a growing share of loyalties among the poor, the preferential base for liberation theology. The option was not for Protestantism in the abstract but rather for specific forms of Protestantism that stressed an intense spiritual and community life rather than a program for long-term political transformation. As for the Protestants themselves, the end of the cold war liberated them not only from the obsessive anticommunism of the past but also from close dependence on foreign (mostly North American) leadership and resources, now directed in growing measure to capture souls in the former socialist bloc.

The new opening to politics along with growing pluralism within the Protestant community has brought several important elements to the scene. New leadership groups and utterly new leadership styles have emerged in the churches. Media skills are notable and careers in religious or other broadcasting are increasingly common stepping stones to political candidacies. In some Protestant groups in Brazil, there is the beginning of what looks like dynasties, with sons of church leaders or founders assuming a directing and leading role in the next phase of church expansion (Fonseca 2008; Freston 2001). There is also a notable revaluation of politics itself: once seen as the realm of corruption and evil, it is now presented as a possible, legitimate, and even necessary field of action for believers. Where once the children of light were enjoined to concentrate above all on personal salvation and building a community of the elect, they now visualize politics, despite the dangers it holds, as a central part of their identity and responsibility.[6] One sees a growing plurality of political positions, undergirded in part by the fact that the explosive growth of the churches has, not surprisingly, drawn in new members with a wide variety of experiences, careers, and orientations. The experience of Brazil is notable, with self-identified evangelicals (many of them adult converts) present in parties and movements all across the ideological spectrum, from the Workers' Party (Partido dos Trabalhadores, or PT) on the left to the Liberal Party (Partido Liberal) on the right.[7]

Politics has its own rules, and as they engage the political world, groups and actors of religious inspiration have proven no more immune to the temptations of the old politics, including corruption and the abuse of power, than anyone else. Evangelical leaders (like Christian Democrats a generation earlier) may have expected their very presence to carry with it a cleansing and moralization of politics, but this has not been the case. Dario López (2004) documents the sad experience of Peru's evangelicals, who swept into office with Fujimori in 1990 and remained bound to the regime until its ignominious collapse a decade later.[8] López distinguishes between the small group of evangelical politicians who were totally compromised by the corruption of the Fujimori-Montesinos regime and the rich experience of activists and ordinary people in civil society, above all in urban survival movements, human rights organizations, and in the Rondas Campesinas, or peasant patrols. He argues forcefully that the new civic capacities and social capital created at the base have a greater chance of nurturing and sustaining democracy in the long run than does the cultivation of official favors and partisan political ties:

> Those evangelicals who supported the regime contributed neither to the articulation of alternative spaces for participation in formal politics nor to the creation of a distinct political ethos. Instead, the experience of the past decade, following the only democratic period of Fujimori's Presidency (1990–92) shows that those evangelicals who served in the Congress during the Fujimori years (1990–2000), all closely tied to the regime, reinforced traditional political practices, adopting with ease all the vices of the old political class, most notably corruption and nepotism. . . . The presence of evangelical believers in social movements presents a very different image. As part of these citizen movements, sharing in the dynamic of civil society, and working collectively with the poor in the settlements that encircle our great cities as well as with peasant communities suffering directly from the violence of those years, evangelicals crafted new forms of "doing politics" which in the long run helped keep democracy from collapsing completely. (López 2004, 124, 125)

The effort to create an effective and effectively democratic political presence has been a continuing thread in the recent public presence of religion in Latin America. The process has a different meaning for elites and the institutions they direct than for grassroots activists and group members. Elites and institutions face the challenge of maintaining a critical presence in a very different political arena. In the 1970s and 1980s religion was pushed and pulled onto center stage by a powerful combination of new ideas, effective leaders, and populations eager to make sense of their situation and find moral sanction and allies in their search for solutions. As circumstances changed, religion moved off center stage, but it is important to be clear that moving off center stage does not mean moving out of the public sphere altogether. The struggle by some church leaders against what they see as "improper politicization" has not kept them from mounting public campaigns on issues such as abortion, contraception, censorship, or other matters they define as moral and thus within their legitimate ambit (Drogus and Stewart-Gambino 2005). Anyway, why expect religion to be depoliticized in Latin America when religious issues and groups flourish in politics all around the world, not least in the United States? At issue is not depoliticization or abandonment of the public sphere but rather a shift in who speaks, where voices are heard, and what they say. Whatever the issue or the specific arena, the fact is that with the restoration of "normal politics," other voices, including those of straightforward political movements along with a range of social movements and new churches, fill public space. The prime focus and level of action has also shifted. Religious spokesmen no longer command immediate attention, and religious discourse no longer occupies center stage. Even if it did, there is no longer a single voice. For their part, activists and especially grassroots members face a more elemental challenge: how to hold on to members and keep organizations alive in the teeth of hard times and a state that is at best indifferent.[9]

Everywhere in Latin America transitions to democracy have been accompanied by demobilization and marginalization of popular movements. By now it is clear that early hopes that a new kind of politics would emerge out of the chrysalis of civil society will not be fulfilled. With only scattered exceptions, the social power and new identities put together in the struggles of the preceding decades proved unreliable bases for organization and action in the new politics of the 1990s. By early in the decade, many groups had burned out: the struggle had been exhausting; organizations divided on partisan political grounds; members lost interest, drifted away, or moved into government or politics; leaders were not replaced; and severe economic decline meant that for numbers of grassroots followers, the struggle to survive took precedence over the political struggle.[10]

The preceding considerations suggest that expectations about how grassroots and popular movements would provide the seedbed for a wholly transformed culture and a new "way of doing politics" were exaggerated when not wholly misspecified. The autonomy of movements (vis-à-vis institutions such as political parties, state institutions, or churches) was overstated, and a romantic image of the "small is beautiful" kind made many observers anticipate that a totally new kind of politics would arise from the seeds provided by these movements. This in turn would provide the basis for a different pattern of representation with new kinds of political parties and altered institutions that would hopefully be more democratic and more fully empowering of citizens than what had hitherto existed. But as I have suggested, in case after case the new politics was easily absorbed into the old, "normal" politics of parties and influences. To be sure, movements often fail or run out of steam: activism is costly and antinomian, and the day-to-day pressures of economic and family survival make any organization difficult to sustain. People are also practical, and new styles of organization and action do not necessarily replace older forms but rather take their place as an alternative to be weighed and perhaps put to use, as circumstances seem to indicate.

The problems that groups have experienced in consolidating and even surviving are reinforced by the combination of neoliberal economics (which throws multiple obstacles in the way of collective organization) with a pattern of institutional reconfiguration that in effect removes arenas that poor people have used to present collective demands and seek redress and resources, which together shrink the available field for groups. Thus, neoliberal reforms that were in theory supposed to enhance participation seem to have ended up further constraining it (Kurtz 2004; Holzner 2004). That many groups ultimately fail should not surprise us, nor does it mean that they leave no trace in the personal lives of activists or in society at large

(Drogus and Stewart-Gambino 2005; Levine and Romero 2004; Tarrow 1994). The key issue here may be less the survival of the group itself than the possibility of creating capacities in one arena and transferring them to other fields of action. Indeed, from one point of view, the most densely structured and provisioned groups may well be less apt venues for the creation of civic capacities and social capital than those with less exclusive and exhaustive internal ties. Granovetter's notion of the "strength of weak ties" is relevant here. He stresses that when the ties within a group are wholly exclusive and demanding, and the group in effect is shut off from others, there are significant problems of survival. In contrast, weaker internal ties facilitate alliances between groups and the group itself remains open to the flow of information (Granovetter 1973).

Although they have been frustrated and cut short in many cases, the hopes placed in civil society as a possible source for a new politics did point to an important reality. The broad spectrum of groups created throughout Latin America in recent decades helped to open public life to hitherto excluded groups and silent voices; they also put in place a series of spaces for public life that in many instances simply did not exist before, including neighborhood associations, human rights organizations, women's groups, survival organizations (such as the communal kitchens of Peru), cooperatives, cultural groups, new unions, micro businesses, *piqueteros* (urban protesters in Argentina who employ disruptive street blockades), and so on. Although only a few of the groups in question were explicitly religious in origin and sponsorship, many had clear links with churches and religious groups with which they shared ideas, agendas, personnel, and resources. These groups did not create democracy or bring it about all on their own. Many are not explicitly political at all, nor can they be understood as social movements if we understand social movements to be groups created to press a claim or secure a good of some kind for their members. But this qualifier may be too stringent for what is a very fluid reality. If we loosen the definition, it is clear that the new presence of multiple groups has important connections to democracy and to the possibilities for a democratic life. Growing pressure for democratization, civilian politics, and restoration of the rule of law was energized and vigorously advanced by the stock of ideas and movements and effective networks of contacts that emerged to link state institutions and political parties to the everyday lives of members of the social groups that had come to maturity in the preceding decades of struggle.

Religiously linked groups turned out to be much more vulnerable to the withdrawal of support from the institutional churches than many enthusiastic observers had imagined. The cumulative weight of changes in Vatican policies over the past few decades—appointment of conservative bishops and reassignment of sympathetic clergy, withdrawal of the institutional church from "undue politicization" (and hence from support for contestatory politics and movements), drastically restricting the flow of human and material resources to grassroots groups, and closing critical institutions like Chile's Vicaría de la Solidaridad, which was shut down in 1992—had a devastating effect on many groups. Drogus and Stewart-Gambino (2005) examine the impact of this new posture by the institutional Catholic Church on grassroots women activists and their movements in Brazil and Chile. Both national churches had been heavily invested in creating and supporting these movements, which had played a key role in earlier struggles for democracy. The distinctive style of each hierarchy's involvement shaped how withdrawal took place, with what effect, how it appeared to group members, and what was left behind. Drogus and Stewart-Gambino show that in Chile, heavy investment of resources was accompanied by more control and direction from the top, making groups more dependent. In Brazil the operative model of the "progressive church" made for more autonomy but fewer resources. As the institutional church backed away from its commitments and support, Chileans were left weaker and more adrift. Brazilian women appear more open to the construction of new alliances and connections but have fewer tools with which to operate in an admittedly difficult environment (Drogus and Stewart-Gambino 2005). The contrast is instructive and ties into earlier work (Levine 1992) on the democratizing potential of religious change, which suggests that less central control may be related to more cultural democratization (and a more open and participatory model of social life) with the down side of fewer resources.

The presence of plurality and plural options within each religious community means that analysts should be particularly careful when drawing inferences from such pluralism in beliefs and memberships to specific political consequences. Although multiple options and resulting choices can be a starting point for democratic politics, this does not mean that any particular group is necessarily internally democratic. Participatory ideals can find it hard going within theocratic structures.[11] At the same time, the very variety of options and the volatility of identities and connections make it unlikely that any unified and sustained political movement will emerge out of the blooming garden of Protestant growth (Steigenga 2001; Warner 1988).

Drawing a Balance of Challenge and Opportunity

It is not easy to draw a balance of challenge and opportunity. Part of the difficulty arises from the dynamic character of our subject matter. The plurality and pluralism that are now so visible were predicted by very few. Change is continuous and comes from multiple sources, and the continued energy and creativity of those on the ground will surely produce as yet unanticipated patterns. Drawing a balance is further complicated by contextual variation. The common thread of pluralism and plurality shapes the actors at play and the resources and orientations at their disposal, but what they do with these varies greatly depending on the structure of opportunity in any specific time and place.

The consolidation of pluralism in religion, in civil society, and in politics presents the churches (Catholic as well as Protestant) with a range of groups and voices that escape control and must be recognized as autonomous if they are to be real, rather than paper, organizations. It is clear in the documents issued by the Catholic bishops at Aparecida (in the fall of 2007) that many equated loss of vitality and influence for the institutional church with loss of loyalty and position (Levine 2008). But control is essential to continuity only if control is built into the very definition of what is being continued, in this case "the church" and the Catholic community conceived in hierarchically dependent terms. But this is not the only Catholic model available on which to build. Romero (chap. 9 in this volume) states it forcefully: "Understanding persons as friends of God is quite different than looking upon them as serfs, in the same way that inviting them to follow

God's project is different than ordering them to follow the law." One way to get at possible futures is to think about how institutional churches reposition themselves to cope with the new realities of plurality and pluralism in religion and politics. Repositioning is partly ideological and, thus, can be found in the statements and actions of those who speak in the name of religion, "authorized and official" or not. Repositioning is also behavioral and resource based, as the examples of Brazil and Chile, noted earlier, make clear. Changes in the public stance taken by the bishops (with backing from the Vatican) threaten to widen the gap between official church policies and many of the activists and groups supported in earlier struggles. But although shifting Vatican policies can clearly undermine the possibilities of grassroots action, it is too late to put that particular genie back in the bottle. Activism will likely not disappear but rather turn to the creation of means and methods of action as yet unknown.

A review of the recent history of religion, politics, and of the relation between them shows a lot of change in little time. Contrary to what classic theories of secularization and modernization lead many to anticipate, the space where religion, society, and politics come together has remained a dynamic source of innovation and continuing transformation with consequences that reach far beyond the confines of any particular institutional sphere. In Latin America today, religion is a buzzing, blooming confusion of possibilities, full of innovation charged with social and cultural energies. The seemingly sudden shift to openness and open competition seems to preoccupy the bishops, but it is also a source of potential energy and commitment in as yet unknown forms. Among the most urgent tasks any agenda for the future must take up will be finding ways to make sense of the multiple consequences of religious pluralism, as much for religion as for politics, and for democratic politics above all. The erosion of Catholicism's religious and cultural monopoly, the new presence of competition among religions, and the coming of real pluralism impact the public image of religion and have a clear feedback effect on the internal life of the community of faith. Whatever the social and political interests or commitments of any given religious community, all experience the impact of incentives that draw new kinds of leaders onto the scene, of innovative forms of organization, and of trying out hitherto unknown alliances.

Notes

The author thanks José Casanova, Paul Freston, Frances Hagopian, Soledad Loaeza, José Enrique Molina, and Timothy Steigenga for their helpful comments and suggestions on earlier versions of this chapter.

1. Uruguay has been the notable exception to this pervasive civic-religious fusion.

2. See, in this context, Romero, who in chapter 9 in this volume underscores the emergence of public space and civil society *within the church*. She writes that "through these different forms of association and the construction of new spaces for encounter and interaction, the church has renovated itself and infused religious meaning in everyday life problems. In the last decade, this space has begun to close once again due to the intervention of a number of bishops who are trying to take back control of public space in the church itself and in the way the church expresses itself and is represented in civil society, political society, and the state." She describes this public space as a space of liberty where believers encounter others (both believers and nonbelievers) in voluntary associations, social movements, and personal development courses, as well as arts, music, expressive mobilizations, the Internet, and mass media. The trend Romero identifies for Peru is visible throughout the region: groups proliferate while many prelates, fearing division and loss of control, have tried to rein them in by cutting funds to dissident groups and striving for greater control over schools, universities, and publications (Drogus and Stewart-Gambino 2005).

3. See, in comparison, David Lehmann's discussion of *basismo* (Lehmann 1996, part 1).

4. See in this regard Chesnut's account (2003) of the Catholic Charismatic Renewal in Brazil.

5. Villa and Mallimaci (2007) make a similar point about Argentina, referring to this group as *"católicos cuentapropistas."*

6. The Latin American process has much in common with the growth of fundamentalism and its move to political activism in the United States, in particular the revalorization of politics.

7. This has been a conscious tactic for the leadership of the Universal Church of the Reign of God, who deliberately locate candidates (clerics or bishops to ensure greater control) in a range of political parties (Fonseca 2008).

8. The fall of Guatemala's evangelical president, Elias Serrano, who was accused of corruption and abuse of power, is another case in point.

9. Detailed examination of the organizations and vehicles of mobilization that the church presumably "controls" and could use to further its agenda (see chap. 1 of this volume) reveals that the bishops' capacity to manage groups and members is much weaker than they would like or than they often imagine. Many

of the "resources" that prelates commonly list or rely upon turn out on closer inspection to be hollow shells, groups that exist more on paper than in reality. Even where groups as such do survive, members prove much less malleable than the evidence of formal ties and documents might indicate. In any case, the effort to ensure loyalty by insisting on separate groups with built-in clerical supervision runs into the problem of control in a world where citizens have too many skills, connections, and possibilities to be treated as sheep by a shepherd or to be controlled or moved *en bloc* in traditional ways. In this world, loyalty is more likely to be secured through provision of spaces and engagement, not by demarcation of boundaries.

10. Recent work has underscored the importance of gender in this process (see Drogus and Stewart-Gambino 2005). Throughout the region, women have been a significant part (commonly a majority) of the members and activists of grassroots groups of religious inspiration. Such activism is costly and difficult and often runs afoul of felt obligations to family, not to mention open pressure from male relatives. Women also encounter a glass ceiling in many churches with positions of influence and authority effectively closed to them. The situation is marginally better in some Pentecostal groups, who believe that gifts of the spirit are open to men and women alike, but here, as in the Catholic Church, Max Weber's (1963) general point holds: as religions institutionalize and consolidate, patriarchal views and male domination become more pronounced.

11. In this regard, see Harris (1999) on religion and African American political activism.

References

Casanova, José. 1994. *Public Religions in the Modern World.* Chicago: University of Chicago Press.

Chesnut, Andrew R. 2003. *Competitive Spirits: Latin America's New Religious Economy.* New York: Oxford University Press.

Drogus, Carol Ann, and Hannah Stewart-Gambino. 2005. *Activist Faith: Popular Women Activists and Their Movements in Democratic Brazil and Chile.* University Park: Pennsylvania State University Press.

Fonseca, Alejandro. 2008. "Religion and Democracy in Brazil: A Study of the Leading Evangelical Politicians, 1998–2001." In Paul Freston, ed., *Evangelical Christianity and Democracy in Latin America,* 163–206. Oxford: Oxford University Press.

Freston, Paul C. 2001. *Evangelicals and Politics in Asia, Africa, and Latin America.* New York: Cambridge University Press.

Garrard-Burnett, Virginia. 1998. *Protestantism in Guatemala: Living in the New Jerusalem.* Austin: University of Texas Press.

Gill, Anthony. 1998. *Rendering Unto Caesar.* Chicago: University of Chicago Press.

Granovetter, Mark. 1973. "The Strength of Weak Ties." *American Journal of Sociology* 78, no. 6: 1360–80.

Harris, Fredrick. 1999. *Something Within: Religion in African American Political Activism.* New York: Oxford University Press.

Holzner, Claudio. 2004. "The End of Clientelism? Strong and Weak Networks in a Mexican Squatter Settlement." *Mobilization* 9, no. 3: 223–40.

Kurtz, Marcus. 2004. *Free Market Democracy and the Chilean and Mexican Countryside.* New York: Cambridge University Press.

Lehmann, David. 1996. *Struggle for the Spirit: Religious Transformation and Popular Culture in Brazil and Latin America.* London: Polity Press.

Levine, Daniel H. 1992. *Popular Voices in Latin American Catholicism.* Princeton, NJ: Princeton University Press.

———. 1995. "Protestants and Catholics in Latin America: A Family Portrait." In Martin Marty and R. Scott Appleby, eds., *Fundamentalisms Comprehended,* 155–78. Chicago: University of Chicago Press.

———. 2005. "Pluralidad, Pluralismo, y La Creación de un Vocabulario de Derechos." *América Latina Hoy. Revista de Ciencias Sociales* 41 (December): 17–34.

———. 2006. "Religión y Política en América Latina. La Nueva Cara Pública de la Religión." *Sociedad y Religión* (Buenos Aires) 26/27, no. 18: 7–29.

———. 2008. "The Future as Seen From Aparecida." In Robert Pelton, ed., *Aparecida: Quo Vadis?,* 173–90. Scranton, PA: University of Scranton Press.

Levine, Daniel H., and Catalina Romero. 2004. "Movimientos Urbanos y Desempoderamiento en Perú y Venezuela." *América Latina Hoy* 36: 47–77.

López, Darío. 2004. *La Seducción del Poder. Evangélicos y Política en el Perú de los Noventa.* Lima: Ediciones Puma.

Smith, Brian H. 1998. *Religious Politics in Latin America: Pentecostal vs. Catholic.* Notre Dame, IN: University of Notre Dame Press.

Smith, Christian. 1991. *The Emergence of Liberation Theology: Radical Religion and Social Movement Theory.* Chicago: University of Chicago Press.

Steigenga, Timothy J. 2001. *The Politics of the Spirit: The Political Implications of Pentecostalized Religion in Costa Rica and Guatemala.* Lanham, MD: Lexington Books.

Stoll, David. 1990. *Is Latin America Turning Protestant?* Berkeley: University of California Press.

Tarrow, Sidney. 1994. *Power in Movement: Social Movements, Collective Action, and Politics.* New York: Cambridge University Press.

Villa, Martha, and Fortunato Mallimaci. 2007. "Las Comunidades Eclesiales de Base y el Mundo de los Pobres en la Argentina: Conflictos y Tensiones por el Control del Poder en el Catolicismo." Available at http://www.ceil-piette.gov. ar/docpub/libros/cebs.pdf.

Warner, R. Stephen. 1988. *New Wine in Old Wineskins. Evangelicals and Liberals in a Small-Town Church*. Berkeley: University of California Press.

Weber, Max. 1963. *The Sociology of Religion*. Trans. Ephraim Fischoff. Boston: Beacon Press.

11 | The Catholic Church in a Plural Latin America

Toward a New Research Agenda

FRANCES HAGOPIAN

In May 2007 bishops and Vatican representatives gathered in Aparecida, Brazil, for the Fifth General Meeting of the Latin American Bishops' Conference (Conferencia General del Episcopado Latinoamericano y del Caribe); the purpose of the meeting was to set a new course for the Latin American Catholic Church. The optimism of the meeting in Santo Domingo fifteen years earlier, which had made credible the notion that Latin America provided fertile ground on which to plant a "new evangelization," had given ground to the reality that the new project to evangelize culture, reconquer civil society, and reclaim the public sphere for faith had not yet borne fruit.

Indeed, the Aparecida meeting came at a moment in which the Catholic Church in Latin America found itself clearly on the defensive; the church was in danger of losing the flock and a distinctively Catholic social and political sphere. In most countries the proportion of the population that calls itself Catholic has continued to decline, in the 1990s by as much as 10 percent, and in some of the larger countries in the region, such as Brazil, by 1 percent a year since then. Recent surveys suggest that the population in

Brazil that self-identifies as Catholic fell from 70 percent in 2002 to 64 percent in 2007 (*Folha de São Paulo* 2007). Even in Mexico, it is estimated that the percentage of the population that self-identifies as Protestant rose from a little over 7 percent in 2000 to nearly 20 percent today,[1] and in Peru the percentage of the population that self-identified as Catholic in surveys declined precipitously just in the five-year period from 2001 to 2006, from 82 to 72 percent (see Romero, chap. 9 in this volume). Not only must the church confront the significant challenge posed by religious competition, but secularization is not the idle threat scholars once believed it to be, even in Latin America. Although most Latin American Catholics still believe in God—at least "in their own way," to use Cristián Parker's evocative term—the globalization and secularization of popular culture has outpaced the church's capacity to hold that ground for a moral public sphere. Religious institutions may have inspired their commitments to social justice, but most Latin Americans also want access to artificial birth control and are removing themselves from religious subcultures. In several countries the proportion of those who claim no religion and who do not practice one is climbing. This trend may be particularly pronounced only in Uruguay, but it is also ever truer in Chile, Argentina, and increasingly in Venezuela and the Dominican Republic. Both religious competition and secularization may pose equal challenges to the institutional health of the church, but the secular threat poses a greater challenge to maintaining a moral public sphere.

How the Catholic Church has responded to the contemporary challenges of pluralism, what the church's strategies are for the new evangelization and beyond, and what the impact of religious pluralism has been on civil society, political participation, and the political behavior of Catholics are pressing questions for scholars of religion, politics, and society in Latin America today. We need to explain church responses to social and political developments in religiously competitive environments, and we need to account for variation in those responses across political and ecclesiastical borders. Indeed, the nature, success, and consequences of church responses have varied to a greater extent than appreciated.

This volume has attempted to identify the nature of the challenges facing the Roman Catholic Church at the outset of the twenty-first century in a democratic Latin America. It represents an attempt at deepening our understanding of those challenges and at developing the skeleton of a new framework for understanding the relationship between religious institutions and belief, civil society, and politics in a time of greater religious and political pluralism than Latin America has ever known. This analysis of Latin American cases, therefore, may illuminate the place of religious institutions in plural and secularizing societies more broadly. The volume's contributors have highlighted a number of global, national, local, and individual-level influences on the religious beliefs of Latin Americans. They have identified institutional and policy challenges—some shared, some distinctive—in many Latin American countries. They have also collectively contributed to a revision of our paradigms for understanding church behavior under conditions of religious and especially political pluralism and to a reassessment of the strategic role of religious institutions and the effects of religious-based participation in the public sphere in Latin America. Undoubtedly, the volume has raised more questions than it has answered. Nonetheless, it is worth reviewing several of its most important themes.

The Church in Civil Society

A central theme of this volume has been that the ability of the Roman Catholic Church to respond to the contemporary challenges it faces, and the way in which it does so, is significantly shaped by the nature of its relationship with civil society. What the previous chapters have shown clearly and without ambiguity is that in the decades since Catholic Action and other lay movements emerged with force in Latin America (in the 1950s and 1960s), the civil society in which the church is embedded has changed in profound ways.

Modernization

It is perhaps paradoxical that just at the time that the process of modernization got underway in Latin America and around much of the globe, modernization as a paradigm was essentially discredited in North American political science circles. Political scientists abandoned modernization in part because they accepted the Latin American critique of that paradigm but also because they rejected Weberian categories and embraced institutional—and rationalist—approaches to politics. Scholars grew skeptical of structuralism and of the possibility that global processes of social change could generate individual-level political action.

The essays in this volume tell a different story, however. In his chapter, richly informed by two decades of World Values Survey data, Ronald Inglehart provides evidence that modernization does produce political effects, although not necessarily in the way traditional modernization theory predicted. People who move to cities and read Western newspapers will not suddenly become more Westernized and less religious; rather, once industrialization begins people develop what Inglehart calls "self-expression values." If socioeconomic development "gives rise to mass self-expression values that give high priority to free choice," these values in turn become a foundation for freedom of action, autonomous choices in public and private activities, and ultimately mass demands for democracy. Inglehart's very important finding about Latin America is that religious attachment is strongly linked with a sense of subjective well-being. In other words, people can retain their religious values *and* develop the values of self-expression that are key to democracy's emergence. Of course, growing self-expression also leads to greater demands for freedom, such as those expounded upon in Blancarte and Loaeza's chapters. Extending Inglehart's analysis solves a paradox: on the one hand, Latin America remains a religious place and Latin Americans appear to retain traditional values about gender roles, divorce, and abortion; on the other hand, demands are growing, from women, youth, and others, for more personal freedom than Latin America has ever known.

In their chapters Soledad Loaeza and Cristián Parker chronicle the momentous changes that modernization brought to Mexico and Chile, respectively. Though their chapters represent case studies, the evidence they uncover concerning the influence of education and workplace opportunities for women and the impact of a secular higher education on young men and women could be repeated in most of the Latin American continent. Drawing from a trove of unique survey data, Parker shows that adherence to the teachings of religious authorities is declining among those with the most privileged access to education, especially young graduates of higher educational institutions. But Parker is quick to point out and unflinching in his emphasis that it is not *religion* or belief in God that has declined among Chile's educated youth but rather their willingness to recognize and submit to religious authority. They want to be "Catholic in their own way" or, as they are referred to disparagingly in the United States, "cafeteria Catholics." It is not the case that students in religious institutions who have received formal religious instruction are immune from this trend. A similar dynamic is in evidence in Mexico among women, who have options available today that earlier generations did not.

A Gender Perspective

It is difficult to overstate that any look ahead in the study of religion in Latin America must incorporate a gender perspective. The chapters by Soledad Loaeza and Mala Htun remind us of some obvious truths that represent, in a sense, bookends of our story: on the one hand, women were the backbone of the church for decades, indeed centuries, in Latin America, but, on the other, the demands articulated by women for what they increasingly define as rights represent perhaps the greatest challenge to the Roman Catholic Church in Latin America today. From the underground soldiers of the Cristero rebellion in Mexico to guardians of the moral education of youth, Latin American women young and old were expected to keep the Catholic faith, and for decades they performed this role spectacularly well. The fact that leftist parties resisted the enfranchisement of women for so long in Mexico and elsewhere on the grounds that women were too close to their priests—an argument familiar to students of French politics—is eloquent testimony to the ideological and cultural proximity of Latin American women to the Catholic Church.

With new options in life now available to Latin American women, the church has lost its torchbearers, in Mexico largely due to education and modernization. Elsewhere, women thrust into leadership roles during military regimes acquired leadership skills and independence from religious leaders (Drogus and Stewart-Gambino 2005). These changes, in turn, have meant not merely that the church has "lost" women as an asset but also that it must now confront women over some of the most contentious issues on the public policy agenda in Latin America today. Women's groups have mobilized in most countries and have made substantial strides in placing female political representatives in high office in the executive and legislative branches of government, especially in those countries where quotas have been introduced to guide selections for appointive positions and nominees for elective office (Baldez 2004; Htun 2004).

Women who now serve in presidential cabinets and in national legislatures have not been as successful in changing public policy—at least not yet—as they have in notably broadening the parameters of political debate, as Mala Htun makes plain in her chapter. Apart from the lower house of the Uruguayan legislature and the state legislature of Mexico's federal district, no legislation liberalizing or even decriminalizing abortion has passed a Latin American legislative body; however, now the potential liberalization of abortion laws can be discussed. Such debates have begun in Venezuela and Argentina, and in Brazil a debate that began in a limited way about restrictions on abortion in cases of anencephaly has rapidly escalated into a wider debate about abortion more generally. On the eve of the visit of Pope Benedict XVI to Brazil to open the Aparecida conference, President Lula sparked tensions when he expressed an openness to discuss the issue, which had been placed on the agenda earlier in 2007 by his health minister, José Gomes Temporão, who had called for a national referendum on abortion.[2] Such debates in Colombia may have persuaded the courts to liberalize abortion in one of the most conservative societies in Latin America. Of course, not all countries are moving in a liberalizing direction. El Salvador and Nicaragua have toughened their laws banning the procedure in all cases, including when the life of the mother is endangered, and El Salvador has imposed stiff prison sentences (six to twelve years) for providers (including medical doctors) and for women (who face two to eight years in prison or from thirty to fifty years if the fetus was more than eighteen weeks old and considered viable).[3]

There is evidence that Latin America's bishops are aware of the challenge they face. While still emphasizing the "essential-spiritual ministry that woman bears within her: receiving life, welcoming it, nourishing it, giving birth to it, sustaining it, accompanying it, and deploying her being as woman in creating habitable spaces of community, and communion" (CELAM 2007b, §457),[4] and that women play an indispensable role in the care and education of children, transmission of the faith, and building the church (§453, 455, 456), the final document to come out of the Aparecida conference hastened to add that fulfilling these roles did not preclude women's professional development and active participation in constructing society. The bishops decried both the "machista mentality" of Latin America and the Caribbean and the "new slavery" of consumer and show-business society (§453), and they unambiguously declared it time for Latin America and the Caribbean "to hear the clamor, so often silenced, of women who are subject to all forms of exclusion and violence in all its forms and in all stages of their lives (§454). The final document proposed specifically "guaranteeing the effective presence of women in Church ministries that are entrusted to laypersons, as well as in planning and pastoral decisions, promoting dialogue with authorities to draw up programs, laws, and public policies that permit women to reconcile their work life with their home and family responsibilities, and discovering and developing in each woman and in ecclesial and social circles the 'feminine genius'" (§458).

Indigenous Peoples

The image of docile indigenous peoples serving as the bedrock of Catholicism—with the now beatified Juan Diego Cuauhtlatoatzin, the Indian visited by the Virgin of Guadalupe, as emblematic—has been shattered by the work of historians showing that indigenous peoples were often Catholic converts in name only. Abandoned on the rural periphery of the empire by the Crown and the church, indigenous peoples concealed their own systems of beliefs—under the watchful eye of the state, clergy, and landlords. Indigenous communities have also been ripe for conversion. In Mexico Protestants claim to have converted half the country's indigenous peoples, and "much the same goes for the highlands of Guatemala."[5]

Recognizing this, Latin American bishops have pursued a two-pronged strategy to reach out to indigenous peoples. First, in many countries bishops have spoken out as advocates of the indigenous, especially when their human and social rights are at stake, and they have loudly and unmistakably backed the land claims of indigenous movements. Patricia Rodriguez's chapter in this volume chronicles the support that episcopal conferences accorded to the claims of the Landless Workers Movement (Movimento dos Trabalhadores Rurais Sem Terra, or MST) in Brazil and Mapuche communities in Chile. At Aparecida the church reaffirmed its commitment to work with indigenous peoples to strengthen their identities and organizations and to defend their territory, intercultural bilingual education, and rights (CELAM 2007b, §530), as well as to support Afro-descendants in their struggle against racism in all its forms and discrimination in education and employment (§533). The bishops forcefully sided with the indigenous and Afro-descendants in their claims for their "legitimate rights" and against the threat of physical, cultural, and spiritual extinction (§89, 90).

If the clergy and at least some members of the hierarchy have supported the demands of the indigenous peoples of the hemisphere for land, health, education, and human rights, what comes through in Rodriguez's chapter is that church authorities, especially in Chile, still struggle with the challenges of recognizing cultural and religious pluralism. Whereas the Chilean bishops have readily supported the demands of the Mapuches for land and dignity, and even asked for forgiveness for the sins committed by Catholic Chileans throughout history, they have balked at embracing another key indigenous demand: respect for Mapuche culture, philosophy, and religion, which comes with a set of beliefs that conform uncomfortably to Roman Catholicism. Some Mapuche groups have viewed the new process of evangelization, which considers indigenous peoples as objects of evangelization, as "racist and oppressive." As the Chilean bishops recognized, the church had not delivered on the call issued in Santo Domingo in 1992 to develop an "inculturated evangelization" that would incorporate native religious and cultural values" (Rodriguez, chap. 5 in this volume). For that reason, the issue was back on the agenda for Aparecida. While the bishops recognized that the indigenous would want to promote theological and liturgical reflection in the context of their own history and culture, they also held firm to pressing ahead with their work of evangelizing among the indigenous. They also warned that they would be attentive to efforts to "eradicate the Catholic faith from indigenous communities," which, in their view, would leave these communities "defenseless and confused" before the clash of ideologies and groups (CELAM 2007b, §530, 531).

The tension between evangelization and respect for indigenous culture is not an easy one to resolve. In a speech delivered during his May 2007 visit to Brazil, Pope Benedict XVI infuriated indigenous groups in saying that native populations had been "silently longing" for the Christian faith brought to South America by the same colonizers who, from the indigenous perspective, converted natives by the sword and were, "with honorable exceptions, accomplices, deceivers and beneficiaries of one of the most horrific genocides of all humanity." Back in Rome, the pope apologized for his remarks but clung to his position that the "Gospel has expressed and continues to express the identity of the peoples in this region, and provides inspiration to address the challenges of our globalized era."[6]

Defending Hegemony and Culture

The challenges of religious pluralism, secularism, democracy, and globalization, which have been the subject of a good deal of this volume, have generated a series of responses by Catholic hierarchies across the region in an attempt to maintain Catholic religious hegemony—over the church's competitors, over society, and, more specifically, over culture. Before we attempt to explain the reasoning behind these responses, we must better understand their exact nature.

Responding to Competition

The greatest challenge of pluralism, according to the church, is stemming the tide of conversions to other denominations and faiths, especially evangelical sects. Indeed, this issue was most in evidence in the discussions leading up to the Aparecida meeting. In scrambling for ways to bring the Gospel to the faithful in a manner that provides a rewarding and ultimately satisfying religious experience, church leaders have revisited and reevaluated old and new forms of worship.

The experiments known as CEBs (comunidades eclesiais de base, or ecclesial base communities) were, of course, originally designed precisely to bring an intense and meaningful religious experience to laypersons who had only rarely participated actively in the life of the church and who lived in isolated or poor communities and saw a priest or received the sacraments infrequently. At one point this experiment—upon which activists and scholars placed so much hope in earlier decades as an emancipationist project that could pull the church into alliance with the poor—was retrospectively judged a failure from the perspective of securing the church's position in society and stemming the tide of defections. As Daudelin and Hewitt put it, "the progressives delivered no more faithful, no more seminarians, no more priests, than their more traditionalist counterparts. In fact, they did not even deliver the 'natural communities' of the poor" (1995, 188). Critics charged that liberationists expected too much of people for whom daily life was a struggle; the poor were not ready to undertake the sort of doctrinal reflection required to participate in the grassroots communities. In Brazilian communities studied by Burdick (1992, 173–80), a heavy emphasis on reading the Bible by literate Catholics silenced illiterates; working mothers with small children did not have the time to meet the ramped-up expectations for church participation; inequality in the realm of politics and production could be discussed but not domestic problems and conflict; and dark-skinned mulattos and blacks felt they were treated like second-class citizens. On a deeply personal level, Burdick argued, liberation theology failed because it did not offer the poor spiritual comfort; struggle against unjust social systems and in the political realm did not bring a satisfactory resolution to people's personal dilemmas. The poor felt it was better to focus on those things they could control, like their drinking, than on politics, which they could not. In explaining why Protestants were able to make inroads in Guatemala and elsewhere, Stoll (1990, 314) similarly charges that liberationists in grassroots movements defined the people only in class terms, not according to their multiple identities as women, as indigenous, and so forth, and really did not listen to the needs of the poor. Stoll (41) also maintains that the crisis of participation that created the hollow pillars of church support in society was real, and if the CEBs, and especially the liberationist message, failed to solve the crisis, they were not responsible for creating it. A reformation was due, and bound to happen, either within the church or outside of it.

Against the backdrop of the perceived failure of progressive theologies and forms of worship, in a gesture consistent with the reasoning of the religious marketplace thesis, the church hierarchy, cautiously at first but subsequently with more enthusiasm, backed the Catholic Charismatic Renewal (CCR), which appeared to hold promise as delivering a product better suited to the demands of poor parishioners. There is certainly anecdotal evidence that the CCR represents a dynamic force within contemporary Latin American Catholicism, as millions flock to services based more on ecstasy than on ritual. At the same time, however, on the eve of the 2007 papal visit to Brazil, news outlets reported what activists and researchers on the ground had long asserted: the announced death of the CEBs is premature; in fact, the "CEBs are doing very well, thank you."[7]

If CEBs and the CCR hold meaning for millions of observant Catholics in Latin America, arguably neither has worked terribly well in stopping the hemorrhage of members leaving the church, and neither church leaders nor scholars really know which has worked better. It could be that whichever way the church chooses, it chooses wrong. Alternatively, it is conceivable that both might be successful in capturing different slices of the market and the church should lend support to both. The Aparecida document favorably referred to the CEBs as schools that have helped to form committed Christians and as the "visible expression of the preferential option for the poor" (CELAM 2007b, §178, 179); the document expressed the hope that in close contact with their bishops and integrated into diocesan life, and taking care not to "alter the precious treasure of Church Tradition and Teaching," the CEBs could be a "sign of vitality in the Church" (§179). At least some Latin American bishops may also recognize that large outdoor Masses and global Catholic media networks such as Lumen 2000, which grabbed attention in theological circles as a way to energize youth (Della Cava 1992), are a poor substitute for the kind of intense discussions held in the nurturing environment of schools, universities, and, especially, in civil society associations, which form leaders and cultivate loyalty. Indeed, at Aparecida the bishops also recognized the "new movements and communities" as "a gift from the Holy Spirit to the Church," whose members are exercising their natural rights of free association, and invited those movements and associations that are showing "a certain fatigue or weakness" to "renew their original charisma" (CELAM 2007b, §311).

Responding to Globalization

Latin American bishops treat globalizing influences in much the same way the military used to treat Marxist ideas: as alien imports that threaten Latin American culture. For the Catholic Church globalization has spread rampant consumerism and a popular culture that promotes immorality. Bishops' conferences across the region officially and forcefully denounced the book and movie version of *The Da Vinci Code* for offending the majority religion and attempting to mislead Catholics about the divinity of Jesus and other core tenets of Christianity. The opposition of church leaders to globalization places them on the political left when they denounce the tyranny of the market but on the right when they express concern about the contamination of Latin American culture.

Will Latin America be a less religious region when living standards and existential security improve, as Norris and Inglehart (2004) suggest? Is Latin America as exceptional as bishops allege? Or, as Parker claims (chap. 4 in this volume), is it open to globalizing cultural influences? In his contribution to this volume, Inglehart finds that Latin America is indeed a distinctive cultural region and that Latin Americans have developed "self-expression" values: they are happier than they "should be" given their level of economic development. They also express more traditional values than the European and postcommunist regions. But it is hard to conclude on this basis, and against Parker's analysis, that Catholicism provides immunity from globalization and its secularizing trends and "New Age" religious expressions.

Responding to Democracy and Liberalism

In 1965 in *Gaudium et Spes,* a document that changed history, the Roman Catholic Church embraced democracy. It is easy to forget, nearly a half century later, that until that time many church theologians preferred monarchies and even authoritarian regimes to democracies.[8] Arguably, since then the church has accustomed itself to democracy but not to the liberalism that usually accompanies democracy, and especially not to the variant that most observers argue best protects civil liberties and minority rights. Countless Catholic websites point out that individualism is an alien concept to Catholicism, and in practice when rights clash with norms, church leaders often take stands against rights because a Catholic conception of the law is very different from a liberal one. In a liberal society the law is something that sets limits and should be enforced. It may, but need not, reflect the median values shared by society. In Latin America traditionally, and still for Catholic bishops, the law should reflect the moral standards of the majority, even if that means denying rights to individuals and regardless of whether or not the law is transgressed in practice. To do otherwise—to permit government distribution of condoms to unmarried youth or to permit legal abortion under any circumstance—would be tantamount to the state desecrating the sanctity of marriage or endorsing the taking of innocent life. The notion of trusting Catholics to uphold Catholic principles in their own lives and allowing non-Catholics to do as their own consciences dictate is an alien one. It may well be the case that the church in Latin America is digging its heels in because it cannot trust lay Catholics not to take advantage of services conferred as rights by the state precisely for reasons that have been the subject of this volume: the erosion of hegemony over the faithful, the changing roles of women, and the institutional weakness of the church's subcultural associations.

This clash of legal philosophy, conceptions of state, society, and nation, and stances on liberal rights are vividly portrayed in Roberto Blancarte's account of the Catholic Church and the lay state in Mexico. Blancarte's chapter opens a window onto the ideological mindset of the hierarchy of the Mexican Catholic Church. For the hierarchy, Mexican society is Catholic and always has been, despite a century of victimization at the hands of a lay state. Its current response to pluralism begins here and cannot be understood without reference to this history. For the Mexican church there can be no separation between Catholic morality and public law. Ordinary Catholics, however, seem to take seriously the less well-known but no less radical admission of *Gaudium et Spes* that human beings have their own individual consciences and Catholics should be free to follow them.

Why Do Churches Respond as They Do?

It is somewhat self-evident that the answer to any question about church responses begins with an age-old question of its own: Is "the church" represented by Rome and its national hierarchy, or its community of baptized believers? I am reminded of a story a colleague told me about attending an evening meeting of relatively recent rural migrants in a low-income neighborhood in Santiago, Chile, nearly four decades ago. The meeting was called by a missionary of the Congregation of the Holy Cross to discuss a sit-in (*toma*) in the downtown cathedral by Catholic University students. As he told it to me, a grizzled old *campesino* rose to say, "I don't see how you can talk about a takeover [also *toma*] of the church. The church isn't that building in the city. The church is us."[9] While this wise *campesino* reminds us that the obvious answer to our question is "both," in practice, whether one privileges the hierarchy or the community affects how one frames her answers. Much of this volume has identified the responses of the hierarchy as "church" responses to pluralism.

Much of this chapter has also spoken of the church hierarchy as if there were one rather than many. If we are to explain how Latin America's Catholic bishops are responding to secularization and eroding religious hegemony in a context of democratic politics, we must recognize, describe, and explain national variation in those responses. This volume has made a start in that direction by providing broadly comparative approaches toward as well as focused comparisons and case studies of the Catholic Church in different countries. It has been the contention of the volume that any explanation for understanding these diverse responses to pluralism must begin with the complicated relationship between the church and the society in which it is embedded and, more specifically, the interaction of the hierarchy with the base and those outside its orbit. Such an approach implies that we should take seriously not merely the capacity of church leaders to enforce their interpretations of dogma among the faithful and even to count on their votes in electing governments that will subsidize parochial schools and prevent ministers of health from making morning-after pills available over the counter in pharmacies; in addition we must consider the capacity of the grassroots to at minimum inform—and perhaps even influence—the hierarchy of the church. Therefore, this emphasis also requires that we look not only to the channels through which the church reaches congressional committees, newspaper editors, university professors, labor activists, and residents of poor neighborhoods but also inside the Catholic Church to the internal institutions that allow the grassroots to transmit information to the hierarchy.

A recurring theme among those who have studied organizations of the laity on different continents over the years is not merely the vitality of their organizations, and their importance in developing leaders and infusing Catholic principles of social justice into national institutions, debates, and policies, but also the function they serve in providing critical feedback to the hierarchy. This theme has been sounded in particular but not exclusively by scholars of Peru and Brazil, who have attested to the fact that the militants of the Catholic Youth Workers and the Catholic University Youth, the often foreign-born parish priests who worked with the rural poor, and the leaders of CEBs contributed to a deeper understanding among episcopal leaders of the ways in which the faithful experienced their religion.

In her chapter Catalina Romero reports that in contrast to the time when clergy and bishops participated in and learned from the apostolic movements of Catholic Action and Christian and ecclesial base communities, today the Catholic hierarchy has closed these privileged spaces of association, participation, expression, and opinion as part of a deliberate attempt to "retake control of public space." Such a closure can have deleterious consequences for the church: without a set of eyes and ears on the ground, it is hard for church leaders to understand the anxieties and aspirations of their base; without priests and lay workers, it is hard for ordinary people to gain the support of the hierarchy in the struggles of their daily lives.

Are there institutions left to provide information feedback and cross-fertilize ideas and beliefs? Patricia Rodriguez's fine chapter shows how pastoral commissions—one form of an organizational structure that connects the institutional church to society—might serve as a conduit through which the church and its faithful influence each other. They have done so to a greater degree in Brazil than in Chile, which has enabled the Brazilian church to adapt faith and its mission to new realities. But we should be cautious about expecting pastoral commissions to substitute effectively for broader forms of lay participation in the church.

Assuming the church has information, what determines national responses to the strategic dilemma of deciding *how* to intervene in politics? Given that church positions on wages and employment, the rights of migrants, reproductive rights, and other issues of moral concern cut across traditional partisan boundaries, and that at any given moment, stressing its social justice concerns could alienate the church from political agents who might be willing to carry out its pro-life policies, on what basis do national hierarchies make choices about which areas of concern to emphasize in their collective as well as individual statements? Chapter 7 proposes a framework for predicting church responses to this strategic dilemma based on its capacity to mobilize civil society, the political orientation of the faithful—which matters more in conditions of declining hegemony—and the degree of political risk it faces. Of equal interest is assessing how successful the church has been, and can be, in having an impact on society and politics. This volume has devoted proportionally less attention to chronicling and developing a separate framework to explain the church's impact in the public sphere in times of religious and democratic pluralism. But it has made a start, which I highlight next.

Church Influence on Society and Politics

Although admittedly only a first step, the framework presented in chapter 7 contains an argument with clear implications for the impact of democracy on the church and for the church's capacity to influence the democratic public sphere. Where the church is constrained by a plural base, it may influence the public debate on economic and moral issues but will not likely decide the outcomes of public policy or reorder political space. Where it can mobilize a Catholic civil society, it may ride the tide of discontent with market reform, constitutionalism, and partisan politics and turn challenge into opportunity. Where national ideological currents move the church toward parties of the right with a religious identity or parties that more generally promote the church's moral agenda, however, national religious authorities could realign their economic ideology to conform to those parties, and the church may increase its influence in politics with significant consequences for electoral outcomes and public policies. Where religious pluralism is low but civil society is weak and disengaged, the church will not likely have a significant presence in public life. A preliminary examination of the church's impact on public policy suggests that we need to consider more seriously the venues of public decisions, the timing of elections, and other factors that potentially could sway the balance of church influence on public policy. Analysis of its impact on politics more broadly will require an even more creative approach, as we see next.

Church Impact on Public Policy: Economy, Environment, and Social Services

As we have seen, the church has vocally opposed neoliberal economic policy, poverty, landlessness, rising inequality, and unemployment and underemployment. It has also condemned environmental degradation in general and in such specific manifestations as gold and silver mining in El Salvador and the Brazilian Amazon. There is little evidence, however, that its opposition to market reforms and unsustainable development has been successful. Where its grassroots activists are also close to government, as has been true in Brazil during the Lula government, its positions in favor of antipoverty programs and in recognition of indigenous land rights have been, not surprisingly, the most successful. But more typically, antineoliberal policies have been carried out by governments with which the church feels little affinity, such as in Venezuela and even Argentina under the Kirchner government, and those governments that conform most closely to the church's positions on life have turned a deaf ear to the church's social justice agenda. In the few bright spots on the continent where moderate market-oriented economic policies have been successful and combined with forward-looking social policies, such as Chile, opposing liberal economic policies is not necessarily a vote-winning strategy; thus, the church has by and large not traveled down that path.

The church has been more successful in backing land reform. Land reform has been a major issue in Brazil, where a powerful movement of the landless has benefited from church support. Church intervention has been especially effective, as Patricia Rodriguez's chapter demonstrates, in protecting the landless from violent attacks by landowners' hired guns; where it has failed to protect the landless from violence, the church has shined a spotlight on human rights violations in the countryside. Successive governments in Brazil have paid more attention to the plight of the rural poor thanks in part to church efforts.

Aside from economic policy, one of the most salient issues on the agenda of politics across Latin America is that of access to quality health care and education. The extension of democracy and the decline of social services after decades of debt service and the privatization of public services aroused mass publics to demand that their children be able to see a doctor and learn to read. Some countries like Chile and Brazil—the latter on a shakier foundation—have made remarkable strides in expanding access to secondary education in the past fifteen years. They are seen as success stories in overcoming resource constraints (often through innovative and targeted tax increases), excessive centralization, inefficient policy designs, and, in the case of Brazil, the use of public services as sources of patronage.

The church has backed the demands of ordinary Latin Americans for access to health care and education as their basic, human rights. But governments and the church do not always see eye to eye on the *sort* of education to which people ought to have a right. The Catholic Church has focused a good deal of its efforts in recent years throughout the hemisphere (including in the United States) on seeking public support for Catholic education. Latin American bishops contend that constitutional guarantees of religious freedom demand that states support Catholic schools; bishops base their argument on the following logic: parents have the right to choose the education they want for their children, and if they choose a private, religious education, the state should be responsible for providing that. To do otherwise is to discriminate against the poor, who cannot afford to pay for the education of their choice for their children. In this instance *rights* are understood not in the liberal sense of freedom from state intervention and regulation but rather in a sense of enabling that which would otherwise not be possible. But in other aspects of education policy, the church seeks liberal protections. Religious orders such as Opus Dei and the Legionaries of Christ, typically associated with the most conservative wing of the church, have taken advantage of the privatization and deregulation of higher education to found new universities with the goal of socializing the layer of the elite that was traditionally educated in Jesuit and Dominican institutions. Bishops have also clashed with government ministers in country after country over the content of public education and the appropriate limits of state authority with respect to regulation of religious education. They have vociferously opposed the availability of sex education in public and religious schools. To the church, programs that introduce knowledge about artificial birth control methods (which also help to stop the spread of sexually transmitted diseases, including HIV/AIDS) violate the rights of parents and encourage promiscuity. National churches have also resisted any government efforts to remove from officials of parochial schools the discretion to offer or deny students admission or the right of attendance on a basis that could be considered discriminatory (such as if girls are pregnant).

The issue of public health has also sparked a clash of perspectives that are even more difficult to reconcile. Although there are instances in which church and women's groups can and have allied, such as over forced sterilization programs in Peru in the 1990s (Romero 2005) and Mexico in the 1970s, more often than not the church stands opposed to the extension of what women around the world define as reproductive rights and women's health. Whereas two decades ago women timidly asked for the right to a legal divorce and access to artificial contraception, today women's groups have placed the issue of abortion on the agenda of politics in Latin America. Proponents of reform frame the issue as one of rights, which are typically decided and protected by the courts; opponents view it from the perspective of enshrining the norms and values of the majority into law, a process that takes place in national and provincial legislatures. The venues in which decisions about public services are made may bias the outcomes.

In her timely essay, Htun starkly poses the paradox between the openness of the public debate about abortion and same-sex unions spearheaded by medical professionals and women's rights groups often backed by international allies—a sharp contrast to the early days of post-transition politics, when politicians did not dare raise such subjects for fear of alienating religious leaders who had been valuable allies in the fight for democracy and human rights—and the essential failure to enact liberalizing legislation. The reason for this disjunction cannot be attributed to the opposition of politicians to policy change. Surveys of politicians show that the majority are personally favorable to extending liberal rights. Htun contends that when democracy places threatening items on the agenda, the church can draw upon its moral authority and public trust (especially compared to politicians and political institutions) to sway outcomes. She concludes that church pressures to block reforms are most effective "when brought to bear on the legislature and other elected (as opposed to appointed) officials; when elections are imminent; and on bicameral legislatures" (chap. 8 in this volume). This is so, she argues, because during the long policy-making process bishops have ample opportunity to "remind politicians of their Catholic roots, mobilize the electorate, and threaten their disapproval." The church has correctly concluded, based in part on its success in El Salvador, Uruguay, and elsewhere, that when the issue of abortion is thrown to the legislature, it has a better chance of defeating liberalization than when the matter is decided in the courts, as it was in Colombia.[10] The state legislature of Mexico City, dominated by members of the leftist PRD (Partido de la Revolución Democrática, or Party of the Democratic Revolution), is the exception that proves the rule. Indeed, bishops now find themselves in the awkward position of opposing their country becoming a signatory to various international treaties for human rights for fear they may be interpreted as guaranteeing rights to women that the church views as violations of life.

Church Impact on Politics and Democracy

This volume has also asked the question of what the impact of the Roman Catholic Church and religious change more broadly has been on democracy in Latin America, but it has to this point offered few answers. Here, I sketch out two sets of ideas that future research might explore more fully: the impact of the statements and campaigns (that if not issued in the name of the hierarchy have its sanction) that focus on what we might think of as building democratic institutions, and the broader impact of religious transformation and especially religious pluralism on building what we tend to think of as a democratic political culture. As Catalina Romero reminds us in chapter 9, José Casanova (2001, 1043) emphasized that the "third wave" of democratization was a Catholic wave (as Huntington [1991] identified it) not merely because the countries it swept over happened to be Catholic but also because the transformation of Catholicism was itself an important independent factor in producing the wave.

Most readers are very familiar with the work of the church in helping to facilitate democratic transitions in Brazil and Chile and in helping to broker peace accords that resulted in the establishment of democracy in El Salvador. The standard version of church activity in the posttransition period is that once democracy was established, the church would be more or less a neutral player; it would be highly improbable that the church would *oppose* democracy in the modern age, yet it would also have less of a role to play in fostering democratization since there would no longer be a need to shelter activists from military repression. Thus, the church would essentially—and appropriately—withdraw from party politics.

These expectations notwithstanding, there are strong reasons to believe that the church has continued to play an active and effective role in promoting democratic institutions. First, not all transitions were "settled" in the 1980s or even the 1990s. The Catholic Church in Cuba finds itself at the center of contention in a decaying communist regime, giving civil society space and support to enhance individual freedom without voicing the sort of overt opposition to the government that would surely bring retaliation upon it (Portada 2009). Catholics in Peru played an important role in supporting the work of the Truth and Reconciliation Commission just a few years ago (see Romero, chap. 9 in this volume). Second, in the past quarter century and especially in the past decade, there have been many examples—off scholars' radar screens—of bishops' conferences issuing strong statements in favor of democracy after the issues of human rights transgressions under military rule were essentially settled. Examples include fighting for fair elections in Mexico, holding parties accountable for pro-poor policies in Brazil, and in both countries encouraging voters to familiarize themselves with party positions and above all not to sell their votes. Today the Venezuelan Catholic Church finds itself in a different sort of dilemma: fending off the authoritarian creep of a democratically elected government.

The second major theme to which we should collectively return is the impact, hypothesized long ago, of religious change on the culture of democracy. We should recall that much of the faith in the future of the liberationist movement lay in the power of its transformative potential for those within its orbit.[11] To review, CEBs approximated the small self-managed groups of believers, with equal rights and capabilities, responsible for following a common set of ethical rules more typically associated with such congregational and ethical Christian denominations as Puritanism than Roman Catholicism (Levine 1993, 213). As such, they carried the hope for a new kind of democracy—one that would take root in local culture rather than floating freely above essentially authoritarian societies that offered no realistic prospect of democratic citizenship to the majority of the population. In creating participatory communities, they were believed to hold the promise to serve as Tocquevillian "schools for democracy." In the most giant of paradoxes for the most rabid anticlericalists, democracy's hope in Latin America appeared to lie with the capacity of the Roman Catholic Church to lay the associational and participatory foundations of modern democracy, an irony not lost on Huntington (1991, 79–80). The hope and expectation was that millions of Catholic activists formed in base and Christian communities across Latin America would fan out to lead other democratic religious and nonreligious social movements.

Did Catholic activists fulfill the promise of laying the foundation for a more democratic political culture only to dutifully retreat from the public stage when ordered to do so? Or might they have shut down their operations merely to set up shop on the other, secular side of the street under new management? In truth we do not know. But we strongly suspect they opted for the latter. Catalina Romero's chapter contends that activists formed by the Vatican II catechists—who continued the intense discussions of grassroots religious communities at an increasing distance from the conservative Peruvian hierarchy—moved into secular civil society with their principles in tow. These are the Catholics responsible for attenuating violence in rural areas and for contributing to the construction of democratic bodies and spaces in civil society. Similarly in Mexico, where Blancarte alleges activists were expelled from the church, and in Brazil, where they remained in the church, grassroots Catholics have been steadily building anticlientelist, participatory democratic structures from the ground up.

An Agenda for Research

In summarizing the questions whose answers require us to know much more than we do, we highlight the following areas for further study:

1. *We need to look inside the hierarchy.* There are close to 1,200 cardinals and bishops in Latin America, some formed in the heady days of Vatican II, others belonging to Opus Dei.[12] Some tend to the poor in Honduras, others to the indigenous from Chiapas to Araucania, and others to the wealthy in the chic neighborhoods of Lima and Buenos Aires. It is implausible that they all see eye to eye on political, social, and eco-

nomic issues with theological import, especially in countries with increasingly diverse dioceses. It is also not likely that they assess the church's best strategies in the same way.

In light of this internal diversity in the most important decision-making bodies in the Latin American church, we need to return to the premise of methodological individualism. We need to understand the individual-level incentives facing members of the episcopate as they jockey for position with each other, the papal nuncio, members of other national episcopates, and Rome itself. Those representing large urban dioceses may attempt to push their weight around in their national conferences. Some may use support from their bases to advance their positions within the hierarchy, while others may attempt to cultivate connections with Rome in order to rise above their peers. As with any elite, some conferences may unite to maximize their autonomy from Rome while others may allow Rome to divide them for personal or factional gain.

It should also be clear that what happens within the hierarchy matters. Patricia Rodriguez's chapter makes vivid the sharp divisions and contradictory statements emanating from within the Chilean episcopate over the Mapuche conflict, with southern bishops who are closer to indigenous communities clashing with the bishop of Santiago. And to return to the important insight of Luiz Alberto Gomez de Souza (2005), in those conferences such as the Brazilian one, in which the liberationist bishops were able to ally with moderates, centripetal forces were set in motion that preserved moderation and internal pluralism, whereas in those such as the Nicaraguan one, where the left was expelled, the church veered to the right but left many behind.

2. More systematic analysis is needed to understand *the particular circumstances under which the church intervenes in these issue areas and what drives it to adopt the positions that it does*. We should begin with a detailed chart of the positions that the church has adopted on key issues, nation by nation. Chapter 7 makes a start by examining the positions national episcopal conferences adopted in pastoral letters and other official communications, but clearly we also need to examine systematically the public positions bishops adopt in press conferences and letters to government officials on issues of the day. We also need to

know *why,* and on what basis, the hierarchy makes its decisions. In addition to a consideration of the beliefs of individual bishops, we especially need to pay more attention to how church officials assess political opportunity and risk. Case studies of particular episcopates and policy areas that draw from interviews with politicians, congressional leaders, leaders of civil society organizations, and the clergy and hierarchy would be especially welcome. Such studies might confirm, dispute, or qualify the theoretical framework advanced in this volume for understanding the roles of religious hegemony, capacity for mobilization, and political risk in the decision-making calculus of church leaders.

3. In order to be able to address these and virtually all other important questions about the responses of the contemporary Roman Catholic Church in Latin America to the challenges of the twenty-first century, *we should place these responses in the context of the church's past.* Social scientists would clearly benefit from an expansion of studies of the institutional, social, and cultural history of religion in Latin America in the nineteenth and twentieth centuries.

4. If we are to understand the contemporary beliefs and aspirations of the laity, *we will need to update our studies of individual-level religious belief among Catholics,* in the same way that many scholars have done for studies of various Protestant faiths in recent years. The contributions of Cristián Parker and Catalina Romero are especially valuable for bringing to light the results of recent surveys of religious beliefs in Chile and Peru, respectively. These rich surveys enable their authors to distinguish between "Catholics" and "Catholics in their own way" (Parker, chap. 5 in this volume); and between "Mel Gibson" Catholics, for whom Christ's life and death is the means to salvation, and Catholics who identify Catholicism primarily as the embodiment of Christ's message of love (Romero 2005). These surveys are also important for what they tell us not merely about *what* Catholics believe, but *which* Catholics, and why. They enable Parker and Romero to shine a light on the influences on the formation of religious beliefs, be they the socialization experiences of higher education or catechetical instruction. The Peruvian surveys suggest that the future is not necessarily one of steady secularization as educational opportunities expand but rather, and more importantly, of different conceptions of Catholicism, and in-

deed a Christianity based on when and from whom the faithful received their religious instruction. In fact, what is striking in the Peruvian case—but probably not limited to Peru—is that there is a generational divide in beliefs. Not only has the content of the message from religious authorities changed in the past quarter century—the church is no longer open to changing unjust social structures—but so, too, has the medium, from intense, small-group discussions to a more traditional, top-down method. Similar surveys exist for Brazil but are sorely lacking in most other Latin American countries.[13] As illuminating as these surveys have been, we also need more *qualitative* research on what religious studies scholars refer to as "lived religion." This is important if we are to understand what it means to be Catholic "in one's own way" or to be a "believer without belonging."

5. We also need to go beyond mass surveys, as important as these are, *to learn more about how beliefs spread in civil society.* We need to look deeply into the myriad social organizations of civil society to determine whether Catholic activists and ideas are found within them or not. Survey research alone will not be able to address such questions as what lasting impact, if any, participation in the CEBs had on individuals, civil society, and democratic politics. Has such participation produced committed Catholics, albeit ones that question church authority on issues that are not dogma? Or have former activists left the church, as Blancarte suggests occurred in Mexico (see chap. 6 in this volume)? Apart from Drogus (1999) and Drogus and Stewart-Gambino (2005), few students of the CEBs have returned to ask what has happened to those that participated in progressive, grassroots communities. Only more intensive studies based on fieldwork will be able to shed light on this glaring deficit.

6. *We need to chart out what impact church action has on democracy*—on the policy debate, election outcomes, and electoral cleavages. What, for example, is the larger impact likely to be for the future course of Venezuela's troubled democracy of the Catholic Church's fairly visible role of opposition to the presidency of Hugo Chávez Frías? Can the church sway elections? Do Catholics today vote according to their pocketbooks or their religious convictions? Researchers have barely scratched the surface of whether or not religious cleavages exist. Most who have

studied the question believe they do not. Soledad Loaeza's claim that the church in Mexico overstated its capacity to mobilize voters has some support in electoral surveys that show Catholics pretty evenly divided in their electoral loyalties. Eloy et al. (1993) have argued that Protestants do not behave differently from Catholics and the religiously nonaffiliated in Central American elections, as previously believed. And Torcal and Mainwaring (2003) have asserted that the religious cleavage in Chilean politics has faded. On the other side of the question and based on new survey data, Valenzuela, Scully, and Somma (2007) claim that there is indeed a religious cleavage in Chilean voting. One study of Brazil has shown that the cleavage that matters is not whether or not one is an observant person or whether one self-identifies as a Catholic or Protestant but rather what kind of Catholic one is— liberationist or charismatic (Pierucci and Prandi 1994).

Is there any possibility of an alliance between Catholics and conservative Christians of other denominations? To this point the Catholic Church has not allied with Protestant churches in an ecumenical movement to renew the public sphere for faith as effectively as it has in the United States to oppose abortion rights and advance a moral agenda, mostly because of its reluctance to accept the role of one church among many. Today, despite some hints of cooperation on particular issues, broader ecumenical cooperation is no more likely than it was twenty-five years ago when Levine wrote that he was often puzzled by the "fear and uncertainty of loss and defection one often encounters among bishops facing the possibility of open dialogue and competition with non-Catholic groups" (1981, 199).

7. *We are especially deficient in our knowledge of how democracy is transforming the church.* Political pluralism can either prompt the church to deepen its roots in society and maintain its own internal plurality, or it can cause the church to return to an alliance with its wealthiest members. Preliminary indications are that the currents within the church that favor the former are not as isolated as many previously thought. The Aparecida final document denounces inequality and injustice, the concentration of power and wealth in the hands of the few, and poverty, exclusion, and misery as effects of globalization (CELAM 2007b, §61, 62, 65). It reaffirms the commitment of the church to the preferen-

tial option for the poor made in previous general conferences (Medellín in 1968, Puebla in 1979, and Santo Domingo in 1992), not merely on a "theoretical" or "emotional" level but also in the form of "concrete options and actions" (§396, 397). We need to know more about what factors tip the church in one direction or another.

We have already discussed several factors that might influence church responses to pluralism—the individual beliefs of members of the hierarchy, the way in which the hierarchy calculates political opportunity and risk, and even the commitments of ordinary Catholics. Here we have something different in mind. We are interested in the institutional channels for lay participation in the church that afford lay persons the opportunity to transmit their concerns and insights to the hierarchy. More work on pastoral commissions, lay councils, and other church structures along the lines of Rodriguez's contribution to this volume would be especially welcome. But we should also be interested in systematically mapping out the networks of engagement within the church, between the church and society, and between society and the church that were alluded to in Romero's chapter. Such an exercise would be especially valuable for enabling an analysis of how Catholic activists shape religious and political pluralism.

8. *We must refine our theories to inform and be informed by the research that lies ahead.* Theory is important to understand the calculations, actions, and effects that might not otherwise make sense. Consider the church that invests a good deal of effort and resources in fighting a public policy battle it is bound to lose. Such an effort would make little sense if church leaders were single-mindedly focused on winning this and other public policy battles. But it might make perfect sense if it had an orthogonal goal of exciting its base. Such a statement may sound rather strange and obvious, but there is an important point to be emphasized. Social scientists studying religion, politics, and society should not be afraid to import paradigms developed for other purposes, and they must not claim exceptionalism due to the extraordinary and special place that religion occupies around the globe and in the hearts of men and women. If some scholars are dismayed by the application of rational choice paradigms to religiously motivated action, they may discover others. Putnam's (1988) thesis of two-level games may, for

instance, hold the promise of illuminating the behavior of religious leaders who must interact with their regional and international counterparts as well as secular authorities, on the one hand, and their faithful, on the other. Alternatively, scholars may invest more strongly in developing their own paradigms.

An Agenda for the Church: From Santo Domingo to Aparecida

The church, too, has a number of pressing, unanswered questions at this historic juncture. It bears repeating that half of the world's Roman Catholics live in Latin America, and for the church, the stakes could hardly be higher. As if to illustrate this point, at a time when the Bavarian-born Pope Benedict XVI was widely viewed as having been excessively focused on Europe during the first two years of his papacy, Brazilian Cardinal Cláudio Hummes sent a loud and clear message: "Latin America cannot be lost. . . . Latin America could be lost. . . . If you lose Latin America . . . it would be a substantial loss that could be irreparable."[14]

This volume has described the challenges facing the church, the society it must win over or win back, the way it has gone about responding initially to the new religious and political pluralism, and what its initial impact has been on society and politics in a democratic Latin America. We have, to this point, steered clear of any normative or prescriptive advice to the church. At this point it seems appropriate to ask how the Catholic Church *should* respond to religious pluralism. How can the church compete with religious denominations whose larger supply of ministers, more flexible doctrine, and promises to heal appear to be more responsive to the needs of the poor than its own? What kind of participation—large open-air Masses or smaller groups that still admit the possibility of intense discussion and religious innovation—will best keep the masses loyal to Catholicism? What kind of service—ecstasy or ritual—can slow the growth of the "sects"? Should the church speak out on human rights and workers' rights, as many among the faithful hope it will, or should it stay out of "politics"? Would the church be better off to acknowledge that its days of religious hegemony are over or soon will be, cede religious pluralism at the mass level, and shift gears to prioritize the formation of ethical civic leaders in elite universities? The evident solutions—to live with a smaller market share or give the people what they want—are unpalatable, indeed anathema, for a church that seeks to defend Latin American soil for the one true faith and, more importantly, that intrinsically believes the word of God is passed from above to the grassroots, not the other way around.

The Roman Catholic Church in Latin America is not yet ready to live with a smaller market share, accept minority status, or fundamentally reorder the institution to allow more internal pluralism and democracy. Instead, it seems bent on pressing ahead with its ambitious, perhaps utopian, post–Vatican II project to evangelize culture. Indeed, the Aparecida meeting was predicated on a strategy for the church to send forth new disciples and missionaries to infuse Catholicism more deeply into everyday public and private life. The problem with this project is that it assumes two preconditions—religious hegemony or at minimum a status of first among equals, not pluralism, as well as a willingness on the part of plural democracies to accept the principle of a public sphere organized on a religiously based morality and ethical code—that do not conform to the contemporary reality of Latin American religious and political pluralism. The collective evidence, theoretical frameworks, and reflections in this volume suggest that the prospects for such a program are not bright. At minimum, they suggest two major questions for the church: What is the appropriate relationship of the church to the state, and how can the church defend its cultural hegemony against further erosion?

Church and State in the New Century

How closely should the church ally with sympathetic state officials in order to accomplish its goals? To this point the church has self-consciously steered clear of strongly identifying with states and governments in favor of society. But to the extent that the project to evangelize society falters and the church perceives it is losing the battle for culture and for political space, the temptation to revive the alliances characteristic of the *patronato* and neo-Christendom that served it in the past will be overwhelming. State support can maintain religious institutions when they cannot mobilize resources within their communities, extend the reach of those institutions into society, and enforce outcomes that the church cannot through moral persuasion. State support, in other words, can serve as a functional substitute for private contributions, compensate for the declining service of female and male religious orders that made parochial school affordable for working-class families, and deny access to birth control and abortion that observant Catholics would choose voluntarily to forego.

What makes the horizontal strategy of forming elite alliances so much more tempting than the vertical one of drawing on support from below is that it is more expedient. It takes a shorter time to achieve institutional goals with friends in high places. In the long run, however, such a strategy can be detrimental to the institution. In a brilliant and searing essay, Francisco Weffort (1989) acknowledged a similar error made on the part of the Brazilian left, which, believing it could seize the state as an agent of social change, avoided the hard work of building support for its projects from below and thus was complicit in strengthening the Brazilian Leviathan. The dream of the left soon became the nightmare of a twenty-one-year dictatorship. From this experience, Weffort drew the lesson that Brazil needed a civil society. Indeed, if we continue with the Brazilian example, the church's contemporary dilemma is akin to that faced by union leaders in Brazil in the twentieth century. For the two decades from 1943 to 1964, accommodating *pelego* leaders of the state-sponsored corporatist unions won concessions from sympathetic government officials in the social welfare institutes, labor ministry, labor courts, and even the presidential palace, but however well protected by laws and subsidies, these unions, which had appeared to be powerful but lacked genuine support from the rank and file, collapsed like a house of cards when the military coup came. The "new" Brazilian unions formed in the crucible of a dictatorship that turned its back on labor, whose leaders, like Lula, had shop-floor support, were more enduring, and ultimately were more effective; they toppled a dictatorship and reinvented the established political order.

Nearly four decades ago, Ivan Vallier (1970) presaged this dilemma. He saw the separation of church and state and the fracture of their historical alliance as a prerequisite for the church to abandon its "traditional styles of control and influence" and strengthen its bonds in society. As church and polity are differentiated and "freed" from each other, "the Church ceases to rely on direct political supports and, concomitantly, the polity or major political groups cease to view the Church as a potential ally and source of legitimation" (9). As if to underscore his argument, the church in Argentina, which remained loyal to state authorities and depended on them, never developed strong roots in society and remained weak. On the other hand, the twentieth-century Brazilian and Mexican churches did well when separated from secular authority. Looking back on the 1890 separation of church and state, the Brazilian National Bishops' Conference wrote in 1996, "the separation created the conditions for the fortifying and the renovation of Catholicism" (qtd. in Cleary 1997, 256). The bishops' autonomy freed them to oppose authoritarianism, and in the democratic order that followed, they retained a reasonable capacity to mobilize Catholic grassroots opinion. If the Colombian church has appeared to date to do better because of its privileged status, time will tell if it will follow the Argentine path or make its own.

This argument has a corollary. There is a clear correlation between the strategy chosen and the type of impact the church can have. If the church accepts protection for its institutional interests, it will not be able to shape the terms of the public debate. Its actions will be circumscribed by the fear of alienating its staunchest defenders, who may be on the political right. But if it can rely on its own social networks, or voters, then it will have more latitude to cross traditional left-right boundaries and address issues of its choice in the public arena. It can champion issues of social justice at the same time it can stay vigilant on issues pertaining to public morality. It will have the opportunity, in other words, to formulate a response that opposes both economic and social but not political liberalism. In order to do so, it must look within. It may even need to change.

In an essay on what he called the "twin tolerations," Alfred Stepan (2001, 216–17) argued that in order to maintain both democracy and religious freedom, religious institutions should not have constitutionally privileged prerogatives that allow them to mandate public policy to democratically elected governments, and, conversely, individuals and religious communities must have sufficient autonomy from government and other religions to worship privately. As individuals and groups, they should also be able to advance publicly their values in civil society and sponsor organizations and movements in political society, as long as their public advancement of these beliefs does not impinge negatively on the liberties of other citizens or violate democracy and the law. This does not always mean, Stepan emphasizes, that the state can never subsidize a religious effort. Among the fifteen member countries of the European Union, all countries with Lutheran majorities have an established Lutheran church, and in Holland, most children attend state-supported, private religious schools. According to Stepan's guidelines, the Catholic Church in Latin America may retain a privileged position with respect to other religious faiths and denominations. But his guidelines also suggest that in a plural democracy the Catholic Church may not be able to dictate law and public policy. The church may be unaccustomed to such a role, but democracy and the pluralism that protects freedom and religious liberty will require no less.

Church and Society in the New Century

If the church is to cut itself off from state life support and take the plunge into society, as the new evangelization implied it should, and if this project is to be viable, the church will need bridges to civil society. It is not at all clear that these exist, or even that civil society everywhere is sufficiently well organized that the church can penetrate and mobilize it. In some countries, especially in those where it opposed dictators or where there was no dictatorship, the church had a start. But the effectiveness of these groups and their capacity for self-sustaining action has varied. Civic associations in Brazil and Venezuela, whose links to the institutional church were weaker from the outset, have been more genuinely vibrant than those in Colombia, which were more tightly controlled but swiftly declined once external support and supervision were reduced (Levine 1993, 192). These civic associations might constitute a platform for engagement. Elsewhere, if the church cannot count on its own organizations, its only option may be to work through the civic, political, and trade associations that already exist. But can the church ally with community organizations that are not led by Catholics but that share some common goals with the church, or must these allied associations demonstrate fealty to Catholic religious doctrine?

The church's mission to evangelize culture, which assumes close contact with civil society organizations, does not specify how Catholic those organizations should be. In decades past, Catholic society erected barricades of self-isolation around its communities at home, at work, and at school in order to intensify belief among baptized Catholics. In Peru and elsewhere around the continent today, Catholics work with representatives of other Christian denominations in lay and even secular organizations in order to live out their faith in public action. If Catholic society is no longer to be segregated, is it realistic to believe that religious activists can assert their hegemony over the rest of society? Although the church is appropriately cautious not to assume it can impose its leadership on autonomous organizations and appropriate the captain's wheel of civil society's ship, ultimately that is precisely what some in the church believe it should do.

As this twenty-first-century project takes form, we should not lose sight of the fact that shaping the public sphere sets the institutional church on a collision course with politics. Whatever the church may have once thought in claiming to abandon politics and leaving the project to the people, eventually the project of reconquering the public sphere for a Christian version of modernity will require legislation and policies, especially since the church cannot actually dominate a plural culture. In the best of circumstances, conquering the public sphere via civil society would be a hard pull for a church that has never really gone it alone without state help. Although the church's option for culture claims that winning over civil society will be sufficient to reclaim and reorder the public sphere according to the principles of faith, in reality that project will require the state regulation of culture. Winning state policy, in turn, requires that the church can mobilize voters. To accomplish its objectives, in short, the church needs political support and willing allies in civil society. Although the church welcomed the opportunity—created by public disgust with the neoliberal economic model and disaffection with the apparent inefficacy of formal democratic institutions—to fill a moral and ethical vacuum, give this swell of discontent shape and purpose, and help to imagine a humane democracy constructed on the principles of social justice, individual rights, and community harmony, thus far neopopulist politicians and economic nationalists have been more successful in winning over the disaffected. The failure to penetrate and preserve Latin American "culture" as Catholic highlights the fact that the church now has diminished hegemony. But that does not mean it has lost its opportunity to influence a plural society with more meaningful commitment on the part of the faithful.

The Opportunity of Pluralism

Perhaps the most important conclusion this volume may draw about the Roman Catholic Church in a plural Latin America is that Catholicism itself has become a plural religion, if it was not always so. The church may ultimately speak with one voice on questions of dogma, but in daily pastoral and institutional life different ideas within the church pull and tug it in different directions. While both the progressive and the conservative wings of the church have backed the idea of the new evangelization, their understanding of it differs considerably. For some Catholics, the church's social teachings require that it never abandon its preferential option for the poor. Many other Catholics do not buy into the social doctrine, understand the principle of subsidiarity very differently, and favor an investment in forming elite ranks as more effective in meeting the goal of evangelizing culture than in bringing along the poor. This is the view of bishops that belong to Opus Dei. The lesson here is that a church embedded in civil society cannot be assured that the transmission of ideas runs in only one direction; to the contrary, the plurality of voices within civil society will inevitably penetrate the church.

In his magisterial reflection in chapter 10 of this volume, Daniel Levine points out that religious pluralism should not be thought of merely as a challenge, and certainly not as a scourge, but also as an opportunity. This important insight may serve as a capstone for this volume, whose essential lesson may be that if the church does not hear the message of its base, and expels its laity as it once did the liberationists within, it releases the laity to build a more democratic layer of civil society, but it also renders the church less plural and ultimately less representative of the broader society and culture it aims to lead, defend, and comfort. Because some may ask whether or not shedding self-styled believers actually matters, it is worth spelling out the ways in which pluralism can be advantageous. Whereas it may be apparent that by empowering ordinary men and women religious pluralism may help democracy to deliver on its lofty promises, it is perhaps harder for the church to see how democracy can be good for even a hierarchical institution.

The research and reflections in this volume point to the fact that the Catholic Church in Latin America was not in good shape after its first five hundred years of existence. Arguably, democracy affords an opportunity for the church to learn from men and women who are more fully aware of their rights and responsibilities and better able to articulate them than they once were. Democracy also affords the laity the opportunity to bring the messages of community and justice to popular discourse and public policy. As if to acknowledge these twin possibilities, remarkably the discussion document for the Aparecida meeting issued a clarion call to promote a more active laity:

> The whole Church is missionary. What is needed for this truth to become reality is that lay people be trained, the Christian and secular character of their vocation be promoted actively without fear, room be made for them in the Church, they be respected in their opinions and initiatives, and that room be opened for them to participate in the decisions of the community; in short *that they be treated as adults in a line of communion and participation*. (CELAM 2007a, 349; emphasis in the original)

Or, as José Casanova has advised, "The answer to pluralism is pluralism."[15]

Notes

1. "Lighting on New Faiths or None," *Economist,* May 5, 2007, 47.
2. Larry Rohter, "As Pope Heads to Brazil, Abortion Debate Heats Up," *New York Times,* May 9, 2007.
3. Jack Hitt, "Pro-Life Nation," *New York Times,* April 9, 2006.
4. All translations of the Fifth General Meeting's final document are the author's.
5. "Lighting on New Faiths or None," *Economist,* May 5, 2007, 47.
6. Ian Fisher, "Pope Softens Remarks on Conversion of Natives," *New York Times,* May 23, 2007.
7. This expression is taken from Luiz Alberto Gomez de Souza, the director of the Brazilian think tank CERIS (Centro de Estatística e Investigações Sociais), who said of the CEBs, "Vão bem, obrigado." See Levine (2001), Lesbaupin et al.

(2004, 35–36), and Larry Rohter, "As Pope Heads to Brazil, a Rival Theology Persists," *New York Times,* May 7, 2007.

8. I am grateful to Fr. Ernest Bartell, C.S.C., for his discussion of the church history of that period in the context of a discussion of his own, pre–Vatican II religious formation.

9. Personal communication from Fr. Ernest Bartell, C.S.C., June 27, 2005.

10. In the Salvadoran legislature, the Farabundo Martí National Liberation Front (Frente Farabundo Martí para la Liberación Nacional, or FMLN), which had in previous rounds asked its delegation to vote against a bill that would raise criminal penalties for providers and women, released its delegation facing a difficult election, with the result that legislators passed a bill so extreme that doctors cannot treat an ectopic pregnancy.

11. In one particularly eloquent passage, Levine and Mainwaring wrote of the personal transformations they had witnessed firsthand: "We have observed countless meetings where once tongue-tied men and women step forward to speak and share experiences. Their capabilities are nurtured in the group, supported and drawn out by friends and neighbors, and then spill over to affect other issues—from agricultural practice to savings, from personal relations to marriage patterns, schools to politics. People who were once afraid to speak out, now do so with confidence and vigor. People who did not even have rudimentary notions of their rights now stand up for them" (1989, 219).

12. One news report placed the number belonging to Opus Dei in Colombia as high as eleven. See Larry Rohter, "Pope and Bishops Set Thorny Agenda to Talks," *New York Times,* May 13, 2007. In Peru the archbishop of Lima, Juan Luis Cipriani, also belongs.

13. The Brazilian surveys have been conducted by CERIS.

14. Larry Rohter, "Brazil Greets Pope but Questions His Perspective," *New York Times,* May 9, 2007.

15. Stated at the conference Contemporary Catholicism, Religious Pluralism, and Democracy in Latin America, University of Notre Dame, Notre Dame, IN, March 31, 2005.

References

Baldez, Lisa. 2004. "Elected Bodies: Gender Quotas for Female Legislative Candidates in Mexico." *Legislative Studies Quarterly* 29, no. 2 (May): 231–58.

Burdick, John. 1992. "Rethinking the Study of Social Movements: The Case of Christian Base Communities in Urban Brazil." In Arturo Escobar and Sonia E. Alvarez, eds., *The Making of Social Movements in Latin America: Identity, Strategy, and Democracy,* 171–84. Boulder, CO: Westview Press.

Casanova, José. 2001. "Civil Society and Religion: Retrospective Reflections on Catholicism and Prospective Reflections on Islam." *Social Research* 68, no. 4 (Winter): 1041–80.

Cleary, Edward L. 1997. "The Brazilian Catholic Church and Church-State Relations: Nation-Building." *Journal of Church and State* 39, no. 2: 253–72.

Consejo Episcopal Latinoamericano (CELAM). 2007a. *Sintesis de los Aportes Recibidos para la V Conferencia General del Episcopado Latinoamericano.* Available at http://www.br.celam.info/sintesis/sintesis-vconferencia-aparecida .pdf.

———. 2007b. *V Conferencia General del Episcopado Latinoamericano y del Caribe: Documento Conclusivo.* Aparecida, May 13–31. Available at http://www .celam.info/download/Documento_Conclusivo_Aparecida.pdf.

Daudelin, Jean, and W. E. Hewitt. 1995. "Churches and Politics in Latin America: Catholicism at the Crossroads." *Third World Quarterly* 16, no. 2: 221–36.

Della Cava, Ralph. 1992. "The Ten-Year Crusade Toward the Third Christian Millennium: An Account of Evangelization 2000 and Lumen 2000." In Douglas A. Chalmers, Maria do Carmo Campello de Souza, and Atilio A. Boron, eds., *The Right and Democracy in Latin America,* 202–22. New York: Praeger.

Drogus, Carol Ann. 1999. "No Land of Milk and Honey: Women CEB Activists in Posttransition Brazil." *Journal of Interamerican Studies and World Affairs* 41, no. 4: 35–52.

Drogus, Carol Ann, and Hannah Stewart-Gambino. 2005. *Activist Faith: Grassroots Women in Democratic Brazil and Chile.* University Park: Pennsylvania State University Press.

Eloy Aguilar, Edwin, José Miguel Sandoval, Timothy J. Steigenga, and Kenneth M. Coleman. 1993. "Protestantism in El Salvador: Conventional Wisdom versus Survey Evidence." *Latin American Research Review* 28, no. 2: 119–40.

Folha de São Paulo. 2007. Special Supplement (May 6).

Gomez de Souza, Luiz Alberto. 2005. "Roman Catholic Church and the Experience of Democracy in Latin America." Paper prepared for the conference Contemporary Catholicism, Religious Pluralism, and Democracy in Latin America: Challenges, Responses, and Impact. University of Notre Dame, March 31–April 1.

Htun, Mala. 2004. "Is Gender Like Ethnicity? The Political Representation of Identity Groups." *Perspectives on Politics* 2, no. 3: 439–58.

Huntington, Samuel P. 1991. *The Third Wave: Democratization in the Late Twentieth Century.* Norman: University of Oklahoma Press.

Lesbaupin, Ivo, Lúcia Ribeiro, Névio Fiorin, and Solange Rodrigues. 2004. "Revisitando as CEBs: Un estudo no Rio de Janeiro e em Minas Gerais." Rio de Janeiro: ISER.

Levine, Daniel. 1981. "Religion, Society, and Politics: State of the Art." *Latin American Research Review* 16, no. 3: 185–209.

———. 1993. "Popular Groups, Popular Culture, and Popular Religion." In Daniel H. Levine, ed., *Constructing Culture and Power in Latin America*, 171–225. Ann Arbor: University of Michigan Press.

———. 2001. "On Premature Reports of the Death of Liberation Theology." *Review of Politics* 57, no. 1: 105–31.

Levine, Daniel, and Scott Mainwaring. 1989. "Religion and Popular Protest in Latin America: Contrasting Experiences." In Susan Eckstein, ed., *Power and Popular Protest: Latin American Social Movements*, 203–40. Berkeley: University of California Press.

Norris, Pippa, and Ronald Inglehart. 2004. *Sacred and Secular: Religion and Politics Worldwide*. Cambridge: Cambridge University Press.

Pierucci, Antônio Flávio, and Reginaldo Prandi. 1994. "Religiões e Voto: A Eleição Presidencial de 1994." *Opinião Pública* 3, no. 1: 20–44.

Portada, Robert. 2009. "The Dissident Cross: The Catholic Church and Political Confrontation in Cuba." Ph.D. diss., University of Notre Dame.

Putnam, Robert. 1988. "Diplomacy and Domestic Politics: The Logic of Two-Level Games." *International Organization* 43, no. 3 (Summer): 427–60.

Romero, Catalina. 2005. "Religion in Civil Society: Building Democratic Institutions in Peru." Paper prepared for the conference Contemporary Catholicism, Religious Pluralism, and Democracy in Latin America: Challenges, Responses, and Impact. University of Notre Dame, March 31–April 1.

Stepan, Alfred. 2001. "The World's Religious Systems and Democracy: Crafting the 'Twin Tolerations.'" In *Arguing Comparative Politics*, 213–53. New York: Oxford University Press.

Stoll, David. 1990. *Is Latin America Turning Protestant? The Politics of Evangelical Growth*. Berkeley: University of California Press.

Torcal, Mariano, and Scott Mainwaring. 2003. "The Political Recrafting of Social Bases of Party Competition: Chile, 1973–95. *British Journal of Political Science* 33: 55–84.

Valenzuela, J. Samuel, Timothy R. Scully, and Nicolás Somma. 2007. "The Enduring Presence of Religion in Chilean Ideological Positionings and Voter Options." Kellogg Institute Working Paper no. 336 (March), Kellogg Institute, University of Notre Dame.

Vallier, Ivan. 1970. *Catholicism, Social Control, and Modernization in Latin America*. Englewood Cliffs, NJ: Prentice-Hall.

Weffort, Francisco. 1989. "Why Democracy?" In Alfred Stepan, ed., *Democratizing Brazil: Problems of Transition and Consolidation*, 327–50. New York: Oxford University Press.

About the Contributors

Roberto J. Blancarte is professor and director of the Center of Sociological Studies at El Colegio de México in Mexico City. He was the founder of the Interdisciplinary Program for the Study of Religions at El Colegio Mexiquense in Toluca; associate researcher with the Groupe des Sociologies des Religions et Laïcités in France; and member of the National Committee of Bioethics and the National Commission to Prevent Discrimination in Mexico. He has been an adviser at the Mexican Embassy to the Holy See; chief of staff in the Vice-Ministry of Religious Affairs; and visiting professor at Dartmouth College and the École Pratique des Hautes Études. His research deals with the sociology of religion, particularly church-state relations, secularization, "laicity," and, most recently, the connection between the secular state and sexual and reproductive rights. He is the author and editor of several books, including *Historia de la Iglesia católica en México* (El Colegio Mexiquense-Fondo de Cultura Económica, 1992), *Religión, Iglesias y democracia* (La Jornada-UNAM, 1995), and *Afganistán, la revolución islámica frente al mundo occidental* (El Colegio de México, 2001), as well as numerous journal articles. He writes a weekly column on politics and religion for a national newspaper and participates actively in local politics on behalf of civil freedoms.

Frances Hagopian is associate professor of political science and a faculty fellow and former director of the Kellogg Institute for International Studies at the University of Notre Dame. She studies the comparative politics of

467

Latin America, with emphasis on democratization, political representation, and the political economy of economic reform in Brazil, Argentina, Chile, and Mexico, as well as religion and politics in Latin America. She is the author of *Reorganizing Political Representation in Latin America* (Cambridge University Press, forthcoming), *Traditional Politics and Regime Change in Brazil* (Cambridge University Press, 1996), coeditor (with Scott Mainwaring) of *The Third Wave of Democratization in Latin America* (Cambridge University Press, 2005), and author of numerous articles and book chapters. In 2007–2008 she was a visiting fellow at the Woodrow Wilson International Center for Scholars.

Mala Htun is associate professor of political science at the New School for Social Research. She is the author of *Sex and the State: Abortion, Divorce, and the Family under Latin American Dictatorships and Democracies* (Cambridge University Press, 2003) and articles that have appeared in *Perspectives on Politics, Latin American Research Review,* and *Politics and Gender,* among other journals and edited volumes. She is currently writing a book on the politics of representing women and ethnic and racial minorities in Latin America and worldwide. Her article "Is Gender Like Ethnicity? The Political Representation of Identity Groups" won the Heinz Eulau Award from the American Political Science Association in 2005, and she has been supported by grants and fellowships from the National Science Foundation, Social Science Research Council, and National Security Education Program. A former fellow of the Kellogg Institute for International Studies at the University of Notre Dame and the Radcliffe Institute at Harvard, in 2006–2007 she was a Council on Foreign Relations International Affairs Fellow in Japan and a visiting fellow at the Institute of Social Science at the University of Tokyo.

Ronald Inglehart is a professor of political science and program director at the Institute for Social Research at the University of Michigan. He helped found the Euro-Barometer surveys and directs the World Values Survey. His research deals with changing belief systems and their impact on social and political change. His most recent books are (with Pippa Norris) *Rising Tide: Gender Equality in Global Perspective* (Cambridge University Press,

2003), (with Pippa Norris) *Sacred and Secular: The Secularization Thesis Revisited* (Cambridge University Press, 2004), and (with Christian Welzel) *Modernization, Cultural Change and Democracy: The Human Development Sequence* (Cambridge University Press, 2005). He also edited *Mass Values and Social Change: Findings from the Values Surveys* (Leiden: Brill Publishers, 2003) and *Human Beliefs and Values: A Cross-Cultural Sourcebook Based on the 1999–2001 Values Surveys* (Mexico City: Siglo XXI, 2004). Author of more than 225 publications, he has been a visiting professor or visiting scholar in France, Germany, the Netherlands, Switzerland, Japan, South Korea, Taiwan, Brazil, and Nigeria and has served as a consultant to the U.S. State Department and the European Union.

Daniel H. Levine is James Orin Murfin Professor of Political Science at the University of Michigan. He has also been chair of the Department of Political Science and director of the Program in Latin American and Caribbean Studies. He has published widely on issues of religion and politics, democracy, and social movements in Latin America. His books include *Conflict and Political Change in Venezuela* (Princeton University Press, 1973), *Religion and Politics in Latin America* (Princeton University Press, 1987), *Religion and Political Conflict in Latin America* (University of North Carolina Press, 1986), *Popular Voices in Latin American Catholicism* (Princeton University Press, 1992), and *Constructing Culture and Power in Latin America* (University of Michigan Press, 1993). He has also published numerous articles and book chapters.

Soledad Loaeza is professor of political science at El Colegio de México, where she was director of the International Relations Center (1990–1994). She has held the Alfred Grosser Chair at the Institut d'Études Politiques de Paris (1999) and fellowships at the Radcliffe Institute of Advanced Studies (2003–2004) and the Kellogg Institute for International Studies at the University of Notre Dame (2005). She is the author of *El Partido Acción Nacional, la larga marcha, 1939–1994* (Fondo de Cultura Económica, 1999) and "Vicente Fox's Presidential Style and the New Mexican Presidency" (*Estudios Mexicanos/Mexican Studies,* 2006). Her current research focuses on the growth of Mexican authoritarianism and presidential power after 1945 as a response to the transformation of U.S. world power.

Cristián Parker Gumucio is professor and director of the Institute for Advanced Studies at the Universidad de Santiago de Chile, where he was previously director of the Department of Scientific and Technological Research (2000–2003). He has also taught at the Diplomatic Academy of Chile, the Foreign Affairs Ministry, and the Chilean War Academy. He has served as consultant to UNICEF, UNDP, and ECLA and has produced studies for various public agencies and ministries. His research interests include science, technology, and education; politics, youth, and democracy; and development, poverty, sustainability, and culture and religion. He has published numerous journal articles and chapters in edited books, as well as monographs and edited volumes. His most recent works include *Universitarios, Ciencia, Tecnología y Conciencia* (Sello Editorial-IDEA, 2007), *Popular Religion and Modernization in Latin America* (Orbis Books, 2006), and *Catolicismos Populares, Globalización, Inculturación* (Center for Mission Research and Study/CERC-UAHC, 2001).

Patricia M. Rodriguez is a Ph.D. candidate in the Department of Political Science at the University of Notre Dame; her work centers on the links between social mobilization and democracy in Latin America. Her dissertation examines the processes of protest and negotiations between peasant and indigenous movement leaders and political elites and their effect on land-related public policies over a period of thirteen years in Brazil, Chile, and Ecuador. It aims at an understanding of why and how movement leaders make the decisions that they do, and how these decisions become (or fail to become) a threat to authorities. The project has been funded through an NSF Dissertation Improvement Grant and a Kellogg Institute Seed Money Grant. Her other research interests include U.S.–Latin American relations and environmental politics. She has taught at the University of California at Santa Barbara (spring 2007) and is currently an assistant professor of politics at Ithaca College.

Catalina Romero is professor at the Pontificia Universidad Católica del Perú (PUCP), where she currently serves as dean of the social sciences faculty and coordinator of the Seminar on Interdisciplinary Studies of Religion. Formerly, she was director of the Instituto Bartolomé de Las Casas.

Her research focuses on religion and politics. She is the coeditor (with Manuel Marzal, S.J., and José Sánchez) of *Para entender la religión* (Fondo Editorial PUCP, 2004), and she has published numerous articles in English- and Spanish-language journals and books, including most recently (with Daniel H. Levine), "Urban Citizen Movements and Disempowerment in Peru and Venezuela," which appeared in *The Crisis of Democratic Representation in the Andes*, edited by Scott Mainwaring, Ana María Bejarano, and Eduardo Pizarro Leongómez (Stanford University Press, 2006). Currently she is exploring the link between civil society organizations and the Catholic Church. She is a member of the research team of the World Values Survey and the European Union's working group on Modernity and Secularization in Europe and Latin America and serves on the editorial boards of *Páginas* and *Elecciones*.

Index